Michaela Maier, Jens Tenscher (Eds.)

Campaigning in Europe – Campaigning for Europe

MEDIEN
Forschung und Wissenschaft

Band 12

LIT

Michaela Maier, Jens Tenscher (Eds.)

Campaigning in Europe – Campaigning for Europe

Political Parties, Campaigns, Mass Media and the
European Parliament Elections 2004

Patrick Dumont & Philippe Poirier
European Elections in Luxembourg:
A Case of Second-Order Campaigning 141

Carlos Jalali
A Yellow Card for the Government, Offside for European Issues?
The European Elections of 2004 in Portugal 155

Athanassios N. Samaras & Giorgos Kentas
Campaigning under the Shadow of the Annan Plan:
The 2004 EP Elections in Cyprus 171

III. National Case Studies on Media Coverage

Lars W. Nord & Jesper Strömbäck
Game is the Name of the Frame:
European Parliamentary Elections in Swedish Media 1995-2004 191

Claes H. de Vreese
Continuity and Change: The 2004 European Elections in the Netherlands 207

Petr Kopáček
More or Less Europe: Media Coverage of
European Parliamentary Elections in the Czech Republic 219

Ágnes Simon
Two Hungaries?
European Parliamentary Elections and Their Media Coverage in Hungary 237

Radoslava Brhlíková, Mária Kočnerová & Tatiana Tökölyová
Europe Stays Distant: Media Coverage and Voting in the
European Parliamentary Elections in Slovakia 251

Rosa Berganza & Javier Beroiz
The Influence of the March 11th Madrid Bombings on the
2004 European Campaign in Spain: An Analysis of Television News 261

Nicolas Demertzis
Europe on the Agenda? The Greek Case 277

Andrew Paul Williams & Lynda Lee Kaid
Media Framing of the European Parliamentary Elections:
A View from the United States 295

IV. National Case Studies on Campaign Effects

Pascal Delwit
The 2004 European Elections in Belgium:
An Election That Went by Unnoticed 307

Peter Filzmaier
Campaigning and Media in Austria: Lessons to be Learned from the
"HPM Phenomenon" in the European Parliamentary Elections 323

Jacques Gerstlé, Raul Magni-Berton & Christophe Piar
Media Coverage and Voting in the European Parliamentary Elections
in France 2004 339

Michaela Maier & Jürgen Maier
Let Us Entertain You! Perception and Evaluation of the
European Election Campaign Spots 2004 in Germany 353

Wojciech Cwalina, Andrzej Falkowski & Paweł Koniak
Advertising Effects: Polish Elections to the European Parliament 371

Mart Raudsaar & Külli-Riin Tigasson
The European Parliament Elections in Estonia 2004:
Party Spots and the Effects of Advertising 387

Preface

Michaela Maier & Jens Tenscher

In June 2004 the sixth direct election of the European Parliament took place. The run-up to the elections was connected with great expectations due to the fact that on May 1st eight "young democracies" from East and Southeast Europe as well as two Mediterranean islands (Cyprus and Malta) had joined the European Union accompanied by highly memorable Europe-wide ceremonies. In was only six weeks later when about 342 million voters from 25 countries were asked to give the "new Europe" a brilliant kick-off. The historical significance of the 2004 European Parliament elections in the light of the proceeding enlargement of the EU, the strengthening of the European Parliament, and the ongoing debate about a European Constitution roused hopes among EU-optimists that a new kind of *EUphoria* would occur. In fact, after the first direct EP elections in 1979 a kind of EP-apathy had slowly spread among political parties, the mass media, and the citizens as shown by low-key campaigns, relatively little media coverage, and fading citizens' interest in and empathy for the EU. Now, the "enlargement elections" were supposed to strengthen both the commitment of the main actors (political parties and mass media) as well as the involvement of the people.

However, such high expectations were disappointed at least to some degree: in most of the countries political parties saw the elections as a compulsory exercise, the media did not exert very much effort on searching for newsworthy stories and offering helpful background information, and turnout fell to an all-time low – on average only 45.7 percent of the eligible EU-citizens cast their ballots, in some of the new member states less than a third of the eligible voters showed up on election day. In fact, after the "enlargement hype" EU-focused attention faded away rapidly and the European elections turned out to be – once again – "second order" for almost all actors involved: EU-wide, many established political parties pursued their campaign activities in a rather traditional and unspectacular manner, not investing much money, time, and creativity in their campaigns, thereby facilitating the unexpected success of some smaller oppositional parties having charismatic political figures. Especially in some of the new member states, EU-excitement had rapidly diminished after the accession referendums, and anti-EU candidates were doing well in attracting media attention and citizen's votes. In many established countries too, EU-opponents were elected to the European parliament. Besides the marginal attention the elections received, in most of the established EU-member states political parties, mass media, and citizens turned the European event to national "test-elections". Consequently, in such countries many citizens seized the opportunity to teach their governing parties a lesson for their performance on the national level. Once more, the European elections were largely domesticated and failed to a great extent in pushing the "European idea" and shaping a transnational "European public sphere".

Given the historic significance of the 2004 European Elections and the rare opportunity to comparatively analyze a single political communication event, the Department of Communication Psychology and the Department of Political Science at the University of Koblenz-Landau hosted an international conference entitled "Campaigning for Europe. Media, Parties, and the European Parliamentary Elections 2004" from October 1-3, 2004, in Landau, Germany, a city located right in the geographic heart of the new European Union. Colleagues from the field of political and communication science from several EU member states and the USA as well as politicians, campaign managers, and media actors discussed the outcome of the 2004 European Parliamentary Elections, the characteristics of the campaigns, and the role of the media. Building on the results of this conference we compiled this volume. It is divided into four parts:

- The three contributions to Part I discuss the 2004 EP elections' turnout, political parties' campaigns, and media structures from a longitudinal and comparative perspective. Special attention is given to the process of an emerging "European public sphere".
- The seven chapters of Part II are national case studies focusing primarily on political parties' campaign strategies in getting public attention and mobilizing voters. All of them refer – at least implicitly – to theories of modernization and professionalization of political communication and examine to which extent political parties made use of "modern" techniques of political campaigning.
- Part III comprises eight country studies which first and foremost discuss the role of the mass media in the run-up to the 2004 EP elections. Mostly using quantitative or qualitative content analyses they investigate to which degree and in which manner the EP elections were covered by the mass media, thereby referring to theories of agenda-setting and framing.
- Finally, the six national case studies of Part IV specifically focus on the consequences of political parties' campaign efforts and mass media's coverage with respect to voters' attitudes towards the EU and their voting behaviour. In addition to "classic" voter studies, special attention is given to experimental studies examining advertisement effects.

In discussing country-specific particularities of the campaigns, media's coverage, citizens' attitudes, turnout, and results of the election in this volume the magnitude of similarities and disparities with respect to the European-wide shared political communication event becomes clear. These can be traced back to country-specific constraints of the political systems and the media systems on the one hand and to divergent political contexts und cultural variables on the other hand. They became especially obvious in the case of the post-communist new member states, but also in countries like Cyprus and Spain in which the 2004 EP elections were overshadowed by either national or international conflicts.

Above all, this volume hopes to stimulate research activities on a periodically reoccurring, but nonetheless unique European-wide political communication event, the European Parliament elections, an area which has hitherto been rather neglected. For the first time, research from almost all 25 EU countries including the brand new member states from Eastern Europe and the Mediterranean is brought together – together with different methodological approaches and scientific traditions. We are proud of the fact that many well-known colleagues from "old Europe" and the USA got involved in this project and that many colleagues from the "new" European countries shared with us their first experiences within the European Union. We would like to thank all colleagues for their important contributions to this book.

Obviously, the success of such a project which occupied us for a whole year greatly depends on the assistance of some helpful people and the support of funding institutions. At this point we would especially like to thank: The Fritz Thyssen Stiftung (Cologne), the President of the University Koblenz-Landau, and the Ministry of Science, Education, Research, and Culture in Rhineland-Palatinate for their financial support of the international symposium as well as this publication. Without their support neither the symposium nor the book would have been possible. And without the assistance of Katharina Hentschel it would have been very difficult to correctly follow out all the regulations connected with administering these funds. We also want to cordially thank the irreplaceable people who helped to smooth and polish the manuscript, namely Annika Breutmann, Carsten Gieselmann, Eleonore Hertweck, Anke Hub, and Christiane Wittmar.

Landau, January 2006   *Michaela Maier & Jens Tenscher*

COMPARATIVE AND GENERAL APPROACHES AND PERSPECTIVES

European Elections' Turnout from 1979 to 2004

Markus Steinbrecher & Sandra Huber[*]

1. Introduction

The first thing of interest after an election is usually not the level of turnout, but the result in terms of which party got most of the votes, which parties lost or won votes compared to the last election, and what this means for the future government. Only in the more detailed analyses following the elections, turnout comes under closer scrutiny. At least this is true as long as turnout lies within the normal range. However, in recent years it has been stated quite often that turnout in European Parliament Elections (EPE) is no longer in the normal range. This is especially the case in some member countries of the EU like the United Kingdom, the Netherlands, Sweden, or Germany, where turnout is very low compared to that in national parliament elections (NPE).

This article tries to explain low turnout in EPE and examines it from two different perspectives. After some theoretical considerations about the meaning of high and low turnout rates, we will describe and analyse turnout in EPE from 1979 to 2004 on the aggregate level in the first part. The multi-level political system of the EU allows a comparison of EPE-turnout with turnout in national parliament elections and accession referenda for all member states of the EU. In the second part we focus on the individual level and attempt to determine the factors which drive voters to participate in EPE using an analytical framework developed by Blondel et al. (1998). Empirical results in this part focus on campaign and media effects on the individual decision to participate and originate from the Fifth Framework Project "Democratic Participation and Communication in Systems of Multi-level Governance" (see Rattinger/Huber 2004). Results in this part refer only to Germany and concentrate on the EPE in 1994 and 1999, since data for the 2004 elections was available to a limited extent only.

2. Turnout and theories of democracy

As turnout rates have been declining for many years and this has not yet come to a halt, political scientists have intensified their research efforts to explain the ongoing changes in electoral behaviour. But the question is: "Can low turnout be called a bad thing in general?"

---

[*] Markus Steinbrecher, Dipl.-Pol. *1978. Project Researcher at the Chair for Political Science II, University of Bamberg, email: markus.steinbrecher@sowi.uni-bamberg.de
Sandra Huber, Dipl.-Pol. *1974. Project Researcher at the Chair for Political Science II, University of Bamberg, email: sandra.huber@sowi.uni-bamberg.de

In theories of democracy two important approaches can be found based on quite contradictory assumptions and postulations with respect to the adequate level of electoral participation (see Scharpf 1975: 21-28). Input-oriented approaches emphasise the need for a maximum turnout to ensure that all interests and demands of society as a whole are represented and articulated in the political process. Hence, on the one hand low turnout rates are considered evidence for declining support and a symptom for the crisis of the political system, because large groups of the population do not provide input anymore; on the other hand citizens express their support of and satisfaction with the state through high turnout rates. In contrast, output-oriented approaches accentuate the quality of decisions in a political system. High turnout rates are not necessarily needed to reach high quality decisions, so that elections are mainly seen as an instrument for the allocation of power and the legitimisation of authority and rule. Under an elite-democratic point of view, participation of each and every citizen is not even appreciated, so that high turnout rates are expected to show dissatisfaction with the political system, whereas low turnout rates show indifferent consent. These contrasting perspectives make a general evaluation of European Elections' turnout quite difficult, but if one compares turnout in elections to the European Parliament (EP) with that in elections to national parliaments, it makes more sense to apply the input-oriented approach.

3. Development of turnout on the aggregate level 1979-2004

In the European Election of 2004, turnout in the EU decreased to an all-time low: only 45.7 percent of the eligible EU-citizens cast their ballots. Differences between the member states appeared to be quite strong. The highest participation rate was reported for Belgium with 90.8 percent, whereas in Slovakia only 17 percent of the electorate went to the polls. In 18 of the 25 member states more than half of the electorate stayed at home. Among the seven states with turnout rates over 50 percent Belgium, Luxembourg, Greece, and Cyprus have compulsory voting. In addition, Italy also enforced compulsory voting until 1992, so there may be still some kind of turnout tradition among Italians. The new member countries showed extraordinarily low turnout rates with the exception of Malta and Cyprus. Turnout in Poland, Czech Republic, Estonia, Slovenia, and Slovakia stayed below 30 percent. Hence, the new instrument of democratic elections to the EP was not able to attract many people.

If one looks at the development over time, turnout in European Elections on EU-level has been declining continuously since the first election in 1979. After a rather small decrease from 63.0 percent to 56.8 percent between 1979 and 1994, the decline intensified in the last two elections. With an electoral participation of 49.8 percent in 1999 and 45.7 percent in 2004, not even half of the eligible voters in Europe participated in the European elections.

Table 1: Turnout in European Parliament Elections 1979-2004

Country	1979	1984	1989	1994	1999	2004	Mean	Standard deviation	Range
France	60.7	56.7	48.7	52.7	47.0	42.8	51.4	6.6	17.9
Belgium	91.6	92.2	90.7	90.7	91.0	90.8	91.2	0.6	1.5
The Netherlands	57.8	50.6	47.2	35.6	30.0	39.3	43.4	10.3	27.8
Germany	65.7	56.8	62.4	60.0	45.2	43.0	55.5	9.3	22.7
Italy	84.9	83.4	81.5	74.8	70.8	73.1	78.1	5.9	14.1
Luxembourg	88.9	88.8	87.4	88.5	87.3	89.0	88.3	0.8	1.7
Denmark	47.8	52.4	46.2	52.9	50.4	47.9	49.6	2.7	6.7
Ireland	63.6	47.6	68.3	44.0	50.5	58.8	55.5	9.6	24.3
UK	32.3	32.6	36.2	36.4	24.0	38.8	33.4	5.2	14.8
Greece	78.6	77.2	79.9	71.2	75.3	63.4	74.3	6.1	16.5
Spain		68.9	54.6	59.1	63.0	45.1	58.1	9.0	23.8
Portugal		72.4	51.2	35.5	40.0	38.6	47.5	15.1	36.9
Sweden				41.6	38.8	37.8	39.4	2.0	3.8
Finland				60.3	31.4	39.4	43.7	14.9	28.9
Austria				67.7	49.4	42.4	53.2	13.1	25.3
Malta						82.4			
Poland						20.9			
Czech Republic						28.3			
Slovakia						17.0			
Estonia						26.8			
Latvia						41.3			
Lithuania						48.4			
Hungary						38.5			
Slovenia						28.3			
Cyprus						71.2			
EU	63.0	61.0	58.5	56.8	49.8	45.7	55.8	6.7	17.3

Source: http://www.elections2004.eu.int/ep-election/sites/de/results1306/turnout_ep/turnout_table.html (turnout rates), own calculations (mean, standard deviation, range)

The member countries show different patterns for the development of turnout. On the one hand, countries like Belgium, Luxembourg, Denmark, and Sweden have quite stable participation rates. But levels for each country are quite different. Luxembourg and Belgium show the most stable turnout patterns because of the compulsoriness of the vote with an electoral participation of almost 90 percent or even more and a standard deviation below 1 percentage point. Denmark's turnout fluctuates between 46 and 53 percent across all European elections with a standard deviation of 2.72 percentage points, while turnout in Sweden is even on a lower level ranging between 38 and 42 percent and a standard deviation of 1.97 percentage points. On the other hand, turnout has been quite variable in Finland, Austria, the Netherlands, Portugal, Ireland, Germany, and Spain. The high standard deviation for all of these countries with the exception of Germany and Ireland results from the extraordinarily high turnout in the respective first European Election that perhaps was caused by a "first-time boost" due to the excitement accompanying the novel experience of European elections (see Franklin 2001: 312; Reif 1984: 7; van der Eijk et al. 1996). Considering the standard deviation, Austria, Finland, the Netherlands, and Portugal show the most unstable development of turnout. Quite interesting developments can be reported for Germany and especially Ireland with a continuous up and down from election to election. Finally, the United Kingdom is the country with the lowest turnout in four of the six European elections, varying between 25 and about 40 percent.

Table 2: Comparison of turnout in European and National Parliament Elections (EU-15)

Country	EPE 2004	Last NPE	Difference last NPE - EPE 2004	Mean EPE	Mean NPE	Difference mean NPE - mean EPE
France	42.8	64.4	21.6	51.4	69.5	18.1
Belgium	90.8	96.3	5.5	91.2	93.3	2.1
The Netherlands	39.3	80.0	40.7	43.4	80.7	37.2
Germany	43.0	79.1	36.1	55.5	82.7	27.2
Italy	73.1	81.4	8.3	78.1	86.0	7.9
Luxembourg	89.0	91.7	2.7	88.3	88.6	0.3
Denmark	47.9	87.1	39.2	49.6	86.2	36.6
Ireland	58.8	62.6	3.8	55.5	70.1	14.7
UK	38.8	59.4	20.6	33.4	71.3	37.9
Greece	63.4	63.2	-0.2	74.3	77.5	3.3
Spain	45.1	75.7	30.6	58.1	74.2	16.1
Portugal	38.6	62.8	24.2	47.5	73.1	25.5
Sweden	37.8	80.1	42.3	39.4	86.8	47.4
Finland	39.4	69.7	30.3	43.7	73.2	29.5
Austria	42.4	84.3	41.9	53.2	84.7	31.5

Source: http://www.elections2004.eu.int/ep-election/sites/de/results1306/turnout_ep/turnout_table.html (turnout in EPE), http://cdp.binghamton.edu/era/index.html, http://www.parties-and-elections.de/index.html (turnout in NPE), own calculations (mean EPE, mean NPE, difference last NPE – EPE 2004, difference mean NPE – mean EPE)

Since European Elections take place in a system of multi-level governance, a comparison with turnout in elections to national parliaments is important for an overall assessment. If one compares the mean turnout in European Elections and national elections for the EU-15, electoral participation in national elections is higher in all countries, even in Luxembourg where both elections are held simultaneously. Differences of the means vary between 0.3 percentage points in Luxembourg and incredible 47.4 percentage points in Sweden (see Table 2). Again, a clear distinction can be made between countries with and without compulsory voting. While Belgium, Luxembourg, Greece, and Italy (as a country with previous compulsory voting) show differences below 8 percentage points between the mean turnout rates of both election types, differences between 25 and 35 percentage points can be reported for a number of countries, namely Germany, the Netherlands, Denmark, the United Kingdom, Portugal, Finland, and Austria. If one compares stability of turnout for both election types, participation rates are normally more stable in national elections than in European elections. Only countries with compulsory voting as well as the United Kingdom and Sweden show a greater stability for turnout in European elections.

Similar patterns, but with larger differences, can be found in the comparison between the last elections on both levels. Only in Greece participation has been (0.2 percentage points) higher in the last European Election than in the last national election. For the other 24 countries differences vary between 2.7 percentage points in Luxembourg and 53.1 percentage points in Slovakia. Differences can be explained by the second-order election model by Reif and Schmitt (1980), originally developed after the first direct election to the EP. The model differentiates between elections to the national legislatures, which are first-order elections, and the European Elections, which consequently are second-order elections.

Table 3: Comparison of turnout in the First European Election, Last National Parliament Election, and Accession Referendum (Accession countries of 2004 and 1995)

Country	Referendum	EPE 2004/1995	Last NPE
Malta	90.9	82.4	96.2
Poland	58.9	20.9	46.3
Czech Republic	55.2	28.3	57.9
Slovakia	52.2	17.0	70.1
Estonia	64.0	26.8	58.2
Latvia	72.5	41.3	71.2
Lithuania	55.9	48.4	58.2
Hungary	45.6	38.5	70.5
Slovenia	60.4	28.3	70.4
Cyprus	-	71.2	91.8
Sweden	83.3	41.6	88.1
Finland	70.4	60.3	71.9
Austria	81.6	67.7	84.0

Source: http://www.elections2004.eu.int/ep-election/sites/de/results1306/ turnout_ep/turnout_table.html (turnout in EPE), http://cdp.binghamton.edu/era/index.html, http://www.parties-and-elections.de/ index.html (turnout in NPE), http://www.europa-digital.de/ (turnout in referenda)

Both types of elections take place in exactly the same political environment and are connected with each other. Reif and Schmitt mention several reasons why turnout is lower in European Elections than in national first-order elections, among which the "less-at-stake"-dimension is the most important (see Reif/ Schmitt 1980: 9-10). This literally means that voters perceive the EP to be less powerful than the national parliaments. Hence, participation in European Elections is less important for the electorate, resulting in a lower willingness to participate.

A good example for the relevance of the "less-at-stake"-dimension can be found in the comparison of turnout rates of the accession referenda and the 2004 European Election in nine of the ten new member countries, with the former always being higher (see Table 3). Differences between 7.1 percentage points in Hungary and 38.0 percentage points in Poland can be reported, showing that there was obviously more at stake for the people in the referenda than in the first elections to the EP after joining the EU. Accession euphoria, if it ever existed, seems to have dissolved after the referenda. The same effect can be detected for the countries that joined the EU in 1995. Participation in the accession referenda was more than 10 percentage points higher in Austria and Finland compared to the subsequent elections to the European Parliament. Sweden even showed a difference of more than 40 percentage points. Especially the example of the latter helps to drive away concerns about the large turnout differences between national and European level in Eastern and Central European countries that otherwise could be interpreted as threats for democratic stability and as a sign of distrust in the political system of the EU.

4. Factors of turnout on the individual level

After giving an overview of the development on the aggregate level, we now turn to the individual level to identify personal motives and reasons for participation. Media consumption and campaign exposure will be in our focus in addition to other variables that have been found to be important determinants of electoral behaviour. In contrast to the data in the last section, the following findings are based on the elections of 1994, 1999, and partly 2004. In addition, we analyse German data only, so that our findings cannot be applied to other countries.

4.1 An analytical framework for the analysis of turnout on the individual level

Due to the great variety of variables that influence people's decision to participate in an election or to stay at home, Blondel et al. (1998) tried to find a simple solution for the classification of variables by arranging these variables in a 2x2-matrix. In differentiating between facilitating factors and mobilising factors, on the one hand, they take up the approach of Milbrath and Goel (1977). On the other hand, they consider the level of influence of these factors, separating individual and institutional effects from each other. Referring to the first dimension, there are two conditions that must be fulfilled: as voting is a low cost-low benefit act (Aldrich 1993), the act of voting must not cost too much, must be "cheap" or "easy." All aspects that make voting easier and therefore "cheaper" are called "facilitation" by Blondel et al. This, however, is not sufficient: people only turn out to vote if they are motivated, if there is some incentive. That is what is meant by "mobilisation". Both facilitation and mobilisation take place at the institutional level and the individual level. A fourfold table results from the two dimensions. Almost all variables used in electoral research can be categorised in one of these cells. The list in Figure 1 is not exhaustive but contains some variables which are mainly related to media consumption and effects of the campaign.

Figure 1: The facilitation-mobilisation framework

	Institutional	Individual
facilitation	• administrative arrangements: holidays, day of voting • cognitive facilitation: neutral info campaign, how media report on neutral campaign, TV-debates	• practical: disposable time, residential stability • politically relevant resources: education, media consumption, knowledge about politics, internal efficacy
mobilisation	• long-term: role of elected body • short-term: campaigns by parties & candidates, partisan media coverage	• long-term: party identification, civic duty • short-term: issue & candidate preferences, election-specific party & candidate differentials

Institutional facilitation is quite obviously dependent on the administrative arrangements, for example, day of voting and opening hours of the polling stations. But not only the practical organisation of the voting procedure can be subsumed under the heading of institutional facilitation. Another factor that makes voting easier for the voters is the availability of easily accessible information about the election. People need to be informed that an election will take place, what the election is all about, how the voting system works, and so on. Cognitive facilitation can be boosted mainly by neutral information campaigns and extensive reporting of these things by the media. That is what is meant by cognitive institutional facilitation.

At the individual level voting is easier for someone, who does not have to work on the day of the election, or for people, who have been living in the area for a longer time because they know where the polling station is and can be quite sure that their name will be on the voting list. Besides these practical things, there are politically relevant resources that make voting easier for some people than for others. For somebody who is well-educated, reads the political section of the newspaper regularly, and is interested in politics, it is easier to cast a ballot.

As said before, merely the fact that the act of voting is "cheap" is not sufficient. Nobody takes part in an election because the election is on a Sunday or because the opening hours last from the early morning to the late evening. There has to be some wish to influence politics, a motivation or incentive. Of course, the incentive to vote is stronger if the body that is elected is powerful. That is usually quite stable. Campaigns by parties and candidates or what is called partisan media coverage have to be seen as short-term factors. They change with every election and are dependent on its specific context. Like institutional mobilisation variables, individual mobilisation variables can be differentiated in long- and short-term variables: party identification or the feeling that it is a civic duty to vote usually do not change from election to election. However, issue and candidate preferences mostly are election-specific and therefore short-term.

This analytical framework is not specific for EPE, but serves well to highlight the specific long-term and short-term factors of one type of election like EPE, in comparison to other types like national or local elections. It is also suited to analyse a particular election, such as the 1994, 1999, and 2004 EPE in this case. This will be done by presenting important empirical results and interpreting them in the terms of the facilitation-mobilisation framework. As mentioned above, the focus will be on results about the campaign and the media and will be followed by the application of multivariate methods (logistic regression) to assess the relative importance of the campaign and the media in relation to other determinants of voting in EPE.

4.2 Factors of turnout on the individual level

With respect to the campaign and its effects, it is more useful to look at the mobilisation dimension of the framework than the facilitation dimension. It would be interesting to distinguish between those who are already mobilised before the election approaches and those who have zero or very low levels of prior mobilisation and who, therefore, are dependent on the campaign as a stimulus to get them to go to the polls. This is not an easy task. The variable best suited for discriminating between these two groups of eligible voters might be general interest in politics. However, data on this variable are available for 1994 only.

Table 4: Interest in politics, 1994

	General interest in politics	Interest in EU-politics
Not at all	13.4	16.7
Not much	46.6	49.9
To some extent	30.9	26.4
A great deal	9.0	7.0
N	1.899	1.906

Source: EB 41.1 (1994)

Sixty per cent of the respondents were not interested (not at all or not much) in politics in general in 1994 (see Table 4). Even more, about 65 percent, were uninterested in EU-politics. One can assume that these figures have not changed dramatically since 1994, although this cannot be confirmed because these variables have not been assessed in more recent surveys. A similar picture appears if one looks at the data concerning knowledge about EU personnel: both in 1994 and in 1999 more than half of the respondents neither knew who the President of the Commission was nor national commissioner. Moreover, more than 70 percent of the respondents are not close to any party or are mere sympathizers. After creating a dichotomous variable of political involvement from the three variables general interest in politics, strength of party identification, and knowledge of EU personnel, 34 percent of the respondents in 1994 were classified as not politically involved. In terms of individual mobilisation, this means that those 34 percent probably lack an intrinsic motivation to vote and need additional incentives to go to the polls. This becomes very clear when the correlation between turnout and the dichotomous involvement variable is analysed: only 58 percent of those not politically involved turned out to participate in the 1994 European election compared to 82 percent of the politically involved respondents. Additional incentives can be triggered, for example, by the parties' campaigns or a very high party differential. A problem for the parties is, however, to reach exactly those persons with their campaign, who are not politically involved.

If we look at campaign exposure, the comparison between 1994 and 1999 shows a kind of polarisation (see Table 5). In 1999 the share of German respondents who were passively reached by the campaign was much lower than in 1994. On the other hand, the share of people who did not notice the campaign at all and the share of people who were actively interested in the campaign were both much higher. In 2004 the picture is different. Germans were much more active: 38.4 percent were partially active, while almost half of the respondents were fully active, meaning that they read the newspaper to get information about the EPE and were discussing the topic with friends and relatives.

Table 5: Campaign exposure

	1994	1999	2004
None	5.0	11.6	1.0
Passive	29.4	13.2	11.5
Partially active	43.6	47.8	38.4
Fully active	22.0	27.3	49.1
N	1.917	1.927	1.000

Source: EB 41.1 (1994), EB 52, FL EB 162 (2004)

Campaigning would be most successful for the parties if they managed to reach those groups of people that normally are less likely to vote. By looking at the socio-demographic correlates of campaign awareness, we can examine if this aim was achieved in the two campaigns. As the data show only minor differences in the awareness of the campaign depending on socio-demographic variables, this does seem to be the case. No socio-demographic group seems to be excluded from campaign information, so that we only display results for age groups as an example here and give short information about the other variables (see Rattinger/Huber 2004: 34-36 for the exact effects of other socio-demographic variables). People older than 66 years are somewhat less aware of the campaign in both election years, which is not very surprising, whereas highly educated persons are somewhat more aware of the campaign. Professional status as well shows only minor differences with slightly higher mean values in those occupational categories that are more interested in politics, as for example managers. This result is not surprising as it is not so much a question of educational or financial resources if a person is exposed to the campaign, rather it is a question of interest if one can remember having seen, read or heard it. Table 6 also reflects the rise in campaign exposure for all age groups as already illustrated by Table 5 for all respondents.

Table 6: Mean Campaign exposure according to age

Age Group	1994	1999	2004
18-25	1.84	1.90	2.31
26-35	1.80	1.87	2.25
36-45	1.78	1.93	2.35
46-55	1.99	1.96	2.49
56-65	1.77	1.98	2.44
66-75	1.74	1.79	2.34
75+	1.75	1.69	2.28
N	1.923	1.941	1.000

Source: EB 41.1 (1994), EB 52 (1999), FL EB 162 (2004)

The crucial question for a successful campaign, however, is if in the end it changes a person's behaviour, in this case, if it boosts participation. This is a very difficult question that cannot be answered by the survey data alone. In addition, political scientific research has disregarded effects of party campaigns on turnout while focussing instead on the effect on the decision which party to vote for. This is quite surprising since the mobilisation efficiency of the campaign has effects on the result of an election (see Finkel 1993: 19). To date, it has not been possible to detect a clear-cut effect of the campaign on turnout (see Norris et al. 1999: 97-113).

Table 7 makes it possible to uncover effects of the campaign on turnout. It shows the cross-tabulation of participation in the 1994 European Election with campaign exposure, controlled for political involvement. Turnout clearly rises with campaign awareness ranging from 24 percent among those not involved and not aware of any campaign to 68 percent among those not involved but fully aware of the campaign, a difference of 44 percentage points. In the case of the politically involved, the turnout difference between the two extreme categories of the campaign variable is only 27 percentage points. Thus, the impact of the campaign seems to be stronger among those less interested in politics. The fact that campaign exposure also has an impact on those persons, who are interested in politics, suggests that the relationship between political interest and campaign exposure is reciprocal. Interest in politics facilitates taking part in the campaign, and conversely being actively involved in the campaign seems to raise interest in the election and consequently turnout.

Table 7: Participation in EPE 1994 by political involvement, controlled for campaign exposure

Campaign Exposure	Voting Behaviour in 1994 EPE	Political Involvement	
		Yes	No
None	Voted	64	24
	did not vote	29	66
Passive	Voted	74	55
	did not vote	21	41
Partially active	Voted	83	63
	did not vote	15	35
Fully active	Voted	91	68
	did not vote	8	28

Source: EB 41.1 (1994)

Our results up to this point are mainly from the EPE in 1994 and 1999. The question is, if the conclusions we drew are still true for 2004. We can use data from the Flash-Eurobarometer 162, conducted in June 2004, that contains the question on campaign awareness. In 2004 79 percent of German respondents read about the electoral campaign in the newspapers compared to 75 percent in 1999 (see Table 8). This indicates a slightly more visible campaign in 2004.

Table 8: Campaign exposure in EPE-Campaigns

	1994 (EB 41.1)	1999 (EB 52)	2004 (FlashEB 162)
Coverage on TV and radio	76	77	94
Coverage in the newspapers	58	66	79
Election leaflets received	38	64	56
Advertising	68	62	85
Family, friends or colleagues	29	37	57
Party workers called	3	11	2
Attend public meetings	-	8	4
Contact by phone	-	5	2
Internet	-	3	10

Source: EB 41.1 (1994), FL EB 162 (2004)

That view is supported if we compare the different forms of campaigning in 1999 and 2004. We see an increase in campaign awareness in 2004 especially for those forms and information channels that have already been popular in 1999. Decreases can be reported for the reception of information leaflets, for calls from party workers, the attendance at public meetings, and contact by phone.

In surveys it is difficult to distinguish between the neutral information campaign and the parties' campaigns, because it is likely that the respondents do not distinguish between the two. The Flash-EB 162 included a question where respondents were asked if they had been aware of a non-party campaign or advertisement encouraging people to vote in the EPE. Twenty-eight per cent said that they had been aware of this neutral campaign (see Table 9). Among those who voted, 32 percent had noticed the neutral campaign, whereas only 25 percent of the non-voters did. It is risky however, to interpret this as a success of the neutral campaign without controlling at least for political interest, which unfortunately was not measured.

Table 9: Awareness of neutral information campaigns by turnout

	All respondents	Voters	Non-voters
Yes	28	32	25
No	71	67	74
N	1.000	429	567

Source: FL EB 162 (2004)

4.3 Multivariate analysis of the factors of turnout

To assess the relative importance of campaign exposure in EPE we calculated logistic regressions with socio-demographic variables, attitudes towards the EU, and campaign exposure for 1994 and 1999 (see Table 10, Appendix). In both years it is the same group of variables that contributes significantly to the explanation of turnout, with the exception of education, which was only significant in 1999. In reference to the socio-demographic variables, age and income contribute to explain turnout (in 1999 education as well).

A look at the attitudinal variables shows that in 1994 being aware of the campaign increased the probability of voting the most, followed by knowledge of EU personnel, and a positive attitude to membership of one's own country in the EU. High party differential has less power of explanation than all other variables with significant effects. The comparison between 1994 and 1999 reveals some interesting shifts in the importance of the different attitudinal variables to explain turnout. Having a high party differential became much more important. The influence of campaign exposure increased as well, whereas knowledge of EU-personnel and the attitude toward membership in the EU both had smaller effects on the decision to turn out.

5. Conclusion

While analysis on the aggregate level more or less showed a decline of turnout in all member states and substantial differences between turnout in national parliament elections and accession referenda on the one hand and EPE on the other, our analysis with individual data for Germany tried to explain these differences and changes. Bivariate and multivariate analyses come to the result that the campaign is an important variable to explain individual turnout in EPE. It has a higher impact on uninvolved voters. Comparison over time shows that campaign awareness has increased from 1994 to 1999 and again from 1999 to 2004, which does not correspond to the development of turnout between both elections. However, the campaign is only one of many other determinants of turnout. A look at the vast literature on the explanation of turnout differences between electoral levels as well as further analyses that could not be discussed in this chapter show the importance of the feeling of a duty to vote (see Kleinhenz 1995: 126-132; Eilfort 1994; Roth 1992). This feeling appears to be not as strong and widespread anymore, especially among younger generations. Looking at Europe-specific variables and attitudes, one must say that these are of minor importance. Hence, the expressive function of EPE (general support of European integration) does not mobilise voters (anymore). This applies to the new member states, too, as displayed by the large turnout differences between the EPE 2004 and the accession referenda, the former obviously appearing much less important than the latter.

Consequently, to enhance turnout it seems essential to promote the important role of the EP. To mobilise the electorate it is necessary to convince people that it is important which parties and candidates are represented in the EP. This underscores the importance of both neutral information campaigns and partisan campaigns as well as the role of the media in bringing these to the voters' minds.

Table 10: Multivariate stepwise logistic regressions. Dependent Variable: Turnout in European Parliament Elections 1994 and 1999

Variables in the regression:	1994			1999		
	B	Exp(B)	entered on step	B	Exp(B)	entered on step	classification result
Age	1.389***	4.010	4	1.882***	6.565	4	70.5
Female	-	-	-	-	-	-	-
Education (age at which full time education was completed)	-	-	-	.383*	1.467	7	71.5
Income (in quartiles, mean sub.)	.802***	2.230	5	.507***	1.661	6	71.5
Retired	-	-	-	-	-	-	-
Left-right self-placement (10 point scale, mean sub.	-	-	-	-	-	-	-
Extremism (derived from left-right scale)	-	-	-	-	-	-	-
Knowledge of EU personnel (does not know anybody / knows either Pres. of Commission or nat. commissioner / knows both)	1.204	3.335	1	.917***	2.501	3	68.5
Satisfaction with democracy in EU (5-point scale, mean sub.)	-	-	-	-	-	-	-
Power of EP (10-point scale, mean sub.)	-	-	-	-	-	-	-
Attitude to membership in EU (bad thing / neither good nor bad / good thing)	1.069***	2.913	2	.792***	2.208	5	70.1
Own country benefited by EU	-	-	-	-	-	-	-
Campaign exposure (none / passive / partly active / fully active)	1.463***	4.320	3	2.021***	7.545	1	63.0
Party differential EU elections (10-point scale, mean sub.)	.743***	2.101	6	2.490***	12.065	2	67.2
Constant	2.276***			-4.747***			
	Nagelkerke's R-Square: 0.214			Nagelkerke's R-Square: 0.327			

Levels of significance: *** α< 0.001; ** α<0.01; * α<0.05
Source: EB 41.1 (1994), EB 52 (1999)

References

Aldrich, John H. (1993): Rational Choice and Turnout. In: American Journal of Political Science, Vol. 37, No. 1, 246-278.
Blondel, Jean et al. (1998): People and Parliament in the European Union. Participation, Democracy, and Legitimacy. Oxford: Clarendon Press.
Eilfort, Michael (1994): Die Nichtwähler. Wahlenthaltung als Form des Wahlverhaltens. Paderborn: Schöningh [The Nonvoters. Electoral Abstention as a Form of Electoral Behaviour].
Finkel, Steven E. (1993): Reexamining the 'Minimal Effects' Model in Recent Presidential Campaigns. In: Journal of Politics, Vol. 55, No. 1, 1-21.
Franklin, Mark N. (2001): How Structural Factors Cause Turnout Variations at European Parliament Elections. In: European Union Politics, Vol. 2, No. 3, 309-328.
Kleinhenz, Thomas (1995): Die Nichtwähler. Ursachen der sinkenden Wahlbeteiligung in Deutschland. Opladen: Westdeutscher Verlag [The Nonvoters. Reasons for Declining Turnout in Germany].
Milbrath, Lester W./Goel, Maden L. (1977[2]): Political Participation. How and Why Do People Get Involved in Politics? Washington D.C.: University Press of America.
Norris, Pippa et al. (1999): On Message. Communicating the Campaign. London: Sage.
Rattinger, Hans/Huber, Sandra (2004): Democratic Participation and Political Communication in Systems of Multi-level Governance. The Case of Germany. Bamberg: BACES Discussion Paper Nr. 2. At: http://www.baces.uni-bamberg.de/Texte/discussion_paper2.pdf, retrieval June 24th 2005.
Reif, Karlheinz/Schmitt, Hermann (1980): Nine Second-Order National Elections. A Conceptual Framework for the Analysis of European Election Results. In: European Journal of Political Research, Vol. 8, No. 1, 3-44.
Reif, Karlheinz (1984): European Elections 1979/81 and 1984. Conclusions and Perspectives from Empirical Research. Berlin: Quorum.
Reif, Karlheinz (1997): European Elections as Member State Second-Order Elections Revisited. In: European Journal of Political Research, Vol. 31, No. 1, 115-124.
Roth, Dieter (1992): Sinkende Wahlbeteiligung. Eher Normalisierung oder Krisensymptom . In: Starzacher, Karl et al. (Eds.): Protestwähler und Wahlverweigerer. Köln: Bund, 58-68 [Roth: Declining Turnout. Rather Normalisation or Symptom of a Crisis. In: Starzacher et al.: Protest Voters and Elections' Denial].
Scharpf, Fritz (1975): Demokratietheorie zwischen Utopie und Anpassung. Kronberg/Ts.: Scriptor [Theory of Democracy between Utopia and Adjustment].

van der Eijk, Cees/Franklin, Mark N. (1996): Choosing Europe? The European Electorate and National Politics in the Face of the Union. Ann Arbor: The University of Michigan Press.

The Long Road to Professionalisation: Campaigning in Europe vs. Campaigning for Europe

Ralph Negrine[*]

1. Introduction

There can be little doubt that the nature of political campaigning in national and European elections has changed considerably over the last three or four decades: new techniques are being used, new principles and strategies are being adopted, and new types of personnel are being employed. Sometimes that change in election practices has been interpreted as a professionalisation of election campaigning; at other times it has been seen as confirmation of the application of political marketing techniques to election campaigning (see Scammell 1996; Lees-Marshment 2001; Gould 1998).

Those sorts of interpretations are quite useful because they point to change – from, say, amateur to professional campaigning – but it is possible to argue that such interpretations not only simplify a much more complex historical process in which political parties continually adapt their practices to changing circumstances, but also mask interesting structural changes within political parties. In this respect, it is often easier to *claim* that there has been a professionalisation of campaigning in Europe than to actually demonstrate its extent, its significance or its consequences. In other words, it is still important to identify more clearly the processes involved and the nature of the change that allows us to use the term professionalisation (see Lilleker/Negrine 2002).

It follows on from this, that there are related questions about whether campaigning in Europe, and for the European elections, can also be described as professional. Do they, for example, make use of expert or professional personnel and techniques, strategies and practices as are used in national elections or are there limits to the professionalisation of campaigning for European elections? Using material drawn from the 2004 European elections in Britain, this paper will argue that there may be certain factors that can act as constraints on the application of fully professional techniques in the European context.

The first part of this paper will explore the broader issue of professionalisation of campaigning. It will look at different interpretations of the use of the phrase and suggest how it can be applied more generally. The second part of this paper will focus on the 2004 European election in Britain in order to develop the

---

[*] Ralph Negrine, PhD. *1951. Professor of Political Communication, Department of Journalism Studies, University of Sheffield, Sheffield, S1 3NJ, email: r.negrine@sheffield.ac.uk

argument that different elections need to be treated differently and pose different sorts of questions and issues.

2. The meaning of professionalisation

Words such as profession and professional are usually used in relation to certain types of occupations that involve lengthy periods of training, codes of ethics which all members of the profession accept, a service ideal, and high levels of autonomy. These characteristics are derived from the 'classic' professions of medicine and law but other occupations that seek to change their status also often make claims to being professions or becoming professionalised (see MacDonald 1996). It is highly unlikely that those who work within election campaigns, say, would be able to justify claims to being professional in the strict sociological sense of the word and this would suggest that the use of the word within the field of political communication is much less strict and applied far more generally (see Webb/Fisher 2003; Scammell 1998).

In common usage, "professionalisation" is most likely to refer to a process of change that, either explicitly or implicitly, brings about a different and more efficient organisation of resources and skills in order to achieve desired objectives. It suggests a 'higher' stage of development or even perhaps an improvement on what went on before. For example, a university that improves its procedures may be said to be more professional than before, and this would apply to nearly all organisational change. In the field of political communication, one could then make a case for saying that improvements in a variety of fields can also be seen as efforts to make things more professional. This could be in relation to the operation of communication facilities (a more skilful use of television techniques), campaigning techniques (employment of consultants, better use of polling data, for example), the re-organisation of political parties themselves (as in centralization), the re-organisation of government communication systems (as in the creation of a centralized communication directorate to co-ordinate publicity) and even in respect of media-politics relations (e.g. as in news management techniques).

But if we are going to use the word in this way, we need to acknowledge that the process we are dealing with is much more complex than simply pointing to the use of newer technologies of communication or to the employment of consultants. These things may be important but in a longer historical sweep, one finds that political parties – and governments, commercial organisations, universities, etc – are nearly always engaged in processes of *self-reflection and self-improvement in order to enhance their organisational and electoral chances* (see e.g. Wernick 1991). In this respect, the changes that take place in the organisation of political parties for the purpose of conducting election campaigns – centralisation, use of consultants, use of new technologies, and the like – could be seen as simply an integral part of a continuous dialogue between political organisations and their environment. In which case, political parties as other organisations need to constantly reshape and reconfigure themselves if they wish to survive and thrive. They cannot afford not to change; they cannot afford not to "professionalise" their activities in order to better their work and performance.

Such an interpretation of the word "professionalisation" as applied to political parties and campaigning is obviously quite different from the use of the word in the sociological literature. One reason it is preferred here is that the sociological use of the word is highly contested and one can easily enter a controversy about what is or is not a profession and what characteristics are or are not applied. Often such discussions can be fruitless and in this particular context unhelpful. What, for example, would one do if it was decided that none of the characteristics of professions apply in the case of political consultants and campaign experts? Do we abandon the use of the words and the idea of the professional campaign or do we think more constructively about how the word is used in this field of political communication. I suggest that latter which is perhaps why the more flexible interpretation is preferred.

A somewhat different interpretation of the concept of „professional campaigning" can be found in a recent paper by Dennis Kavanagh. He has approached the topic from a different perspective, and perhaps using a much stricter interpretation than may be appropriate. According to Dennis Kavanagh, „the concept of campaigning professionalisation is defined largely in marketing terms. A professional party is one that has clear objectives, is disciplined, adheres to a message which has been shaped by research, implements its communications effectively, and is united".

There can be little doubt that these are truly properties of professional parties. However, this interpretation, if taken very literally, would probably *exclude* nearly all political parties before the emergence of *New Labour* in Britain from the late 1980s onwards. This is in part because none were as disciplined, as efficient, or as market oriented as *New Labour* and so could not necessarily be labelled as a "professional party". Another reason would be that political parties have continually tried to improve themselves – to professionalise themselves, in common parlance – even before such words or language were in common use to describe that very process.

Where Dennis Kavanagh is absolutely correct, though, is in his analysis of the consequences of political parties "professionalizing" themselves. In centralizing their structures, in becoming more elite focused, using marketing research tools to develop policies, and disconnecting from their memberships, they cease to be mass parties and begin the long process of decline as viable mass organisations.[1]

It could be, of course, that the process of "professionalisation" takes root precisely because political parties no longer have the allegiances of their traditional electoral base and so need to find alternative means to persuade and mobilise potential voters.

However one analyses the processes of transition for political parties, the end results across most European countries are fairly similar: they are now more centralised, more elite centred parties, and they use external strategic and technical help (consultants, pollsters, TV producers) to persuade and mobilise voters who no longer have firm allegiances (see Farrell et al., 2001; Norris 2000). As Plasser and Plasser (2002: 310) put it, "professionalisation and its concomitant orientation of strategic vote management probably represents one of the most momentous *reaction strategies* of political parties in the long run".

The most obvious and outward indicators of "professionalisation" in respect of political parties is the use of consultants or experts to give direction to their election campaigns, to produce strategies and to provide levels of technical support that political parties themselves could not, or are unable to, provide. This is implied in most interpretations of "professionalisation" though it is important to ask why precisely such "outsiders" are employed: is it a "logical" or "rational" progression and adaptation to the modern world of politics or is it something that is qualitatively different from the past? Put differently, if we were to find examples of 'outsiders' being used by political parties in the 1950s, say, would this mean that those political parties were professional and so no different from the contemporary parties, or are there other changes of an institutional or organizational kind that differentiate today's more professional party from an older one? Furthermore, and perhaps more critically, how do such outside experts interact and relate to party workers, and who has ultimate control over the development of strategies for campaigning and over policy-development? Again, how one answers these questions impact on how we interpret the moves towards professionalisation, as well as the characteristics of that process.

One way to try and answer these sorts of questions is to use Maggie Scammell's suggestion based on her study of the US and Britain that one aspect of professionalisation is the idea of *displacement*, that is,

"*party strategists have been displaced by non-party 'professional' strategists. Employed at first for their expertise with the technologies (arising from specialization), the professionals become increasingly central to campaign strategy and even policy-making*" (Scammell 1998: 256).

Such "experts", in other words, take over tasks that were formerly carried out by party members. With *displacement*, it is also likely that the ideological profile of a political party will change and that it will become less ideological as the emphasis switches to winning votes from a larger constituency than would normally be supportive of that political party. In effect, this analysis points to a general move away from the "traditional mass party" and towards the modern "electoral-professional party" in which professionals (pollsters, marketers, consultants, media advisers) drawn from outside the party come to occupy key positions, often replacing party bureaucrats and leaders in key campaign and organisational roles (see Mair 1998). The "professional" political party is thus no more than an organisation permanently seeking electoral advantage, along the lines suggested by Kavanagh (2003: 3).

Whilst this form of analysis is useful, the changes alluded to are perhaps more complex and less straightforward than suggested. It is certainly the case that British political parties have used a host of professionals – strategists, pollsters, and advertisers for example – but this is not a recent phenomenon. It stretches back at least to the 1950s and their use does raise the question of how they are inserted into political parties and how much direction they give the campaign and its constituent parts. For example, in recent British national elections, "professionals" have tended to lend support to political and party leaders, rather than take over and control all aspects of the campaign – and the evidence does suggest that political parties use them to extend their potential to persuade and mobilise voters (see Cook 2002; Gould 1998). Perhaps it is less of a matter of displacement than a reconfiguring of roles and tasks within election campaigns.

More critically, it is still an open question as to whether changes in party organisation have come about because of the increased use of "professionals" or whether the increased use of professionals reflects the changing nature of (party) politics in contemporary societies brought about by socio-political and technological change?[2]

So, whilst it is generally accepted that consultants/experts are increasingly used in key campaign roles and that more attention is being paid to campaigning issues, the extent, significance and meaning of these developments remain open to discussion and further research. Indeed, if one adds the historical dimension and notes the use of advertisers and pollsters in the recent past, there is then a further set of questions about how contemporary use differs qualitatively and quantitatively from use in the recent past.

3. Understanding campaigning and professionalisation in, and for Europe?

At a general level, the evidence that is available regarding changes in the Netherlands, Sweden, Germany, Italy, Greece and the UK lends support to the view that parties are becoming more centralized and more elite oriented.[3]

To return to an earlier point, they are becoming "electoral-professional" parties. They are "more capital-intensive party organisations" than before; the party leadership is more "remote from the everyday life of the citizen" and the role of the membership is much more limited (Mair 1998: 11, 37).

But as has already indicated, these are tendencies; not all parties in all countries exhibit all the tendencies and there may be other factors to take into account when looking at how one interprets these developments. For example,

- "experts" usually claim to provide the background research only and they claim not to make the final decisions (see Gould 1998). In which case, politicians are still determining the direction of development. It is, however, also possible that politicians share responsibility for certain decisions but not for

others. In which case there may be different levels of professionalisation within different countries as parties do not always move at the same speeds.
- political parties are also constantly changing and may be in the process of improving themselves or professionalising themselves so complicating the distinction of what is an external or internal influence (see Farrell/Webb 2002, for a brief discussion of the *Labour Party*). A good example of this comes from Britain where the *Labour Party* has begun to recruit, train and employ "professional organizers". Under the "Trainee Organizer Scheme", as it is known, the party recruits individuals who spend time in the party and get "intensive training. If they are successful, they will have the chance to work for the party as professional organizers until after the next general election" (Labour Party 2003: 28). This does raise the possibility that political parties may decide to pick and choose what sorts of tasks can be completed professionally from within and what tasks can be undertaken by outsiders. Consequently a different set of relationships is established between the political party and its chosen "outside" and "inside" experts.

More generally, political parties can probably use a number of different organisational arrangements to obtain that expert advice they need: they might employ full-time permanent employees – although this is probably rare since it is expensive when elections are contested so infrequently – or they might prefer to "buy-in" or contract out services. In some circumstances these professionals do not necessarily have an exclusive relationship with one political party, but the available evidence suggests that, by and large, professional advisers/experts/consultants work with politicians and parties with whom they have some affinity (see Kolodny 2000).

It may be, then, that political parties continue to be run by party employees and their political masters – some of whom may have obtained or may have improved their "professional skills" – but that the task of mobilising the party leads to the use of a individuals who have developed skills in those particular areas, e.g. polling, vote-management, and so on. Their main task is then to coordinate the campaign and lend support to its progression over the election campaign itself. In other words, they take on the role of promoting the party in both strategic and practical/technical ways. Given that modern democracies are media saturated, it comes as no surprise that dealing with the media takes on an added significance. And the more independent the media, the greater the dependence of the political party on professionals who can help it communicate with the outside world.

How far does this model and the suggestions of a more gradualist approach as parties adapt to changing circumstances apply to the European context? The evidence is mixed though, by and large, some aspects of campaigning have been placed in the hands of outside marketing and polling experts or, at the very least, parties have been aided by outside help. This is not a new phenomenon but it may be a tendency that has accelerated in recent years. Yet it is a tendency whose intensity is uneven. It is more likely to take place in national than local elections, or national elections than "second order elections". In the case of Italy, Paolo Mancini (2006) has suggested that the national level is better organised than the local level; in the case of Germany, Holtz-Bacha (2006) has suggested that professionalisation "proceeds at two speeds. When it comes to campaign communication, professionalisation has developed quite extensively, but the process has developed less in respect of routine political communication". Similarly for Sweden where the political "parties have more people working with communication issues than ever before and most modern practices in political marketing are used, especially during election campaigns. However, the parties are still characterized by a value-based or ideological organisational structure. The campaign party has not as yet replaced the party of ideas or the issue party, but all parties are gradually becoming more market-oriented, and are thus also becoming more professionalized" (Nord 2006).

In Britain, we have also seen a continuing use of professionals and experts – pollsters, advertisers, and strategists – but there is as yet no clarity as to whether these have completely displaced party officials/employees or are simply lending support and offering advice. Contributions to a study of the 2001 election show how the *Conservative Party* leader, William Hague, appeared to ignore informed advice on how he should run the campaign and what issues he should campaign on (see Cooper 2002) and one *Labour Party* employee and polling expert has written that "the fatuous suggestion that government policy is directed by polls or by the mythical focus group is a caricature of the process and its role" (Cook 2002: 87).

Nevertheless, it is obvious that political parties use outside experts and/or professional help in a number of different ways in order to achieve their main objective, namely election victory. And in the process of the campaign, the experts – either from outside or from within – are able to devise strategies that create a profile, a message and a set of policies that will be to the advantage of their party and to the disadvantage of all opposing parties. National elections provide the setting for the professionalised campaign: they are critical elections, use up enormous resources and generally occupy a high level of importance in the minds of both politicians and the electorate. By contrast, the European elections are regarded as being somewhat less important. Historically, they have attracted fewer voters, for example, and they generally do not have the same high profile as national elections. In this respect, they do fit into the category of "second order" elections (Reif/Schmitt 1980). But the fact that European elections are regarded as "second order" elections does not mean that they cannot necessarily be conducted in a professional way. Nevertheless, as the next section of this paper suggests, there may be certain important factors in European election campaigns that limit the extent to which they can be deemed to be professional campaigns.

4. The 2004 European campaign in Britain

As has been argued above, it is unlikely that the European elections will occupy the attention or the resources of politicians and the public that national elections do. In this respect, European elections are seen to be less important and less critical than national elections and this has consequences for the way European elections are funded, organised and run. The same would also be true of sub-national elections such as local, regional and even mayoral elections.

It is a safe bet, then, to observe that the EU election campaign is unlikely to engage the attention of professional consultants, at least in a paid capacity. For example, it is difficult to envisage internationally known political communication consultants such as the American Stanley Greenberg or the Australian Lynton Crosby flying in to offer advice on how to run an EU campaign, not because it would not be a formidable challenge but because the dynamics of the EU campaign make it very unlike the sorts of campaigns that attract professional experts, not least because the issues tend to cut across traditional party lines. At least five factors make those dynamics very different, and it is useful to consider them bearing in mind the main characteristics of a professional campaign. The five factors are:

The first factor is the difficulty of clarifying to the voters what "campaigning for Europe" actually means. This is a continuing problem that journalists, but to a lesser extent politicians also, face. Journalists write little about "Europe" and find it harder to write about "Europe" in a way that points out the importance of the elections and the choices that have to be made.[4] Although British journalists did attempt to deal with this task by producing the customary "what has Europe done for you" articles such as 'Let's wise up to Europe' (Leicester Mercury, May 26th 2005), it was not an easy task: the issues do not stand out very clearly or distinctively and the complexities of Europe and the European Union cannot be easily simplified for the reader or viewer.

So, did the public get a sense of what the 2004 European elections were about? Preliminary research carried out for the Electoral Commission has found that the campaign reached more people and that the public felt better informed than in previous elections. It also found that people were more likely to identify differences between the policies the parties were offering and that "the media played an important part in providing the public with election information" (www.electoralcommission.org). At this stage, the details of these studies are not available. At first sight, they emphasise the role of the media and the public's ability to distinguish between the major party policies, although this point might need further elaboration since one of the parties – the *Conservatives* – adopted a very unclear policy towards Europe (see below). One other piece of evidence regarding the election is worth noting, and this sits uneasily next to the study noted above: according to a content analysis of 'opinion-leading (print and broadcast) media of the twenty-five member countries' of the EU carried out by

Media Tenor most of the information received by the public through the media was negative in tone (http://www.mediatenor.com/Euproj.html).

As these studies roll out, we will begin to get a better sense of the way the media fed the debates, the public's perceptions of the debates and, more important for our purposes, the extent to which the messages were indeed clear and obvious.

One other point is worth taking note of in respect to the clarity of the campaign. The EU elections in Britain took place on the same day as some local and mayoral elections. This may also have caused some confusion amongst voters, more so given that voting preferences in these other elections are influenced by national politics, so that the European elections were not fought exclusively on their own behalf. Admittedly, there were attempts by the Electoral Commission to highlight the issues for the three elections but this only illustrates how difficult it is to make European elections distinctive.

The second factor is that the EU campaign in Britain was run and reported as an extension of British domestic politics. This may be something that also happened in other European countries but in Britain, at least, some of the campaign appeared to have distinctly national and domestic priorities. A number of things illustrate this point.

1. The first *Labour Party* television election broadcast was entirely about Michael Howard, the leader of the *Conservative* opposition. With the background music titled "If you don't know him by now", the broadcast sought to remind voters that a vote for the *Conservatives* was a vote for a 1990s politician. Europe and European issues did not feature in this broadcast and it was considered a particularly negative broadcast aimed at discrediting the leader of the opposition. But *Labour* was not the only party to use national politics to engage the attention of voters: the *Liberal Democrat* broadcast was about the Iraq war and, hence, about the questionable policies of the *Labour Party* in government.
2. The leaflets produced by the political parties reflected both a concern with national and domestic politics – e.g. "*Labour* cannot be trusted" – but also indications that the parties would all work for a "better" Europe. Inevitably, this "better" Europe would be one in which jobs were protected, the environment improved, and so on... all fairly general statements of intent that sat alongside the strong message that national and domestic politics would indicate how much one trusted the message on Europe.
3. Finally, the political parties – especially the *Conservative Party* and *UKIP* (*United Kingdom Independence Party*) – had to play a tactical game. The *Conservatives* had to tread a fine line between asking for withdrawal (so alienating its pro-EU voters and members) and asking for continued membership (so pushing its voters and members into the arms of *UKIP* which called for withdrawal from Europe). The result of the posturing was a lack of clarity, something that was very much in evidence in one of the party's newspaper advertisements which declared that "We don't want to live in a

country called Europe". Not surprisingly, the *Labour Party* played both sides of this particular political divide against one another.

The election result showed, however, that *UKIP*'s simple message of withdrawal from Europe did have some considerable support, though the other major parties fared well in their traditional heartlands. *UKIP* achieved an overall average of 16.1 percent of the votes as against the *Conservatives* 26.7 percent, *Labour*'s 22.6 percent and the *Liberal Democrats* 14.9 percent. U-KIP won ten new seats in the 2004 elections (BBC 2004).

The third factor relates to resources. Do parties spend hard earned money when general elections are looming, as is the case for Britain with the general election expected in the spring of 2005? During the 2001 general election, the parties spent nearly £30 million (approximately 44 million Euros) on their campaigns but only about one-third of that during the 2004 EU elections. The *Labour Party* spent nearly £11 million (approximately 16 million Euros) and £1.7 million (approximately 2.5 million Euros) respectively (see Electoral Commission 2005). Given the spending limits imposed on electioneering, it is hardly surprising that these can also be taken as an indication of the extent to which political parties are prepared and willing to "professionalise" their EU campaigns.

What is clearer, though, is that generally speaking there are few resources to devote to publicising European issues. In July 2004, the Minister for Europe revealed that he only had £200.000 (approximately 300.000 Euros) to spend on making the case for the EU constitution. This was one fifth of the amount to be spent on publicising the Home Office's drugs policy, and a miniscule amount compared to the £138 million (approximately 212 million Euros) that the government spent on publicity in 2003 (see The Guardian 2004).

The fourth factor is that the EU elections use a list system. In other words, who is elected is decided through a list system, that is, the party publishes a list of candidates in descending order and the number of candidates elected is dependent on the votes cast for the party, not the individual. In this way there is less opportunity to *personalise* the campaign, and to work with individuals. The "ideal-type" "professional" campaign tends to feature prominently one individual – the President/ Challenger; leaders of the parties, etc. – and to build campaigns around the individual or, at most, a core team. This is not possible under a list system although the profile of the party leader and his/her fortunes in national and domestic politics can often impact on the share of the vote. Nevertheless, the basic point remains that professional campaigns tend to personalise the contest and that this is something that is much more difficult to do under a list system. Interestingly, Britain did have one high profile, ex-*Labour* MP and ex-TV chat show host (Robert Kilroy-Silk) stand for election and, perhaps not surprisingly, he – and the party he stood for (*UKIP*) – attracted considerable media attention nationally and regionally. He was elected as an MEP, although he subsequently used his high profile to mount an (unsuccessful) challenge for the leadership of the party.[5]

The fifth point is that it is more difficult to identify the key issues for parties, the unique selling points, in European elections. The *UKIP* party might have had an advantage: its message was clear and distinct. The other parties' messages were much less so, with the *Conservative Party*'s message particularly unclear because of its own domestic agenda and internal divisions. This connects with the first factor – mentioned above – but it does have the effect of making it much more difficult to devise and / or design those simple and clear messages that are so commonplace in "professionalised" election campaigns.

One final point needs to be added to this list but is dealt with as an additional point rather than a more general one because it did not apply to the whole of the UK. In certain regions of the UK, the European election was conducted as a postal ballot only. Voters received their ballot papers through the post about ten days prior to the election date of June 10th and they could vote anytime up to that election date. Although the turnout was higher than usual on account of this change in voting systems – in the East Midlands regions it was 43.4 percent as against a national average turnout of 38.2 percent (see BBC 2004) – one important effect of all-postal ballots is that voters can vote at any time and may therefore cast their votes without seeing any of the messages the parties produce in the immediate run-up to election day. More generally, such a voting system alters the dynamics of campaigning and may complicate traditional practices of canvassing and knocking on doors.

If we place these points together, and we could probably add to this list, we can see how different the EU campaigns are from the classic professionally run campaigns in the US, with their high-cost, television-driven and personalised characteristics. The dynamics are different, the processes are different and so there are limits to the way the EU campaign can be marketed to the public, difficulties that can be interpreted as limits to "professionalisation".

5. Conclusion: Was this a professional campaign?

The obvious answer is that, at least in Britain, it was more "politics as usual" than a professional campaign as usually defined. During the European elections of 2004, there was little that the ordinary voter could remotely describe as evidence of extreme "professionalisation". The publicity campaigns were not up to their usual general election standard and tended to focus on domestic issues. It may be that behind the scenes the best party strategists were at work silently pulling strings but there was no real evidence of this in the public realm. The parties had obviously planned their strategies but one should properly question whether they had planned the *right* strategies, at least in terms of meeting head-on the European agenda.

Unless European Elections acquire the same level of resources devoted to other campaigns, they will rarely acquire the importance of other campaigns in the eyes of the public or the media. Or, and this is also a distinct possibility, unless the political parties are able to persuade voters that European elections are not only distinctive but of critical importance, they are unlikely to acquire large amounts of resources. Paradoxically, we may need to move towards more "professionalised" European campaigns before the European Elections emerge as important campaigns in themselves.

References

BBC (2004): http://news.bbc.co.uk/1/shared/bsp/hi/vote2004/euro_uk/html/front.stm, retrieval Oct. 21th 2004.

Cook, Greg (2002): The Labour Campaign. In: Bartle, John/Atkinson, Simon/Mortimore, Roger (Eds.): Political Communications. The General Election of 2001. London: Frank Cass, 87-97.

Cooper, Andrew (2002): The Conservative Campaign. In: Bartle, John/Atkinson, Simon/Mortimore, Roger (Eds.): Political Communications. The General Election of 2001. London: Frank Cass, 98-108.

Electoral Commission. At: http://www.electoralcommission.org.uk/mediacentre/newsreleasecorprate.cfm/news/364 and http://www.electoralcommission.gov.uk/mediacentre/newsreleasecorporate.cfm/news/412, retrieval February 2005.

Farrell, David M./Kolodny, Robin/Medvic, Stephen (2001): Parties and Campaign Professionals in a Digital Age. In: Harvard International Journal of Press/Politics, Vol. 6, No. 4, 11-30.

Farrell, David/Webb, Paul (2002): Political Parties as Campaign Organizations. In: Dalton, Ronald J./Wattenberg, Martin P. (Eds.): Parties Without Partisans. Political Change in Advanced Industrial Democracies. Oxford: OUP, 102-128.

Gould, Philip (1998): The Unfinished Revolution. London: Abacus.

Holtz-Bacha, Christina (2006): Professionalization of Politics in Germany. In: Negrine, Ralph/Mancini, Paolo/Holtz-Bacha, Christina/Papathanassopoulos, Stylianos (Eds.): The Professionalization of Political Communication. Bristol: Intellect Publishers (forthcoming).

Kavanagh, Dennis (2003): Democracy and Political Marketing: No Place for Amateurs. Paper delivered in Germany.

Kolodny, Robin (2000): Electoral Partnerships: Political Consultants and Political Parties. In: Thurber, James/Candice J. Nelson (Eds.): Campaign Warriors. Political Consultants in Elections. Washington: Brookings, 110-132.

Labour Party (2003): 'The Professionals' *Inside Labour*. London: Labour Party.

Lawson, N./Thompson, P. (2004): The Stakes are too High. In: The Guardian, 9th August, 11.

Leicester Mercury, (2005): Let's Wise up to Europe, May 26th 2005 Lilleker, Darren/Negrine, Ralph (2002): Professionalisation: of What? Since When?

By Whom? In: Harvard International Journal of Press/Politics, Vol. 7, No. 4, 98-103.
Mair, Peter (1998): Party System Change. Approaches and Interpretations. Clarendon Press. Oxford.
Media Tenor (2004): Media Coverage of Europe and Union's Parliament Before June 13 Insufficient and Highly Negative in Tone. At: www.mediatenor.com/EUproj.html, retrieval September 2004.
Mancini, Paolo (2006): Old and New Political Professionalism in Italy. In: Negrine, Ralph/Mancini, Paolo/Holtz-Bacha, Christina/Papathanassopoulos, Stylianos (Eds.): The Professionalization of Political Communication. Bristol: Intellect Publishers (forthcoming).
Negrine, Ralph/Mancini, Paolo/Holtz-Bacha, Christina/Papathanassopoulos, Stylianos (Eds.) (2006): The Professionalization of Political Communication. Bristol: Intellect Publishers (forthcoming).
Nord, Lars (2006): The Swedish Model Becomes Less Swedish. In: Negrine, Ralph/Mancini, Paolo/Holtz-Bacha, Christina/Papathanassopoulos, Stylianos (Eds.): The Professionalization of Political Communication. Bristol: Intellect Publishers (forthcoming).
Norris, Pippa (2000): A Virtuous Circle. Cambridge: Cambridge University Press.
Plasser, Fritz/Plasser, Gunda (2002): Global Political Campaigning. Praeger: London.
Reif, Karlheinz/Schmitt, Hermann (1980): Nine Second Order National Elections: A Conceptual Framework for the Analayis of Eureopan Election Results. In: European Journal of Political Research, Vol. 8, No. 1, 3-44.
Scammell, Maggie (1996): Designer Politics. How Elections Are Won. Basingstoke: Macmillan.
Scammell, Maggie (1998): The Wisdom of the War Room: US Campaigning and Americanization. In: Media, Culture and Society, Vol. 20, No. 2, 251-276.
Webb, Paul/Fisher, Justin (2003): Professionalism and the Millbank Tendency: the Political Sociology of New Labour's Employees. In: Politics, Vol. 23, No. 1, 10-20.
Wernick, Andrew (1991): Promotional Culture, London: Sage.
Wintour, Patrick (2004): I've Only £200.000 to Make Case for Europe – Minister. The Guardian, 7th August 2004. At: http://politics.guardian.co.uk/eu/story/0,,1278087,00.html, retrieval Aug. 7th 2004.

---

[1] Interestingly, this is precisely the debate now taking place within the *Labour Party* in the UK. In the pursuit of electoral success, does the professional electoral party inevitably leave its members (and ideology) behind (see Lawson/Thompson 2004: 11)?

² A separate issue is whether the increased use of professionals simply reflects a "professionalisation" of everyone as roles become more specialised and hence just a different way of carrying out a series of functions.
³ The discussion here draws on Negrine et al. 2006. It also draws on work carried out on ESRC project, R000223540 *MPs and the Media: a study of professionalization in political communication.*
⁴ Of 27 items in the local midlands paper, Leicester Mercury, 13 were about the procedural concerns over how to vote and the postal ballot scheme, seven were generally about politics and Europe, and seven dealt with the different positions of the political parties. These appeared in the month before the election date.
⁵ He left the party late in 2004 and then stood – unsuccessfully – for a parliamentary seat in the general election of 2005.

Media Structures as an Obstacle to the Europeanization of Public Spheres? Development of a Cross-National Typology[1]

Silke Adam & Barbara Berkel[*]

1. Media structures and Europeanization

European campaigns – as any other electoral campaign – need mass media to reach citizens. The special challenge is that European campaigns cannot build on a functioning European media system, but have to transmit messages in 25 different national media systems. Research on this fundamental problem is conducted in a wider context that investigates the openness of national public spheres for European actors and issues (see Gerhards/Neidhardt 1991: 42-43; Pfetsch 1994: 12). Content analyses reveal doubts whether national media have the potential to serve as a platform for European campaigns. Until 1995, national media were found to have a strong national focus and thus withstand the political changes (see Gerhards 2000: 288; Sievert 1998: 241). However, recent studies reveal inconsistent results: Risse and van de Steeg (2003: 3) conclude that the salience of Europe is generally increasing in the media, while Peter and de Vreese (2003: 23) reject this claim with regard to national TV news across Europe. In sum, the Europeanization of public spheres proves to be a complex process that varies among different media types (see Kevin 2003), issue fields (see Koopmans/Erbe 2003), and nations (see Peter 2003).

To better understand the multiple changes, researchers have shifted their concern to the analysis of the factors that contribute to or hinder a process of Europeanization. On the one hand, reasons for the lack of Europeanization are seen in conditions inherent in the political process, for example that most European decision-makers such as the members of the European Council or the European Commission are legitimised by national electorates and thus are not interested in publicity work (see Gerhards 2000: 297-298). On the other hand, conditions inherent in the national mass media systems are held responsible. In this regard, some researchers point out the lack of mass media's infrastructure in Brussels (see Meyer 2002; Kevin 2003). Others regard the working logic of mass media as inadequate for depicting the European political process (see Gerhards 2000: 298). However, these general arguments neglect the differences between national media systems in European countries. Despite the interest of

---

[*] Silke Adam, Dipl. rer.com., M.Sc. *1976. Researcher at the University of Hohenheim, Germany, email: adamsilk@uni-hohenheim.de
Barbara Berkel, Dipl. Sozw. *1974. Researcher at the University of Hohenheim, Germany, email: barbara.berkel@web.de

many researchers in the role of mass media, the relation between the structures of media systems and Europeanization has so far not been investigated systematically.[2] This article seeks to fill this gap by taking a macro-analytical point of view. The aim is to derive hypotheses that show which media systems are prepared to deal with European campaigns and which are likely to withstand European information input.

Our general assumption is that different European media systems offer varying opportunities for the Europeanization of public spheres. The study therefore aims to show which mass media systems of EU member countries provide which potentials for a process of Europeanization. In this connection, we reject the idea of a unifying force of the political and economic integration of the EU on the nation states. Instead we follow an idea that was developed in political science: Risse et al. (2001) show that the impact of EU integration on national political institutions and collective understandings varies among member countries. With regard to the national political systems they speak of a 'domestic adaptation with national colours' that depends on the goodness of fit between European processes and national political institutional settings, rules, and practices (see Risse et al. 2001: 1). Extending this argument, public spheres' Europeanization depends (at least partly) on the goodness of fit between the political process in the EU and characteristics of national media systems: The better a country's media system fits the requirements to depict European politics, the greater the potential is to find a Europeanized public sphere.

How is the political process in the EU characterized? It can be described as a multi-level policy-making system, in which actors from different political levels interact to solve problems (see Weßels et al. 2003: 9). The increased complexity of policy-making that is characterized by dispersed and sometimes unclear responsibilities (see Peter/de Vreese 2003: 20) makes it rather difficult for national media to present and explain European politics. Thus, specific features of national media systems are required. We assume that the two major dimensions that determine the chances for Europeanization are *the chances of access* a national media system offers to the actors in the multi-level game and the *capacity of the media system to convey complex and abstract political information*. The first criterion refers to the inclusiveness of media systems and the openness for European and transnational actors. It is backed by all democratic theories which stress that at least those accountable for political decisions should have access to public debates, as political decisions must be subjected to the will of the people (see Ferree et al. 2002: 19). The second criterion captures the type of information a media system can convey. We assume that only a specific type of media culture can contribute to the Europeanization of national public spheres. Media cultures influence the process of news selection and presentation and vary in their primary logic which can be predominantly commercial or political.

Are national media an impeding or a driving force for the Europeanization of national public spheres? To answer this question, we will firstly identify indicators for the two relevant dimensions that shape the possibility of a media system's Europeanization – namely the access points and the capacity for complexity and abstractness regarding political matters. In a second step we will try to measure these indicators in six major countries of the European Union, namely France, Germany, Italy, the Netherlands, Spain, and the United Kingdom. To summarize our findings we will develop a typology that categorizes the different European countries with regard to their potential for a Europeanization of their public spheres. As European campaigns need a platform for dissemination, this typology may help to identify chances and problems that those trying to reach a broader audience with European topics may face. It has to be noted that such a categorization of countries contains the problems of all comparative methods: Differences and commonalities are always part of a complex environment, and thus the chosen characteristics of the media systems are not the only causes that could possibly explain different forms of Europeanization (see Donges 2002: 266). However, a theoretically driven reduction of the many intervening factors is crucial to deduct hypothesises that can be validated. In this respect, the later developed macro-theoretic approach shall enrich the reflection on the role of mass media in a process of Europeanization. This approach thus focuses on the structural preconditions within the various media systems for the success of European campaigns.

2. Chances of access to national media systems

Our first criterion refers to the openness of national media systems in terms of the possibilities they provide for European and transnational actors to access a national public sphere. These chances of access highly depend on the degree of plurality of a media system. A plural media system is assumed to reflect a full picture of varying interests, opinions, and attitudes and therefore also of actors and issues. Structural conditions in a media system can support or hamper this ideal free flow of political information (see McQuail 1992: 160-165). The literature on media performance differentiates between internal and external plurality. Internal plurality refers to the range of opinions that a single medium represents, whereas external plurality measures the degree of diversity that the media offer altogether. Internal plurality of a media system is given if different political opinions are equally represented in the contents of a single medium. This form of plurality is usually measured by content analyses of media items.

From our macro-analytical point of view, external plurality is the relevant aspect. External plurality of a media system can be assessed by studying the diversity of media outlets in general and their geographical diversity. As a first step we shall focus on the *diversity of media outlets*. We hypothesize that this form of plurality will affect national public spheres' Europeanization in that the more pluralistic a national media system is, the more opportunities it will offer European and transnational actors and issues to access national public spheres. The more plurality a media system exhibits, the more one can expect that the diversity of publicly discussed interests, opinions, and attitudes will come to the fore. This criterion has been put forward by theorists of democracy who regard the diversity of media outlets as one central precondition for a functioning democracy because only the plurality of media can provide a complete picture of the differing views (see Almond 1960; Dahl 1979; Voltmer 1997).

Going beyond a purely quantitative measure of external plurality, we assume that with regard to Europeanization the *geographical diversity of media systems is of crucial importance*. The scope of a media system is decisive for a process of Europeanization as regional and local media are expected to focus less on the EU or other European countries than national or even Pan-European media. In sum, the plurality of a media system indicates its general openness to political issues and opinions. The higher the degree of plurality of a national media system, the higher the chances for Europeanization of a media induced public sphere. With regard to the geographical diversity of media systems it can be assumed that the less a media system is focused on local or regional levels, the higher the chances for Europeanization are.

2.1 Diversity of media outlets

As a first step, we will compare the diversity in terms of the number of media that actors who want to shape politics can access. The external plurality in the system of daily newspapers can be measured in terms of numbers of titles (see Table 1). By far, the most daily newspapers of the analysed countries are published in Germany, followed by Spain and the United Kingdom. The fewest number of newspapers are circulated in the Netherlands which is evidently related to the size of the country in comparison to the others studied.

Table 1: Offer of daily newspapers and television programmes

	Number of titles		Number of TV channels
	Absolute[1]	Relative[2]	> 50% Technical Penetration[3]
France	81*	1.8*	7
Germany	382	6.0	21
Italy	88	1.8	8
Netherlands	35	2.7	20
Spain	136	4.1	4
United Kingdom	104	2.2	6

*) Numbers from 1998 or 1999
1   Source: World Association of Newspapers 2001
2   Number of Titles/Adult Population (Titles per Million), Source: World Association of Newspapers 2001
3   Own calculation based on IP 2001, own research

An indicator that takes the size of national consumer markets into account is the relative offer of daily newspapers measured by the number of titles per million of the adult population. In this respect Germany shows the richest press system: Six newspapers per one million German adults are published every day. Spain ranks second as the relative offer is four newspapers, and the Netherlands with nearly three newspapers ranks third. The offer in France, Italy, and the United Kingdom is smaller.

The external plurality in television systems depends in the first place on the opportunity to access information free of charge. We will therefore focus our analysis on television channels that are free of charge and that at least partly broadcast political information. Pay TV as well as channels that solely broadcast films, music, or the like are excluded. The flow of free information is highly determined by technical preconditions. In principle, television reaches nearly the entire citizenry in Europe: According to European Key Facts nearly all households in the countries we investigate own a television set (between 93.6 percent in France and 99.7 percent in Spain). However, the plurality in free television systems relies heavily on the penetration rates of cable and satellite distribution as these technologies offer viewers a far bigger choice of programmes.

The rates of TV distribution divide the countries clearly into two groups. In Germany and the Netherlands it was a political decision to heavily invest in the cable infrastructure and satellite distribution to allow the audiences access to more programmes and to foster the free flow of information. As a consequence thereof, most households can access a rather large variety of free television programmes. In contrary, the vast majority of television households in France, Italy, Spain, and the United Kingdom depend to a much higher degree on terrestrial distribution.

To get an understanding of the plurality of a television system we only counted those television channels that a majority (more than 50 percent) of all television households are able to receive. If channels that only a minority of households have technological access to were included, the plurality of a television system would be overestimated. As a consequence of the different national situations, the audiovisual offer varies strongly between countries (see Table 1). In Germany and the Netherlands the majority of television consumers can choose between up to five times more free television channels than in France, Italy, Spain, and the United Kingdom. Thus, the plurality is obviously independent from the size of a television system, but dependent on technical preconditions.

In sum, concerning the relative external plurality four types of media systems can be distinguished. Compared to the other countries under study, the German media system is the most plural. The plurality of the Dutch television system is relatively strong, but the plurality of the Dutch newspaper system is rather low, whereas in Spain the opposite tendency can be found. Relatively less pluralized are both media systems in Italy, France, and the United Kingdom. Accordingly, when comparing the countries under study, Europeanization is more likely to occur in the German media systems, the Dutch television, and the Spanish newspaper system.

2.2 Geographical diversity

So far external plurality is measured in terms of sheer quantitative plurality. With regard to Europeanization one has to pay additional tribute to the question, which actors and issues will presumably profit from these access opportunities. Of vital importance is the degree of external plurality in terms of the representation of regions that a media system exhibits. Depending on their level of organization and orientation, one can distinguish local, regional, national, Pan-European, and foreign media. Depending on the dominant scope of a media system, one can assume that accordingly local/regional, national, or foreign actors and issues will have better opportunities to access public discourses.

At first sight however, regarding the set-up of a media system in terms of geographical diversity, two contrasting hypotheses come into play. On the one hand, one can look at geographical diversity as a core element of external plurality of the media system and assume that the higher the degree of representation of regions in the media, the more diverse the scope of a media system, and the higher the chances of a broad representation of actors of all political levels to appear in public discourse will be. This assumption applies in particular to countries with strong federal elements in the political system where European politics are also processed in regional or federal institutions. On the other hand, since European politics is a policy area which principally falls into the competence of the national government, one could assume that a media system that roots on strong national media is more open to European issues and actors. The second hypothesis is additionally supported by the fact that the scope of a medium heavily influences the focus of its political coverage, its organizational structure, and last but not least its possibilities of investigation.

The attention of broadsheet newspapers to international affairs, their transnational orientation, exceeds by far that of the tabloid newspapers (see Gerhards 2000: 294). Typically broadsheet newspapers belong to the supra-regional category. The organizational structure of most regional/local newspapers reveals their emphasis on regional and local affairs in form and content. Usually their editorial offices for regional/local affairs are at least as well staffed as those responsible for (inter)national affairs (see Moss 1998). Moreover, many regional/ local newspapers purchase by subscription the general coverage of (inter)national politics and limit their own research to local and regional affairs (see Schütz 2000).

With regard to television channels the effect of scope is less obvious. Many broadcasting companies are organized on a regional level because of political and economical reasons (see Heinrich 1999: 331). Public broadcasting companies especially, focus on (inter)national politics independently from their scope. To measure the geographical diversity of television systems we therefore chose another indicator. We analysed the relevance of foreign and Pan-European channels in national television systems. According to the definition of Europeanization that takes place if national public spheres open up for European and transnational actors and topics (see Habermas 2001: 120-121), it is plausible to assume that television systems in which foreign channels play an important role provide better opportunities for Europeanization. This effect certainly plays an equivalent role in newspaper systems, but unfortunately comparative statistics on the relevance of foreign newspapers in the countries under study do not exist.

To sum up this point, we argue that the wider the scope of a media system is, the better the opportunities of access for European and foreign actors and issues. In press systems we will therefore basically analyse the relevance of national compared to regional newspapers; in television systems we will analyse the relevance of foreign compared to national/regional channels.

To analyse the scope of press systems we broke down the titles into the two categories 'national' and 'regional/local' and measured their plurality in terms of circulation. The circulation of titles (see Table 2) shows the distribution rate of national newspapers compared to the regional/local ones. Two types of press systems are revealed: Whereas the press system of the United Kingdom and Italy is characterized by the dominance of national newspapers, in the Netherlands, Spain, and France regional outlets predominate. The German press system turns out to have an exceptionally strong regional orientation with a share of more than 90 percent regional outlets.[3]

Table 2: **Scope of Media Systems (2000/01)**

	Distribution of regional newspapers	Relevance of domestic TV channels
	Proportional Distribution (%)[1]	Index (0-1)[2]
France	71.2*	0.83
Germany	93.1	0.79
Italy	39.3	0.97
Netherlands	54.8	0.47
Spain	65.1	0.99
United Kingdom	29.9*	0.94

* Figures for France from 1998; for the United Kingdom from 1999
1 Shares on Dailies Circulation, World Association of Newspapers2001
2 Own Calculation based on number of channels and their technical penetration, IP 2001
   Index 0-1 (0 = no relevance, 1 = total dominance)

To analyse the scope of television systems all channels can be differentiated into domestic (including regional and national) and foreign (including Pan-European, supranational, and others) channels, depending on their level of organization. The number of channels and their average technical penetration[4] show that most television systems have predominantly national scopes. Though numerically foreign channels are well represented in most countries, the technical penetration rates reveal the real relevance of foreign channels which only a minority of TV households can receive. Apart from the Netherlands with penetration rates over 50 percent, foreign channels play an inferior role in all countries.

To get a realistic evaluation of the scope of television systems we created a standardized index of relevance that considers the numbers of channels and their penetration rates.[5] The index ranges between zero and one. For instance, an index of 'zero' in the category 'foreign channels' would mean that no foreign channels can be received in a country, whereas an index of 'one' would imply that television households can only receive foreign channels. This index allows the comparison of the spread and relevance of domestic and foreign channels in the countries under study (see Table 2). The data confirm that foreign channels play a serious role only in the Dutch television system. Here the majority of television households have a broad choice of different channels which yields an overall equivalent importance of foreign and domestic channels. The other countries are dominated by domestic channels, whereby the role of foreign channels can be neglected particularly in Italy and Spain.

In sum, concerning the scope of media systems in the countries under study, three types can be distinguished. In comparison, the Dutch media system is characterized by geographically wide scopes, including television and newspapers. The British and Italian press systems are firmly grounded on national newspapers, whereas foreign channels play an inferior role. The German, French, and Spanish media systems, however, are characterized by relatively narrow scopes.

3. The media systems' capacity for abstractness and complexity of political information

So far we have analysed the possibilities a media system offers European and transnational actors to access a national public sphere. The plurality of a media system however contains no information about the contents of media reports. The outcome of a media system is heavily influenced by a country's media culture. "Indeed, culture is not simply mediated through mass media; rather, culture – in both form and content – is embodied in mass media" (Altheide/Snow 1988: 196). Differences in media cultures have grown historically. The development of mass media shows two major forces that still heavily influence the form and content of discourse. In an early stage of mass-mediated communication, politics was the influential power. Later on, as publishers realized that a broader audience could be reached by complying to professional news values instead of following a specific political line, the commercial logic became a second driving force of the media systems. These two major forces behind media systems – the political and commercial logic – are still the most relevant features not only to distinguish media cultures, but also to explain the possibility of a system to convey complex and abstract political information. They precede and limit what is communicated, whether political information or entertainment is dominant, whether abstractness or simplicity prevails (see Altheide/Snow 1988: 218). In the following paragraphs we will argue how the dominant logic of a media system shapes its output.

The *commercial logic* prevails in a media culture if mass media are heavily dependent on advertisers. A multitude of media channels through which advertisers can reach their target audience leads to strong competition between media outlets. As the attractiveness to advertisers and thus the income from advertising depends on audience shares, general interest media try to attract as many readers or viewers as possible. Audience taste thus becomes the crucial variable for the content and the form of its presentation in the media. We assume that in highly commercialized systems those aspects of events that target audience tastes are more highly emphasized than in non-commercial systems (see Hallin/Mancini 2003: 51; Altheide/Snow 1988: 211). Empirical research supports this claim (see, e.g., Blumler et al. 1986; Bens et al. 1992; Gerhards et al. 1999; Peter/de Vreese 2003).

The *political logic* prevails in a media culture if the political elite influences, dominates and/or controls substantial parts of the media system. The main means can be distinguished into legal regulations, monetary subsidies, and the disposal of knowledge (see Donges 2002: 213-214). This political influence contrasts the commercial influence. Political influence makes the media less dependent on market pressure and more dependent on the political elite. The orientation of the media towards the political elite gives political actors a better starting position from which to get their ideas on the media agenda. This agenda-setting of the elites (see Kriesi 2001: 8) leads to a stronger focus on political information in the media system (see Pfetsch 1993: 114). An elite focus also enhances the chances for transferring abstract and complex issues, because of the media's focus on topics of the elite and on the political process with its complex and long-lasting bargaining procedures. As EU integration is regarded as elite-driven, we expect a stronger Europeanization of the public sphere in media systems with a strong political logic. Nevertheless, as in these systems the elite uses the media to achieve their own goals,[6] the Euro-sceptic British elite may contradict Europeanization.

3.1 The commercial logic

To measure the degree of commercialisation of a media system, we take the share of advertising compared to public spending as an indicator for the television system. In parallel, we analysed the share of advertising compared to sales revenues for all daily newspapers of a country. Regarding the daily newspapers system, only the French newspapers earn more through sales than advertising (see Table 3). The most commercialized press systems can be found in Germany and the United Kingdom. These countries are characterized by a very strong popular press. In Germany tabloids have a circulation of more than 22 percent, in the United Kingdom of more than 53 percent.

Table 3: Commercial and political logic (2000)

	Share of advertising (%)		Importance of public revenues / Share of public funds	
	Print[1] (%)	Television[2] (%)	Print[3] (Index Points)	Television[4] (%)
France	41*	73	4	56
Germany	65	60	1.5	80
Italy	58	76	5	46
Netherlands	59	63	0.5	59
Spain	53	97	1	22
United Kingdom	63*	61	1	81

* Figures for France from 1998; for the United Kingdom from 1999
1 World Association of Newspapers 2001
2 European Audivisual Observatory 2002
3 World Association of Newspapers 2001, own research
4 European Audivisual Observatory 2002

The analysis shows that the Netherlands, the United Kingdom, and Germany have a less commercialized television system, as public spending takes a share of more than 35 percent compared to advertising. Spain has the most commercialized television system: The share of public finance amounts only to 3.3 percent. Italy and France take a middle position.

In sum, concerning commercialization one expects a Europeanization of the public sphere in the less commercialized broadcasting systems like Germany, the United Kingdom, and the Netherlands. Accordingly, regarding the countries under study, one can expect that processes of Europeanization are more likely to occur in the French newspaper system and to a lesser degree in the Spanish, Italian, and Dutch newspaper systems.

3.2 The political logic

How strongly the political logic impacts a media system cannot be revealed easily as there are several possibilities by which the political elite exerts influence. Classic steering instruments are regulation mechanisms like content constraints for private stations, monetary subsidies, and knowledge transfer.

Newspapers usually experience less political influence than public broadcasters. Nevertheless, all countries under study support the functioning of their press system by monetary subsidies. Regarding state support for daily newspapers, three forms of politicisation can be distinguished: tax reductions for sales/composition/newsprint, secondly reduced post/rail/fax/telephone rates, and finally direct state subsidies. Direct state subsidies allow for the strongest political influence. To compare the degree of political influence, an index for politicisation can be calculated by focusing on the public money that is transferred to daily newspapers. We calculated 0.5 points for each 10 percent tax reduction, for each 50 percent of discounts, and for each 20 million Euro direct subsidies (see Table 3).

Regarding the politicisation of the press system only two countries have a strongly politicised system: France and Italy. These countries have tax reductions for sales, newsprint, and composition. Additionally, they grant discounts for postage, partly for rail, fax, and telephone and give direct subsidies to newspapers. In France these direct subsidies amount to 39.8 million Euro (in 2000). The Italian state spends 56.8 million Euro for newspapers published by parties, movements and newspapers managed by cooperative companies or published by linguistic minorities (in 2000). Within the other countries under study, state steering by transferring money is limited to tax reductions for sales and to discounts on postage.

Regarding the television systems one can distinguish two principal instruments: first, regulations and controls on the content and second, the establishment and financing of a public television system (see McKinsey 1999: 15-16). Despite the emergence of private competition in broadcasting systems, the latter is still regarded as the most powerful instrument of the political system. As all countries under study can be characterized as dual systems with public and private broadcasters, we do not take the sheer existence, but the form of financing of public broadcasters as an indicator for politicisation. This indicator takes into account that it is up to the political elite to decide how strongly public broadcasters are freed from commercial pressure. Thus we analyse the shares of public revenues of the total income of public television stations.[7]

The chosen indicator for politicisation of national television systems only takes one part of a television system into account: the public broadcasters, whose market share lies between 37.4 percent in the Netherlands and 50.3 percent in Spain. Thus, in most countries under study more than 50 percent of the television system is privately organized. For this part, different regulations and laws that make private channels abide to specific standards and types of programmes would be another relevant indicator.[8] As legal regulations are hardly quantifiable and difficult to compare between countries, we limit our analysis of politicisation to the instrument of monetary subsidies. This shortened perspective must be kept in mind when interpreting the results.

To justify our indicator for politicisation of the television sector, we want to emphasize that public broadcasters with a sufficient market share and public funding, can impose their elite orientation on the media system in general. As various studies show, less commercialized public TV stations support a better quality of reporting not only in the public sector itself, but also in the private sector as the quality standards of the entire market are raised (see Mattern et al. 1998; McKinsey 1999: 4; Bens et al. 1992: 95).

An exceptional case that needs further commenting is the Italian television system. The Italian Prime Minister Silvio Berlusconi controls the major private television channels and at the same time exerts a strong influence on the public channels. In addition to the means of monetary subsidies, Berlusconi practices political control that includes even personal decisions in the management board of public channels. This specific form of politicisation however, does not contribute to a Europeanization. In contrary, the form of elite orientation in Italy leads to a de-politicisation of public broadcasting: Long existing information programmes have been degraded, and infotainment has substituted substantial information (see, e.g., Neue Züricher Zeitung 2002).

The results show that Germany, the United Kingdom, the Netherlands, and France show a relatively politicised television system (see Table 3). Far more than 50 percent of the total income of their major public television stations comes from public sources. In Germany and the United Kingdom this amounts to more than 80 percent, in the Netherlands to nearly 60 percent, and in France to around 55 percent. Public broadcasters in Italy and Spain depend more strongly on advertising: Public funding in Italy amounts to 46 percent, in Spain to only 22 percent of their total income.

In sum, concerning politicisation one can expect a Europeanization of the public sphere in the more politicised broadcasting systems in Germany, the United Kingdom, and to a lesser degree in the Netherlands and France. As politicisation refers to a stronger reflection of the elites' attitudes, we assume that the prospects for Europeanization in the United Kingdom are less promising keeping in mind the strong rejection of further integration by a substantial part of the elite. The strong (non-monetary) influence of politics on the Italian television system will not push the Europeanization of the public sphere (see above). Regarding the countries under study, one can expect processes of Europeanization more likely to occur in the French and Italian newspaper system, whereas the other newspapers systems are assumed to hinder Europeanization.

4. Conclusion: Typology of countries

The goal of this cross-national analysis is to investigate the connection between media structures in the countries under study and the potential for Europeanization of the media-induced national public spheres. We therefore formulated tendencies regarding the ways in which opportunity structures of national media systems can push or hamper Europeanization. Herewith we identified two major dimensions: the *chances of access* a national media system offers and the *information capacity of national media systems* which refers to the complexity and abstractness that media allow for in public discourses.

To bring together the results, we created an indicator of opportunities for Europeanization that sums up the relevant dimensions. This allows us to come up with a final typology of the press and television systems under study. Though one might assume that, for example, the geographical diversity of a media system has a bigger influence on Europeanization than the sheer quantitative diversity, there is no definite knowledge on the interplay of these structural forces. As a basis we therefore assumed that the four analysed aspects, the external plurality in terms of quantitative[9] and geographical diversity[10] and the media culture in terms of commercialization[11] and politicisation,[12] have to be treated equivalently. The country that scored best in all aspects was placed as number one, the other countries were placed in relation to it. Thus, an indicator for the press and television systems under study was calculated which ranges from zero to one, whereby 'zero' expresses relatively no chances and 'one' relatively the best chances for Europeanization. Evidently, the resulting typology does not claim absolute validity. Instead, it can only be interpreted as a relative statement with regard to the countries under study. As soon as another country is included, the overall picture could change. In addition, it is obvious that in order to explain Europeanization the analysed media opportunity structures must be regarded as being closely connected to specific political opportunity structures in a country. Only the interplay of both forces can entirely capture and explain the differences in the processes of Europeanization of national public spheres.

The typology of media opportunity structures (see Figure 1) shows that in all countries under study either the press and/or the television systems hold a potential for Europeanization. The United Kingdom and France have chances for Europeanization within the television as well as the press sectors.

Figure 1:   Typology of media systems in six European countries

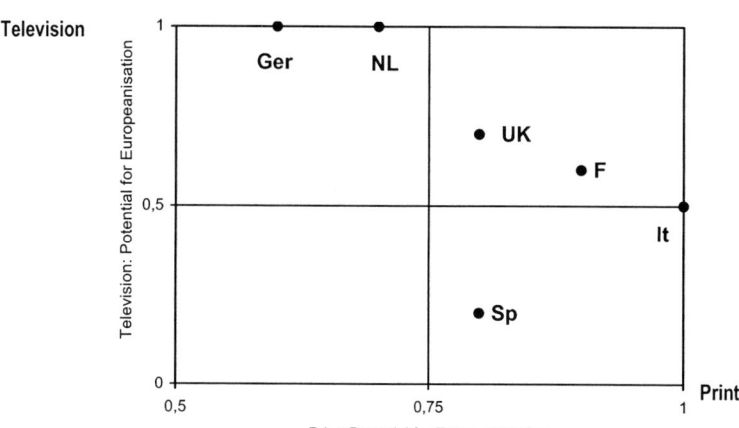

The United Kingdom has better chances for Europeanization within the television system, as it shows a relatively strong political and thus a weaker commercial logic. As argued before the elite-orientation leads to a stronger focus on the elites' attitudes. This could oppose the effect of Europeanization as there is a strong rejection of further European integration in the UK. France reveals high chances for a Europeanized press system as it shows the lowest commercialisation and at the same time scores very high on politicisation.

Germany and the Netherlands show high potentials for a Europeanization of their television systems that can be characterized by a rich diversity, strong politicisation, and low commercialization rates. The Dutch system profits particularly from the high relevance of foreign channels and the German system from a strong politicisation. Maybe surprising is the result that the German press system provides the least chances for Europeanization, mainly due to the fact that it is strongly rooted in regional outlets. Research that shows a relatively high degree of Europeanization in the German press system (see Kevin 2003: 70) often overestimates the relevance of national newspapers that hold less than seven percent of the overall circulation in Germany.

Italy and Spain have a higher potential for a Europeanization in their press systems compared to their television systems. The reason behind this is that the Italian press system is highly politicised and is firmly rooted on national media. The Spanish press system is politicised and at the same time weakly commercialized.

In sum, the presented typology takes the structural characteristics of the media systems under study into account. Extending the focus to the audience who represent a crucial actor of a public sphere reveals the relevance of the media-induced public spheres under study: Not all of them refer to the mass. The press systems in Italy, France, and Spain show the highest potential for Europeanization. In these countries, however, only a minority of the people read daily newspapers. Eurobarometer data for 2001 reveal that only 26 percent of the French, 24 percent of the Spanish, and 30 percent of the Italian adults read a newspaper daily. In contrast, those press systems, in which daily newspapers can truly be regarded as ways of mass communication, provide smaller chances for Europeanization. This is the case in Germany and in the Netherlands where about 60 percent of the population read a newspaper daily.

The United Kingdom must be treated separately. The British press system holds relatively good chances for Europeanization, and at the same time 49 percent of the people are daily readers. Whether a Europeanized British press has the potential to reach the mass must be questioned, as 53.6 percent of the daily newspaper circulation can be attributed to tabloids. Thus, the readership shares show that a process of Europeanization in press systems concerns mainly elite publics. Press systems that are addressed to a broader audience obviously provide less chances for Europeanization.

Television in contrast has the potential to reach the mass. Eurobarometer data for 2001 reveal that the majority of people in all our countries under study watch TV news programmes every day. The figures vary between 62 percent in France and 83 percent in Italy. This means that those countries which have a high potential for a Europeanization of the TV sector, namely the Netherlands, Germany, and the United Kingdom,[13] could potentially reach a broader audience with Europeanized contents. This has consequences for the often cited democratic deficit: Europeanized television systems create a better chance of connecting ordinary citizens with the integration process of the EU.

The overall potential for Europeanization in press compared to television systems however develops on different levels. Researchers have pointed out that newspapers have a much greater capacity to convey information than television channels (see Altheide/Snow 1988; Meyer 1988). 'Newspapers are believed to be far more effective than television for conveying the detailed information necessary to understand complex and detailed policy issues' (Norris 2000: 63). Taking into consideration that a television report of two minutes can only transfer the information of 50 lines of a newspaper article (see Graber 1996: 93), the results of Kevin (2003: 55) are not surprising: On average even tabloids show more Europeanized reporting in all countries compared to television.

Thus, the Europeanization of press systems could probably develop in a substantial way, but can be regarded as the continuation of the elite project 'European integration'. The Europeanization of television systems however, as weak as it may be, could possibly reach the majority of ordinary citizens.

References

Almond, Gabriel A. (1960): Introduction. A Functional Approach to Comparative Politics. In: Almond, Gabriel A./Coleman, James S. (Eds.): The Politics of Developing Areas. Princeton: Princeton University Press, 3-64.
Altheide, David L./Snow, Robert P. (1988): Toward a Theory of Mediation. In: Anderson, James (Ed.): Communication Yearbook. Thousand Oaks: Sage 194-223.
Bens, Els de/Kelly, Mary/Bakke, Marit (1992): Television Content. Dallasification of Culture? In: Siune, Karen/Truetzschler, Wolfgang (Eds.): Dynamics of Media Politics. Broadcast and Electronic Media in Western Europe. London/Newbury/New Delhi: Sage, 75-100.
Blumler, Jay G./Brynin, Malcolm/Nossiter, Thomas J. (1986): Broadcasting Finance and Programme Quality: An International Review. In: European Journal of Communication, No. 1, 343-372.
Dahl, Robert A. (1979): Procedural Democracy. In: Laslett, Peter/Fishkin, James (Eds.): Philosophy, Politics and Society. Oxford: Blackwell, 7-133.
Donges, Patrick (2002): Rundfunkpolitik zwischen Sollen, Wollen und Können. Eine theoretische und komparative Analyse der politischen Steuerung des Rundfunks. Wiesbaden: Westdeutscher Verlag [Broadcasting Politics between Normative Ideas, Wishes and Possibilities. A Theoretical and Comparative Analysis of the Steering of Broadcasting Systems].
European Commission (2001): Eurobarometer. Spring.
European Audivisual Observatory (2002): Statistical Yearbook. 1.

Ferree, Myra Marx/Gamson, William A./Gerhards, Jürgen/Rucht, Dieter (2002): Shaping abortion discourse. Democracy and the Public Sphere in Germany and the United States. Cambridge: Cambridge University Press.
Gerhards, Jürgen/Neidhardt, Friedhelm (1991): Aspekte moderner Öffentlichkeit. Strukturen und Funktionen moderner Öffentlichkeit: Fragestellungen und Ansätze. In: Müller-Dohm, Stefan/Neumann-Braun, Klaus (Eds.): Öffentlichkeit, Kultur, Massenkommunikation. Oldenburg: bis, 31-89 [Gerhards: Aspects of Modern Public Spheres. Structures and Functions of Public Spheres: Questions and Approaches. In: Müller-Dohm/Neumann-Braun: Public Spheres, Culture, Mass Communication].
Gerhards, Jürgen (2000): Europäisierung von Ökonomie und Politik und die Trägheit der Entstehung einer europäischen Öffentlichkeit. In Bach, Maurizio (Ed.): Die Europäisierung nationaler Gesellschaften. Opladen: Westdeutscher Verlag, 227-305 [Gerhards: Europeanisation of the Economy and Politics and the Lacking behind of a European Public Sphere. In: Bach: The Europeanisation of National Societies].
Gerhards, Maria/Grajczyk, Andreas/Klingler, Walter (1999): Programmangebote und Spartennutzung im Fernsehen 1998. In: Media Perspektiven, No. 8, 390-400 [Supply of Programs and Usage of Specific Formats in Television 1998].
Graber, Doris A. (1996): Say it with Pictures. In: Jamieson, Kathleen Hall (Ed.): The Media and Politics. The Annals of the American Academy of Political and Social Sciences. London: Sage, 85-96.
Habermas, Jürgen (2001): Zeit der Übergänge. Kleine Politische Schriften IX. Frankfurt am Main: Suhrkamp [Time of Transition. Political Writings IX].
Hallin, Daniel C./Mancini, Paolo (2003): Amerikanisierung, Globalisierung und Säkularisierung. Zur Konvergenz von Mediensystemen und politischer Kommunikation in westlichen Demokratien. In: Esser, Frank/Pfetsch, Barbara (Eds.): Politische Kommunikation im internationalen Vergleich. Grundlagen, Anwendungen, Perspektiven. Wiesbaden: Westdeutscher Verlag, 35-55 [Hallin/Mancini: Americanization, Globalization and Secularization. Understanding the Convergence of Media Systems and Political Communication in the U.S. and Western Europe. In: Esser/Pfetsch: Comparing Political Communication. Theories, Cases, and Challenges].
Heinrich, Jürgen (1999): Medienökonomie. Band 2: Hörfunk und Fernsehen. Opladen: Westdeutscher Verlag [Media Economy. Volume 2: Radio and Television].
IP International Marketing Committee (CMI) (Ed.) (2001): Television 2001. European Key Facts. September. Köln.
Kevin, Deirdre (2003): Europe in the Media. A Comparison of Reporting, Representation, and Rhetoric in National Media Systems in Europe. Mahwah, NJ: Lawrence Erlbaum Associates.

Koopmans, Ruud/Statham, Paul (2002): The Transformation of Political Mobilisation and Communication in European Public Spheres: A Research Outline. At: http:europub.wz-berlin.de, retrieval May 2004.

Koopmans, Ruud/Erbe, Jessica (2003): Towards a European Public Sphere? Vertical and Horizontal Dimensions of Europeanised Political Communication. Paper Presented at the International Conference „Europeanization of Public Spheres". Wissenschaftszentrum Berlin. June.

Kriesi, Hanspeter (2001): Die Rolle der Öffentlichkeit im politischen Entscheidungsprozess. Ein konzeptueller Rahmen für ein international vergleichendes Forschungsprojekt. In: Discussion Paper P01-701. Wissenschaftszentrum Berlin für Sozialforschung [The role of the Public Sphere in Political Decision-Making. A Concept for an Internationally Comparative Research Project].

Mattern, Klaus/Künstner, Thomas/Zirn, Markus (1998): Fernsehsysteme im internationalen Vergleich. In: Hamm, Ingrid (Ed.): Fernsehen auf dem Prüfstand. Aufgaben des dualen Rundfunksystems. Gütersloh: Bertelsmann Stiftung, 13-50 [Mattern et al.: Broadcasting Systems in Comparison. In: Hamm: Benchmarking Television. Tasks of Dual Broadcasting Systems].

McKinsey & Company (1999): Public Service Broadcasters Around the World. A McKinsey Report for the BBC. At: http://www.bbc.co.uk/info/bbc/pdf/McKinsey.pdf, retrieval April 2002.

McQuail, Denis (1992): Media Performance. Mass Communication and the Public Interest. London: Sage Publications.

Meyer, Christoph O. (2002): Europäische Öffentlichkeit als Kontrollsphäre. Die Europäische Kommission, die Medien und politische Verantwortung. Berlin: Vistas [The European Public Sphere as Sphere of Control. The European Commission, the Media and Political Responsibility].

Meyer, Timothy P. (1988): On Mediated Communication Theory. The Rise of Format. In: Anderson, James (Ed.): Communication Yearbook. Thousand Oaks: Sage, 224-229.

Moss, Christoph (1998): Die Organisation der Zeitungsredaktion. Opladen: Westdeutscher Verlag [The Organisation of Editorial Offices of Newspapers].

Neue Züricher Zeitung online (2002): Berlusconis Schatten über der RAI. At: http://www.nzz.ch/2002/12/06/em/page-article8K3MV.html, retrieval June 2003 [Berlusconi Shadowing RAI].

Norris, Pippa (2000): A Virtuous Circle. Political Communications in Postindustrial Societies. Cambridge/New York: Cambridge University Press.

Peter, Jochen (2003): Why European TV News Matters. A Cross-Nationally Comparative Analysis of TV News about the European Union and Its Effects. PhD. University of Amsterdam.

Peter, Jochen/de Vreese, Claes H. (2003): In Search of Europe. The European Union in National Television News. Paper presented to the Political Communication Division at the Annual Meetings of the International Communication Association. San Diego. May 2003.

Pfetsch, Barbara (1993): Politische Fernsehwelten: Die Politikberichterstattung in privaten und öffentlich-rechtlichen Sendern. In: Jarren, Otfried (Ed.): Politische Kommunikation in Hörfunk und Fernsehen. Elektronische Medien in der Bundesrepublik Deutschland. Opladen: Westdeutscher Verlag, 111-122 [Pfetsch: Political Worlds within Television. The Reporting of Politics of Private and Public Broadcasters. In: Jarren: Political Communication in Radio and Television. Electronic Media in Germany].

Pfetsch, Barbara (1994): Themenkarrieren und politische Kommunikation. In: Aus Politik und Zeitgeschichte, No. 39, 11-20 [Issue Carreers and Political Communication].

Pfetsch, Barbara (2001): „Amerikanisierung" der politischen Kommunikation? Politik und Medien in Deutschland und den USA. In: Aus Politik und Zeitgeschichte, No. 41-42, 27-36 ["Americanisation" of Political Communication? Politics and Media in Germany and the US].

Risse, Thomas/Cowles, Maria Green/Caporaso, James (2001): Europeanisation and Domestic Change: Introduction. In: Cowles, Maria Green/Caporaso, James/Risse, Thomas (Eds.): Transforming Europe. Europeanisation and Domestic Change. Ithaca/London: Cornell University Press, 1-20.

Risse, Thoams/Steeg, Marianne van de (2003): An Emerging European Public Sphere? Empirical Evidence and Theoretical Clarifications. Paper presented at the International Conference „Europeanization of Public Spheres". Wissenschaftszentrum Berlin. June 2003.

Schütz, Walter J. (2000): Deutsche Tagespresse 1999. Ergebnisse der fünften gesamtdeutschen Zeitungsstatistik. In: Media Perspektiven, No. 1, 602-642 [The German Daily Press 1999. Results of the Fifth German Press Statistics].

Sievert, Holger (1998): Europäischer Journalismus. Theorie und Empirie aktueller Medienkommunikation in der Europäischen Union. Opladen/Wiesbaden: Westdeutscher Verlag [European Journalism. Theoretical and Empirical Considerations Regarding the Actual Media Communication in the European Union].

Weßels, Wolfgang/Maurer, Andreas/Mittag, Jürgen (2003): The European Union and Member States. Analysing Two Arenas Over Time. In: Weßels, Wolfgang/Maurer, Andreas/Mittag, Jürgen (Eds.): Fifteen Into One? The European Union and its Member States. Manchester/New York: Manchester University Press, 3-28.

World Association of Newspapers (Ed.) (2001): World Press Trends 2001. The Definitive Guide to the Changes Taking Place in the Press Industry around the World. Paris: zenith media.

Voltmer, Katrin (1997): Structures of Diversity in Press and Broadcasting Systems. Manuscript. Wissenschaftszentrum Berlin für Sozialforschung.

1. This article derives from a larger research project entitled 'The transformation of political mobilisation and communication in European public spheres' which is sponsored by the European Commission in the context of its Fifth Framework program (see further details at http://europub.wz-berlin.de). We would like to thank the British, Dutch, French, Italian, Spanish, and Swiss country teams who contributed to this article by complementing the official sources with additional statistical information.
2. So far analyses of media structures have mainly been conducted within a more general theoretical framework of media and democracy (see Voltmer 1997).
3. 373 regional and nine national dailies were published in Germany in the year 2000 (world press trends).
4. As we are interested in the plurality of political information we again focus our analysis on television channels that are free of charge and that at least partly broadcast political information. Pay TV as well as channels that solely broadcast movies, music or the like are excluded.
5. The index was calculated in the following way: Firstly, all channels were weighted with their average penetration rate and summed up. Secondly, the share of regional, national, and foreign channels on the thus created television landscapes was calculated, and thirdly converted to a standardized index between 0 and 1.
6. This idea reflects the party-oriented media culture of Pfetsch (2001), which she distinguishes from a media-oriented culture.
7. Additionally one can distinguish if the public money that is transferred to broadcasters is raised by fee or tax/grant. A tax-based factoring is subject to stronger political influence, as its budget is included in the annual political budget decisions, whereas a fee-based factoring normally rests upon longer licence agreements (see McKinsey 1999: 31). As this differentiation cannot be measured in a reliable quantitative way, we did not take it into account, thus possibly underestimating the politicisation of the tax-based systems in the Netherlands and in Spain.
8. An example for that can be found in the United Kingdom, where Channel 4 is completely financed by advertising revenues but has similar obligations as a classic public channel.
9. The quantitative plurality was included by a simple valuation system: 1 point per newspaper titel/per adult population and 1 point per 4 channels/>50 percent techn.pen. This conversion was necessary in order to not give too much weight to the aspect of quantitative external plurality.
10. Geographical plurality: for the press systems the circulation shares of national daily newspapers was included, for television systems the index of relevance of foreign channels.
11. Commercialisation: for the press systems the shares of sales revenue was included, for television systems the shares of public spending.
12. Politicisation: for the press systems the circulation shares of national daily newspapers was included, for television systems the print index of politicisation.
13. As the British television system is strongly politicized we must qualify this statement. As we hypothesized that politicisation allows the political elite to push their attitudes on European integration, we assume that the British elite pushes the national agenda instead of a commitment to European politics.

NATIONAL CASE STUDIES ON CAMPAIGN STRUCTURES AND STRATEGIES

Between Absence and Populism: The British 2004 EP Election

*Pontus Odmalm**

1. Introduction

The 2004 European Parliament election in Britain displayed a number of interesting features compared to previous elections. Firstly, electoral participation went up significantly compared to the 1999 election. Secondly, the unexpected electoral success of the *UK Independence Party* (*UKIP*) and the relative electoral failure of the *Conservatives* and *Labour*.

This article discusses some of the reasons behind these two particulars by referring to the role of the election campaign and what party strategies the competing parties adopted. In addition, the article utilises ideas stemming from literature on political marketing. It argues that the main parties (*Conservatives* and *Labour*) did not make sufficient use of the campaign since the EP election was by and large seen as a second-order election. Furthermore, the campaign was dominated by the issue of Britain's EU membership which put these parties in a difficult position given their prevailing ambivalent attitudes towards Europe which played in favour of *UKIP*. The previous use of successful political marketing techniques was to a large extent absent in the EP election amongst the mainstream parties, whereas the main challenger, *UKIP*, used an explicit Eurosceptic and populist rhetoric in combination with a strong media presence which contributed to its electoral success. This article suggests that even though the election campaign proved to be a 'success' due to effective *political marketing* and getting more people to vote, there was also a 'failure' in achieving the expected votes by the more established parties due to insufficient campaigning and underestimating the opposition. The empirical part of this article is based on a structured questionnaire survey done amongst representatives who were closely involved in the EP campaign, either as MEPs or as campaign strategists[1]. The interviews were conducted over a three-month period (May – July 2004) and aimed to identify changes in the election campaign by conducting three different sets of interviews with the respondents at different points of time. In addition, informal conversations about the election were held with the representatives following the completion of the questionnaire.

---

* Pontus Odmalm, PhD. *1974. Lecturer in Politics, Sussex European Institute, University of Sussex, email: g.p.odmalm@sussex.ac.uk

2. The UK context

Despite Britain being somewhat notorious for its comparatively high levels of Euroscepticism, both in terms of public sentiments and from a party point of view (see Evans 1998; Taggart 2004), turnout in the 2004 UK EP election rose to 38.8 percent. This was a significant increase compared to the 1999 election (24 percent) but is roughly similar to levels shown in previous elections (1979: 31.6 percent; 1984: 32.6 percent; 1989: 36.2 percent and 1994: 36.4 percent). In comparison to the national election, which shows a general decline in voter turnout (from 71.4 percent in 1997 to 59.4 percent in 2001), the EP election shows an interesting increase in voter turnout.[2] In addition to the EP election other concomitant elections included the Greater London Authority, London Mayor, and English municipality election. The coinciding of several elections may also have contributed to the relatively higher degree of voter turn-out in that the cost of voting would have been higher if the elections had been held separately.

However, these figures must be viewed in conjunction with the overall political climate in the UK. The EP elections were held during a time of *Labour* dominance on the national level. Having won its second consecutive general election in 2001, the EP election represented a mid-term test of *Labour*'s popularity at a time when it was still unclear whether *Labour* would win a third term. Although being a popular government, Tony Blair had seen his popularity drop in the aftermath of British participation in Iraq with a May 2004 poll showing 32 percent being satisfied and 56 percent being dissatisfied with his leadership (ICM Research 2004). On the other hand, the *Conservative Party* – the main opposition party at the Westminster level – has gone through a number of leadership changes since they relinquished power in 1997 (William Hague, 1997-2001, Ian Duncan Smith, 2001-2003) until Michael Howard took over in November 2003. 'Europe' has been a source of division for the Conservatives since Thatcher and has, in one way or the other, been on the political agenda since then.

Given this background, the EP election could be judged as an important electoral barometer of a popular government with an unpopular PM and an opposition that had problems making itself a viable party of government (Taggart 2004). In terms of the issues that dominated the campaign, Taggart singles out two: the Constitutional Treaty and EU enlargement. Although a main feature in the media, the emphasis on these could be said to have shifted towards the more populist slogan of staying in or withdrawing from the EU (Carey/Burton 2004; Anderson/Weymouth 1999). This was made apparent following the sudden switch in *UKIP* support and the inclusion of TV-personality Robert Kilroy-Silk.[3] This in turn created a number of spin-off issues relating to the UK such as (illegal) immigration and asylum-seekers, the Euro, lack of sovereignty, corruption within EU institutions, etc. all of which were related to EU membership.

This new political cleavage – membership or non-membership – created difficulties for the mainstream parties in terms of how to profile their campaign. As a pre-emptive measure, the *Labour* campaign moved into 'traditional' *Conservative* areas and pointed out the need for further integration and co-operation to address and combat cross-border crime and, especially, illegal immigration. Furthermore, the *Tories* were portrayed as Eurosceptics, and several references were made back to the negative aspects of the *Conservative* regime under the heading of 'Britain is working, don't let the Tories wreck it again'. As such, the campaign's main focus was the economy and to criticise the Conservatives, while the European dimension was largely absent.

The issue of Europe has been considerably problematic for the *Conservatives*. Firstly, the party had to accommodate three different attitudes within the party, the 'hard' and 'soft' Eurosceptics and the pro-Europeans. Secondly, their plans to call for a referendum on the Constitutional Treaty was hi-jacked by the *Labour party* when Tony Blair unexpectedly decided to call for one. Finally, the hard Eurosceptic vote that was previously monopolised by the Tories was now under threat by *UKIP*.

The smaller parties, the *Liberal Democrats* and the *Greens*, chose to emphasise Britain's involvement in the Iraq war as their major campaign issue. The *Liberal Democrats* stand out from the other mainstream parties in being clearly pro-Europe and pointing to Blair's support of the US as having an isolating effect with the rest of Europe. In addition, their manifesto highlighted *Liberal Democrat* achievements on the European level by their existing MEPs. The EU, in the eyes of the *Lib Dems*, is and was the best means by which to ensure economic growth and to promote justice, security, and peace.

The *Greens*, on the other hand, focused more on using the election as a way of showing dissatisfaction with the Blair government and being, like the *Lib Dems*, openly anti-war, but their campaign was further characterised by other issues that were not directly related to the EP such as university top-up fees and public transport failures.

3. The EP Election and British voters

Previous research on British EP elections has mostly focused on voter abstention in the EP election, especially when put in relation to the national election. Both the 1994 and 1999 elections conformed to the theory that these were "second-order elections" (Reif/Schmitt 1980), almost on level with local elections. Several aspects of second-order elections were present in previous elections: low turnout, an anti-government swing, and a relatively high support for smaller parties. Important to note also is that the domestic, rather than the European arena dominated the campaigns (Curtice/Steed 2000; see also Negrine in this volume). In general, the EU elections tended to attract less voter interest than general elections. However, it would be oversimplifying to refer to the EP election merely as a second-order election, and scholars in the field have suggested three additional explanatory factors.

Firstly, there are formal aspects of voting to consider, such as whether voting is compulsory or not, choice of election day, access to voting (postal or ballot), etc (van der Eijk et al. 1996). It is important to note here that the electoral procedures have changed somewhat in the UK over the years. For the 1999 election, a proportional representation list was introduced (which replaced the 'old' simple plurality, single ballot vote) using a closed regional list system for the regions. Another change was the merger of the 84 single-member constituencies into eleven regions (nine for England, with Scotland and Wales serving as separate districts) with varying district size (the smallest being the North East with four seats and London, the North West (ten seats) and the South East (eleven seats) being the largest). Voting can also be done either by a postal vote or at the polling station (the latter being subject to a new legislation which relaxed postal voting) and is not compulsory. The second reason refers to the priority given to EP elections by voters. These elections tend to be considered as less 'important' compared to national elections, and thus citizens abstain from voting. However, as Blondel et al. (1998) point out, this ranking is far from systematic, and turnout is not solely influenced by national political attitudes (see also Scully 2001; Marsh 1998). Thirdly, there appears to be a public perception that the EP and its MEPs lack legitimacy and that the parliament suffers from a democratic deficit (Franklin/Eijk 1996). This perception, however, might be misleading since the EU representatives stem from democratically elected member-states.

On the other hand, Taggart (2004) focuses on the British regions in order to understand the current trends in British EP elections. Here, different patterns of competition emerge, and it becomes useful to analytically think of Britain as composed of six different party systems based on regionalism with the six divisions being the South and Midlands; Northern England; London; Wales; Scotland and Northern Ireland. This is especially relevant for EP elections due to the greater size of the constituencies but could also be seen as indicative for the national elections, thus challenging the traditional view of Britain as a two-party system.

This partition, however, has also created a two-tier intra-division in England between the North (Yorkshire and Humber; the North West and North East constituencies) and the South (South East; South West; East of England; East and West Midlands but excluding London). Northern England has had a strong *Labour* dominance with the *Conservatives* in second place followed by the *Liberal Democrats*. In this region, *UKIP* came fourth in 2004 with 12.8 percent of the votes. This region is also a stronghold for the *British National Party* (*BNP*) who gained its highest level of voter support with almost 7 percent of the votes. In contrast, the South has a strong *Conservative* dominance where the competition for EP vote came mainly from *UKIP* rather than from *Labour*. The South is also where *UKIP* had a majority of its supporters; here the average votes amounted to 22.6 percent (compared to the national average of 16.1 percent) with *Labour* performing exceptionally poor with 17.8 percent of the vote (national average of 22.6). London and Scotland have a more traditional two-party dominance between *Labour* and the *Conservatives* in the former and between *Labour* and the *Scottish National Party* in the latter. This division, Taggart continues, shows that single party dominance seems to be rare in the UK and different parties dominate different regions with the *Liberal Democrats* standing out by having less regional variation compared to the other parties.

More traditional explanations have also been suggested which relate to elections more generally. These are lack of political interest, lack of political knowledge, and a scepticism or dislike of the EU project as a whole. The three variables are related to each other in the sense that holding one attitude ('lack of political interest') usually indicates holding another ('lack of political knowledge') (Bicchi et al 2003). The role of these three factors is made more relevant if one considers the possible impact that the election campaign can have on them. As Bicchi et al. (2003) further suggest, the election campaign is crucial since it is the one political activity which is specifically devoted to boosting both political knowledge and political interest. An active campaign exposure is more likely to stimulate political interest and political knowledge, thereby decreasing the level of voluntary EU election abstention.

4. Political marketing in the UK

Political marketing has had a long history in British political life dating back to the early 20th century (see Wring 1996). This approach, Wring suggests, is particularly useful for analysing the strategic development of a political party as well as making it easier to understand how changes in campaign practices can be motivated by factors other than mass media or technological innovation. The claim is that "marketing is a specific form of economic rationality that offers insights into the strategic options and behaviour of parties" (Scammell 1999: 719; see further Faucheux 1995; Maarek 1995). The novelty of the term lies in what Kavanagh (1995) refers to as a new professionalisation of campaign communications, that is the election campaign is now, to a much higher degree, relying on effective advertising, public relations, opinion polling, and marketing strategies.

More closely defined, Lees-Marshment suggests that political marketing is "about political organizations adapting business-marketing concepts and techniques to help them achieve their goals" (Lees-Marshment 2001: 692). By adopting these techniques political parties, interest groups, and local councils can identify citizen concerns and change their behaviour in accordance with their demands and thus communicate their product, as it were, more effectively.

Both the *Conservative* and *Labour Party* set up specific party units in order to deal with this propagandist orientation, the former in 1911 and the latter in 1917. Political marketing then took on a more professionalised appearance in the

1979 election when the *Conservatives*, and especially Margaret Thatcher, utilised marketing as a specific tool (see Scammell 1995). *Labour* embraced a market orientation sometime later (during the Policy Review) following the 1987 defeat, its legacy being the appointment of the media friendly Tony Blair as well as the re-writing of *Labour's* 75-year-old Clause Four[4] (see Lees-Marshment 2001; Wring 1996).

Although having downplayed the media so far in this article, its role, especially in the UK context, should not be overlooked. As Carey and Burton (2004) point out, newspapers in Britain are highly partisan and usually make their political views very clear and have also tended to be very Eurosceptic (Anderson/Weymouth 1999). However, the impact of the media on attitudes and behaviour appears to be relatively small. In addition, as Carey and Burton note, there are also differences regarding newspapers' partisan alignment and their views on the EU. Newspapers in the UK can e.g. be both pro-*Labour* and anti-EU, and thus *Labour* supporters can be expected to read *The Sun* (anti-EU) or *The Mirror* (pro-EU). In addition, television seems to have an ever lesser significance when it comes to influencing voting or voting choice (Norris et al. 1999). Since paid political advertisements are not allowed, competing parties are restricted to two to five minutes of party election broadcasts which are given to all of the main parties and shown on all channels.

However, these broadcasts often have more to do with image creation than putting forward a political message (Franklin 1994). Therefore, one can argue, it is the election campaign that seems to be of crucial importance for getting the *political* message across. But in a similar way, the election campaign has developed into a more professional and media-orientated direction. As Scammell (1999) points out, the modern election campaign is capital intensive, relying less on volunteers and more on non-party experts from media and marketing with a tighter central direction of campaign operations, less face-to-face communication with voters, and increased targeting of floating voters.

A key element in the marketing of politics is thus to build up a profile in order to maximise the number of votes by establishing name recognition for the candidate among the electorate. Candidates may also need to establish an image which sends out the message of being an effective representative (see Lilleker/ Negrine 2003). Therefore, election campaign exposure in which the party, or increasingly so the candidate, manages to effectively market its profile will have a positive effect on the electorate's political knowledge and stimulate voting.

5. But where's the campaign?

However, given these theoretical assumptions, the overall picture that stems from the UK election campaign seems to suggest that only one party – *UKIP* – picked up the importance of political marketing for the campaign, especially in terms of exploiting the media to put forward their anti-EU message. The data collected for the CIVICACTIVE project supports the notion that the EP election was not a high priority issue for the established parties. This was displayed both in terms of campaign efforts, recruitment of staff for the campaign, and the tactics that were used in order to make voters aware of the election and the party profiles. The parties started to prepare for the EP election six to nine months prior to the election with the most intense phase of the campaign being the three to four weeks before election day. Most parties stated that they concentrated their efforts on the entire voting population, although some interviewees stressed that they were also interested in voters who tend to abstain and the voters of their main rival party. Only the *Green Party* made deliberate efforts to target specific segments of voters, including homosexual voters but also young/elderly, ethnic minorities, and disabled people.

In general, it appears that only *UKIP* was satisfied with the efforts made, whereas the other parties were dissatisfied with their targeting of voters. Although the *Conservatives* seemed to have put more effort into the campaign, their voting support was 8 percent less than in the previous EP election. As pointed out above, the impression given by the *Labour Party* was that the EP election was not a main priority (compared to the national election), but this did not seem to affect the party in a negative way since *Labour* 'only' got 5.4 percent less votes than in the last election. However, all parties (apart from *Labour*) stated that the campaign did 'really start' between two to four months prior to election day, which suggests that the election was given some importance. *Labour*, on the other hand, stated that their campaign 'really started' only three weeks before election day.

Given the emphasis placed on the media for effective political marketing it is somewhat surprising to observe what campaign strategies the parties chose as their main channels or sources of communication. According to the interviewees, the main campaign activities seemed to be mailing or delivering of leaflets for all parties with general public events and face-to-face canvassing coming in second and third. The exception is *UKIP* which relied heavily on billboards and posters for their campaign (which was identified as the crucial factor for their success) with the simple, yet effective, slogan 'Say No'. Furthermore, there appeared to be little to no adjustments of campaign tactics by *UKIP* during the course of the election, instead the party relied consistently on billboard campaigns (which few of the other parties utilised), and this appeared to have given them an advantage over the other parties.

In addition, the main issue for the British parties was undoubtedly Britain's membership in the European Union. This was especially apparent after *UKIP* showed high levels of electoral support. The *Labour Party* found this aspect of the campaign difficult since their strategy had been to highlight the importance and benefits of being a member. The pro-EU *Liberal Democrats* alongside the *Greens* attempted to make the campaign focus on Britain's involvement in the Iraq war and also to make a point about criticising the *Labour* government. The *Conservatives*, on the other hand, appeared to find it hard to decide what their main campaign priorities should be, given their ambiguous attitudes towards the EU, and their campaign thus focused primarily on criticising the existing government and raising the issue of corruption within EU institutions (see also Negrine in this volume).

As a consequence, it is difficult to talk about a solid, national EP election campaign but rather a fragmented and localised campaign dominated by a single issue: EU membership or not. *UKIP* was here in a more favourable position compared to the other parties when Britain's EU-membership became the main issue; by using populist rhetoric in their campaign (e.g. the five freedoms emphasised in one of their leaflets: freedom from the EU, crime, overcrowding, too much government, and political correctness) they claimed to voice the concerns of the 'silent majority'.

The lesser importance given to the EP election is to some extent also reflected in the composition of the group in charge of the campaign. The size of the regional campaign staff showed great variance between the different parties ranging from 3 (*UKIP*) to 165 (*Conservatives*). The average size of the campaign teams, or the 'strategic unit' as the interviewees referred to, was around 12 to 30 people with an overrepresentation of males (around 66 percent to 80 percent). Most teams had an age spread from late-20s to late-50s apart from *UKIP* which on average had more older team members (in their 50s and 60s). A majority of the campaign teams had personnel with responsibilities for European issues, but in terms of previous EP campaign experience there was a lot of variance. Some parties (e.g. the *Conservatives*) had recruited younger team members with little or no experience, whereas the *Greens* and *Labour* had some staff with previous experience. *UKIP* saw a dramatic increase in party membership and activists, but these were, as already mentioned, older on-the-street campaigners of a volunteer type as opposed to the more professionally-oriented staff in the major parties. External personnel were used by all parties but only to a lesser extent.

On the occasions that they were used, these tended to be call centres (although in the majority of cases these were in-house rather than external) and used during the whole campaign, whereas public opinion polling and media consultants were employed occasionally. The relative lack of professional consultants is interesting to note since the current development in terms of *national* elections point in the opposite direction (see Scammell 1999; Shaw 1999).

Similarly, the developments towards a more market-oriented approach also point to party campaigns starting to display a higher degree of centralisation with party headquarters being the main area of activity (Franklin 1994). Despite increased national level concentration, local level campaign teams in the EP election displayed a certain degree of autonomy. These teams were mostly concerned with representing and promoting the constituency representative rather than going for a strategy which involved promoting the party position as such. As a consequence, the party campaign took on a more personal appearance in which the candidate became the focus of attention. In addition, these regional teams operated under the broad themes adopted at headquarters (although the *Green Party* teams were more decentralised in comparison to the other parties), which indicates relatively lower levels of control and steering of the regional teams and a greater degree of freedom to pursue the marketing of the regional candidate.

Campaign spending seemed to vary considerably between the parties. Most of the interviewees had vague perceptions of the total amount and gave merely rough estimates. According to figures given by the interviewees, these ranged from £ 100.000 to 150.000 (i.e. 140.000 to 215.000 €) (*Greens* and *Lib Dems*) to £1 to £4 million (~ 1.4 to 5.5 million €) (*Labour* and *Conservatives*). *UKIP* had relatively small campaign expenditures which were covered by high donations (around £250.000, i.e. 355.000 €) compared to £36.000 (~ 50.000 €) (*Greens*) and £947.000 (~ 1.4 million €) (*Liberal Democrats*). As another comparative measure, campaign expenditure for national elections was around four times the size of the EP campaign (see Negrine in this volume). These lower figures could be indicative of the importance placed on the EP election by the parties on a central level and gives some support to the argument about the EP election being of a second-order nature.

In terms of how the campaign money was spent this appeared to be geared towards printing and mailing out leaflets to households rather than using established marketing techniques as e.g. polling and phone canvassing. Again, *UKIP* stands out from the rest of the parties having devoted a majority of their expenditures on billboards and posters which contributed to the awareness of the party and its candidates.

As mentioned above, British media and especially the printed press play an important, although not decisive, role when it comes to communicating politics to the population as well as supporting or criticising the government (Carey/Burton 2004). In addition, issues relating to EU membership (sovereignty, immigration, the Constitution, etc.) were rarely off the headlines[5]. Therefore, the relationship that the parties had with the media during the campaign could be a significant factor when trying to explain the particular strategies adopted during the campaign. A majority of the parties stated that they had average to very good relations with the media. *UKIP* stands out from the other parties in the sense that they noted a significant shift in media attention from mid-May onwards when the right-of-centre Daily Telegraph announced surprisingly high levels of electoral support for *UKIP*. Up to that point, *UKIP* had been more or less absent from the media and was not considered to be a serious contender. In combination with recruiting the TV-personality Kilroy-Silk, this situation led to a virtual domination of media coverage by *UKIP* and its candidates which made it very difficult for the other parties to acquire sufficient space in the media. In the weeks before the election, *UKIP* thus took advantage of the sudden opportunity handed to them through an increase in media exposure which had dramatically positive effects on electoral support and the recruitment of on-the-street volunteers. Therefore, as Taggart (2004) suggests, *UKIP* can be seen as the 'winner' in terms of the media game. After the election results displayed *Labour*'s and the *Conservative*'s 'failure', the media focused instead on the unexpected electoral success of *UKIP* and its twelve new MEPs. Kilroy-Silk was quick to exploit this attention and keen to inform about *UKIP*'s plans for the EU – that is to 'wreck it' and expose what was considered to be a haven for corruption, waste, and a threat to British sovereignty.

6. Concluding remarks

The British 2004 EP election displayed some interesting developments. On the one hand, voting levels rose significantly compared to 1999. On the other, support for the mainstream parties decreased in favour of the Eurosceptic *UKIP*. The reasons, this article argues, can be found in the difficulties regarding the parties' profiling during the election campaign as well as in the relative lack of extensive political marketing. The campaign was not given a high priority by the mainstream parties relating to the perception of the EP election being of second-order relevance. The main issue of the campaign was undoubtedly Britain's membership in the European Union. The *Labour Party* found this aspect of the campaign difficult since their strategy had been to highlight the importance and benefits of being a member. The pro-EU *Liberal Democrats* alongside the *Greens* attempted to make the campaign focus on Britain's involvement in the Iraq war and also to make a point about criticising the *Labour* government. The *Conservatives*, on the other hand, appeared to find it hard to decide what their main campaign priorities should be, given their ambiguous attitudes towards the EU. Consequently, the *Conservative* campaign took the opportunity to primarily criticise the existing government and raise the issue of corruption within EU institutions. As such the campaign displayed an interesting case of being both *absent* in the sense that little effort was made to actually campaign on EU-related issues as well as being highly *populist* and playing on perceived fears of EU membership and Britain's involvement in the Iraq war.

As an effect of the low priority given to the election, traditional political marketing techniques were not used to a high degree as during national elections. Instead, the mainstream parties relied on leaflets and phone canvassing and other labour intensive strategies. *UKIP*, on the other hand, seized the opportunity given to them through increased media attention and relied heavily on the media friendly and populist figure of Kilroy-Silk for their campaign. However, at the same time they were also more prone to invoke traditional electoral techniques such as billboards and posters in their campaign, making them a highly visible party. Finally, with the conflict dimension revolving around national sovereignty vs. EU decision-making, this focus proved to be a successful voter attracter but less successful in terms of making the election a high priority for both voters and parties.

The EU continues to be a problematic project for British politics. Following the Dutch and French rejection of the constitution, *Labour*'s Eurosceptics joined forces with *Conservative* backbenchers urging the foreign secretary, Jack Straw, to announce its demise or launch the promised referendum (Branigan 2005). The repercussions of *Labour*'s low-key approach towards the benefits of EU membership during the 2004 election, in combination with accusations from Europe that Britain is trying to turn the EU into a free-market, Anglo-Saxon welfare model, has put Britain in a difficult position of whether to be in, out, or on the margins of the EU system.

References

Anderson, Peter.J/Weymouth, Antony (1999): Insulting the Public? The British Press and the European Union. Harlow: Longman.
BBC, 'European Election: United Kingdom Results'. At: http://news.bbc.co.uk /1/shared/bsp/hi/vote2004/euro_uk/html/front.stm, retrieval Jan. 12th 2005.
BBC, 'European Election: Northern Ireland Results'. At: http://news.bbc.co.uk/ 1/hi/northern_ireland/3766315.stm, retrieval Jan.12th 2005.
Bicchi, Federica/Blondel, Jean/Svensson, Palle (2003): The European Parliament Campaign. At: http://www.ucd.ie/dempart/workingpapers.htm, retrieval Nov. 8th 2004.
Blondel, Jean/Sinnott, Richard/Svensson, Palle (1998): People and Parliament in the European Union. Oxford: Oxford University Press.
Branigan, Tania (2005): MPs Warn Straw not to Smuggle in Treaty by Back Door. At: http://politics.guardian.co.uk/eu/story/0,9061,1500818,00.html# article_continue, retrieval Jun. 8th 2005.
Carey, Sean/Burton, Jonathan (2004): Research Note: The Influence of the Press in Shaping Public Opinion Towards the European Union in Britain. In: Political Studies, Vol. 52, 623-640.
Curtice, John/Steed, Michael (2000): Appendix: An Analysis of the Result. In: Butler, David and Westlake, Martin (Eds.): British Politics and European Elections 1999. London: MacMillan, 240-256.
Dearlove, John/Saunders, Peter (2000): Introduction to British Politics. Cambridge: Polity Press.
Evans, Geoffrey (1998): Euroscepticism and Conservative Electoral Support: How an Asset Became a Liability. In: British Journal of Political Science, Vol. 28, No. 4, 573-590.
Faucheux, Ron (1995): The Road to Victory: the Complete Guide to Winning in Politics. Washington DC: Campaigns and Elections.
Franklin, Bob (1994): Packaging Politics: Political Communication in Britain's Media Democracy. London: Edward Arnold.

Franklin, Mark/Eijk, van der, Cees (1996): Choosing Europe? The European Electorate and National Politics in the Face of the Union. Ann Arbor, Michigan: University of Michigan Press.
ICM Research (2004): Are You Satisfied or Dissatisfied With the Job Tony Blair is Doing as Prime Minister? At: http://www.icmresearch.co.uk/reviews/vote-intention-reports/politician-satisfaction-trends.asp, retrieval Jan. 12th 2005.
Kavanagh, Dennis (1995): Election Campaigning: The New Marketing of Politics. Oxford: Blackwells.
Lees-Marshment, Jennifer (2001): The Marriage of Politics and Marketing. In: Political Studies, Vol. 49, 692-713.
Lilleker, Darren G./Negrine, Ralph (2003): Not Big Brand Names but Corner Shops: Marketing Politics to a Disengaged Electorate. In: Journal of Political Marketing, Vol. 2, No. 1, 55-74.
Maarek, Philippe (1995): Political Marketing and Communication. London: John Libbey.
Marsh, Michael (1998): Testing the Second-Order Election Model after Four European Elections. In: British Journal of Political Science, Vol. 28, 591-607.
Norris, Pippa/Curtice, John/Sanders, David/Scammell, Margaret/Semetko, Holli (1999): On Message: Communicating the Campaign. London: Sage.
Reif, Karlheinz/Schmitt, Hermann (1980): Nine Second Order National Elections: A Conceptual Framework for the Analysis of European Elections Results. In: European Journal of Political Research, Vol. 8, 3-44.
Scammell, Margaret (1995): Designer Politics: How Elections are Won. Basingstoke: MacMillan.
Scammell, Margaret (1999): Political Marketing: Lessons for Political Science. In: Political Studies. XLVII, 718-739.
Scully, Roger (2001): Review Article: Voters, Parties and Europe. In: Party Politics, Vol. 7, No. 4, 515-523.
Shaw, Eric (1999): The Labour Party Since 1979: Crisis and Transformation. London: Routledge.
Taggart, Paul (2004): 2004 European Parliament Election Briefing No.14: The European Parliament Election in the United Kingdom 2004. At: http://www.sussex.ac.uk/sei/1-4-2-2.html, retrieval Nov. 11th 2004.
van der Eijk, Cees/Franklin, Mark/Marsh, Michael (1996):What Voters Teach Us About Europe-Wide Elections: What Europe-wide Elections Teach Us About Voters. In: Electoral Studies, Vol. 15, No. 2, 149-166.
Wring, Dominic (1996): Political Marketing and Party Development in Britain: A "Secret" History'. In: European Journal of Marketing, Vol. 30, No. 10/11, 92-103.

[1] The UK survey was part of the larger pan-EU Framework 6 project, 'The Determinants of Active Civic Participation at European and National Level' (CIVICACTIVE), co-ordinated by Federica Bicchi, Fredrik Langdal and Jean Blondel. The breakdown of interviews/party is as follows: *Conservatives* (3), *Labour* (2), *Lib Dems* (1), *Green Party* (2) and UKIP (3).

[2] In terms of the election results, the *Conservatives* got 27 seats (26.7 percent), followed by the *Labour Party*'s 19 seats (22.6 percent), the *UK Independence Party*'s 12 seats (16.1 percent), and the *Liberal Democratic Party*'s 12 seats (14.9 percent). The rest of the seats were divided among the *Greens* (2 seats; 6.3 percent), *Scottish Nationalist Party* (2 seats; 1.4 percent), Plaid Cymru: *Party of Wales* (1 seat; 1 percent); *Democratic Unionist Party* (1 seat; 28.4 percent in N. Ireland); *Social Democratic* and *Labour Party* (1 seat, 28.1 percent in N. Ireland) and the *Ulster Unionists Party* (1 seat; 17.6 percent in N. Ireland) (BBC website, 2005). The party in power is the *Labour Party* with the *Conservatives* and the *Liberal Democrats* in opposition.

[3] Kilroy-Silk left *UKIP* in January 2005 to set up his own party, *Veritas*, only to resign in July 2005 following disappointing general election results.

[4] Clause 4 of the *Labour Party* constitution was drafted at the party's 1918 conference and had a huge symbolic significance (especially Paragraph 4) in that it marked *Labour* as a socialist party when it promised common ownership of the means of production, distribution, and exchange; popular administration and control as well as the most equitable distribution that may be possible (see Dearlove/Saunders, 2000).

[5] E.g. a keyword search for 'EU' and 'immigrants' revealed 26 articles in *The Sun*; 57 in *The Guardian* and 29 in *The Times*; between April and June 2004.

Between Medialization and Tradition: Campaigning in Finland in a Longitudinal Perspective

*Tom Moring**

1. Introduction

A main focus in research on political communication during the last decades has been the changing role of media in the democratic process. Research on the concept of medialization and related conceptualizations has suggested fundamental changes in the relations between parties, individual candidates, and voters due to the changes in the media sphere. This chapter discusses the European Parliamentary Election in Finland in 2004 against the background of the medialization hypothesis and empirical findings from a longitudinal study carried out since 1991, at which time paid political advertising was allowed on Finnish national television. The voter survey was one in a series of panel surveys that have been conducted since 1991, allowing for measurement of voter behaviour and preferences at different occasions: some weeks before the election and immediately after the elections.[1] While the domestic parties still seek their role in European elections, many voters in 2004 shifted away from "American style politics" characterized by a personalized voting system and a permissive media system, which is favoured in Finland. Though the Finnish context seems to be an ideal playing ground for financially resourceful charismatic political actors who operate in a professional way seeking individual success, results indicate that such features had a rather limited effect in this election.

2. The medialization hypothesis

The conceptual framework of medialization has established its position in Nordic studies since the mid-1980s. The concept relates to a broader scientific debate, where other concepts are also used for basically the same phenomenon: mediatization, mediazation, Americanization, modernization, mediacracy etc. The term "medialization" has frequently been used in Scandinavia (Asp 1986; 1990; Asp/Esaias-son 1996; Moring/Himmelstein 1996; Carlson 2000; Ruostetsaari 2001), whereas in recent years the term "mediatization" appears to have become established on the continent (Schulz et al. 2005; Wurff 2005). Both concepts are used to describe more general tendencies in society and within media development. In connection with political communication, however, they have

---

* Tom Moring, PhD. *1952. Professor of Communication and Journalism at the Swedish School of Social Science, University of Helsinki, email: tom.moring@helsinki.fi

been used in parallel with the concept of "Americanization" in combination with the so-called diffusion theory, while objections against this theory have been raised under the so-called "modernization theory" (for a discussion, see Schultz et al. 2005: 60). Here I will use the term "medialization" as this term was originally used in some Scandinavian studies for the conceptualization of the so-called "medialization hypothesis" (Asp 1986, 1990; Asp/Esaiasson 1996).

The medialization hypothesis builds on a market metaphor: there is a surplus of information and a deficit of attention in society, leading to competition for attention. Editors and journalists are in a crucial position, as they are gatekeepers of the news- and entertainment media that attract daily attention of large audiences. In accordance with theories on anticipated action, politicians would seek ways to by-pass critical media, but also to act in a way that attracts the attention of journalists and entertainment editors in order to affect the electorate (see Asp 1990).

From this follows that the medialization of society would tend to increase under two conditions: 1) Medialization increases if volatility within the electorate grows, as this would give more "room for effects". Increased volatility would be an expected outcome of socio-political development in society leading to decreased class voting. 2) Medialization would also tend to increase if the autonomy of the media sphere increases. This, again, would be an expected outcome of decreased political dependence of the news media and increased concentration and market-based ownership of the big mass media outlets that increasingly act according to internal media logics. According to the hypothesis, when these prerequisites are met, the readiness of political actors to include expectations regarding media response when planning their behaviour will tend to grow. This, again, gives different forms of media expertise an increased role in political planning, including the planning of election campaigns. The increased media-hype would be expected to further increase volatility within the electorate, which would lead to a self-reinforcement of the process.

In practical terms, what would we expect to happen? At the outset of our research, we identified seven expected outcomes:
- The voters would disengage themselves from class- and socially determined behaviour that previously had tied them to certain parties within a traditional party structure. The "personalization" of elections would increase.
- This would lead to increased voter mobility and a wider "influence interval", i.e. the possibilities to influence the electorate through media would increase.
- As mobile voters tend to make their voting decisions later than steady voters, election campaigns would matter more.
- The media would develop a higher level of autonomy as earlier ties to political parties are severed and the media professionalize within a relatively homogeneous discourse ("professional code").
- The entertainment value of media would become more important with increased media competition. As a result, political actors would try to get more

access to entertainment television, and voters would increasingly base their voting decisions on information received through entertainment TV.
- An outcome would be higher turbulence in political life as the election results would shift the power constellations more frequently.

Other studies have proposed further expectations. Schulz et al. (2005: 62) suggest negative effects on the voters such as increased television dependency, fragmentation of the public sphere, and political malaise (apathy). Schulz et al. have also pointed to positive effects (as, for example, Patterson and McLure in 1976), such as mobilization (or at least increased knowledge of issues) among unsophisticated citizens and greater access to information sources.

The medialization hypothesis was operationalized through specific indicators, which have been assessed in repeated measurements sine the 1990s.
- Personalization is measured as choice according to party vs. choice according to candidate.
- Voter mobility is measured by comparing individuals' voting choices (for the big parties) across elections.
- The influence interval during the election campaign is assessed through changes in the time of voting decision (late decision-making indicates a higher potential voter mobility during the campaign).
- The level of media professionalization and autonomy is assessed through content analysis of campaign programmes and political journalism (see Rappe 2004; Holmberg 2004).
- The effect of entertainment programmes is assessed with the help of self-reported influence on voters from entertainment programmes on TV.
- The turbulence within politics and fragmentation of the public sphere are measured by changes in the issue hierarchy of voters.

3. The Finnish context

Due to the fact that this study has been carried out in Finland, four particular contextual features relevant to the medialization hypothesis should be kept in mind. These are the rapid socio-demographic changes in Finland since the Second World War, the level of personalization of the voting system, the consensual tradition of the Finnish multi-party system, and the deregulation of the media system since the 1990s.

3.1 The Finnish context 1: A rapidly modernized society

In many states, the structural change of society has led to a shift from party structures based on social cleavages towards "Catch All Parties" (Kirchheimer 1966). This shift follows a socio-demographic change in society that makes old party structures obsolete (see Carlson 2000). The socio-demographic development underpinning this change has been particularly rapid in Finland. Until the Second World War, Finland was a predominantly agricultural country. This structure profoundly changed after the war. In reference to the occupation of the head of the household, by 1998 less than 4 percent of the Finnish population were farmers, some 25 percent workers, 35 percent blue- or white collar employees, 7 percent entrepreneurs, somewhat more than 20 percent pensioners, and 5 percent unemployed. This corresponds to the typical structure of a European post-industrial society. By the mid-1990s, almost 60 percent of the population was living in urban areas. In general, the social development of the Finnish society appears to fulfil the preconditions for the medialization hypothesis rather well (see Häkkinen/Peltola 2001: 309-328; Uusitalo 1998: 15).

3.2 The Finnish context 2: A personalized voting system

The Finnish electoral system is personalized, and thus well tuned to medialized politics. Parties or constituency associations present candidates. Parties may form electoral alliances and constituency associations may form joint lists (although joint lists and constituency associations were of no relevance in the Finnish EU Parliamentary election 2004). The personal vote of each candidate decides his/her rank within the party (for a detailed description, see the Ministry of Justice Finland, www.vaalit.fi/21959.htm). This system allows more room for individualised voting than the different list methods used in the other Nordic states and in many other states in Europe.

In national parliamentary elections, the country is divided into electoral districts. In EU parliamentary elections, the country as a whole constitutes the electoral district; any voter may vote for any candidate in any part of the country. As voters cast their votes for individual candidates, there is good ground for personalization of the election to nationally profiled well-known candidates and nation-wide campaigns on the media.

3.3 The Finnish context 3: A multi-party system fostering consensus

Finland is a multi-party system. Since there are no thresholds, small parties may get seats in local and parliamentary elections. Presently, eight parties have seats in the Finnish parliament. There has been, however, a clear difference in size between the three biggest parties (*NCP*, *CP* and *SDP*) and the three smaller parties that succeeded in getting a seat in the European Parliament in 2004 (*GL*, *LA*, *SPP*) that has been prevailing since the early 1980s.

From the multi-party structure, it follows that coalition building is a prerequisite for governing. Any two of the three big parties may together form the backbone of a Finnish government. Usually such a coalition would also need at least one of the smaller parties to secure its majority in the parliament. As this is the case, parties tend to refrain from tying themselves to radical demands in election campaigns; they never know which type of coalition will form the next government, and as any combination is possible, radical demands in the campaign may become a burden in the government formation process. This pragmatic tradition (in Finland often called "consensual") has an effect on all types of elections. Thus, parties could be tempted to lean more toward image building instead of pursuing conflictive issues in their campaigns – again a feature that fits together well with medialization.

Table 1: Parties, their abbreviations, and affiliation

Party	Abbreviation	European Parliamentary group affiliation
National Coalition Party	NCP	Conservatives, PPE-DE
Centre Party	CP	Liberals, ELDR
Social Democratic Party	SDP	Socialists, PSE
Green League	GL	Greens, Verts/ALE
Left Alliance	LA	GUE/NGL
Swedish People's Party	SPP	Liberals, ELDR
Christian Democrats	CD	no seat in the European Parliament
True Finns Party	TF	no seat in the European Parliament

4. The Finnish context 4: A deregulated media system

A particular feature of the Finnish media system is that the regulations and constraints of media with respect to political content are relatively relaxed. Finland has a strong public service radio and television, *Yleisradio* (*Yle*). When our study started, in the beginning of the 1990s, the only commercial broadcaster in Finland at that time (*MTV3*) operated on *Yle*'s operating license. The public service broadcaster had a tradition of rather strictly controlled political debate programmes during the election campaign. The commercial broadcaster *MTV3* broadcasted its first political debate during the National Parliamentary election campaign in 1991.

During the following years, the Finnish media system was rapidly deregulated. *MTV3* got its own license to broadcast. A new commercial channel (*Nelonen*) was established. These channels were not tied to constraints regarding political programmes. Today, the public service broadcaster operates two of the four main channels (*TV1* and *TV2*), together collecting somewhat more than 40 percent of the viewing time. The biggest commercial operator, *MTV3*, collects close to 40 percent of the viewing time on its main channel. The programme content of *MTV3* is commercial mainstream, covering a full range of programme categories (including news and election debates). The newcomer *Nelonen* (*TV4*) collects somewhat more than 10 percent of the total viewing time, but it is oriented toward a younger audience (see Aslama 2004).

Regulations of the public service broadcaster's political programmes during election campaigns were lifted in the early 1990s (see Moring/Himmelstein 1993). Since that time, professional journalists have produced party presentations and debates. The journalists are tied to certain principles of fairness. These principles are, however, of a self-regulatory character decided by the broadcasters themselves according to what they define as "programming" or "journalistic" principles.[2] With the deregulation of television, rules regarding the appearance of politicians on television during the election campaign also became more relaxed. Politicians frequently appear in all types of TV-programmes during the campaign, including entertainment formats.

Whereas the deregulated broadcasting system in principle forms a good platform for a medialized system in which television plays a predominant role, this feature is counter-balanced by another factor: as in Norway and Sweden, also in Finland the newspapers have a relatively strong position in the media landscape. 82 percent of the Finns of voting age read a newspaper on a daily basis (compared to 94 percent for TV, 82 percent for radio, and 43 percent for Internet, see Intermediatutkimus 2004 survey). Most daily newspapers are subscribed morning papers. This makes for a strong impact of traditional printed media. The newspapers that were originally tied to political parties have gradually freed themselves from such constraints. This process was completed in the early 1990s, and today there are only occasional traces of the old political bindings in the reporting of the bigger newspapers. At the same time, the salience of political issues (and political personage) has decreased in the press, particularly in news footage (see Holmberg 2004).

Contrary to many other European states, in Finland parties get no free advertising time on public or private television stations. Since 1991 however, parties can use paid political advertising on the commercial channels. In this respect, the Finnish system deviates dramatically from other Nordic states (except for Iceland) and many other states in Western Europe.[3]

Political advertising on radio and television in Finland is not constrained by spending limits, time limits, or content limits (see Moring 1995). The only content limits applied, in particular to paid political television advertising, are set voluntarily by the biggest commercial television station (*MTV3*). The station does not allow personal attack ads or mixed product/political ads. As *MTV3* is the market leader on the commercial side, the standards set by this channel have consequences beyond the channel itself. Parties and candidates normally produce their spots to be broadcasted on this channel, and use the same spots on other channels.

5. The Finnish campaigns in practice: Not so medialized after all in 2004?

The political parties in Finland actively started to use paid political advertising on television as soon as it was allowed. The attention value of political television advertising was also high from the start. The Gallup Finland surveys (see Note 1) show that in domestic elections from 1995 onwards, 70 to 80 percent of the voters were able to identify ads from all three big parties.

The 2004 EU Parliamentary election was a strict exception to this development. All parties but one (the *Social Democratic Party*) decided not to use television advertising as they considered the campaign candidate-driven. The relative importance of the individual candidate campaigns in Finland has also more generally led to a situation where the cumulative size of the candidate campaigns is significantly bigger than the size of the party campaigns. Only a few candidates, however, placed their trust in TV-campaigns in the EU Parliamentary election 2004. The main reason for this is that the number of repeats required to impact an audience is difficult to achieve within the campaign budget of a single candidate. According to party campaign managers,[4] a viewer must be confronted with a television campaign five to six times before it "sinks in". However, the candidates simply cannot afford the costs of an extensive television campaign and turn to other media instead.

While most parties moved away from television ads in the campaign in 2004, all parties invested more – in terms of both organization and resources – in the 2004 EU Parliamentary election campaign than in earlier EU election campaigns. The state supported the increased use of resources by almost doubling its support for the campaign in comparison with the last election. Five of the six campaign managers estimated the level of professionalization and modernity of the EU Parliamentary campaign to be at the same level as the national parliamentary campaign one year earlier (two responses) or even higher (three responses). In comparison with these two last-mentioned campaigns, the campaign managers considered the professional level of the previous EU Parliamentary election campaign in 1999 to have been very low. Thus, while the level of professionalization was higher in 2004 in comparison with earlier EU Parliamentary election campaigns, it does not necessarily mean that professionalization in general has increased, but that the parties now take the EU-level campaigns more seriously.

The interviews with the campaign managers show that the campaign strategies of the parties in the European Parliament election campaign were mainly built on national issues, in spite of some emergence of general European themes. All campaign managers stressed Finland's position within the European Union as a main feature of the campaign. The main themes of the three biggest parties related directly to this theme, but partly in different manners.[5]

The *National Coalition Party* and the *Social Democratic Party* stressed the importance of Finnish participation in the inner circles of the Union. These two parties were also overtly playing on the influence of their European Parliamentary group affiliations (*NCP* with the conservative group *PPE-DE*; *SDP* with the socialist group *PSE*) and the right-left cleavage of the Union. In addition, the Chair of the *Finnish Social Democratic Party* had decided to run for the Chair of the European Commission. The *Centre Party* (affiliated with the less influential

ELDR) was understandably less comfortable with these topics, which left this party outside the debate. Their main party slogan was the deliberately ambiguous "More of EU". The party evidently wanted to signal readiness to fight for EU subsidies that would benefit its rather influential agrarian wing, while at the same time allowing for a more pro-active campaign in the cities.

The three smaller parties all stressed their particular issues in the campaign. The *Green League* participated in the pan-European campaign of the *Greens* in Europe. Reflecting this, their slogan pointed out that when voting for the *Greens*, the voter knows what he or she would get. The *Left Alliance* focused mainly on the need for social responsibility in Europe. The *Swedish People's Party*, afraid to lose its only seat, called for solidarity among the Swedish speakers in Finland relying on the classic slogan from The Three Musketeers, "one for all and all for one".

When comparing different media platforms for their campaigns in the EU Parliamentary election 2004, the campaign managers generally stressed the importance of the advertisement campaign in the newspapers. They also considered this medium to have increased its importance since the EU Parliamentary election in 1999. In addition, they believed that the Internet had become more important than in earlier EU Parliamentary Elections, whereas only (for obvious reasons) the campaign manager of the *Social Democratic Party* thought that television advertising had increased its importance in this campaign. *The National Coalition Party* mentioned their election tour and the *Centre Party* their radio ads broadcast shortly before the election. Among all parties, billboard advertising was perceived as important, though not more important than in earlier campaigns. New techniques used were e-mail, Intranet, and mobile phone (SMS) messages. However, in all cases these types of messages were sent only to well-known active party members, as the parties were afraid of the backfiring effect of spam.

The campaign managers generally considered writings in the newspapers and fact-related TV-formats on television to have been the most influential campaign media. Compared to these, they considered entertainment programmes on television, for example, to be of marginal importance. They were somewhat divided on whether or not the Finnish campaign culture showed signs of further "Americanization" in the 2004 campaign; three of the managers were of this opinion, one saw little change, and two stated that this was not the case.

6. Only small changes in voting behaviour over time

Our longitudinal study that started in 1991 shows remarkably little change in the Finnish political culture in view of the rather dramatic structural changes of the social context and the deregulation of Finnish media, and in the context of a personalized voting system and consensual political culture. In the first Finnish EU Parliamentary election in 1996, there were signs of a more "American style voting" compared to local and national parliamentary elections. The same kind of media hype was also clearly visible in the Presidential elections in 1994 (see Moring 1998). But over the period that has elapsed, such behavioural patterns assumed to result from medialization have stabilized or even decreased. We see this in the development of volatility in the electorate, in the timing of the voting decision, in the priority given to party vs. person, in the development of media contents, and in a general stability in issue priorities.

The political stability of the electorate over the studied period has been remarkable. In our interview surveys (see Note 1), we have not detected indications of increased mobility among parties in pair-wise comparisons between elections. Our measures of the share of respondents who voted for the same party in two subsequent elections of the same type (the local elections 1988 and 1992 and the parliamentary elections 1991 and 1995) show an average voter stability for the three biggest parties of 71-75 percent (Moring 1997: 92). A comparison between the National Parliamentary elections in 1999 and 2003 shows an average voter stability of 78 percent for the three biggest parties. The stability between the National Parliamentary elections in 2003 and the EU Parliamentary elections in 2004 was even greater, a remarkable 86 percent.[6] The low turnout in EU Parliamentary elections probably explains this finding. In elections with low turnout, more loyal voters cast their ballots.

The stability in Finnish voting gets further support in analyses of the voting results themselves. In all Finnish national elections since 1983, the three biggest parties together have accumulated between 64.5 and 68.3 percent of the votes. Gains and losses of the parties are best explained by the activation factor. Turnouts at the polls have been decreasing, and the parties have been more or less able to activate their potential supporters in different elections. Recently, the development toward decreasing turnout has also stabilized and has even shifted to a slight increase in participation (see Moring 2005).

Though voting activity in the 2004 European Parliament election in Finland remained low in comparison with national elections, it did increase substantially in comparison with the earlier EU Parliamentary election in 1999 (see Table 2). The first election in 1996 after Finland had become a member of the Union the previous year coincided with the local elections. Most of the voters that participated in this local election also cast their vote in the EU Parliamentary election. This fact explains the comparatively high turnout in the Finnish EU Parliamentary election in 1996. Since then, the EU Parliamentary elections have been run independently of other elections. The results of the EU Parliamentary elections in comparison with national elections are largely explicable in terms of changes in turnout. Those parties that have loyal voters or a greater share of voters within the higher and more educated social layers that are more likely to vote show a higher degree of participation and thus better results (see Table 2).

Table 2: Results and turnout of the European Parliament elections in Finland

	European Parliament 1996	European Parliament 1999	European Parliament 2004	Seats in the EP[7] 2004 ('99)		Local 1996	National Parliament 2003
NCP	20.2	25.3	23.7	4	(4)	21.6	18.6
CP	24.4	21.3	23.4	4	(4)	21.8	24.7
SDP	21.5	17.9	21.2	3	(3)	24.5	24.5
GL	7.6	13.4	10.4	1	(2)	6.3	8
LA	10.5	9.1	9.1	1	(1)	10.4	9.9
SPP	5.8	6.8	5.7	1	(1)	5.4	4.6
Other	10	6.2	6.5	-	(1)	10	9.7
Total	100	100	100	14	(12)	100	100
Turnout	60.0	31.4	41.1			61.3	69.7

Source: Statistics Finland.

Our second indicator of volatility in the electorate is the timing of the voting decision. The trend towards later decision-making that we detected in the mid-1990s has stabilized or even turned around (see Figure 1). In the first Finnish EU Parliamentary election in 1996, many voters had difficulties in applying earlier experiences to the new situation. In 2004, among those who voted, this did not seem to be such a big problem anymore.

Figure 1: The time of the voting decision has become more stabile[8]

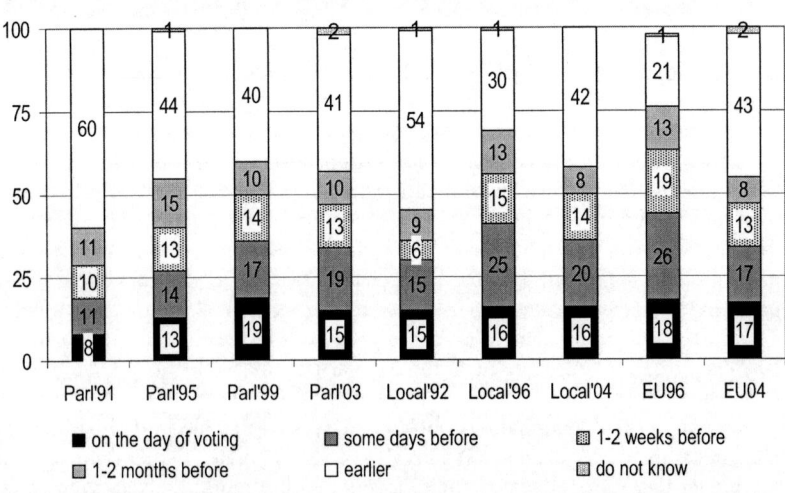

Source: Gallup Finland, see Note 2

Comparisons of elections of the same type show that there was an increase in the share of late deciders in the mid- and late 1990s. The share of late deciders, however, has decreased during recent years in all types of elections. Irrespective of type of election, about half of the voters have decided how they will vote already one to two months before they cast their vote, which is well before the heated part of the election campaign starts (in Finland this part of the campaign normally starts approximately 3 weeks before Election Day).

Figure 2: Parties are favoured over persons[9]

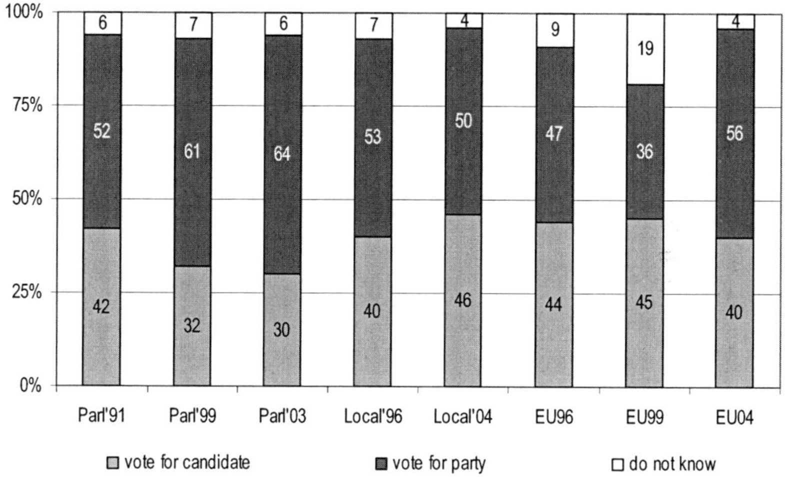

Election	Vote for candidate	Vote for party	Do not know
Parl'91	42	52	6
Parl'99	32	61	7
Parl'03	30	64	6
Local'96	40	53	7
Local'04	46	50	4
EU96	44	47	9
EU99	45	36	19
EU04	40	56	4

Source: Gallup Finland, see Note 2

A similar pattern appears if we compare the percentage of votes cast primarily for the party with the percentage cast primarily for the person (see Figure 2). This measure is an indicator of the balance between a cleavage-oriented part of the electorate voting for the party on the one hand and a personality-driven part of the electorate that is more easily attracted by personal images on the other hand. With the exception of the local elections in 2004, all types of elections show an increased party-vote in most recent elections compared to similar type elections in the 1990s.

7. Issue preferences: In defence of the welfare state

In light of the development within the electorate regarding issue preferences, the expectations (raised by Schulz 2005 and others, see above) of a fragmented public sphere also get less support from our findings. In elections in the early and mid-1990s, economic factors such as *state economy* and *taxes* were among the top-rated issues, given very high priority by approximately 40 percent of the voters[10], along with *social security* and *employment*. This was rather logical, considering the deep economic crisis that Finland passed through during the early 1990s. However, while the hard economic issues fell back in the latter part of the decade, the social issues, such as *health care* and *education,* remained high in salience and further social issues rose over the 40 percent mark.

The same priorities also prevailed in the EU Parliamentary election in 2004. In addition, we found a major concern among voters regarding the Finnish influence on EU-policies and the need to ensure a safe environment. As has been noted, the campaigns of the parties supported these values. The main message is, however, that there was broad support among all parties, with the exception of the conservative *NCP,* regarding the importance of maintaining the Finnish public service system. This indicates that also the high priority given by voters to Finland's position in the EU might have tied into the same issue: there were – and still are – large groups of voters that want their Finnish representatives to defend Finnish welfare and public service schemes within an EU context. There are also parts of the electorate (particularly from the political right) that do not see this as a main question, but consider the EU to be important more on the basis of free market logics. Thus, EU Parliamentary elections have become more clearly politicized within the Finnish electorate, with a focus on rather common goals that are furthered by the public domain.

One further observation that would indirectly support the conclusion that the common public sphere remains central to Finnish voters was the low level of success for pure celebrity candidates. Several parties ran such candidates. As noted, the voting system in Finland is personalized; however, pure celebrity candidates were not elected. A win-win combination seems to be for the celebrity-politician; a combination of popularity through media, good image-work, and good political credibility based on a long-time record has proven effective. In some cases, also strong regional campaigns were successful.

8. The channels of information: News media rule, some young voters lean on the internet

Most voters have a preference for news media of the conventional type when seeking information to support their voting decision. When considering the – in a Scandinavian context – unusual level of deregulation of Finnish broadcast media (see Moring 2004), this is somewhat counterintuitive. The position of traditional sources, such as television news and current affairs programmes and newspapers, has been strong not only among older voters, but among young voters as well (see Table 3). These media have also maintained their position in the most recent European-level election. In addition, the contents of television coverage before elections are presented in a serious manner. Axel Rappe (2004: 208-209) found little evidence of alleged tendencies towards popularization of the television contents in his analysis of the election campaigns of 1991, 1995, and 1999. Both the public service television (*Yle*) and the main commercial channel (*MTV3*) have maintained predominantly serious news coverage, and signs of dramatization of news were not detected in the contents of news, current affairs programmes, and election debates. The public service broadcaster had increased the amount of entertainment programmes featuring politics, but these were mainly satirical programmes, in which politicians did not participate in person.

Table 3: Importance of different media for the voting decision of young voters (18-34 years old)

	Local 92	Parl95	EU/local96	Parl99	Parl03	EU04
TV news, current affairs	22	22	31	25	23	32
Newspapers	18	25	33	30	24	26
TV-ads	5	7	12	11	6	3
Newspaper ads	15	11	21	26	19	11
TV election programmes	13	17	24	20	15	11
TV entertainment	*	*	3	6	3	4
Web candidate selectors	*	*	*	9	31	31
Campaign meetings	5	3	4	5	4	4
Friends, relatives	21	15	13	16	17	14

* missing observation; the variable was not included in the survey covering the election
Source: Gallup Finland, see Note 2

A new phenomenon that had already emerged in the National Parliamentary election 2003 was that a growing proportion of the younger voters (here: 18-34 years old) actively sought information from candidate selectors on the Web as a basis for their voting decision. The same was also true in the 2004 European Parliament Election Campaign. This finding was further confirmed in the Local elections in autumn 2004. The high figure (31 percent in both the National Parliamentary election 2003 and the European Parliamentary election 2004) is partly explicable by the fact that the data were collected through home-based computers. The figures should thus not be read as a point estimate for the entire population within the age bracket, but as elements of a time-series showing a dramatic rise in the importance of internet-based information sources among young people in computerized environments.

The differences in media use in order to support voting decisions between voters of different ages are not very dramatic. Internet of course makes a difference; according to the surveys by Gallup Finland after the Parliamentary election 2003 and the EU Parliamentary election in 2004, somewhat less than 10 percent of the older voters (35 plus) considered the Candidate Selectors important. Among older voters newspaper reporting has a narrow lead compared to television news and current affairs, whereas the order is opposite among the young. Although the role of political television advertising started to rise in the mid 1990s, it has fallen back since. Political television advertisement or television entertainment programmes have not started to play a major role as an information base for the voting decision in any age group. The newspapers have maintained their strong position as an information source also among young voters. This contradicts the expectation, presented at the outset of this chapter, of an increased predominance of television in the election campaign. Overall, traditional habits of media use have remained astonishingly stable, which again is one more argument against the medialization hypothesis.

9. Conclusion

In line with the medialization hypothesis, we expected a development where a contextual change of the political and media system would lead to a less politically stable society. As voters disengage themselves from class- and socially determined behaviour, they become more prone to media influence. As the media develop a higher level of autonomy, with increased competition and the severing of earlier ties to political parties, media logics would become more important. Furthermore, as the Finnish voting system is personalized, Finland was expected to be an "ideal case" of brave new electoral politics.

According to our findings, the basic preconditions for medialization are present in Finland. These include the social development in the Finnish society at large, the growing independence of media from political influence, the introduction of political advertising and entertainment programmes on television, and a personalized voting system.

However, what we did not find in our research were the consequences originally predicted by the medialization hypothesis. Voter stability has not decreased. The time of the voting decision initially developed as the hypothesis predicts: voters delayed their voting decision closer to the voting day. However, this tendency levelled out or even turned in the other direction, also in the new type of European Parliamentary elections. Our measure of personalization of the campaign, choice according to party vs. choice according to candidate, developed the same way in National and European Parliamentary elections. In most elections, personalization decreased and prominence of parties grew. How can we explain this development?

The findings indicate that differences between types of election seem to affect the voters more than long-term changes in the campaign culture or in the media. Experiences from the 2004 European Parliamentary election, however, indicate that the new setting has gradually become more familiar. Though the turnout has remained relatively low, it still has increased from the European Parliament election in 1999. At least partly, this appears to be a result of voters connecting more closely to European level politics, though this connection seems to be strongly coloured by national interest. A conclusion from the study of the 2004 election campaign in Finland in the light of the longitudinal study of

Finnish election campaigns is that as European-level politics become more familiar, Finnish campaign culture also better integrates this new type of election. Parties learn to relate European level politics and issues familiar to the voters, playing on issues relating to internal national interest.

In addition, a longer perspective, including different types of elections, reveals that constraints in the political system counteract structural changes in the media and tendencies towards increased medialization. One major feature seems to be the consensual tradition in Finnish politics. In combination with a relatively homogeneous value-pattern among voters, this has lowered the interest among the bigger parties to seek adversarial strategies. This, again, has contributed to a long-lasting equilibrium between the main forces in Finnish politics. What we thus see, contradicts the belief that the medialization of politics has to be a one-way road.

References

Aslama, Minna (2004): Suomalainen tv-tarjonta 2003. Liikenne – ja viestintäministeriön julkaisuja 58/2004 [A Content Analysis of the Finnish Television Channels 2003 Commissioned by the Finnish Ministry of Communication].

Asp, Kent (1986): Mäktiga massmedier. Studier i politisk opinionsbildning. Stockholm: Förlaget Akademilitteratur [Powerful Mass Media. Studies in Political Opinion Formation].

Asp, Kent (1990): Medialisering, medielogik, mediekrati. In: Nordicom information, No. 4, 7-11 [Medialization, Media Logic, Mediacracy].

Asp, Kent/Esaiasson Peter (1996): The Modernization of Swedish Campaigns. Individualization, Professionalization, and Medialization. In: Swanson, David L./Mancini Paolo (Eds.): Politics, Media, and Modern Democracy. An International Study of Innovations in Electoral Campaigning and their Consequences. Westport: Praeger, 73–90.

Broberg, Jenny (2004): De invaldas valfinansiering i riksdagsvalet 2003. Master's Thesis. Helsinki: University of Helsinki [A Study of the Distribution of the Campaign Financing of Elected Members of the Finnish Parliament 2003].

Carlson, Tom (2000): Partier och kandidater på väljarmarknaden. Studier i finländsk politisk reklam. Åbo: Åbo Akademi [Parties and Candidates on the Voter Market. Dissertation].

Diamond, Edwin/Bates Stephen (1989/revised edition 1988/orig. 1984): The Spot. The Rise of Political Advertising on Television. Cambridge, Massachusetts: The MIT Press.

Hernes, Gudmund (1983): Media; Struktrur, vridning og drama. In: Nordicom information No. 3-4, 2-13 [Media: Structure, Bias and Drama].

Holmberg, Jukka (2004): Etusivun politiikkaa. Yhteiskunnallisten toimijoiden representointi suomalaisissa sanomalehtiuutisissa 1987-2003. Jyväskylä: Jyväskylä Studies in Humanities, No. 30, University of Jyväskylä. [News Representation of Social Actors in the Finnish Newspapers 1987-2003. Dissertation].

Holtz-Bacha, Christina/Kaid, Lynda Lee (1995): A Comparative Perspective on Political Advertising. Media and Political System Characteristics. In: Kaid, Lynda Lee/Holtz-Bacha, Christina (Eds.): Political Advertising in Western Democracies. London: Sage, 8-18.

Häkkinen, Antti/Peltola, Jarmo (2001): On the Social History of Unemployment and Poverty in Finland 1860-2000. In: Kalela, Jorma/Kiander, Jaakko/Kivikuru, Ullamaija/Loikkanen Heikki A./Simpura, Jussi (Eds.): 1990s Economic Crisis. The Research Programme on the Economic Crisis of the 1990s in Finland: Down from the Heavens, up from the Ashes. The Finnish Economic Crisis of the 1990s in the Light of Economic and Social Research. Helsinki: Government Institute for Economic Research, 309-345.

Intermediatutkimus 2004 survey, Gallup Finland. At: www.sanomalehdet. fi/index. php?valittu_id=3&valittu_aid=66&aaotsikko_id=67&paaotsikko_id =3&sisaltoid=41&kieli=englanti, retrieval Jul. 21st 2005.

Kirchheimer, Otto (1966): The Transformation of West European Party Systems. In: LaPalombara, Joseph/Weiner, Myron (Eds.): Political Parties and Political Development. Princeton, NJ: Princeton University Press, 177-200.

Ministry of Justice Finland web-site. At: www.vaalit.fi/21959.htm, retrieval November 21st 2004.

Moring, Tom (1995): The North European Exception. Political Advertising on TV in Finland. In: Kaid, Lynda Lee/Holtz-Bacha Christina (Eds.): Political Advertising in Western Democracies. London: Sage, 161-185.

Moring, Tom (1997): "Amerikaniseras" politiken? Medieförändring, väljarmobilitet och nya former för val i samverkan. In: Lindberg, Steve/Molin, Yngve (Eds.): Festskrift till Sten Bergklund. Vasa: Samhälls- och vårdvetenskapliga fakulteten vid Åbo Akademi, Pro Facultate No. 2, 77-114 [Moring: Are Politics Becoming Americanized? Media Change, Voter Mobility and New Forms of Elections in Finland].

Moring, Tom (1998): Election Effects on Campaigning in Finland. Paper presented at the Political Communication Research Section. International Association for Mass Communication Research. Glasgow, UK, 26-30 July 1998.

Moring, Tom (2003): Between Ban and Laissez Faire. Nordic Strategies to Political Television Advertisements. Paper presented at the European Consortium for Political Research. Marburg, 18-21.9.2003, Section: Political Communications and the Media, Panel on political advertising.

Moring, Tom (2004): Finland: A Reality Check. 10 Years of Political Advertising on TV. In IRIS Special: Political Debate and the Role of the Media. The Fragility of Free Speech. Strasbourg: European Audiovisual Observatory, 83-86.

Moring, Tom (2005): Europawahlkämpfe in Finnland. Eine vergleichende Analyse. In: Tenscher, Jens (Ed.): Wahl-Kampf um Europa. Analysen aus Anlass der Wahlen zum Europäischen Parlament 2004. Wiesbaden: Verlag Sozialwissenschaften, 269-292 [Moring: European Election Campaign in Finland. A Comparative Analysis. In: Tenscher: Campaigning for Europe. Analyses on the Occasion of the 2004 European Parliament Elections].

Moring, Tom/Himmelstein, Hal (1992): The New Image Politics in Finnish Electoral Television. In Ruoho, Iiris (Ed.): Finnish Papers Presented at the IAMCR Conference, Brazil 1992. Tampere: University of Tampere, Department of Journalism and Mass Communication, Series B 37/1992, 99-134.

Moring, Tom/Himmelstein Hal (1993): Politiikkaa riisuttuna. Helsinki: Oy Yleisradio Ab [Politics in the Nude. A Political Campaign Culture in the Age of Television].

Moring, Tom/Himmelstein, Hal (1996): The New-Image Politics in Finnish Electoral Television. In Paletz, David L. (Ed.): Political Communication Research: Approaches, Studies, Assessments. Volume II. Norwood: Ablex, 117-143.

NOU 2004: 25. Penger teller, men stemmer avgjør Om partifinansiering, åpenhet og partipolitisk fjernsynsreklame Utredning fra et utvalg nedsatt ved kongelig resolusjon 17. oktober 2003. Avgitt til Moderniseringsdepartementet 29. November 2004. Norges offentlige utredninger 2004: 25. At: www.odin.dep.no/ mod/norsk/dep/utvalg/002001-991455/dok-bn.html, retrieval July 22nd 2005 [Report From the Norweigian Party Financing Committee, November 2004].

Paloheimo, Heikki/Sundberg, Jan (2005): Puoluevalinnan perusteet. In: Paloheimo, Heikki (Ed.): Vaalit ja demokratia Suomessa. Helsinki: WSOY, 169-201 [Paloheimo: The Basis for Party Choice].

Patterson, Thomas E./McLure, Robert D. (1976): The Unseeing Eye. The Myth of Television Power in National Politics. New York: G.P. Putnam's Sons.

Pesonen, Pertti/Sänkiaho, Risto/Borg, Sami (1993): Vaalikansan Äänivalta. Helsinki: WSOY [The Context, Rhythm and Audience of the 1991 Election Campaign].

Rappe, Axel (2004): Valbevakning i förändring. 1990-talets riksdagsval i finsk television. Åbo: Åbo Akademis förlag [Election Coverage Undergoing Change. The Parliamentary Elections of the 1990s in Finnish Television. Dissertation].

Ruostetsaari, Ilkka (2001): In the Euro-Elite or in the Wilderness of Politics? Recruitment of MEPs from a New Member State to the European Parliament. The Case of Finland. Paper prepared for Presentation at the 29th joint session of the European Consortium for Political Research, 6-11 April 2001. Grenoble, France. Workshop "Political Careers in a Multilevel Europe".

Schulz, Winfried/Zeh, Reimar/Quiring, Oliver (2005): Voters in a Changing Media Environment. A Data-Based Retrospective on Consequences of Media Change in Germany. In: European Journal of Communication, Vol. 20, No. 1, 55-88.

Tiilikainen, Teija/Wass, Hanna (2004): Puolueiden vaalikampanjat vuoden 2004 europarlamenttivaaleissa. In: Politiikka, Vol. 46, No. 4, 250-263 [The Election Campaign of Finnish Parties in the 2004 Europarliament Elections].

Uusitalo, Eero (1998): Elinvoimaa maaseudulle. Miksi, kenelle ja miten? Maaseutupolitiikan perusteet. Helsinki: Otava [Vitality for the Countryside. Why, for Whom and How? The Basics of Rural Politics].

Wurff, Richard Van Der (2005): Impacts of the Internet on Newspapers in Europe. Conclusions. In: Gazette, Vol. 67, No. 1, 107-120.

---

[1] The first survey was a two-round panel (1.326 respondents, see Pesonen et al. 1993). From 1992 onwards these panel surveys were conducted by Gallup Finland through a system of computers placed in the homes of the respondents (the "Finland-Channel"). The number of respondents was 1.326 in the 1991 panel survey. In the first electronic panel survey in 1992, it decreased to 680, but has since increased to between 1.000 and 1.600 in subsequent elections. In 2004, there were 1.362 respondents of which 928 voted.

[2] The politically elected administrative council of *Yle*, however, does approve the schedule of election programmes.

[3] In a Nordic context, Finland and Iceland have so far been the odd cases. In Sweden, broadcasters operating for the Swedish market but broadcasting from abroad have broadcasted only some single political ads. In Denmark, there is no formal ban, but the parties have agreed not to use political advertising on television in political campaigns. In Norway, the authorities have so far not allowed political advertising on television, but recently a party financing committee has made suggestions on how the ban of paid political advertising on television can be lifted (NOU 2004: 25).

[4] The campaign managers Juha Kirstilä (*NCP*), Vesa Mauriala (*SDP*), Markku Rajala (*CP*), Aulis Ruuth (*LA*), Ari Heikkinen and Panu Laturi (*GL*), and Berth Sundström (*SPP*) were interviewed for this chapter after the National Parliamentary election 2003 and again after the European Parliamentary elections 2004. The latter interview was conducted in cooperation with Professor Jens Tenscher, comparative results will be published later.

[5] These results correspond well with results from another research project based on repeated interviews with the campaign leadership during the election campaign (see Tiilikaine/Wass 2004).

[6] These results are in line with results from a longitudinal analysis of parliamentary elections 1975-2003 in Finland showing little variances in voter mobility. Pair wise comparisons between elections show the mobility to be within the range 20-30 % of the voters, with the highest scores in the mid-1990s, 1975 and 20003 scoring 24 and 26 percent respectively (see Paloheimo/Sundberg 2005: 198).Voter surveys, as point estimates, are notoriously unreliable in measuring voter stability, because of a post-hoc rationalization effect. The time-series, however, are a sure enough indication of the changes over time.

[7] Because of the re-distribution of MEPs between EU member states in connection with the enlargement of the Union, the total amount of MEPs elected from Finland was reduced from 16 to 14 in 2004.

[8] The phrasing of the question was "When did you finally decide which party's candidate you will vote for? The same day you voted; Some days before voting; About a week or two before voting ; About a month or two before voting; Earlier; I do not know." Note that

there is an unrestricted right to advance voting some weeks before the election, thus a considerable share of the voters does not vote on the Election Day.

[9] The phrasing of the question was "How did you act? I chose between the best candidates irrespective of party; I first selected the party and then the best candidate on its list; I do not know".

[10] The voters were offered a four-point scale: very important; important; not so important; not important at all.

Halfway there?
The Danish 2004 European Parliament Campaign

*Anders Esmark & Mark Ørsten**

1. Introduction

This article analyses the Danish election to the European Parliament in 2004 from the dual theoretical perspective of *professionalization* and *Europeanization*. Even though voter turnout went down 2.6 percent from 50.5 percent in the 1999 election to 47.9 percent in 2004, the analysis presented in this chapter will argue that the election campaign viewed as a whole showed convincing evidence of both professionalization and Europeanization. However, professionalization was clearly confined by an overarching trend towards personalization of the campaigns conducted for the EP-2004 elections in Denmark. Similarly, the level of Europeanization in terms of salience given to the EP-2004 election in the media was also subject to an important restriction: the limitation of the attention span of the Danish media to a hot phase of only two weeks.

According to a number of observers, professionalization is one of the most important trends in current political communication, constituting a new mode of political campaigning which can be described as "permanent" or "postmodern" (Norris 2000), as simply "professional" (Gibson/Römmele 2001), or as the increased dependence of politicians on media professionals in the "third age of political communication" (Blumler/Kavanagh 1999). However, as Ralph Negrine argues elsewhere in this volume, the term professionalization is not used in any strict sense within the field of political communication studies (see also Lilleker/Negrine 2002). In the context of this chapter the term professionalization is closely linked to political parties and the concept of a 'professional campaign' characterized by a more centralized campaign structure, campaign discipline in relation to a common strategy and the issues of the campaign agenda, as well as the use of external consultants and experts to provide technical or strategic support (see Negrine in this volume). Understood in such terms, recent studies have found evidence for the fact that political communication in Denmark has clearly gone through a process of professionalization (see Esmark/ Kjær 2000; Kjær/Carlsen 1999). Taking into account the multi-party structure of the Danish political system, as opposed to the bi-party system of the countries in which the process of professionalization has been most distinct, such as U.S.A.

---

* Anders Esmark, PhD. *1971. Assistant Professor at the Department of Social Sciences, Roskilde University, Denmark, email: esmark@ruc.dk
Mark Ørsten, PhD. *1967. Assistant Professor at the Department of Communication, Journalism and Computer Science, Roskilde University, Denmark, email: oersten@ruc.dk

and Britain, however, it should be noted that overall professionalization – not just limited to EP-elections – is more significant in the larger Danish parties, the Liberal Party, the Social Democrats, and the Conservatives. In the case of the 2004 EP-election, however, professionalization was clearly less evident than in the case of elections for national parliament.

The second core issue at stake in this article is the *Europeanization* of political communication, meaning the extent to which both mediated and non-mediated political communication deals directly or indirectly with the European Union (see Koopmans/Statham 2002; Kevin 2003; Trenz 2004). Europeanization of media content refers to two central criteria: a) an increased focus on European themes and actors, and b) an evaluation of theses themes and actors from a non-nation state dominated point of view (see Gerhards 2002). According to such criteria, recent Danish studies have documented a significant level of overall Europeanization of Danish media at the level of media content (see Ørsten 2004; Lund/Ørsten 2004), supplementing the Europeanization of political and administrative institutions such as parties, parliaments, ministries, agencies, and private organizations (see Esmark 2002, 2003; Blom-Hansen/Christensen 2004). However, Europeanization in relation to the EP-2004 election is limited by the fact that amongst the political institutions of the EU the European Parliament is the body which is least covered by the media.

The following sections of this article deal with a number of aspects. First, election results are presented and commented using traditional quantitative data. Secondly, the specific characteristics of the conducted campaigns are analyzed with respect to the issue of professionalization. The analysis includes a section on campaign strategy and issues and a section on campaign organization. The analysis is based on semi-structured interviews with one representative from the secretariats of each of the parties and movements involved, printed material on the organization of parties and movements, and campaign programs. Finally, media coverage of the election campaign is analyzed using qualitative content analysis.

2. Reversal of fortune – winners and losers

Of the parties represented in the Danish parliament at the time of the EP-2004 election, only the leftist and EU-sceptic *Unity List* ("*Enhedslisten*") chose not to run candidates, primarily because two anti-European protest movements which catered more or less to the same voter base as the *Unity List* also ran candidates: the *Peoples Movement against the EU* ("*Folkebevægelsen mod EU*") and the *June Movement* ("*Junibevægelsen*"). The social movements provided the major anti-European input. The only party based on an anti-European agenda were the *Nationalists*. The remaining parties all entered the election on the basis of official pro-European agendas, but none the less had to deal with less than enthusiastic voter bases and in some cases even full-fledged anti-Europeans. The overall results are presented in Table 1 below.

Table 1: EP 2004 Election results – Denmark[1]

	Votes – nominal		Votes – percent		Mandates	
	2004	Compared to 1999	2004	Compared to 1999	2004	Compared to 1999
The Social Democrats ("Socialdemokraterne")	618.412	+294.156	32.6	+16.1	5	+2
The Liberalists ("Venstre")	366.735	-94.099	19.4	-4.0	3	-2
The Conservatives ("Konservative Folkeparti")	214.972	+48.088	11.3	+2.8	1	0
The June Movement ("Junibevægelsen")	171.927	-145.581	9.1	-7.0	1	-2
The Socialists ("Socialistisk Folkeparti")	150.766	+10.713	7.9	+0.8	1	0
The Nationalists ("Dansk Folkeparti")	128.789	+13.924	6.8	+1.0	1	0
The Social-Liberals ("Det Radikale Venstre")	120.473	-59.616	6.4	-2.7	1	0
The Peoples Movement against EU ("Folkebevægelsen mod EU")	97.986	-45.723	5.2	-2.1	1	0
The Christian Democrats ("Kristendemokraterne")	24.286	-14.842	1.3	-0.7	0	0
TOTAL	1.894.346	-75.930	100		14	-2
Percent of all registered voters	47.9 %	- 2.6 %				

Source: EU-information office of the Danish Parliament

The undisputed winner of the election was the *Social Democrats*: this party received nearly 33 percent of all cast votes, which corresponded to a gain of over 16 percent compared to the last EP election. The *Social Democrats* received two more mandates, making a total of five mandates. Among the traditional parties, the *Liberalists* had the worst results, loosing 4 percent of the votes and two mandates. What makes the results all the more remarkable is the fact that in the last two elections to the Danish parliament the picture was exactly the opposite. Between 1993 and 2001, a coalition of *Social Democrats* and the *Social-Liberals* headed by the *Social Democratic* Prime Minister Poul Nyrup Rasmussen formed the government, backed by the parliamentary support of the *Socialists* and the *Unity List*. Since the election of 2001, governmental power has been in the hands of the *Liberal-Conservative* coalition headed by the liberal Prime Minister Anders Fogh Rasmussen, backed by the parliamentary support of the Nationalists.

In the election of 2001, the *Liberalists* furthermore ended the longstanding reign of the *Social Democrats* as the nation's biggest party. In the last elections to the Danish parliament in February 2005, the *Social Democrats* got the second lowest share of votes in recent history. Although the *Liberalists* lost a minor share of the votes won in 2001 (primarily to the conservative coalition partner), they easily remained both the largest party and the dominant partner in the governmental coalition. Thus, in reference to the two largest and most important parties in recent Danish political history, the overall results of the EP-2004 election was clearly a "reversal of fortune", compared both to the most recent elections to the national parliament and the EP-1999 election.

How might such a reversal be explained? One particularly important reason for this may be the aforementioned Social Democratic Prime Minister Poul Nyrup Rasmussen. After having lost the national election of 2001, Poul Nyrup Rasmussen resigned his chairmanship, and soon after speculations arose that he would be heading to Brussels. By summer 2003 his candidacy was formally announced. Poul Nyrup Rasmussen ended up receiving 404.966 personal votes, more than the entire list of liberal candidates. Although it is too early to know if history will bestow a specific name upon the EP-2004 election, the term "Nyrup-election" does not seem to be too far-fetched.

3. National profiles

The case of Poul Nyrup Rasmussen demonstrates one thing very clearly: the importance of having a strong leading candidate. Although the case of Mr. Rasmussen is truly special, it is indicative of a more fundamental feature of the EP-2004 election in Denmark: the tendency of the political parties to focus campaign activities on leading candidates with well-established profiles in the national political setting – and not least the relative success of such a strategy.

The tendency to focus on a single or a few top-ranked candidates was in no small measure related to the simple electoral calculus of a small country with a very limited number of mandates in the EP-elections. In the EP-2004 election, Denmark was allotted 14 seats in the European Parliament – a loss of two seats compared to the EP-1999 election. Seats were few and getting even fewer, and most organizations simply campaigned to win a single mandate. The interviews conducted support the simple calculus and show that there were hopes for more than one mandate only in three cases: the *Social Democrats* and the *Liberalists* targeted three to four candidates with an outside chance of five mandates, and the goal of the *June Movement* was to hold on to the three mandates from the previous election.

In most cases, the position as a leading candidate was based on a career in the national parliament. In this respect, the career of Poul Nyrup Ramussen clearly stands out. But it should be noted that the *Social Democrats* actually ran two candidates with ministerial experience. The second-ranked Henrik Dam Kristensen was also in the Danish parliament at the time of election and the only other candidate to have served as minister (Minister of Agriculture and Foodstuffs from 1996 to 2000 and Minister of Social Affairs from 2000 to 2001). The social democratic campaign was based very clearly on two leading candidates who had no previous experience in the European Parliament, but long careers at the highest level in the national political setting.

None of the other parties could muster candidates with ministerial experience, but a number of the other leading candidates running in the EP-2004 election had substantial experience from the national Danish parliament. The top-ranked candidates of the *Conservatives* and the *Socialists* had both been elected to the national parliament for ten years or more, the leading candidate of the *Social-liberals* for six years. As shown below, the approach seems successful: two of these candidates made it to the upper half on the list of most personal votes, and the conservative candidate Gitte Seeberg even came in second – well ahead of the leading candidate of the much larger governmental coalition partner, the *Liberalists*.

However, there were also exceptions to the rule of choosing leading candidates elected to the Danish parliament to run in the EP-2004 election. Both the *Liberalists* and the *Nationalists* ran a leading candidate already serving as a member in the European Parliament. In fact the entire liberal top three were already elected to the European Parliament upon entering the EP-2004 election. A possible lesson to be learned, then, is that candidates already based in the European Parliament are probably not the best choice when entering into a new EP-campaign as the case of the *Liberalists* shows. Their choice of a leading candidate based in the European Parliament and with no prior experience from the national political system did not lead to a positive outcome: losing two mandates and having the lead candidate beaten by the lead candidate of the considerably smaller conservative party and nearly beaten by the second-ranked candidate of the *Social Democrats* is hardly satisfactory for the nation's biggest and reputedly most professional political party.

Whereas a strong national profile was synonymous with a notable career in the national parliament in the case of political parties, the same cannot be said in the case of the social movements. The movements have always tended to run candidates without experience from the national parliament, who nonetheless may have had a very well-established profile in the national media. Both movements appointed leading candidates already in the European Parliament, but in contrast to the case of the conventional parties, both have established national profiles based on campaigning in relation to referendums and to some extent also to EP-elections. The historical importance of the movements in the Danish EU-debate, which has been framed by six referendums oscillating between yes and no, has provided a different kind of platform for establishing profiles within the movements than the one offered to conventional parties. However, even though the leading candidates were elected, both movements clearly obtained poor election results, showing a combined loss of 9.1 percent and a loss of two mandates for the June Movement.

Table 2:   Personal votes and position of the 14 mandates. Denmark

		Personal votes	Danish parliament	EP
1.	Poul Nyrup Rasmussen (Social Democrats, ranked 1)	407.966	1988-2004	2004-
2.	Gitte Seeberg (Conservatives, ranked 1)	125.436	1994-2004	2004-
3.	Karin Riis-Jørgensen (Liberalists, ranked 1)	91.348	No	1994-
4.	Henrik Dam Kristensen (Social Democrats, ranked 2)	91232	1990-2004	2004-
5.	Jens Peter Bonde (June Movement, ranked 1)	75.363	No	1979-
6.	Magrete Auken (Socialists, ranked 1)	73.709	1979-2004	2004-
7.	Anders Samuelsen (Social-Liberals, ranked 1)	60.458	1998-2004	2004-
8.	Mogens Camre (Nationalists, ranked 1)	53.714	1968-1987	1999-
9.	Anne E. Jensen (Liberalists, ranked 2)	49.912	No	1999-
10.	Niels Busk (Liberalists, ranked 3)	44.575	1995-1998	1999-
11.	Ole Krarup (Peoples Movement, ranked 1)	34.719	No	1994-
12.	Britta Thomsen (Social Democrats, ranked 3)	12.756	No	2004-
13.	Ole Christensen (Social Democrats, ranked 8)	10.460	No	2004-
14.	Dan Jørgensen (Social Democrats, ranked 5)	10.430	No	2004-

Source: Various homepages of parties, movements, and candidates

In conclusion, all organizations involved in the EP-2004 election singled out a top-ranked candidate or a small core team based on the simple electoral calculus of a small country. Since the parties and movements ran as many as 20 candidates and no fewer than nine, the results show a clear distinction between a small number of top-ranked candidates and the rank and file candidates which more or less just filled the lists. With the exception of the *Liberalists* and the *Nationalists*, the leading candidates were elected on the basis of a career in the national parliament, including ministerial experience in the case of the *Social Democrats*. The clear distinction between a few leading candidates with strong national profiles and the rank and file candidates makes personalized campaigns the obvious tactical choice.

4. Personalizing campaign strategy and issues

Campaign planning for the EP-2004 election was initiated in the second half of the year 2003 in most cases. Only the *Social Democrats* opted for a longer period, beginning their campaign planning as early as spring 2003. In most cases, preliminary meetings and brainstorming sessions concerning major themes of the campaign were held before candidates were nominated. But the real starting point of campaign activities was, not surprisingly, the formal decision on the candidates list. The decision which candidates were to be placed on the list was made between September and December 2003 in various general assemblies of the parties and movements. Most parties and movements targeted the beginning of May 2004 as the starting point of their campaigning activities, leaving a time period of four to seven months for strategic planning and preparation of the campaign.

All parties and movements organized "candidate seminars", which included the rank and file candidates. These candidate seminars had several functions: training in press relations, information about the EU, study trips to Brussels, and in some cases also debates on topics and issues of the campaign. In this way, these seminars helped to build a strong team spirit and cohesion among the candidates making up the party or movement list. Furthermore, the candidate seminars may be interpreted as an attempt to professionalize the rank and file candidates during early stages of campaign planning by providing training in both training in press relations and aspects of overall coordination in relation to the campaign strategy.

However, during the later stages of campaign planning and preparation, taking place roughly from the last months of 2003 to May 2004, campaign activities became increasingly focused on the leading candidates. More specifically, the final choice of campaign strategy and issues was made through discussions with leading candidates and built around their established profiles. Of course, the campaign agendas also reflected the overall party programmes and therefore were also shared by the rank and file candidates. But the specific choice of campaign agenda and issues within the overall party programme was in most cases based on the profiles of the leading candidates and in this sense took the form of personalised campaigns.

Interviews and campaign material display two broad strategies of personalised campaigns. One strategy consisted of making the leading candidate him- or herself the centre of the campaign agenda itself. Such a strategy represents the most pure form of personalization in the sense that the person becomes the campaign. In a broader perspective, the most well-known example is of course presidential campaigns, and accordingly, the tendency to personalise campaigns in such a way has been called presidentialization (see Hallin/Mancini 2004). The most clear-cut example of this trend was the *Conservatives* who commissioned a consultant agency to conduct an analysis of how the general public perceives its leading candidate, and planned the campaign as a branding exercise in reference to the leading candidate, particularly aimed at rallying support from female voters. The use of Mr. Rasmussen in the *Social Democratic* campaign also displayed clear "presidential" traits. The second strategy did not imply making the leading candidate him- or herself the explicit focus of the overall campaign, but rather in matching the choice of specific policy issues on the campaign agenda to the established profile of the leading candidate. Such an approach was displayed very clearly by the *Socialists*, who chose environmental issues as the dominating theme of the campaign to match the very strong profile of the leading candidate in this area. A similar approach was conducted by the Social-liberals.

As already stated, the *Liberalists* chose leading candidates already elected to the European Parliament rather than candidates with strong national profiles. In relation to the degree of personalisation of the leading candidates, the *Liberalists* were also the odd one out among the conventional parties. The liberal candidate did display a certain degree of personalisation, although in another way than the candidates of the other campaigns. Rather than relying on the leading candidates themselves, the campaign made use of Prime Minister Anders Fogh Rasmussen and thus attempted to generate a spill-over effect from the clout of the party leader and Prime Minister. The leading candidates as well as the rank and file candidates were presented as a unified team headed by Anders Fogh Rasmussen in the campaign material. Another important element in this strategy was the decision not to tie the specific issues on the campaign agenda to the top-ranked candidates, but rather to present a broad range of priority issues of the party within an overall framework of an ideological battle between the blue (liberal) and red (socialist) Europe. This resulted in a much less personalized campaign in the case of the liberalists.

With regard to the choice of campaign strategy and issues, the social movements obviously differ from political parties. The historical background of the social movements is the mobilization of opposition to the EU in the context of referendums. Consequently, the approach of the social movements has traditionally been to transform EP-elections into referendums. The result in the EP-2004 campaign as well as earlier campaigns was what might be designated as *polity* campaigns, that is to say a campaign based on broader institutional issues, such as the undemocratic nature of the governance system of the EU, the appropriate competencies of the EU-institutions vis-à-vis national governments etc. A particular important element in the polity campaigns of the social movements in the EP-2004 elections was the draft constitutional treaty.

However, the EP-2004 election displayed a clear – and successful – tendency of the political parties to distance themselves from the polity approach of the social movements. The strategy of the political parties was clearly to mould their campaigns as *policy* campaigns, meaning campaigns based on presentation of problems and future solutions within specific policy areas – in most cases matched with the profiles of the leading candidates. Interviews suggest that the decision to conduct policy campaigns was based on the analysis that the social movements have previously had too much success in framing the agenda as a question of "yes" or "no" to the EU and thus transforming the EP-elections into de facto referendums. The EP-2004 election marked a decisive departure from this development. In such terms, the EP-2004 was actually the first "proper" EP-election in Denmark, meaning an election not transformed into a de facto referendum.

In sum, personalization of campaigns was clearly a dominating trend in the EP-2004 election in Denmark, although not completely without exceptions. It has been argued that personalization is a more or less integral part of professionalization in the sense that the ideal-type of professional campaigns, such as the British *Labour* campaigns of the Blair-era, has been built around a single person or a core team (see Negrine in this volume).[2] No doubt, there is a clear link between professionalization and personalization in many empirical cases. However, personalization should be seen as a trend in its own right rather than something endemic to professionalization. Thus, the relation between personalization and professionalization may turn out very differently in empirical cases. In this regard, the planning stage of the EP-2004 campaign in Denmark proves to be a case where professionalization is clearly circumscribed and limited by personalization. First, it is only the top-candidates that receive the professional guidance and economic support that, among other things, characterize a professional campaign. Second, even for the top-candidate this support and guidance is limited. Rank and file candidates were largely excluded from campaign planning after the initial candidate seminars and increasingly were left to conduct their own uncoordinated campaigns without much support from the campaign management and without any strict campaign discipline in reference to a clearly defined campaign agenda. This trend became even more apparent during the final stages of intensive campaigning.

5. Campaign organization and coordination

The campaign management during the operational period of the campaign was in most cases a loosely organized group of people within the party or movement organization. In the case of the parties, the group consisted of three to five people from the party secretariat located in the building of the Danish parliament. Only the *Christian Democrats* conducted their campaign from party headquarters rather than from the secretariat of the parliamentary group. The members of the campaign group were typically people from the press section, experts in EU-matters, and in some cases experts from policy areas given priority in the campaign. In the case of the social movements, campaign activities were directed from the central offices by a somewhat smaller professional staff, but with the aid of different non-paid volunteers.

The campaign groups were in constant contact with the leading candidates, whereas the rank and file candidates were more or less left to their own devices or, alternatively, their local party organization. Although the rank and file candidates received campaigning material such as posters and flyers as well as continuous updates per email during the campaign, the organizational resources were almost entirely devoted to the leading candidates. The assistance offered to the leading candidates included, in most cases, the appointment of one of the members of the campaign group as an adviser and personal assistant to the leading candidate. Campaign busses and public debates were also planned for most leading candidates, but given the fact that the turnout was moderate to say the least, this particular activity was seen more as "going through the motions" than a vital element of the campaign. The central activity of the campaign group during the actual campaign obviously was press relations. Although such findings suggest a level of professionalization in reference to the leading candidates, it is evident that various elements of what is usually considered to be part of a professional campaign were missing.

First, a distinct feature in all campaigns is the lack of "campaign general". In all cases, the organizational model of the campaign management is a loosely coupled group without clear day-to-day leadership. As regards the overall strategic decisions and the general framework, the campaign management obviously answers to the steering committees of parties and movements. But the day-to-day management of the campaign is conducted by a small collective of mid-level employees of the party secretariat with no clear hierarchy among them. Thus, the mythical figure of the spin doctor is completely absent, at least if we take a spin doctor to be a person who singularly exerts control over decisions on communication strategy in a particular organisation. As Negrine notes in his contribution to this volume, the Stanley Greenbergs of the political communication world flying in to run an EP-campaign is an unlikely scenario. But even settling for less, professionalization in terms of strong overall leaders of campaign activities seems absent in the EP-2004 campaign in Denmark. The head of the press section, which is the most likely person to earn the title of spin doctor within the party structure, did take part in campaign planning is most cases, but more as an on/off member than the leader of the group.[3] Secondly, the period of actual campaigning is characterized by the declining importance of the overall campaign strategy as the election itself drew nearer, and the media attention remained low. Most campaigns were kicked off during the first half of May, but all interviews conducted convey the experience that the media had no intention of spending more than a maximum of two weeks on the EP-election. A banal, but important factor in this decision, besides the widely voiced idea that media always takes little interest in EP-elections, was the fact that the Danish Crown Prince was married on May 14th 2004. The wedding consumed an extreme amount of journalistic resources in both the weeks before and after the wedding and shortened the already brief attention span of the media when it comes to EP-elections (see Leroy/Siune 1994; Lund/Ørsten 2004). As a consequence, the period of actual campaigning was limited to two weeks, and the well-planned campaigns were gradually abandoned for a more simple dogfight simply to get the leading candidates airtime and headlines. This, however, brings up the issue of the EP-2004 election as it was covered by the media.

6. Europeanization and the European Parliament

The lack of media interest observed by campaign workers should be seen against the background of recent studies of political journalism in Denmark that have indicated a growing level of Europeanization in the Danish media in recent years (see Ørsten 2004; Lund/Ørsten 2004).[4] The term Europeanization refers to Gerhards' (2000) two criteria that the development of European politics should lead the media to a) an increased focus on European themes and actors, and b) an evaluation of these themes and actors from a non-nation state dominated point of view.

Ørsten (2004) analyzes EU-coverage in the Danish news media from 1991 to 2001. The study finds that throughout the ten-year-period a relatively large number of European issues are covered by the media, but more so by the press than by television. In general, 7 to 13 percent of all news items in the morning papers are connected to the EU, on television the number of EU news stories vary from just 3 percent (Ørsten 2004: 347) to 9 percent (de Vreese 2002: 107).[5] Ørsten (2004) also finds that even though there is a dominance of national actors in EU-coverage especially the Commission, but also the Counsel, are important actors in media coverage. More important, however, is the change in the way issues and actors are framed by the media. Here Ørsten (2004) shows that in 1991 conflict between the Danish government and the EEC was the most prominent news frame. Through a detailed framing analysis Ørsten (2004) shows that the conflict frame is the result of a nation-sate dominated news discourse that almost exclusively casts the EEC in the role of the 'other'. For this reason almost all European initiatives in 1991 were seen by the media as a threat to the harmony of Denmark as a sovereign nation state. In 1996 and especially in 2001 the conflict frame lost its dominance, and to a larger part the EU became accepted as an equal player in the game of politics.

However, throughout the analysis one major European player receives almost no media coverage: the European Parliament. Throughout 1991 the European institutions (The Commission, The Court, etc.) were mentioned a total of 148 times by the written press. The Commission was mentioned 31 times, whereas the Parliament was only mentioned seven times. In 2001 the European institutions were mentioned a total of 133 times. Here the Commission was mentioned a total of 42 times, but the Parliament was still only mentioned seven times. On television the Parliament as an institution was not mentioned at all during the analyzed period of 2001 (see Ørsten 2004). When interviewed on this subject, both reporters and editors agree that on a day-to-day basis the Parliament receives little or no media coverage (see Ørsten 2004). Adding insult to injury, studies have show that even during European elections the coverage of the Parliament has, historically, been minimal. Leroy/Siune (1994) show that the first European Election in 1979 did receive some coverage in the Danish news media because as a first time election it was considered to have at least some news value. However, the subsequent elections in 1984, 1989, and 1999 were not considered as important events by the national Danish televisions stations (see Leroy/Siune 1994; de Vreese 2002). Thus, even though some evidence of Europeanization can be found in the Danish news media so far, this has not helped the Parliament to be identified as an important European institution by either the press or television.

7. The EP-2004 campaign and the window of opportunity

With the aforementioned facts in mind, it comes as some surprise that a content analysis of the 2004 European Elections shows that the elections did receive substantial coverage (see Lund/Ørsten 2004).[6] Even though there are difficulties comparing the studies, the results shown in Table 3 indicate an increase in election coverage when compared to earlier studies (see Leroy/Siune 1994, de Vreese 2002). It is, however, important to note that most of the media coverage is concentrated on the last fourteen days prior to the election, with more than fifty percent of the coverage appearing only in the last week before the election. Previous studies have suggested a so-called 'hot phase' for the coverage of an election; i.e. a period of time within which the media intensifies its news coverage. In Denmark this hot phase spanned three weeks during both the 1979 and 1984 European elections according to Leroy/Siune (1994). This study, however, indicates that the hot phase is now almost down to just one week. So even though there are signs of a quantitative leap in media coverage, this leap only really became visible in the final week of the election campaign.

Looking at the overall coverage (see Table 3) the written press, the national telegram agency, and the two public service television stations had a total of 1.430 items concerning the EP election. Of the three large morning papers, *Politiken* had the largest number of items covering the election, which was perhaps not surprising as the paper (see Tjernström 2001) was found to be the leading paper regarding news on the EU in a comparative study of Scandinavian newspapers. More interestingly, the two Danish tabloids (*B.T.* and *Ekstra Bladet*) both covered the election extensively even though both papers traditionally write very little about the EU. 63 percent of the TV-coverage on the EP-election was generated by the long-standing public service station (*DR 1*), whereas *TV 2*, the more commercial of the two channels, only generated 37 percent of the coverage.

Table 3: Media coverage of EP-2004 campaign in Denmark

Media outlet	Election coverage (number of items)	Election coverage (percent of total)
B.T.	184	12.9
Ekstra Bladet	256	17.9
Politiken	322	22.5
Berlingske Tidende	212	14.8
Jyllands-Posten	271	18.9
Ritzau	106	7.4
DR 1 (TV) (21:00)	50	3.5
TV 2 (TV) (19:00)	29	2.1
TOTAL	1430	100

Source: Lund/Ørsten 2004: 8.

8. Actors and issues in the media

The analysis also shows some evidence of Europeanization in regard to issues and evaluations. As for the actors, the content analysis shows few surprises: the most frequently cited sources were either new candidates seeking election or present members of the European Parliament seeking re-election. As for the political parties the *Liberalists*, the largest party in the coalition government, and the *Social Democrats*, the largest opposition party, were the most frequently covered political parties in both press and television. Third place was the *June Movement*, the larger of the two social movements running in the election. As for the specific candidates, the study examined whether or not items could be found for which one candidate could be said to be the dominating source. In 37 percent of the articles/news stories it was possible to isolate one dominating source. In 9.6 percent of the articles/news stories this dominating source was found to be the top candidate for the *June Movement*, while in another 9.6 percent of the articles/news stories the dominating source was found to be the top candidate for the *Liberalists*. In only 6.4 percent of the articles/news stories the dominating source was found to be the top candidate for the *Social Democrats*, which is somewhat surprising since the top candidate for the *Social Democrats* was the former Prime Minister. So even though Poul Nyrup Rasmussen 'won' the election, he did not get special treatment by the media.

Table 4: EP 2004 election framing. Denmark (in percentages)

Media Outlet	Strategy	Substance	Character	Other	TOTAL
B.T.	67	17	15	1	100
Ekstra Bladet	51	33	15	1	100
Politiken	35	58	5	2	100
Berlingske Tidende	35	52	6	7	100
Jyllands-Posten	41	51	6	2	100
Ritzau	53	42	4	1	100
DR 1 (TV) (21: 00)	52	46	0	2	100
TV 2 (TV) (19:00)	52	38	7	3	100

Source: Lund/Ørsten 2004

Turning to the themes discussed in the election campaign, the content analysis distinguishes between three main categories (see Table 4): 'Political strategy' meaning a focus on the campaign itself, voter turn-out, the battle between candidates, etc. 'Political substance' meaning a focus on specific political issues such as the European Constitution, the role of the Parliament, the enlargement of the EU, etc. Finally, the focus can be on 'Character' meaning the qualifications, ethics etc. of the particular candidate. Looking at the three themes from the point of view of a political campaign, it is interesting to note that only under the headline 'substance' it is possible to focus on the actual polity and policy of the election. This means that in the media outlets which focus on strategy and/or character there is actually very little space left in which to discuss the political aspects of the debate. The results show that television and the tabloids focused more on political strategy than on political substance, whereas the broadsheet papers focused more on substance than on strategy. This was truer of the tabloids and less true of *DR 1*, the more traditional of the two public service stations that had an almost equal focus on both strategy and substance.

Under the headline of strategy the specific focus was most commonly on voter turn-out, a subject that has also played a significant role in prior elections (see Leroy/Siune 1994). The election campaign itself was also a frequent issue under this headline addressing such topics as campaign financing and the inner-party competition among the candidates. Under the headline of 'political substance' the focus was most commonly on the role of the Parliament, the European Constitution, and the Enlargement of the EU. Together these issues represent a shift away from the three previous elections (1984, 1989 and 1999), where other studies indicate a strong focus on national subjects, to a stronger focus on major European issues. There are two further indicators of a shift in the media evaluation of the importance of European Elections. One was the large number of editorials that dealt directly with the election. In both *Politiken* and *B.T.*, which was rather remarkable since the latter is a tabloid, there were nine editorials discussing the election. Some concerned the growing political importance of the Parliament, others encouraged voters to make use of their democratic right to go out and vote although European politics and the role of the EU might be difficult to understand. Another sign of the media shift in evaluation was the tendency to discuss notions of democracy in a European perspective rather than a strict national perspective, as was commonly done in the findings of Ørsten (2004). The content analysis of the campaign shows that in 305 items out of a total of 1430 items there were manifest discussions in the texts concerning the nature of democracy as either European or purely national. In 86 percent of the items a European notion of democracy was evident, indicating that the national discourse found to be dominant by both Ørsten (2004) and Leroy and Siune (1994) is no longer the dominate way European issues are framed in the media.

9. Conclusion

The result of the analysis of the Danish EP-2004 campaign is ambiguous in reference to two of the otherwise most important trends in political communication – in Denmark and elsewhere. Concerning professionalization, two specific limitations can be observed. The first limitation concerns the number and the profile of the candidates. *First*, insofar as professional political communication is an aspect of the EP-2004 election, this only applies to a few leading candidates. The EP-2004 election campaigns predominantly focused on a few leading candidates with well-established profiles in the national political system. Consequently, support from the central campaign management of the parties and movements is directed at a few leading candidates, whereas the vast majority of candidates is mostly left to their own devices and the occasional support of the local party offices. The *second* limitation concerns the difference between the period of strategic planning and the period of operative campaigning. Put briefly, professionalization of political communication tends to be limited to the period of strategic planning and preparation, whereas the – extremely short – period of active campaigning is characterized more by fragmentation and last-minute solutions rather than by the highly disciplined campaign associated with professional political communication. These limitations have to do partly with some institutional features endemic to the EP-election itself, but also to a very high degree with the role of the media as a gatekeeper. A *third* and final conclusion is that the lack of Europeanization on the part of the media specifically in reference to the institution of the European Parliament established a sort of mutual deadlock between professionalization and Europeanization.

Thus, the study suggests that the process of Europeanization has opened up a window of opportunity in the Danish news media, where a more substantial and European discussion of the EP-election can take place. This window, however, is so short, one to two weeks, that it is not possible to run a full-blown professional campaign. The parties having obviously sensed this and working with at best only a handful of top-candidates instead opt for a more moderate campaign, focusing more on the planning phase than on the actual execution, which to a large part is left to the candidates themselves. From a positive point of view, one can say that Denmark is about half way on the road to a professional European Election campaign. If Denmark is to conduct a fully professional European election campaign in the future, the dual process of professionalization and Europeanization must continue, so that more well-established candidates make it to the party lists, thus pushing open the window of opportunity in the media for a European debate a bit further.

References

Blumler, Jay/Kavanagh, Dennis (1999): The Third Age of Political Communication. In: Journal of Political Communication, No. 16, 209-230.
Carlsen, Erik Meier/Kjær, Peter (1999): Diagnoser af den politiske journalistik – Indtryk fra en interviewrunde'. In: Carlsen, Erik Meier/Kjær, Peter/Pedersen, Ove K. (Eds.): Magt og fortælling. Center for Journalistik og Efteruddannelse [Carlsen/Kjær: Diagnosis of the Political Journalism in Denmark. In: Carlsen et al.: Power and Story-Telling).
De Vreese, Claes H (2002): Framing Europe. Aksant.
Esmark, Anders/Kjær, Peter (2000): Den sidste mediepolitik og den politiske journalistik'. In: Pedersen, Ove K. (Ed.): Politisk journalistic. Ajour: Mod-

tryk [Esmark/Kjær: The Last Media-Policy and Political Journalism. In: Pedersen: Political Journalism].

Gerhards, Jürgen (2000): Europäisierung von Ökonomie und Politik und die Trägheit der Entstehung einer europäischen Öffentlichkeit. In: Bach, Maurizio (Ed.): Die Europäisierung nationaler Gesellschaften. Wiesbaden: Westdeutscher Verlag, 227-305.

Hallin, Daniel C./Mancini, Paolo (2004): Comparing Media Systems. Three Models of Media and Politics, Cambridge University Press.

Koopmans, Ruud/Statham, Poul (2002): The Transformation of Political Mobilisation and Communication in European Public Spheres: A Research Outline. In: http://europub.wz.berlin.de.

Leroy, Pascale/Siune, Karen (1994): The Role of Televison in European Elections: The Cases of Belgium and Denmark. In: European Journal of Communication, Vol. 9, 47-69.

Lund, Anker Brink/Ørsten, Mark (2004): Nyhedsmediernes dækning af valget til Europa-Parlamentet 2004, Working Paper No. 11. Modinet [News Coverage of the EP-2004 Election].

Mazzoleni, Gianpietro/Schulz, Winfried (1999): Mediatization of Politics: A Challenge for Democracy. In: Political Communication, No. 16, 247-261.

Negrine, Ralph/Lilleker, Darren G (2002): The Professionalization of Political Communication. In: European Journal of Communication, Vol. 17, 305-323.

Norris, Pippa (2000): A Virtuous Circle. Political Communication in Postindustrial Societies, Cambridge University Press.

Ørsten, Mark(2004): Transnational politisk journalistik, Ph.d.-Series at Roskilde University, No. 1 [Transnational Political Journalism].

Tjernström, Vanni (2001): Europa Norrifrån. Umeå University [Europe Seen from the North].

Trenz, Hans-Jörg(2004): Media Coverage on European Governance In: European Journal of Communication, Vol. 19, No. 3, 291-319.

Zimmerman, Ann,/Koopmans, Ruud (2003): Political Communication on the Internet Report March 2003. At: http://europub.wz.berlin.de.

---

[1] Denmark forms a single constituency divided into 103 electoral counties. The counties only have an administrative purpose – they do not form constituencies in themselves. Mandates are distributed according to the D'Hondt method, which calculates the number of votes in relation to the number of seats already given (initially 0 for all lists) and the divisors 1, 2, 3, 4, etc. The D'Hondt method favours large lists and except for the *Nationalists*, all parties and movements committed themselves to electoral pacts. The four pacts were: the *Social Democrats* together with the *Socialists*, the *Liberalists* together with the *Conservatives*, the *Social-Liberalists* together with the *Christian Democrats*, and finally the two anti-European Movements forged a pact. All lists used the equal-chance principle rather than a prioritized order, which is to say that that the internal distribution of mandates on each list were conducted according to the number of personal votes given to each candidate.

2   Interestingly, Negrine argues that the list system of EP-elections provides less opportunity to personalize campaigns. Clearly, the Danish case does not corroborate such an argument in the sense that campaign activities simply proceeded from a clear division between the leading candidates and the rank and file candidates on the list in most cases.
3   The absence of spin doctors has to do with an important feature of the Danish political system: persons fitting the profile of spin doctor do not work within the party, but rather as civil servants directly under a particular minister. Since 1998, the formal category of "civil servants under special conditions" has been in effect to establish formal guidelines for civil servants who are not bound by the otherwise strict criterion of party neutrality in the Danish central administration. The spin doctor is clearly a part of the professionalization in Denmark, but he or she is found in the central administration rather than in the party structure as is also the case in other countries covered in this volume (e.g. Germany).
4   In Denmark the written press is typically divided into two groups consisting of the broadsheet papers (also known as the morning papers) and the tabloids. Included in the analysis are also the national telegram agency (Ritzau) and the two national TV-stations: *DR 1* (public service) and *TV 2* (Public service and commercial). The broadsheet papers include *Politiken*, *Jyllands-Posten*, and *Berlingske Tidende*. Politically *Politiken* is a center-left newspaper, whereas *Berlingske Tidende* is center-right, and *Jyllands-Posten* is a regional center-right newspaper. Of the two tabloids, *Ekstra Bladet* and *B.T.*, *Ekstra Bladet* is traditionally placed somewhat to the left, whereas *B.T.* is placed more firmly to the right. The daily readership numbers (Monday-Friday in June of 2004) are *Politiken* (565.000), *Berlingske Tidende* (430.000), *Jyllands-Posten* (608.000), *Ekstra Bladet* (553.000) and *B.T.* (525.000).
    In general the Danish media system, according to Hallin/Mancini (2004), is characterized by a high degree of public service (television), as well as a state subsidised written press. In general the media is less commercial than for instance the British and American press.
5   Coverage of European news in the Danish media during so-called routine weeks (see de Vreese 2002; Ørsten 2004).
6   The study was conducted as a comparative study of Danish, Swedish, and Finnish news coverage of the election during a four week period (May 17 to June 13) leading up to the election. Based on a previously tested Swedish coding schedule, quantitative and qualitative content analyses were conducted on the media mentioned in Footnote 1. A total of 1.430 news items, i.e. articles/news stories, letters to the editor, editorials etc. concerning the election were coded by a single coder. The coder was trained at the University of Southern Denmark and followed strict coding guidelines.

Low Heated and Half-Hearted: The 2004 European Parliament Campaign and Its Reception in Germany

*Jens Tenscher**

1. Introduction

There seem to be three main and interconnected features which were typical for each of the six European Parliamentary (EP) campaigns between 1979 and 2004. Foremost, in the run-up to elections all of them were burdened with high expectations regarding the political and symbolic function of the only direct, legal, and recurring way for the European people to express their support for an evolving supranational political system and for the idea of an expanding European community. However, while the European political elite has steadily pushed forward the European integration process and the European Union (EU) has rapidly grown from originally six to currently 25 nations, the people of Europe seem to be less and less motivated to *participate* in this process.[1]

In fact, turnout at EP elections shrank from a European average of 63.0 percent in 1979 (with nine member states) to a record low of 45.7 percent in 2004 when, for the second time after 1999, turnout failed to pass the "50 percent pain threshold" of democratic legitimacy (see Delwit 2002: 208-209). Not only the voters of the ten new EU member states from East Europe and the Mediterranean region which joined the EU on May 1st, 2004 were exceedingly reluctant to cast their vote (see Weßels 2005), but also in some of the "established" EU nations like Germany more than half of the voters did not participate. Consequently, to a far extent the "founding elections" simply failed to kick off the start of a bright new future for a geographically extended and politically strengthened EU.

There are several explanations for the *traditionally low turnout* in EP elections – the principal characteristic of all EP elections –, which mainly focus on the low salience of these elections for *voters* (see e.g. Reif/Schmitt 1980). Most of them seem to frame EP elections as just another contest within the *national* arena, but with less being at stake because they do not directly influence the composition of the EU "government" (i.e. the European Commission) and because of the widespread *indifference* with which the EU is observed compared to the national level of politics. This indifference is expressed in relatively low rates of interest in and knowledge of EU institutions (see e.g. Blondel et al.

---

* Jens Tenscher, PhD. *1969. Junior Professor for Political Sociology at the Department for Social Sciences of the University of Koblenz-Landau, Germany, email: tenscher@uni-landau.de

1998: 85ff.) as well as in a comparatively small number of people who actively look for European-related information – even during EP campaign times (see Bicchi et al. 2003: 15ff.; EOS Gallup Europe 2004: 15ff.).

Such low levels of attentiveness might be directly connected with the mass media as the main linkage between citizens and the (European) political realm. As several studies point out, EU-related news coverage has generally been insufficient, "ephemeral", infrequent, marginalized, negative, nationally "domesticated", "faceless", and event-driven (see e.g. Semetko et al. 2000; de Vreese 2002; Kevin 2003; Eilders/Voltmer 2004). Even in election campaigns, one of the main events on the European level, European coverage has always been – and increasingly is – low in visibility and low in 'Europeanness' in all EU countries (see Medien Tenor 2004; de Vreese et al. 2005). Thus, the second key feature of the six EP campaigns so far has been their *second-rate character* from the point of view of the media and the citizenry.

Confronted with such a difficult context, namely a – compared to national elections – rather disinterested and uninformed citizenry plus a relatively restrained media, political campaigning for the EP has always been an extremely challenging task. Political parties have been urged to bypass the rather passive mass media and to trust the broad spectrum of "paid media" activities (see Esaisson 1991) to reach the voters. Consequently, even in such Western European countries in which modern techniques of political campaigning have become more important in national elections over the last decade (e.g. Great Britain, France, Germany, Italy, Sweden, see, e.g. Norris 2000), it seems that they have been transferred to EP campaigns only to a moderate extent and with reluctance (see e.g. Gerstlé et al. 2002: 61ff.; Bicchi et al. 2003: 33ff.). Therefore, it seems that *second-order campaigning* has recently become the third key feature of EP elections distinguishing them from elections on the national level of modern democracies.

To test this assumption this article focuses on the 2004 EP campaign in Germany, one of the founding nations of the European Union and one of the mainsprings of the EU's integration process. After a brief look at the German turnout and parties' results, the hypothesis of a *half-hearted, old-fashioned, and low heated* – i.e. second-order – campaign will be tested by investigating the structures and strategies of the parties' campaigns. Afterwards, the *second-rate character of the campaign* from the point of view of the media and the citizenry will be examined. The results are primarily based on 1) a written questionnaire answered directly after the EP elections by the campaign managers of the parties represented in the German national parliament[2], and 2) on an analysis of several representative opinion polls conducted in the run-up and directly after the EP elections.

2. Turnout and Party Results

Like in most of the "old" EU member states, turnout in Germany fell to a historical low with only 43.0 percent of the German voters participating in the EP elections on June 13th, 2004 (see Weßels 2005). Although turnout has continuously shrunk at federal elections for the national parliament too – as it has in almost all democracies over the last decade (see Dalton 2002: 37) – EP elections seem to fail to attract and mobilize German voters in an unusually accelerated way (see Figure 1).

Figure 1: Turnout at Federal and European Parliamentary Elections in Germany

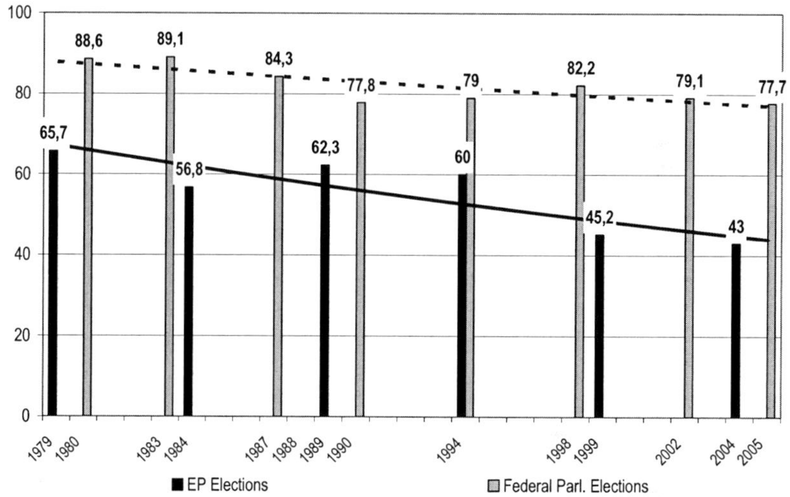

[Bar chart showing turnout percentages. Federal Parl. Elections: 88.6 (1979/80), 89.1 (1983/84), 84.3 (1987/88/89/90), 77.8 (1994), 79 (1998/99), 82.2 (2002), 79.1, 77.7 (2004/05). EP Elections: 65.7, 56.8, 62.3, 60, 45.2, 43.]

Source: Statistisches Bundesamt

Only about half of the people that cast their vote at the last Federal Parliamentary elections showed up at the 2004 EP election. One of the main reasons for such a high level of non-appearance seems to be the relatively low interest in the European dimension of politics, even during EP campaign times. Concerning this just a few days before election day, so to say a the campaign's climax, 57 percent of the German voters claimed to be hardly or not at all interested in European politics – compared to only 41 percent when asked about their general political interest (see Infratest dimap 2004: 70).[3] In addition to that, 36 percent of the eligible voters stated that the EP elections were unimportant as the EU was too complicated (see Infratest dimap 2004: 10).[4] Such answers provide strong empirical proof for the basic assumption of the "second order election" model as regards the lower salience EP elections have for German citizens compared to "first-order" federal parliamentary elections (see Reif/Schmitt 1980).

Furthermore, and in accordance with the assumption, most of the German voters framed the 2004 elections more nationally than EU-related: in the run-up to the elections the majority of the German voters (61 percent) stated that their voting decision would primarily depend on the national dimension of politics, while only 34 percent found the European dimension more important (see Infratest dimap 2004: 7). Thus, election outcome was supposed to predominantly reflect voters' (dis)satisfaction with the *domestic* performance and achievements of the parties represented in the German parliament.

Figure 2:   Party Results at the last Federal and European Parliamentary elections in Germany (percentages)

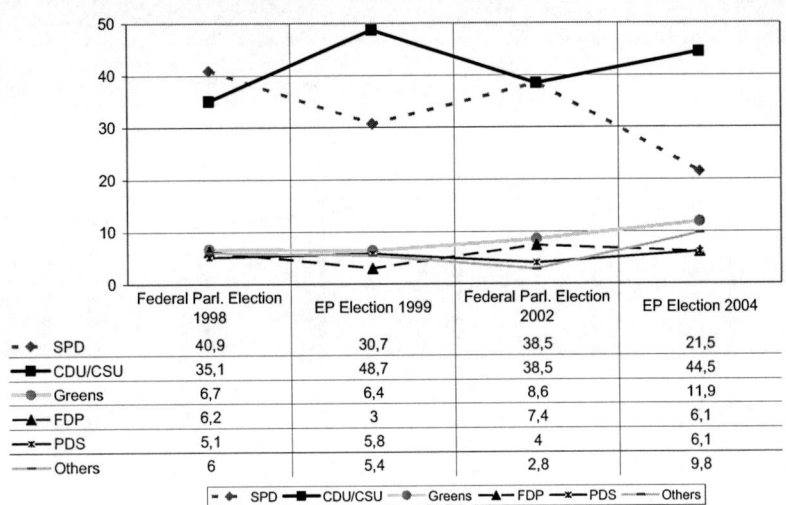

Source: Statistisches Bundesamt

The growing dissatisfaction with the leading governmental party, the Social Democrats (SPD), was expressed by a tremendous loss of 9.2 percent compared to the EP elections 1999 and a record minus of 17.5 percent compared to the previous Federal Parliamentary elections in 2002 (see Figure 2). This kind of overt protest against the performance of the leading governmental party was known from previous EP elections; it had repeatedly happened not only in Germany (see Kornelius/Roth 2005: 97) but in several other EU member states too (see Marsh 2005). Not surprisingly, the 2004 EP elections also turned out – at least in the vast majority of the 25 EU states – as a day of reckoning for the nationally governing parties (see N.a. 2004).

In the case of Germany, it has to be mentioned that although the *SPD* ended with a historical low, the major opposition party, the so-called *"Union" of the Christian Democratic Party (CDU)* and the *Christian Social Party (CSU)*,[5] did not benefit directly: it also lost votes compared to 1999 (minus 4.2 percent) but still got its second best result at EP elections ever (44.5 percent). So, the protest against the leading government party basically resulted in gains for the smaller parties: the co-governing *Green Party* (*Bündnis 90/Die Grünen*) received its best result ever at a nationwide election (see Hirscher 2005), the *Liberal Party* (*FDP*) re-entered the EP after a ten-year absence, and the former communist party *PDS* also jumped easily over the five-percent threshold. They and the other parties not represented in the German Parliament (combined 9.8 percent) obviously profited most from the low turnout and a domestically inspired protest against the leading governing party.

Besides the parties' results, low turnout and a continuous low degree of interest in the European dimension of politics (see above) clearly indicate that the 2004 EP campaign as a whole widely failed in attracting public attention and in mobilizing potential voters in Germany. To test this assumption two "sides" of the 2004 EP campaign will be examined in the following: the political parties' campaigns and the mass media's campaign coverage.

3. Second-Order Campaigning

3.1 Modernization Limited?

Like many other post-industrial democracies Germany has witnessed some significant transformations in political campaigning on the national level especially during the last decade which indicate an accelerating process of "mediatization", professionalization, and modernization: there has been a rise in "symbolic politics", in professional news and event management (including "spin control"), in television-focused, candidate-centered, capital-intensive campaigns which also incorporate target-group-oriented, "post-modern" techniques of "narrow-casting" via direct mailings and e-mailings, canvassing etc. (see Tenscher 2003: 80ff.). In addition to that, politicians have become more professional in dealing with the media, particularly interested in "new" and entertaining platforms, such as television talk shows.

Such changes in the way national electoral campaigns in Germany have recently been carried out stem from deeper transformations on the *structural* level of political organizations that can be linked to a *global phenomenon of political marketing* (see Butler/Collins 1999). In the two most recent Federal elections in Germany, crucial campaign activities such as polling, advertising, media planning etc. have been transferred to specialized political communication agencies and experts (see Holtz-Bacha 1999; Tenscher 2005). Still, it seems unlikely that this trend of *externalization and commercialization* of political communication activities will further expand: due to a party-centred parliamentary system and rather strict regulations on campaign financing, the process of party-unaffiliated professionalisation is self-limited.[6]

While political campaigning has changed considerably at federal elections, prior to 2004 the EP campaigns in Germany had not only been unspectacular but – in marketing terms – quite *traditional*. The parties invested much less money, time, and attention in European elections than in federal elections, they limited themselves to mass activities (especially billboards) and ignored modern techniques like personalization strategies, direct communication, narrow casting, etc. (see e.g. Wilke/Tangemann 2004). In this regard, however, German parties always acted very similar to their European neighbors, which also gave the EP elections low priority compared to their national equivalents (see Gerstlé et al. 2002: 61ff.; Bicchi et al. 2003: 26ff.). With regards to Germany there are several contextual reasons for this second-rate treatment:

1. While national parliamentary elections directly decide over governmental positions, the allocation of power and, therefore, the positioning and development of German political parties within the national realm, at EP elections much less is at stake. Accordingly, most financial and personal resources are invested into national campaigns (see Niedermayer 2005: 48).
2. Not only voters' interest, but especially media attention towards EP campaigns has traditionally been relatively low in Germany (see Brettschneider/Rettich 2005), thereby reducing potentials for elaborated and capital-intensive news management as well as for candidate-oriented presentations.[7]
3. In contrast to federal parliamentary elections, only one – party-related – vote is cast at EP elections. Thus, the potential for candidate-centered campaigns is reduced, especially since most of the European parliamentarians are in any case – compared to the national political elite – rather unknown actors (see Wilke/Tangemann 2004).

Obviously, such an environment reduces *per se* potentials for conducting sophisticated and modern campaigns as a whole. However, they are not excluded from the start – and for *single parties* the chances are theoretically even higher that they can position themselves if they use an unanticipated, attention-driven, modern campaign in a situation where other parties apply more traditional campaign methods.

Therefore, to test how "modern" German parties' 2004 EP campaigns were, their individual *commitment* towards their own campaign has to be explored. Respective indicators must cover the organizational level as well as the strategic level. Concerning this, high degrees of commitment (and, consequently, modernisation) would particularly be reflected in 1) appropriate budgets allowing 2) the involvement of campaign professionals, and 3) target-group-oriented "narrow-casting" via mass media and direct communicative activities. With respect to strategies "modern" campaigns would be characterized by 4) high degrees of personalisation, 5) elaborated and coordinated news and event management activities, and 6) an appropriate mixture of free media and paid media channels (see Norris 2000: 138; Plasser/Plasser 2002: 25-26).

3.2 Parties' Campaign Structures

To start with, all parties radically reduced their *campaign budgets* compared to the 2002 Federal Parliamentary election: they cut back fifty to eighty percent of their 2002 amounts (see Table 1). Thus, most of the parties' expenditures approximated their 1999 EP elections budgets. Only the *Greens* invested (on a very low-key level) much more money in the 2004 campaign compared to 1999 due to the fact that the party was integrated in the first pan-European campaign of the European *Greens*.

Table 1: Campaign Budgets 1999, 2002, and 2004 (in Euro)

	SPD	CDU/CSU	Greens	FDP	PDS
European Election 1999	12.3	13.0	0.25	1.0	3.0
Federal Election 2002	28.0	28.0	2.5	5.1	5.8
European Election 2004	12.5	11.5	1.2	1.0	3.0
Difference in percent FE 2002 – EP 2004	-55%	-59%	-52%	-80%	-48%
Difference in percent EP 1999 – EP 2004	+2%	-13%	+380%	0%	0%

Sources: Gerstlé et al. 2002: 61; Niedermayer 2005: 48; Tenscher 2005a: 114-117; ECP

The small budgets had various consequences for the organization and conduction of the campaigns. First, the number of persons professionally involved in the campaigns was drastically reduced compared to 2002 (see Tenscher 2005) and primarily restricted to party-affiliated activists that routinely worked at the parties headquarters. While the "strategic units" in charge of the national campaigns of the *CDU/CSU*, *FDP*, *Greens*, and *PDS* consisted of ten to twenty persons, the *SPD*'s campaign was coordinated and conducted by the biggest campaign team of more than forty people (see Niedermayer 2005: 48ff.; ECP). Consequently, the *SPD*'s "war room", the so-called "Eurokampa", was, as in 1999 (see Wilke/Tangemann 2004), the most differentiated one – divided into nine task areas. In addition to that, the party engaged four external agencies responsible for event management, advertising, and the party's internet platform. In doing so, the *SPD* showed the highest degree of *externalisation* as the other parties only recruited two agencies at most.

Only a regional party – the CSU – worked together with external pollsters, while its competitors missed that chance for modern political campaigning, i.e. the analysis of voter markets and specific target groups (see Butler/Collins 1999). Furthermore, with one exception, the parties also did not employ external, party-independent experts to consult their leading candidates. Only the *FDP*'s front-runner, the politically rather inexperienced Silvana Koch-Mehrin, was continuously consulted, trained, and coached with respect to her public performance.

3.3 Parties' Campaign Strategies

As a whole, the low budgets and the low degree of externalisation underline the assumption that the parties were not very much committed to the EP elections and were prepared to conduct – in marketing terms – rather traditional campaigns. This assumption is above all supported by the campaign managers' post-evaluations of the 2004 EP campaign (see Table 2). Almost all had the impression that the parties' campaign strategies were hardly innovative and rather uninspired. Insofar, the EP campaign was – as the respondents noted – not another step in the process of "Americanization", but rather a break with regards to the modernization and professionalisation of political campaigning observed for German parliamentary elections at the national level (see Holtz-Bacha 1999; Tenscher 2005).

Table 2: Post-Campaign-Evaluations of the Parties' Campaign Managers
(Scale: 1 = disagree completely > 5 = agree strongly)

	SPD	CDU	CSU	Greens	FDP	PDS
Parties' campaign strategies were innovative.	3	3	3	3	2	1
The EP campaign proved that political campaigns become more "Americanized".	2	1	2	1	3	1
National issues dominated the campaign.	5	4	4	4	4	5

Source: ECP

There is also a far-reaching agreement among the parties' campaign managers that the national dimension of politics extremely dominated the campaign (see Table 2). In fact, especially the two main competitors, *SPD* and *CDU/CSU*, "domesticated" the campaign: as in previous EP elections (see, e.g., Schulz 1999), the leading party in opposition, this time the *CDU/CSU*, trusted in an attack strategy against the national governmental coalition and their achievements (see Niedermayer 2005: 56ff.). They said that EP election day would be the "day of reckoning" against the *SPD/Greens*-coalition in Berlin which allegedly brought Germany, particularly in economic terms, up the European rear. In addition to attacks, the *CDU/CSU* presented itself as *the* competent alternative – both nationally and EU-wise.

Its main opponent, the *SPD*, tried to dodge this confrontation in reference to its unsound socio-economic balance and trusted primarily in its role as a strong European "peace force" that was successful in refusing to participate in the Iraq war. However, while this stance was a decisive issue in the 2002 Federal parliamentary elections (see Tenscher 2005), it was of marginal importance for German mass media and German voters in 2004. The top issues which were said to influence the voter's party decision in the EP elections were, in fact, tax and economic policies, social policies, and labour policies (see Infratest dimap 2004: 58) – in other words, domestic issues pushed by the *CDU/CSU*.

While the senior partner of the electoral alliance of *CDU* and *CSU*, the *CDU*, almost completely ignored European issues, its junior partner, the *CSU*, tried – although rather unsuccessfully – to introduce a highly emotional and populist EU-specific issue: the question of Turkey's accession to the EU. Besides the *CSU*, the Greens and the *FDP* also introduced a unique European perspective – but by different means. As mentioned above, the German *Greens* were integrated in the first European-wide political campaign, allowing them to position themselves as the only "European party of Germany" and pushing "typical" *Greens* issues like the protection of the environment, energy policies, peace policies, etc. These were all, by nature, trans-national topics (see Hirscher 2005), and they were personified by two European-wide well-known politicians: the leading candidate and Co-President of the Green Group in the European Parliament, German-French Daniel Cohn-Bendit, and German Foreign Minister Joschka Fischer.

Even more than the *Green party* it was the *FDP* which transported its message above all via a widely acknowledged personalisation strategy. The *Liberals* promoted a new face: the unspent, young, and eye-catching Silvana Koch-Mehrin, a political newcomer of whom it was expected that she would bring movement into the antiquated male-dominated European Parliament. The *FDP*'s core issues – namely the fight against EU's bureaucracy and the plea for a referendum on EU's constitution – were not only transported by *FDP*'s frontrunner; in fact, Koch-Mehrin became the core issue of the Liberals.

In pushing (and using) persons instead of issues, the *Liberals* and the *Green* party introduced a key element of modern campaigning to German EP campaigns, in which prior to 2004 the personal component had either played a marginal role or had been covered by the national political elite, due to the party-oriented voting system and the widely unknown European parliamentarians (see Wilke/Tangemann 2004; Niedermayer 2005: 40). Their strategies were faring quite well as clearly shown by the rising prominence of Koch-Mehrin and Cohn-Bendit – and their gains in votes – (see Infratest dimap 2004: 86). Quite the opposite happened to *PDS*'s front-runner Sylvia-Yvonne Kaufmann, who remained widely unknown, probably as a result of a half-hearted and inconsistent campaign which highlighted the national dimension of the elections (*PDS* as the unique "social alternative").

3.4 Parties' Campaign Channels

It can be assumed that the mentioned differences in budgets and in strategies would also be reflected in the means by which the parties tried to get public attention. To test this assumption, the parties' campaign managers were asked to evaluate the importance of diverse "free media" and "paid media" channels (see Esaisson 1991).

To start with the importance of the presence of parties and candidates in free media channels, a clear division among the party campaign managers' commitments becomes obvious: while *CDU*, *CSU*, and *FDP* believed in multi-channel-presence, as concepts of modern campaigning propose (see Plasser/Plasser 2002: 24), the *SPD* did not give any of the free media channels high priority (see Table 3). This rather "orthodox" disregard for mass media capacities had been typical for German EP campaigning *so far* (see e.g. Schulz 1999). It also might explain the *SPD*'s relatively low mass media visibility compared to its position as leading governing party (see Brettschneider/Rettich 2005) and – at least to some part – its weak election result.[8] Compared to such extremes, the *Greens* and the *PDS* differentiated the most between specific mass media channels, taking into account their potentials to reach voters.

Table 3: Importance of Parties' and Candidate's Presence in free media channels
(Scale: 1 = completely unimportant > 5 = extremely important)

	SPD	CDU	CSU	Greens	FDP	PDS
Public TV in general	2	5	5	4	5	4
Private TV in general	1	5	5	3	5	2
Political talk shows	2	5	5	3	5	3
TV shows	1	4	3	3	4	1
Radio	2	5	5	2	4	4
Internet	3	3	5	3	4	5
News magazines	1	5	5	2	5	3
Yellow press	1	4	5	2	5	2
Newspapers	2	5	5	4	5	5

Source: ECP

For all parties, with the exception of the *SPD*, newspapers and public television – two rather "traditional" mass media channels – turned out to be the main channels of the 2004 EP campaign. While all parties also gave the internet – i.e. the party's campaign websites – high or highest importance, a medium which was used for the second time at an EP election after 1999 (see Wilke/Tangemann 2004), another "new" platform in Germany did not receive high recognition: with the exception of the *CDU* and the *FDP* the diverse entertaining formats of the "free media" were rather ignored. In fact, the *FDP* gave political and other talk shows, TV shows, and the yellow press highest priority in promoting the candidate's image and presenting the party's positions – a winning strategy which ensured the front-runner much media presence and positive evaluations (see Brettschneider/Rettich 2005).

All parties, however, only poorly used direct campaign forms to get in touch with specific target groups. Compared to the previous Federal Parliamentary election, the amount of direct callings, direct mailings, and canvassing actions mentioned by the campaign managers was marginal (see Tenscher 2005). Although this widespread neglect of narrow *campaigning techniques* might also have been a consequence of the relatively small budgets which did not allow capital- and labour-intensive activities, it obviously underlines the assumption of half-hearted, rather traditional campaign styles ignoring some basic principles of modern political marketing.

On the other side, it seemed that German parties still trusted in some of the "traditional" means of mass advertising. All campaign managers gave billboards high or highest priority (see Table 4) – a paid media channel with comparatively low importance at the last Federal Parliamentary elections, but typically used in German EP campaigns (see Tenscher 2005; Schulz 1999). All parties were airing campaign spots, but only the *SPD* and the *CDU* could afford to buy extra airtime on the private TV channels (see Niedermayer 2005: 52-53). Furthermore, with the exception of the *CDU*'s and *CSU*'s campaign managers, TV spots were not given high priority as effective campaign channels. Such assessments seem to reflect the risk of placing high priority on TV spots, because – especially at "second rate elections" – the viewer may simply ignore them or zap them away.

Table 4: Importance of paid media channels
(Scale: 1 = completely unimportant > 5 = extremely important)

	SPD	CDU	CSU	Greens	FDP	PDS
Spots on public TV	3	5	1	3	3	2
Spots on private TV	3	5	4	-	-	5
Spots on radio	3	3	4	3	3	4
Spots in cinemas	-	4	1	-	4	4
Billboards	4	4	5	4	5	5
Ads in news magazines	-	5	-	-	-	5
Ads in yellow press	-	5	3	-	-	4
Ads in national newspapers	2	4	5	-	-	5
Ads in regional newspapers	4	3	5	-	-	5

Source: ECP

Evidently, the parties trusted in a more or less complex set of paid media activities, depending on their budgets. While the *CDU*'s campaign manager highlighted the importance of almost all "traditional" paid media forms (as he did with regard to free media platforms), the *SPD* once again seemed to underestimate their value, restricting itself to billboards and advertisements in regional newspapers. The *Greens* and the *Liberals* mentioned only three resp. four paid media activities as being important at all. Especially the latter one added just a few selected paid media channels to its free-media-oriented personalisation strategy and believed, above all, in the importance of billboards and cinema spots through which it could reach a specific audience.

In doing so, the *FDP* conducted with regard to its degree of mediatization, media-variation, target-group-orientation, and personalization, the most *modern* campaign in 2004 and – with the smallest budget of all parties represented in the national parliament – the most effective one in promoting its leading candidate (see Infratest dimap 2004: 86). The real winner of the election however was the *Green Party*: with the second lowest budget and integrated in the first real pan-European campaign this party obviously benefited from pushing its two highly prominent European politicians, German Foreign Minister Joschka Fischer and German-French MEP Daniel Cohn-Bendit (see Hirscher 2005).

4. Media Coverage and Public Attention

From the very first EP election, it has been repeatedly shown that a certain degree of visibility of the campaign is required to attract voters' attention and to launch a mobilization process based on augmented levels of interest in European affairs and a broader knowledge base. To put it in simple terms: the more political parties are actively campaigning via direct and mass mediated means of communication and the more the mass media is covering the EP campaign, the more people are attracted and actively involved and the more they are – at least potentially – eager to cast their vote (see Blumler 1983; Blondel et al. 1998: 160ff.; Bicchi et al. 2003: 21ff.; Medien Tenor 2004).[9] Thus, turnout depends on the political parties' commitment to conduct mass-attractive campaigns *as well as* on the mass media to cover campaign activities adequately and in a mass-appealing way.

As seen above, German political parties' efforts to *penetrate* the mass media and to *bypass* them via diverse means of advertising and narrow-casting were rather low heated and half-hearted in 2004 compared to the last federal parliamentary elections; however, at least some parties introduced new techniques of modern campaigning to the EP election arena (namely personalisation and entertainment strategies). The German mass media, however, treated the EP elections – once again – like a *quantité négligeable*:

- As known from previous EP elections and from other EU member states (see Peter 2003; de Vreese/Peter 2005), the amount of EU-related news increased only slightly for the time of the campaign, but remained on a barely noticeable level: only 2 percent of all print and television news in the first half year of 2004 referred directly to the EP elections (see Brettschneider/Rettich 2005). Even on Election Day, TV coverage focused more strongly on the European Soccer Championships than on the results of the "founding elections".[10]
- With regard to the content of coverage, the German mass media almost "ideally" reflected the political parties' efforts in focusing mainly on the national dimension of politics. As in earlier German EP elections more than half of the EP-campaign-related articles referred to domestic issues, only about a third focused on the EU dimension (see Wilke/Reinemann 2005).
- Although the key institution at stake – the European Parliament – was covered considerably more than during non-election times, it was still mentioned less than the EU Commission. Furthermore, due to the far-reaching scandal

of some MEP's in connection with expense-account fiddling, media coverage was predominantly negative in tone until May 2004 (see Medien Tenor 2004).
- Finally, *national* political actors – especially government politicians – dominated the campaign coverage: less than a fifth of the news coverage referred to the running EP's candidates (see Brettschneider/Rettich 2005). And, with the exception of *FDP*'s front-runner Koch-Mehrin, all national and European actors were given negative coverage.

To sum up, the 2004 EP's media coverage continued a trend known from previous EP elections. It was – compared to Federal Parliamentary elections – low in visibility, focused on domestic issues resp. the national dimensions of European issues, and predominantly negative. It seems that the rather unspectacular, half-hearted, and domestically oriented party campaigns were – in a negative sense – "perfectly" portrayed and transported to the public. Nevertheless, 60 percent of the German voters felt that they were sufficiently informed to cast their vote (see EOS Europe Gallup 2004: 26).

Almost every German voter (94 percent) reported that he/she had seen or heard something about the EP campaign at least *once* on television or radio.[11] In fact, as in other EU countries, broadcast media were the primary source of information on the EU campaign, followed by party advertisements and newspaper coverage (see Table 5). Such answers logically also reflect the political parties' "media mix", mostly relying on billboards and – with the exception of the *SPD* – (public) television's and newspapers' campaign coverage (see above). On the other side, due to their neglect of capital- and labour-intensive means of narrow-casted campaigning, the vast majority of voters did not have the chance to directly and interactively get in touch with political parties and candidates as the results of Table 5 indicate. Thus, there is still a high potential – not only, but especially in Germany – which has not been exhausted and which is most promising in mobilizing undecided and passive voters (see Weßels 2005).

Table 5: Exposure to the Electoral Campaign in Germany and the EU (in percentages, Answers "yes")

	Germany	EU
Saw/heard about campaign on TV or radio	94	89
Saw advertisements for parties and candidates	85	82
Read about campaign in newspapers	79	65
Discussion with family/friends/acquaintances	57	56
Received leaflets at post boxes	55	68
Saw non-party advertisements encouraging people to vote	28	36
Talked to political parties and candidates on the street	13	12
Searched for information on the internet	10	7
Took part in public gathering/campaign meetings	4	5
Contact via canvassing	2	6
Contact via direct calls	2	5

Source: EOS Gallup Europe 2004

To sum up, although confronted with an imperfect and nationally biased campaign context, most German voters felt they were sufficiently be informed about the 2004 EP campaign. The majority simply did not expect and was not interested in a "high-density", EU-oriented campaign resp. campaign coverage as the comparatively low degrees of interest in European politics and in the 2004 EU campaign indicated. The low turnout of 43 percent was therefore *not* a sign of distrust towards European institutions, but rather the logical consequence of low-keyed and nationally focused campaigns, accompanied by the same kind of media coverage, which were not able to attract and mobilize voters since they largely framed the EP elections as second-order *national* elections (see Infratest dimap 2004: 70-71).

5. Conclusion

Being one of the founding nations of the European Community, Germany has always been a striving force in pushing forward the European integration process. However, as unsparingly revealed by the last EP elections, although the German political elite has continuously been supporting – at least in the European arena – the "European idea", the strengthening of EU's trans-national institutions (including the European Parliament), and the expansion of the European community, more and more of the German people have seemingly lost their interest in and sympathy for participating in the "European project". Thus, the 2004 EP elections in Germany essentially marked an all-time low with respect to a widespread indifference and apathy towards the European level of politics. However, this was neither a unique German phenomenon – as the low turnouts EU-wide indicate (see N.a. 2004; Weßels 2005) – nor a sign of growing dissatisfaction with *EU institutions* or *EU actors* (see Infratest dimap 2004: 71-72; EOS Europe Gallup 2004: 17ff.).

As the results of the analysis suggest, the historical high level of abstention was most probably a result of a *ménage à trois* of the political parties, the mass media, and the citizenry. Compared to national federal elections, most of the actors involved showed relatively low degrees of commitment, empathy, and interest in the European dimension of politics. The political parties conducted more or less unspectacular, uninspired, and traditional campaigns which – with few exceptions (*FDP*, *Greens*) – domesticated the issues at stake. Some of them (especially the *SPD*) simply seemed to ignore the necessity to conduct "first-order" campaigns, which would have been able to attract media's and voters' attention at a "second-order election". They did not spend sufficient money and/or chose rather "traditional" techniques and channels to get in touch with the citizenry. In particular, the direct forms of mobilizing potential voters – a key element of modern political marketing and heavily used in the 2002 German Federal Parliamentary election campaign – were almost entirely neglected. Consequently, the two parties with the smallest budgets but the most inspiration and sympathy for target-group-oriented, candidate-centered modern campaigning techniques and with the highest degree of "Europeanness" – the *FDP* and the *Greens* – received, in relation to their political status, the most (positive) attention from the mass media and the voters (see Brettschneider/Rettich 2005; Hirscher 2005).

The mass media itself not only covered the EP campaign rather reluctantly but also seemed to reinforce the image of an election being supposedly of minor importance and of greater relevance for the national than the EU arena. As in earlier EP elections, its coverage was low in visibility, concentrated primarily on national actors and topics, and was negative in tone – especially the latter aspect could have diminished voters' interest in the campaign and their willingness to cast their vote, as it did at previous EP elections (see e.g. Butler 1983; Banducci/Semetko 2003). In its low degree of "Europeanness", the campaign's coverage, however, seemed to meet the expectations of the voters, who were also more interested in national politics and who turned the EP elections into a day of reckoning for domestic (mis)achievements.

Obviously, a *vicious circle* has developed among political parties, mass media, and the people in Germany (but also in other EU member states): shrinking interest in and empathy towards the EU on the side of the citizens resp. "the consumers" seem to have induced political parties and the mass media to reduce their efforts in communicating EU-related, "first level" campaigns. In doing so, they have risked alienating voters even more as shown by dwindling turnouts (see e.g. Schulz/Blumler 1994; Blondel et al. 1998; Bicchi et al. 2003).

In order to stop this – from a democratic point of view, dangerous and unsatisfying – vicious circle in the long-run, the main intermediary powers should be called to account, i.e. on the one hand, the mass media as a principal linkage between citizens and the per se distant European level of politics, and on the other hand, the political organisations (political parties, interest groups, national and EU institutions). Not limited to electoral times but continuously, the mass media must augment and re-focus the currently low and domesticated EU coverage (see Semetko et al. 2000; de Vreese 2002), while the political organisations should intensify their mass media-oriented and narrow-casted, interactive, EU-oriented information campaigns. In doing so, citizens' apathy towards the EU and their preoccupation with the national arena of politics could slowly be transformed – an indispensable prerequisite for the on-going process of European integration.

References

Banducci, Susan A./Semetko, Holli A. (2003): Campaign Engagement in a Cross-national Comparative Perspective: The Importance of Context. Paper Presented at a Conference on Mass Communication and Civic Engagement at the Anneberg School for Communication. University of Pennsylvania, August 27th 2003.

Bicchi, Federica/Blondel, Jean/Svensson, Palle (2003): The European Parliament Campaign. Working Paper.

Blondel, Jean/Sinnott, Richard/Svensson, Palle (1998): People and Parliament in the Europenian Union. Participation, Democracy, and Legitimacy. Oxford: Clarendon Press.

Blumler, Jay G. (1983): Communication and Turnout. In: Blumler, Jay G. (Ed.): Communicating to Voters. Television in the First European Parliamentary Elections. London/Beverly Hills/New Delhi, 181-209.

Brettschneider, Frank/Rettich, Markus (2005): Europa – (k)ein Thema für die Medien. In: Tenscher, Jens (Ed.): Wahl-Kampf um Europa. Analysen aus Anlass der Wahlen zum Europäischen Parlament 2004. Wiesbaden: Verlag Sozialwissenschaften, 136-156 [Brettschneider/Rettich: Europe – (Not) a Media-Issue. In: Tenscher: Campaigning for Europe. Analyses on the Occasion of the 2004 European Parliament Elections].

Butler, Patrick/Collins, Neil (1999): A Conceptual Framework for Political Marketing. In: Newman, Bruce I. (Ed.): Handbook of Political Marketing. Thousand Oaks/London/New Delhi: Sage, 55-72.

Dalton, Russell J. (2002): Citizen Politics. Public Opinion and Political Parties in Advanced Industrial Democracies. New York.

de Vreese, Claes H. (2002): Framing Europe. Television News and European Integration. Amsterdam: Aksant Publishers.

de Vreese, Claes H./Lauf, Edmund/Peter, Jochen (2005): The Media and European Parliamentary Elections: Second-Rate Coverage of a Second-Order Event? In: van der Brug, Wouter/van der Eijk, Cees (Eds.): European Elections and Domestic Politics: Lessons from the Past and Scenarios for the Future. University of Notre Dame Press (in print).

Delwit, Pascal (2002): Electoral Participation and the European Poll. A Limited Legitimacy. In: Perrineau, Pascal/Grunberg, Gérard/Ysmal, Colette (Eds.): Europe at the Polls: The European Election of 1999. New York: Palgrave, 207-222.

Eilders, Christiane/Voltmer, Katrin (2004): Zwischen Marginalisierung und Konsens. Europäische Öffentlichkeit in Deutschland. In: Eilders, Christiane/Neidhardt, Friedhelm/Pfetsch, Barbara (Eds.): Die Stimme der Medien. Pressekommentare und politische Öffentlichkeit in der Bundesrepublik. Wiesbaden: Verlag Sozialwissenschaften, 358-385 [Eilers/Voltmer: Between Marginalization and Consensus. European Public in Germany. In: Eilders et al.: The Voice of the Media. Press Commentaries and the Political Public Sphere in Germany].

EOS Gallup Europe (2004): Europe Flash Eurobarometer 162 "Post European Elections 2004 Survey" (21/06/2004-30/06/2004). Report.

Esaisson, Peter (1991): 120 Years of Swedish Election Campaigns. A Story of the Rise and Decline of Political Parties and the Emergence of the Mass Media as Power Brokers. In: Scandinavian Political Studies, Vol. 14, 261-278.

Forschungsgruppe Wahlen (2004): Europawahl. Eine Analyse der Wahl vom 13. Juni 2004. Berichte der Forschungsgruppe Wahlen e.V. No. 115. Mannheim [European Elections. An Analysis of the Election of June 13th 2004].

Fuchs, Dieter (2003): Das Demokratiedefizit der Europäischen Union und die politische Integration Europas. Eine Analyse der Einstellungen der Bürger in Westeuropa. In: Brettschneider, Frank/van Deth, Jan/Roller, Edeltraud (Eds.): Europäische Integration in der öffentlichen Meinung. Opladen: Leske + Budrich, 29-56 [Fuchs: The Democracy Deficit of the European Union and the European Integration Process. An Analysis of Citizens' Attitudes in Western Europe. In: Brettschneider et al.: European Integration and Public Opinion].

Gerstlé, Jacques/Semetko, Holli A./Schönbach, Klaus/Villa, Marina (2002): The Faltering Europeanization of National Campaigns. In: Perrineau, Pascal/ Grunberg, Gérard/Ysmal, Colette (Eds.): Europe at the Polls: The European Election of 1999. New York: Palgrave, 59-77.

Hirscher, Gerhard (2005): Zum Zustand des deutschen Parteiensystems. Eine Bilanz des Jahres 2004. Aktuelle Analysen. No. 36. München: Hanns-Seidel-Stiftung [The State of the German Party-System. Balancing the Year 2004].

Holtz-Bacha, Christina (1999): Bundestagswahlkampf 1998. Modernisierung und Professionalisierung. In: Holtz-Bacha, Christina (Ed.): Wahlkampf in den Medien – Wahlkampf mit den Medien. Ein Reader zum Wahljahr 1998. Opladen/Wiesbaden: Westdeutscher Verlag, 9-44 [Holtz-Bacha: Federal Parliamentary Election Campaign 1998. Modernization and Professionalization. In: Holtz-Bacha: Campaigning within the Media – Campaigning with the Media. A Reader to the Election Year 1998].

Infratest dimap (2004): Wahlreport. Wahl zum Europäischen Parlament. 13. Juni 2004. Berlin [Election Report. Elections to the European Parliament June 13th 2004].

Kevin, Deirdre (2003): Europe in the Media. A Comparison of Reporting, Representation, and Rhetoric in National Media Systems in Europe. Mahwah/ London: Lawrence Erlbaum.

Kornelius, Bernhard/Roth, Dieter (2005): Europawahl in Deutschland: Kein Testlauf für 2006. In: Niedermayer, Oskar/Schmitt, Hermann (Eds.): Europawahl 2004. Wiesbaden: Verlag Sozialwissenschaften, 94-123 [Kornelius/Roth: European Elections in Germany. Not a Test for 2006. In: Niedermayer/Schmitt: European Elections 2004].

Marsh, Michael (2005): European Parliament Elections and the Loss of Governing Parties. In: van der Brug, Wouter/van der Eijk, Cees (Eds.): European Elections and Domestic Politics: Lessons from the Past and Scenarios for the Future. University of Notre Dame Press (in print).

Medien Tenor (2004): First Pan-European Election Analysis by Media Tenor: Media Coverage of Europe and Union's Parliament Before June 13 Insufficient and Largely Negative in Tone. At: http://www.mediatenor.com/EUproj.html.

N.a. (2004): Denkzettelwahl. Die Europäer bestrafen ihre Regierungen. At: http://www.spiegel.de/politik/ausland/0,1518,304043.html, retrieval Jun. 14th 2004 [Teaching a Lesson. Europeans Punish Their Governments].

Niedermayer, Oskar (2005): Europa als Randthema. Der Wahlkampf und die Wahlkampfstrategien der Parteien. In: Niedermayer, O./Schmitt, H. (Eds.): Europawahl 2004. Wiesbaden: Verlag Sozialwissenschaften, 39-75 [Niedermayer: Europe Marginalized. The Election Campaign and the Parties' Election Campaign Strategies. In: Niedermayer/Schmitt: European Elections 2004].

Norris, Pippa (2000): A Virtuous Circle. Political Communication in Post-Industrial Democracies. New York: Cambridge University Press.

Peter, Jochen (2003): Why European TV News Matters. A Cross-Nationally Comparative Analysis of TV News about European Union and its Effect. Doctoral Dissertation. University of Amsterdam.

Plasser, Fritz/Plasser, Gunda (2002): Global Political Campaigning. A Worldwide Analysis of Campaign Professionals and Their Practices. Westport: Praeger.

Reif, Karlheinz/Schmitt, Hermann (1980): Nine Second-Order National Elections. A Conceptual Framework for the Analysis of European Election Results. In: European Journal of Political Research, No. 8, 3-44.

Scheuer, Angelika/van der Brug, Wouter (2005): Locating Support for European Integration. In: van der Brug, Wouter/van der Eijk, Cees (Eds.): European Elections and Domestic Politics: Lessons from the Past and Scenarios for the Future. University of Notre Dame Press (in print).

Schulz, Winfried (1999): The Campaign for the 1999 European Election in Germany. A Contribution to the European Elections Study of the Centro Interuniversitario di Communicazione Politics. Universitá Studi Perugia.

Schulz, Winfried/Blumler, Jay G. (1994): Die Bedeutung der Kampagnen für das Europa-Engagement der Bürger. Eine Mehr-Ebenen-Analyse. In: Niedermayer, Oskar/Schmitt, Hermann (Eds.): Wahlen und europäische Einigung. Opladen, 199-223 [Schulz/Blumler: Campaign-Effects for European Citizens' Engagement. A Multiple-Level-Analysis. In: Niedermayer/Schmitt: Elections and European Unification].

Semetko, Holli/de Vreese, Claes H./Peter, Jochen (2000): Europeanised Politics – Europeanised Media? European Integration and Political Communication. In: West European Politics, Vol. 23, 121-141.

Tenscher, Jens (2003): Professionalisierung der Politikvermittlung? Politikvermittlungsexperten im Spannungsfeld von Politik und Massenmedien. Wiesbaden: Westdeutscher Verlag [Professionalization of Political Communication? Political Communication Experts Torn between Politics and Mass Media].

Tenscher, Jens (2005): Bundestagswahlkampf 2002. Zwischen strategischem Kalkül und der Inszenierung des Zufalls. In: Falter, Jürgen/Gabriel, Oscar/Weßels, Bernhard (Eds.): Wahlen und Wähler. Analysen aus Anlass der Bundestagswahl 2002. Wiesbaden: Verlag Sozialwissenschaften, 102-133 [Tenscher: Campaigning 2002. Between Strategy and the Production of Coincidence. In: Falter et al.: Elections and Voters. Analysis on the Occasion of the German Federal Parliamentary Elections 2002].

Thomassen, Jacques/Schmitt, Hermann (1999). Political Representation and Legitimacy in the European Union. In: Schmitt, Hermann/Thomassen, Jacques (Eds.): Political Representation and Legitimacy in the European Union. Oxford: Oxford University Press, 3-21.

Weßels, Bernhard (2005): Europawahlen, Wählermobilisierung und europäische Integration. In: Tenscher, Jens (Ed.): Wahl-Kampf um Europa. Analysen aus Anlass der Wahlen zum Europäischen Parlament 2004. Wiesbaden: Verlag Sozialwissenschaften, 86-104 [Weßels: European Elections, Mobilizing Voters and the European Integration Process. In: Tenscher: Campaigning for Europe. Analyses on the Occasion of the 2004 European Parliament Elections].

Wilke, Jürgen/Reinemann, Carsten (2005): Zwischen Defiziten und Fortschritten. Die Berichterstattung deutscher Tageszeitungen zu den Europawahlen 1979-2004. In: Tenscher, Jens (Ed.): Wahl-Kampf um Europa. Analysen aus Anlass der Wahlen zum Europäischen Parlament 2004. Wiesbaden: Verlag Sozialwissenschaften, 157-176 [Wilke/Reinemann: Between Deficits and Progresses. German Newspapers' Coverage of the European Parliament Elections 1979-2004. In: Tenscher: Campaigning for Europe. Analyses on the Occasion of the 2004 European Parliament Elections].

Wilke, Jürgen/Tangemann, Jens (2004): Wahlkampfkommunikation zur Europawahl 1999. In: Knieper, Thomas/Müller, Marion G. (Eds.): Visuelle Wahlkampfkommunikation. Cologne, 13-44 [Wilke/Tangemann: Campaign Communication at the European Parliament Election 1999. In: Knieper/Müller: Visual Election Campaign Communications].

Wüst, Andreas M./Roth, Dieter (2005): Parteien, Programme und Wahlverhalten. In: Tenscher, Jens (Ed.): Wahl-Kampf um Europa. Analysen aus Anlass der Wahlen zum Europäischen Parlament 2004. Wiesbaden: Verlag Sozialwissenschaften, 56-85 [Wüst/Roth: Political Parties, Party Programs and Electoral Behaviour. In: Tenscher: Campaigning for Europe. Analyses on the Occasion of the 2004 European Parliament Elections].

1   Although in almost all EU countries participation in EP elections and EU-related referendums has usually been lower than in national equivalents, *support* for the European integration process has not shrunk significantly over the last two decades (see Thomassen/Schmitt 1999; Fuchs 2003). However, there are considerable differences among the average support rates of different countries indicating legitimacy deficits particularly among the Scandinavian countries, Britain, Austria, and the Flemish part of Belgium (see Scheuer/van der Brug 2005).
2   The questionnaire was part of a comparative analysis of campaign strategies (European Campaign Project, ECP) conducted by Jens Tenscher and Tom Moring (University of Helsinki, Finland). I want to kindly thank the campaign managers Achim Post (*SPD*), Laurenz Meyer (*CDU*), Markus Söder (*CSU*), Steffi Lemke (*Greens*), René Hagemann-Miksits (*FDP*), and André Brie (*PDS*) for their participation.
3   At another opinion poll, conducted at the same time, general political interest and interest in European politics were reported to be significantly higher – but this might also be just a result of using different scales (see Forschungsgruppe Wahlen 2004: 28). However, the distances between the general and the European dimension were reflected in this measure also.
4   Asked for the main reasons for abstaining from voting in European elections, however, Germans – similar to the voters in other EU member states – primarily referred to a *general* dissatisfaction with politics and not to the European dimension specifically (EOS Gallup Europe 2004: 17ff.).
5   The *CSU* represents an autonomous party settled in the state of Bavaria, the only state in which the *CDU* has – for historic reasons – not established a regional branch. The two parties usually conduct their own, but tightly coordinated campaigns, and their elected members join the same faction at the German and the European Parliament.
6   In fact, and contrary to the United States, campaign *management* activities are devised and conducted from within the party organization itself. Consequently, campaign "war rooms" are managed either by high-ranking party officials or by temporarily recruited political communication experts with a strong affiliation to the political party or – at least – to the candidate (see Tenscher 2003: 83).
7   There is an apparent reciprocity: the mere expectation that the attention of the media will be low leads to less media-oriented activities on the side of the parties, which consequently leads to almost zero campaign coverage by mass media.
8   However, it has to be mentioned that these answers – given right after the EP election – might also reflect under- and overestimations of the success or failure of the parties' campaign efforts.
9   Yet, it has to be mentioned that there have always been differences between countries with regard to the amount of correlation between the degree of campaigning, the level of campaign exposure, and the willingness to vote. Furthermore, on the micro-level of the individual voter, campaign effects depend highly on the degree of general and EU-oriented political interest and on the voter's general support of the EU (see e.g. Blumler 1983; Schulz/Blumler 1994: 213ff.; Bicchi et al. 2003: 21ff.).
10 Election forecasts and results were only briefly presented between the live transmission of two soccer games, displayed on split screens and by rolling teletexts. At a confidential document, the responsible TV station, *ZDF*, said that the combination of sports and elections was very "successful" since it reached more viewers than at any previous EP-election-day-coverage.
11 Only a third of the voters stated that they had *frequently* seen or heard things concerning the electoral campaign on television, and another 39 percent claimed to have frequently

read something about the campaign in the newspapers; in the last federal parliamentary campaign these numbers were almost double as high (see Wüst/Roth 2005).

European Elections in Luxembourg: A Case of Second-Order Campaigning

*Patrick Dumont & Philippe Poirier**

1. Introduction

The standard theoretical view on European elections is that they are of a second-order type (see Reif/Schmitt 1980; Schmitt 2005), meaning that voters care less for this political level than for national contests and that they tend to make party choices according to domestic government performance rather than European policy issues. According to this common theory, lower turnouts should ensue whilst governmental parties and bigger parties should suffer losses at second-order elections and opposition and smaller parties should do better than at the latest national elections. The theory of second-order elections however also implies a specific type of campaign: If voters consider that there is "less at stake" in European elections, there is supposedly "less at stake" in the first place *in the mind of the leaders of political parties* (Reif 1985), who do not put much effort in campaigning for Europe as an important and specific political arena. We should, therefore, also see systematic differences between campaigns for first-order and second-order elections, such as in the budgetary and personnel resources of party campaigns, the themes developed (EU issues or not), the types of candidates selected on party lists, and whether they eventually sit in Strasburg or not. This chapter analyzes the campaign for the European Parliament election of June 2004 in the Grand Duchy of Luxembourg. After a first section devoted to the analysis of electoral results, evidence for the second-order election hypothesis relating to the electoral campaign is presented in the second section, mainly drawn from interviews with party campaign leaders of the main six parties and opinion surveys gathered for the Elect 2004 project.[1] In the third section it is argued that in Luxembourg the campaign itself is of a second-order type. In a nutshell: Due to the simultaneity of national and EU elections ever since 1979, there was no opportunity for a genuine political, let alone public debate over the EU, as the concurrent national campaign completely overshadowed the European one. In the conclusion, reference to the campaign for the July 2005 referendum on the constitutional Treaty for Europe is made, as the latter represented the first occasion for a separate debate on the EU in Luxembourg.

---

* Patrick Dumont, PhD. *1971. Researcher in political science at the Université du Luxembourg, email: patrick.dumont@uni.lu
Philippe Poirier, PhD. *1971. Researcher in political science at the Université du Luxembourg, email: philippe.poirier@uni.lu

2. The main lessons of the 2004 EP elections in Luxembourg

In Luxembourg, voting is compulsory for all citizens aged eighteen or older.[2] Hence, turnout, even for European elections, is not a crucial issue. In 2004 turnout was 91.3 percent, but 10.184 people voted blank, and 7.320 had their vote invalidated. Therefore, valid votes were given by 83.7 percent of the registered voters (and 91.65 percent of votes cast). These figures can be compared with those of the 1999 elections: In 2004 turnout was the highest in the history of the six direct elections of the European Parliament, as figures for previous ones ranged between a low of 83.3 percent (1999) and a high of 88.9 percent (1979); moreover, for the first time in 2004 more than 200.000 people participated in the elections. Notice also that the electoral system allows for a strong impact of preferential votes: For European elections as well as for national elections, the voter has the same number of votes as there are seats to be filled (six) and may cast them for a single party list (list vote) or may vote for candidates of one or more than one party (the latter possibility is referred to as inter-party "panachage").[3]

Table 1: Results Luxembourg EP Elections 2004

Party	List Votes	Preferential Votes	Total Votes	% of Votes	Diff 1999	Seats	Diff 1999
ADR	60.144	27.522	87.666	8.0 %	-0.9%	-	-
DP	76.086	85.978	162.064	14.9 %	-5.6%	1	-
LSAP	139.740	100.744	240.484	22.1 %	-1.4%	1	-1
Déi Gréng	108.246	55.508	163.754	15.0 %	+4.3%	1	-
CSV	231.144	173.679	404.823	37.1 %	+5.5%	3	+1
Déi Lénk	10.962	7.383	183.45	1.7 %	*	-	-
KPL	8.706	4.094	12.800	1.2 %	*	-	-

* In 1999, Déi Lénk and the KPL presented joint lists; altogether they gained 0.1 percent in the 2004 elections.

The 2004 European elections were a landslide victory for the *Chrëschtlech-Sozial Vollekspartei* (*CSV*; Christian Democrats), the incumbent Prime Minister's party (see Table 1). With 37.1 percent, a result it had never reached in any former European election – an increase of 5.5 percent compared with 1999 results – it managed to get half of the six Luxembourg MEP seats (one more than in 1999). The 41.535 votes cast for Prime Minister Juncker constitute the highest personal result ever recorded in Luxembourg, another indicator of this indisputable victory.[4] The *Demokratesch Partei* (*DP*; Liberals), which was the *CSV*'s governmental partner for the 1999-2004 term, on the other hand, lost votes heavily but managed to keep its seat.

For the first time the *DP* came in only fourth in these European elections, as *Déi Gréng* (*The Greens*), who always fared better in European elections than in national elections,[5] managed to reach 15 percent of the votes and thus was assured a seat in Strasburg for the third time in a row. The other two main parties in opposition at the national level were the *Lëtzebuerger Sozialistesch Ar-*

bechterpartei (*LSAP*; *Socialists*) and the *Aktiounskomitee fir Demokratie a Rentegerechtegkeet* (*ADR*; *Sovereignists*). Both lost votes in these European elections and were also disappointed in terms of seats: Although it retained 22.1 percent of the votes, the Socialists lost their second *MEP*, and the *ADR*, who always fared worse in European elections than in national elections,[6] did not manage to get one of their candidates elected.[7] The two extreme-left parties *Déi Lénk* (*The Left*) and *Kommunistesch Partei vu Lëtzebuerg* (*KPL*; *Communists*) together accounted for less than 3 percent.[8] The two clear winners in votes were thus the *Christian Democrats* (in the incumbent national government) and the *Greens* (in opposition at the national level); due to the small amount of seats to be distributed there was only one winner in terms of seats, as the *Christian Democrats* managed to get one *MEP* seat more to the disadvantage of the *Socialists*.

Figure 1: 1979-2004 EP Elections Results in Luxembourg

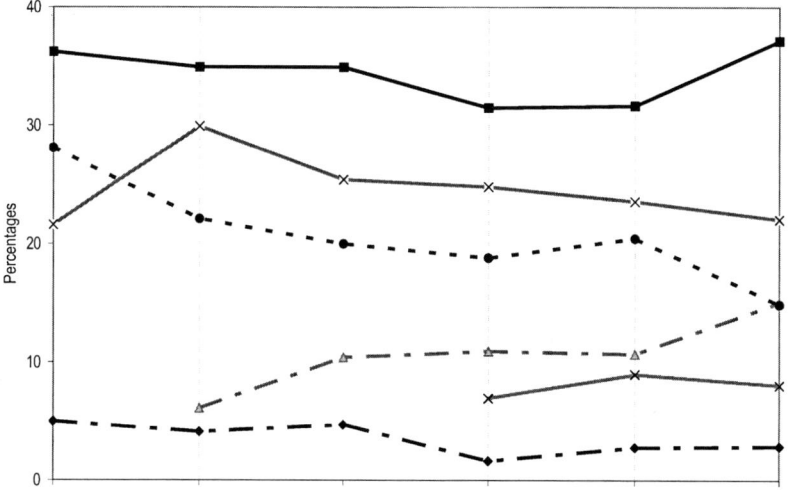

Hence, the main hypotheses of the second-order election approach regarding turnout and electoral results do not seem to be validated in Luxembourg in 2004. Compulsory voting explains high turnout, but the overwhelming success of the largest party in government and the losses of both the main party in the opposition and the smaller parties that are the least EU-enthusiastic run contrary to expectations. In the next section an analysis of the EP elections campaign is provided that may give another picture of the second-order election view.

3. The 2004 EP elections campaign

Mainly due to its size and its dependency on foreign markets, Luxembourg has traditionally favoured participation and loyalty to larger political and economic settings. This position has also traditionally given it a specific role in EU institutional integration. As it is regarded as non-threatening by larger and more powerful countries, through its repeated presidencies of the EU Council of Ministers, important reports written by its political heavyweights, or the presidency of the Commission (already twice given to a Luxembourger) Luxembourg often helped to reconcile diverging interests in the European Union. Given the positive aspects of EU membership in terms of political weight on the international scene (for instance, through the rotating presidency of the Council of the EU, or the seat in the EU Commission) and economic development (for instance, through the presence of EU institutions in the capital city), Luxembourg is generally seen as a *pro-European* country, both at the level of political elites and in terms of popular support for European integration. Indeed, there is no real cleavage and certainly no polarisation at the party political level on European issues (see Ray 1999).[9] For instance, in the context of the July 2005 referendum on the Constitutional Treaty for the European Union only extreme-left movements (that no longer have national MPs) and the *ADR* campaigned against the adoption of the Treaty. The *ADR*, which is the most sovereignist party, had even supported the draft Treaty in the 2004 EP election campaign (although it would have actually favoured a strengthening of the role of national parliaments) but opportunistically changed its mind in the weeks preceding the 2005 referendum campaign. Together these forces gained about 11 percent of the votes but never had seats in the EP (they represent 8.3 percent of the seats in the Chamber of Deputies).

Public opinion surveys also show that the resident population of Luxembourg ranks first in Europe when it comes to satisfaction with democracy in the EU and is well above the EU average in terms of confidence in EU institutions or evaluation of the benefit from membership (amongst others, see Eurobarometer 2004).[10] However, Luxembourg residents also identify the EU with an increase of organized crime and drug traffic, and fears concerning loss of identity and practice of the national language rank higher than for the EU 15 average. In general, Luxembourgers were amongst the least enthusiastic with regard to the latest enlargement.

In spring 2004, 28 percent of Luxembourg's population felt that the national press gave a too positive image of the EU, whereas the EU 15 average was 23 percent. Although nowadays the most-read newspapers are more critical to the traditional parties they used to have links with, the written press is still politicized. For instance, *Le Journal* is the official newspaper of the *DP*; the two largest newspapers are the *Wort*, with connections to the *CSV*, and the *Tageblatt*, which is the official newspaper of the *Socialist* trade union (*OGBL*) and also the newspaper that the *LSAP* still recommends to its members in the official statutes of the party.[11] Even though the latter two newspapers are becoming increasingly critical towards these parties, the wide pro-EU consensus amongst parties may account for the slight pro-EU bias perceived by the residents. Positions taken by a number of pressure groups (for instance, the powerful banking sector association) during the debate over the project of the EU constitution also reveal that Luxembourg's society is moving from a sincere Europhile credo to much more nuanced and sometimes Eurosceptic sentiments (see Poirier 2005).

Despite these growing sentiments in the population and the civil society, there was no discernible overarching theme or conflict dimension politicized by parties during the 2004 EP electoral campaign. In interviews of the people in charge of the EU campaign, three parties (the *CSV*, *DP*, and the *ADR*) mentioned the enlargement of the EU as one of the main issues of their European election campaign, and the sovereignist party tried to capitalize on the fears expressed by the population by linking enlargement with immigration and insecurity issues. According to the election results, it did not succeed in this task. The aim of protecting national interests in EU institutions (keeping one commissioner and six MEPs) and in EU policies (protection of the Luxembourg social model; position on the question of fiscal harmonization) was pointed out by the *DP* and the *LSAP*, but these issues most certainly benefited the party of the Prime Minister at the polls. In 2003 the latter indeed had managed to strike a good deal for Luxembourg with its EU partners, Switzerland, and the Channel Islands concerning the problematic question of the preservation of banking secrecy laws in Luxembourg.

Smaller parties put forward either more global or more national issues, such as economic growth (for both the *ADR* and the *Greens*), education (*Déi Lénk* and the *Greens*) or unemployment (*Déi Lénk*) and the protection of environment (the *Greens*). Interviewed in May 2004, people in charge of the campaign for the two largest parties (respectively the *CSV* and the *LSAP*) even declared that there was no EU campaign at all or lamented that it had not yet started. Others said that it had only started one month before the elections.

There was only one TV debate, with one national leader for each party, dedicated to the European elections on each of the two main Luxembourg channels (*RTL Tele Lëtzebuerg* and *Tango TV*, a private channel recently installed in Luxembourg). Notice that *RTL Tele Lëtzebuerg* belongs to the large *RTL* Group (whose seat is in Luxembourg) and is a private operator that has "public service" obligations in Luxembourg, such as airing a TV journal and a few other programmes (sports, culture, information for the foreign communities present in the Grand Duchy) in Luxembourgish or about Luxembourg's social life.[12] Further, there is a governmental mandate ordering *RTL* to set up debates ("*tables rondes*") during electoral campaigns: In 2004 there was only one such debate devoted to the EU.[13] Each party was also allowed to broadcast one State-paid TV spot for the EU elections. Overall, there was not much EU campaigning on the screens, as only the three largest parties could afford to buy other media space. The post-electoral survey conducted for the Elect 2004 project corroborates this overall impression of lack of campaign: 65 percent of the respondents said they were hardly or not at all interested by the EU campaign, and more than 60 percent declared that the campaign was more about strategy than about European content.[14]

After the elections, most parties declared that the predominant topic, if any, of the European campaign was Prime Minister Juncker's personal fate. The potential appointment of Jean-Claude Juncker as President of the European Commission was indeed high on the European campaign agenda. Luxembourg's Prime Minister, backed by most European centre-right governments, was asked to be the *European People's Party* candidate for the presidency of the Commission. He declined this offer in April, but the main opposition party (*LSAP*) tried to orientate the political debate on the alleged double role of Jean-Claude Juncker, arguing that the latter was still campaigning for this prestigious EU position behind the scenes and that if he had the opportunity of taking it he would renege on his promise to the electorate to remain Prime Minister. The result was detrimental to the *LSAP*, at least for the European elections. On the other hand, the *CSV* reached a score (37.1 percent) it never had received since the first direct elections of the European parliament, and voters supported it even more in the EU elections than in national elections (36.1 percent). The role of the Prime Minister and his party in the agreement reached on banking secrecy, thus protecting national interests, certainly accounted for this *CSV* victory in a country concerned with a slowing down of its economy and a rise in unemployment. The party indeed concentrated its campaign on its leader, amongst other things with meetings all over the country under the banner "Juncker on Tour".

What is interesting is that in the post-electoral survey conducted for the Elect 2004 project the *CSV* was seen by the population as the most pro-European one, whereas the average self-rating of *CSV* voters for the EP elections on EU integration was closer to that of the most sovereignist party, the *ADR* (which lost at the polls). Together with the above-mentioned survey data showing that the European campaign led by parties was not given much attention by voters, this inconsistency between preferences over EU integration and voting behaviour further supports the hypothesis that the European election campaign in Luxembourg was of a second-order type. In any case, what was apparently at stake for voters in 2004 was the confirmation of the EU mandate for the largest party and its leader as representatives of Luxembourg on the European scene. The *CSV*, which is the "party of the State" (*staatstragend*) due to its quasi permanence in power at the national level since Second World War, evidently has reasons to protect the few national interests of the Grand Duchy despite its pro-EU credo. With its experience in EU affairs, the party was able to reach advantageous agreements in the field of fiscal harmonization some months before the elections. Jean-Claude Juncker, its leader since the mid-1990s, who is both the Prime Minister and Minister of Finance with the greatest experience in the EU Council, personifies this stability and pursues the tradition of smaller countries' skilful negotiators (his *CSV* predecessors were Jacques Santer, who resigned from his Prime ministership after ten years in this position to become President of the Commission, and Pierre Werner, who was Prime Minister for twenty years). Voting for the *CSV* and Juncker thus represented a "safe vote" in the EP elections.[15]

4. Explaining second-order campaigning in Luxembourg

Evidence regarding the electoral campaign presented in the previous section is consistent with the view of European elections as second-order ones in Luxembourg. A key institutional feature arguably renders the campaigns themselves "second-order": Ever since 1979, the EP election date coincides with the election date of national elections, as national political elites preferred to couple these elections for pragmatic reasons (avoiding the extra costs of organizing separate elections). As citizens and parties fighting for executive power consider elections in the national political arena as the most important ones, electoral campaign issues have always been mixed, to the clear advantage of national political issues. At the party organizational level of the campaign, there is usually no specific person assigned with the mission of coordinating the European campaign; for all parties except the *Greens*, the person in charge of the EU campaign was actually in charge of both the national and the EU campaigns.[16] In terms of resources, parties declared that only about 10 percent to 15 percent of their general campaign budget (that is partially financed by the State – due to the small number of MEPs to be allocated, the lump sum parties get for the European elections is proportional to the percentage of votes they receive and not the number of seats they get, see Table 2) had been devoted to the European election.[17]

Table 2: Public financing of European electoral campaigns

Result in % of votes at preceding election	Amount awarded in Euros
5-10%	12.500
10-15%	25.000
15-20%	37.500
20-25%	50.000
Above 25%	74.500
Additional amount per MEP elected	12.500

In most other member states, even though EU elections can be seen as much less important than national elections, there is at least a "physical" distinction between national and EU campaigns, as they are not held at the same time. In Luxembourg, not only national issues invade the European campaign like in many other countries, but the latter campaign is not given the party and media attention as in the concurrent national one. At the media and written press level, the time and place devoted to politics is limited, and the EU campaign is the main victim of this zero-sum game (the space devoted to the EU campaign would arguably be more important if elections were not simultaneous). Overall, there is almost no European electoral campaign per se, and other specific electoral system features directly or indirectly reinforce this tendency and the characterization of EU elections in Luxembourg as second-order:

- First, although the MP and MEP mandates are incompatible, it is allowed to candidate for both the national and the European elections (under the condition that the regulations pertaining to the elections of MPs, such as nationality, are fulfilled); candidates who are elected at both levels must therefore choose between the national or the European mandate. As there are only six MEP seats, and there is a possibility to run out of candidates willing to go to Strasbourg, it was decided from 1979 on to have twelve candidates on the EP election lists. Candidates who are not directly elected may therefore replace elected MEPs who choose to stay on the national political scene; in 2004, 70 of the 84 candidates (58 out of the 60 candidates for the five largest parties) running for a seat in the European parliament were also candidates for the *Chambre des députés*.
- Second, whereas for national elections the country is divided into four constituencies, for the European elections there is a single, national constituency. Hence, for "heavyweights" of the large parties, who are also candidates for the position of Prime Minister, EU elections are a good popularity test as it allows them to campaign throughout the country and compare their scores, whereas for national elections they may compete in different constituencies. There is thus a clear personal incentive for these leaders to candidate in both the national and the EP elections; if they manage to become part of the parliamentary majority at the national level, they will resign from their MEP seat and become Prime-Minister for the senior party of the coalition and Vice-Prime Minister for the junior party of the coalition.[18]
- Third, given the highly personalized character of the electoral system, parties tend to put all their well-known figures (either because they were incumbent ministers or other visible leading figures of the party, such as incumbent chairmen of parliamentary party groups, mayors of large cities, etc.) on their European list in order to attract inter-party panachage votes with these names. With this type of vote, a traditional voter of the *DP*, for instance, who may want to support the leader of the *CSV*, has the possibility to both give preferential votes to candidates of his favourite party and also cast a vote for the head of the *CSV* list. The incentives for putting heavyweights on European lists are thus reinforced by this original electoral system feature.

On the other hand, although almost all parties included foreign candidates on their list for the 1994 EP elections, which were the first since the adoption of the Maastricht Treaty allowing for the candidature of EU citizens in any member State, the main parties gradually realized that non-Luxembourg candidates have not yet been able to attract panachage votes in the single national constituency and as a result refrained from selecting such candidates from one election to another. In 2004 only three (the *Greens*, the *Left*, and the *KPL*) of the seven parties that fought in the EP elections presented EU residents on their lists. Altogether the latter accounted for only 12 percent of EP candidates (and there was only one EU candidate amongst the 60 candidates of the five main parties).

The electoral system thus motivates parties to place heavyweights on their lists in order to attract more votes and to avoid selecting EU residents because of their lack of panachage-potential. This has a number of consequences regarding the representation of Luxembourg in the European parliament and the nature of European elections in the Grand Duchy. First, as most of the elected MEPs resign in order to become members of the national government team,[19] MEP positions are filled by candidates that were not directly elected. Governing parties tend to send older former ministers to Strasbourg in order to inject fresh blood in the new government and at the same time provide these former ministers with an honourable office at the end of their political career.[20] The Luxembourg delegation to the European parliament in 2004 is quite typical in terms of these features (see Table 3). Second, as by far most candidates for the EP are active in national politics and also compete in the national elections, voters may either reward or punish parties and candidates for their national political performance. Since 1979, electoral results at the national and European level were indeed very rarely contradictory: In the 23 cases of coupled elections for the five current main parties in Luxembourg, only four times were their results contradictory (winning votes at one election and losing at the other with at least one percent difference). Moreover, the analysis of the electoral campaign reveals that European issues have been almost absent. The lack of EU residents on EP lists further reduces the electoral campaign to debates amongst Luxembourg candidates on national issues.

Table 3: Luxembourg's members of European Parliament 2004

Name	Party	Gender	Age	Position held before 2004 elections
Spautz, Jean	CSV	M	75	Speaker of the Parliament
Hennicot-Schoepges, Erna	CSV	F	63	Minister of Culture, Higher Education and Research, Minister of Public Works
Lulling, Astrid	CSV	F	75	Member of European Parliament
Goebbels, Robert	LSAP	M	59	Member of European Parliament
Polfer, Lydie	DP	F	52	Vice-Prime Minister and Foreign Affairs Minister
Turmes, Claude	Déi Gréng	M	44	Member of European Parliament

To draw on that last aspect, another feature of the electoral system is detrimental to the selection of non-Luxembourg candidates and to the opening of the campaign to more EU issues: Contrary to nationals, who are automatically enrolled on the electoral register, EU citizens who have been domiciled for at least five years in Luxembourg have the right to vote for the European Parliament if they have registered on time (for the 2004 elections, the deadline was March 31st,

2003, that is fourteen months before the elections). Considering the prerequisites to obtain the right to vote, the inconvenient process of registration, the obligation to vote once one is registered, and of course the possibility of voting in their own country, it is not surprising that only 11.615 EU citizens, that is 8.8 percent of all the adult EU citizens living in Luxembourg, registered for the European elections. From another perspective: Although EU citizens represent roughly 36 percent of the adult population living in Luxembourg, the proportion of non-Luxembourgers voting for the 2004 EU elections was a mere 5 percent. Notice however that the number of EU citizens registered for the 2004 elections was 20 percent higher than for the 1999 EU elections and that the figures concerning the 2006 local elections show a further increase in the number of registrations. The participation of EU residents in Luxembourg's political life is likely to become a key element in parties' future electoral strategies.

5. Conclusion

In this chapter, we first evaluated whether the hypothesized consequences of second-order elections materialized in the 2004 EP election results in Luxembourg. Unlike in many other member States, in 2004 turnout was very high, and the party of the Prime Minister did very well at the polls. According to the persons in charge of parties' campaign and opinion polls, the role of the campaign was however negligible with regard to these results. Indeed, we showed that institutional regulations and their consequences for the behaviour of political parties largely account for both these results and for the virtual absence of any EP campaign. The decision to hold EP elections simultaneously with national elections, a single national constituency for EP elections, and the possibility of multiple candidatures have had disastrous consequences for the probability of having a proper campaign on European issues, as all national heavyweights were present on both lists. The necessity of selecting candidates with high personal vote potential has further reduced the incentives for parties to include EU residents on their lists or make lesser known EU specialists (such as incumbent MEPs) more visible on their lists and in the campaign. This was never as clear as in 2004, and the consequences this behaviour had for the type of representation sent to Strasbourg were again far-reaching.

The new government specified in its July 2004 coalition agreement that it would amend the electoral system by prohibiting multiple candidatures. It is not clear whether this reform will have the desired impact on the second-order character of both the EP campaign and the EP elections in Luxembourg. Voters will still be influenced by the national political debate held simultaneously, and the very small number of MEPs to be elected will still lead many of them to cast a safe, tactical vote for the party that is likely to represent them best on the overall EU scene. Hence, parties may not change much of their strategic views in terms of the allocation of resources for and the organization of the campaigns, thereby leaving the EP one as it is now, a second-order type of campaign. This issue is more than ever on Luxembourg's political agenda, as the first occasion of holding a political and public debate specifically devoted to the European Union came in 2005 with the campaign concerning the referendum on the adoption of the Constitutional Treaty for Europe. Although the vast majority of political parties and the media and press system campaigned in favour of the adoption of the Treaty, and the latter was not very high on the agenda in the beginning of 2005 when Luxembourg took over the presidency of the EU Council of ministers, opinion polls showed that after the French and Dutch public rejections of the Treaty, the "No-camp" in Luxembourg could be as high as 45 percent. The Treaty was eventually adopted by a majority of 56.5 percent, but the implication of Prime Minister Juncker (who threatened to resign as Luxembourg's Prime Minister if the No-camp won) certainly played an important role.[21] The bottom line is that an important discrepancy in reference to the Treaty and other EU-related issues between the population and major institutions (political parties, press, trade unions, etc.) was revealed for the first time through this public debate on Europe and the future of the Union. This calls for a profound reflection on the future of such debates in the Grand Duchy.

References

Dumont, Patrick/De Winter, Lieven (2003): Luxembourg. Stable Coalitions in a Pivotal Party System. In: Müller, Wolfgang C./Strøm, Kaare (Eds.): Government Coalitions in Western Europe. Oxford: Oxford University Press, 399-432.

Poirier, Philippe (2005): Les élections européennes au Luxembourg. Une société entre europhilisme et euroscepticisme. In: Delwit, Pascal/Poirier, Philippe (Eds.): Parlement puissant, électeurs absents? Les élections européennes de juin 2004. Bruxelles: Editions de l'Université libre de Bruxelles, 131-156 [Poirier: European Elections in Luxembourg. A Society between Europhilia and Euroskepticism. In: Delwit/Poirier: Powerful Parliament, Absent Voters? The June 2004 European Elections].

Ray, Leonard (1999): Measuring Party Positions on European Integration: Results from an Expert Survey. In: European Journal of Political Research, No. 36, 283-306.

Reif, Karlheinz (1985): Ten European Elections: Campaigns and Results of the 1979/81 First Direct Elections to the European Parliament. Aldershot: Gower.

Reif, Karlheinz/Schmitt, Hermann (1980): Nine Second-Order National Elections. A Conceptual Framework for the Analysis of European Election Results. In: European Journal of Political Research, No. 8, 3-44.

Schmitt, Hermann (2005): The European Parliament Election of June 2004: Still Second-Order? In: West European Politics, No. 28, 650-679.

van der Eijk, Cees /Schmitt, Hermann (1996): Luxembourg. In: van der Eijk, C./ Franklin, M.N. (Eds.): Choosing Europe? The European Electorate and National Politics in the face of Union. Ann Arbor: University of Michigan, 201-208.

---

[1] This project was conducted by the University of Luxembourg and financed by the Chamber of Deputies.
[2] Since 2004, the age limit for compulsory voting has been raised to 75 (before 2004, people over 70 were not obliged to vote).
[3] In the national elections, voters who opt for preferential voting, whether intra-party or inter-party, may cast a maximum of two votes for each candidate (though the maximum number of preference votes equals the total number of constituency seats). For the European elections, only one vote per candidate is allowed.
[4] To these 41.535 preferential votes no less than 38.524 list votes must be added. Altogether then, almost 42 percent of the valid votes for the European elections comprised either a vote for the *CSV* or its leader.
[5] A result consistent with the second-order elections hypothesis, as the *Green Party* was until now a rather small party with no governmental experience. As trying to solve environmental problems is more realistic at the EU level than at the level of the country (especially a very small country), it does not come as a surprise that the Greens are consistently more successful in EU elections.
[6] Probably due to the long-standing pro-EU commitments of their leaders and the advantages of membership for such a small country as Luxembourg, voters seem to be unwilling to send EU-skeptic MEPs to Strasburg.
[7] On the national political scene, the *ADR* is a rightist party originally fighting for the improvement of benefits for private sector pensioners so that they correspond to those of public sector pensioners.
[8] The latter, which was represented in the national Chamber of Deputies from 1945 to 1994, backed the former in the 1999 elections. In 2004 the *KPL* fought elections on its own, as its members felt that the national leaders of the *Left* betrayed the communist and revolutionary heritage.
[9] According to Ray's survey, the range of positions with regard to EU integration has decreased from the 1980s to 1996. The conversion of the *Greens* to a more pro-EU position has made the four largest parties largely, even though with internal nuances, favourable to further EU integration.
[10] Notice however that the Eurobarometer samples for the Luxembourg population include more than 20 percent of non-Luxembourgers (although the proportion of foreigners residing in the Grand Duchy is even higher), whilst in the 2004 EU elections only about 5 percent of the voters were not nationals (see below), and the population allowed to vote in the 2005 referendum was restricted to Luxembourg nationals.
[11] Most of the articles in these three main newspapers are written in German, although some are written in French; in 2001 two newspapers fully written in French appeared (*La Voix*, which is owned by the same editing group as the *Wort* and *Le Quotidien* and has structural ties with the *Tageblatt*, and the French newspaper *Le Républicain Lorrain*).
[12] The notion of "public service" is supposed to be defined under the current government, as it was up until now laid down in vague and media-specific conventions. For instance, cur-

rently *RTL Radio Lëtzebuerg* must also perform "public service" missions, such as broadcasting weekly political tribunes. Hence, every week a party is given a spot lasting a few minutes (paid by the State) so that they can communicate their message to the audience. Both *RTL* and *Radio 100.7* ("*Honnert, 7*" also called "socio-cultural radio") are part of the government's mandated official campaign and thus broadcast radio "tables rondes" (with different guests and slightly different topics than on TV).

[13] In 2003, the *Conseil National des Programmes* (a 25-member organ created in 1991 to advise the government on the regulation of TV and radio programmes' contents through the surveillance of the latter) asked the Communication Department of the University of Trier (Germany) to analyze Luxembourg's media system. In 2004 a project of code of conduct was drafted, and a content analysis of the main TV and radio programmes was conducted during the electoral campaign in order to check whether parties and candidates were given a fair treatment in their journals and other programmes. From March 26th to June 12th it appeared that although some degree of proportionality was respected with regard to the electoral strength of the different parties, clear deviations existed from one media to another. For instance, the small party *Déi Lénk* was given much more broadcasting time on *RTL TV* and especially on the socio-cultural radio than what would have been expected from their electoral position. On *RTL Radio* on the other hand, the three main, traditional parties (*CSV*, *LSAP*, and *DP*) were given about 85 percent of broadcasting time, and other parties were consequently underrepresented. Further, this analysis shows that the *DP*, which was the junior party in government (and thus could have been favoured in media coverage through the actions of their ministerial personnel) and second party in parliament, received less coverage than expected in the examined media (see http://www.gouvernement.lu/salle_presse/communiques/2004/12/23CNP/Abschlussbericht.pdf?SID=424c97a7 9fa7811322fe545eb9933312). Unfortunately the coding scheme adopted did not allow for an evaluation of the presence of European issues in the electoral campaign.

[14] This was a telephone survey conducted in June-July 2004 with a random sample (with quotas for region, age, sex, and occupation) of Luxembourg nationals. There were 1.335 respondents in this post-electoral survey.

[15] Besides the personalization of the campaign around Juncker, another choice made by the *CSV* was to capitalize on this s*taatstragend* character for its campaign slogan (the same for both the national and European ones): *De Séchere Wee* (the "safe way").

[16] In 2004, the *Green Party* was also the only party which officially received financial and technical support from its European party federation. Its spots, conceptualized by a German advertising agency, were similar to those of the Austrian and German *Green Parties*.

[17] In 2004 the *CSV* received a total of 562.000 Euros from the State (this is the overall amount of money received for both the EP campaign and the national campaign for which parties receive public financing according to another scheme), whereas their declared campaign expenses were 1.342.000 (more than 40 percent thus came from public subsidies), and the *Greens* received 219.500 Euros for declared expenses of 660.000 Euros (roughly one third was thus paid by the State). Hence, according to our interviewees, the amounts devoted to EU elections were around 150.000 to 200.000 Euros for the *CSV* and 70.000 to 100.000 Euros for the *Greens*.

[18] Since World War II, no party ever managed to gain a majority in parliament on its own. Hence, since 1945 Luxembourg has always been governed by coalition governments. For a thorough study of government formation, maintenance, and termination in the post-war era (see Dumont/De Winter 2003).

[19] In 2004, four of the six elected MEPs, that is all of the MEPs of the parties of the new governmental coalition, resigned at the first meeting of the European parliament for this reason.

[20] In parties that are not part of the new government, either the elected heavyweight keeps the seat and thus moves away from national politics or European specialists fill the position. In 2004, Lydie Polfer who was Vice-Prime Minister from 1999 to 2004 decided to keep her EP seat.

[21] A Eurobarometer post-electoral survey in August 2005 revealed that almost 80 percent of the *CSV* electorate voted Yes in the referendum, whereas pro-EU parties like the governmental partner *LSAP* or the *Greens* displayed equally split electorates. For other analyses of socio-demographic characteristics of the Yes and No camps and for an evaluation of the campaign by opinion polls respondents (see http://europa.eu.int/comm/public_opinion/flash/fl_173_postref_lux_fr.pdf).

A Yellow Card for the Government, Offside for European Issues? The European Elections of 2004 in Portugal

*Carlos Jalali**

1. Introduction

The 2004 European elections provide perhaps the most recent example of the continued prevalence of domestic considerations in European election campaigning in Portugal. Despite the emergence of a number of significant European issues onto the Portuguese agenda during the months preceding the June 2004 elections (such as the economic impact of enlargement or the proposed European constitution), the election was to ultimately centre on the domestic record of the ruling centre-right coalition. This is borne out both by the parties' campaign and by available individual level data on voter interest in the campaign. As such, the European election campaign of 2004 in Portugal provides stark confirmation of the second-order election theory not only on voter choices, but also on parties' campaign strategies (see Marsh 1998: 607; Ferrara/Weishaupt 2004: 289). The Portuguese experience thus highlights how campaign strategies at the very least reflect – and potentially even accentuate – the second-order election dynamic in voter choice. While the dramatic death of the *Socialist* candidate on the campaign trail was to increase media attention on the elections, once again this was directed very much at national level (intra) party dynamics.

This chapter is structured as follows. After briefly outlining the theoretical background for the second-order election model and existing evidence in Portugal, a description of the Portuguese party system and electoral system will be provided. As will be shown, there are strong (and increasing) similarities in the national legislative and European levels in terms of voting behaviour and its institutional determinants. The European election campaign of 2004 will then be analysed. As will be demonstrated, the second-order effect was strongly in evidence in the parties' campaign strategies, which overtly sought to make this election a plebiscite on the ruling coalition's domestic record. As the *Socialist* campaign slogan put it, the election was an opportunity to "show the government a yellow card". This campaign strategy – followed by the other relevant parties also – was to further remove European issues from the election trail, certainly not contradicting and seemingly reinforcing second-order election consid-

---

* Carlos Jalali, PhD. *1974. Assistant Professor at the Autonomous Section of Social, Political and Juridical Sciences and Centre for Studies in Governance and Public Policy, University of Aveiro, and Institute for Social Science, University of Lisbon, email: cjalali@csjp.ua.pt

erations in voting behaviour. This is visible in the actual election results, which are then presented. By all accounts, the defeat of the ruling coalition – the lowest combined vote total for the two parties in any election since democratisation, legislative or European – appears to have reflected the voters' castigation of the continued economic downturn. Despite being plagued by a succession of rumours and scandals, and the untimely death of its leading candidate on the election trail, the *Socialists*' victory served to reinforce the notion of a *marais*[1] electorate, generally swayed by short-term factors, and particularly by pocket-book voting.

2. Theoretical background

The European elections are often seen as the leading example of the second-order election model of Reif and Schmitt (1980). The implications of this model are normally analysed at the voter choice level. The argument here is that second-order elections, by having "less at stake as compared to first order elections" (Reif 1985: 8) are likely to be characterised by lower turnout – because the election simply matters less – and distinctive voting behaviour patterns. In particular, the model suggests these elections will be more readily used to express discontent with the governing party. The notion of using the vote to evaluate an incumbent is obviously not a novel one. However, as Marsh (1998) has posited, the second-order model implies a greater willingness of insincere voting against underperforming incumbents by their traditional voters, who would have otherwise supported the incumbent in elections 'that matter'. As such, the model predicts losses for incumbents at European elections, given that these often coincide with the mid-term slump for incumbents' popularity; and that smaller parties will tend to fare relatively better – at the expense of larger parties – in European elections *vis-à-vis* legislative plebiscites (see Marsh 1998: 592-593). The depressing effect of second-order elections on larger parties is accounted by the lower costs of "expressive voting" in second-order elections (see Marsh 1998: 593). As Mair (1997) suggests, (legislative) elections are 'about' choosing governments, and in that sense constrain voter choice. Unconstrained by such demands on their decision, voters are able to cast their ballot more sincerely and less instrumentally.

If the impact of the second-order model on voting choice at European elections has been amply examined – and, by-and-large, confirmed (see van der Eijk/Franklin 1996; Marsh 1998) – the model does also have important implications on party strategies in second-order elections. In particular, to the extent that second-order elections are seen by voters as plebiscites on incumbent performance, the model suggests that parties will (rationally) centre their electoral appeal on domestic issues. Slender electoral benefits can be expected from appealing on issues that voters consider irrelevant. As such, the tendency will be for campaigns that focus on domestic matters at the expense of European ones.

As Marsh (1998: 607) puts it, "parties themselves work to make European elections second-order national elections", even if the direction of causality between voter interests and party campaigns is naturally open to debate. As will be shown, the Portuguese elections of 2004 amply confirm this assertion.

3. Portuguese parties and the party system

Four parties have dominated political choice in Portugal, and are the only to have consistently gained parliamentary representation since democratisation – both at legislative level since 1976 and European level since 1987. These four parties are the rightist *Party of the Democratic Social Centre – Popular Party* (*CDS-PP*); the misleadingly named centre-right *Social Democratic Party* (*PSD*); the centre-left *Socialist Party* (*PS*); and, to the *Socialists'* left, the *Portuguese Communist Party* (*PCP*).

Overall, Portuguese parties have relatively weak organisational bases if the mass party model is taken as the standard. However, despite weak social and organisational bases, parties in Portugal remain "the key political institutions" (Bruneau 1997: 19), largely thanks to their monopoly of political representation in parliament and their capacity to tap and distribute state resources – thus accounting for patterns of inter-party co-operation but also of voter disillusionment and disaffection with politics identified by Cabral (2004) and Magalhães (2004).

Portuguese parties are thus hybrid organisations, combining elements of different party models. While presenting some features of mass parties – e.g. statutory requirements for internal democracy – these coexist with patterns of modern cadre (notably a low member/vote ratio and maintenance of the apparent structure of a mass party providing for easily manipulated formal internal democracy) and cartel party typologies (see Koole 1994: 298-299; Katz/Mair 1995), and their older patronage machine predecessors.

The *PS* and *PSD* (and, on a different scale, the *CDS*) are essentially "*partis de electeurs*" (Sousa 1983: 634-635; Barroso 2001: 11, citing Charlot 1971): catch-all parties, with their characteristic ideological flexibility and indeterminacy. This obviously impacts on electoral behaviour; in particular, it may help explain relatively high levels of block volatility from the mid-1980s (see Freire 2001: 23-24; Jalali 2002), as voters switch from one moderate centre-right party to another moderate centre-left party.

The partial exception to this picture is the *PCP* – a reflection also of its longer history. Formed in 1921, the *PCP* is the only party to significantly pre-date of the April 25th 1974 "Carnation Revolution" that brought down the authoritarian *New State* regime erected by António de Oliveira Salazar in 1933. Organisationally, it retains the largest number of mobilised militants, and has traditionally presented the most coherent and clearly-defined social bases of support. Yet in Portugal, as elsewhere in Western Europe, the *Communist Party* has been unable to achieve uniform territorial support from industrial and agrarian workers; and greater ideological consistency has gradually led the ossification of its support into a sizeable, but diminishing and excludable ghetto. It also underpins internal divisions between eurocommunist reformers and the orthodox Marxist-Leninist believers, a conflict that occasionally boils over into expulsions and withdrawals of prominent party members and is likely to impact on the mobilisation of traditional *Communist* voters.

While a plethora of other parties exists – many of which the remnants of the explosion of political participation in the revolutionary context of 1974/75 – smaller parties have traditionally been unable to obtain (let alone maintain) parliamentary representation – be it at the national or European level. However, this pattern has changed since the 1999 legislative elections with the emergence of the *Bloco de Esquerda* (*BE*, *Left Bloc*), an alliance of the Maoist *UDP* (*Popular Democratic Union*), *Trotskyite PSR* (*Revolutionary Socialist Party*) and disillusioned Marxist-Leninist *Política XXI*. The *Bloco* obtained two seats in the 1999 elections – probably costing the *Socialists* the parliamentary majority they had anxiously sought – and were to gain an additional parliamentary seat in the 2002 elections.

In terms of the legislative party system, two very clear patterns can be discerned from relatively early on in Portuguese politics. The first is the emergence of the competition between *PS* and *PSD* as the main dimension of competition within the party system. The 'language of politics' in Portugal has thus effectively been dominated (and constrained) by a choice between these two parties since 1975, which has largely developed as the "overriding electoral choice" in terms of who governs. Indeed, these two parties have led every government since democratisation (bar the brief unsuccessful experiment with presidential governments in 1978/79).

The other key pattern has been the permanent exclusion of the *PCP* from government since 1976. Though arguably now not as polarising as in the 1970s and 1980s, the exclusion of the *PCP* remains a central feature of the party system and also of electoral alignments. Two related aspects thus emerge. First, the anti-system role assigned to the *PCP* in the post-1974 party system; second, and closely related, the cleavage between *PCP* and *PS*, precluding any national-level entente between the two main parties of the left.

Both of these aspects were largely entrenched during the democratisation period, reflecting the increasing polarisation of the revolutionary period, which culminated in the 'Hot Summer' of 1975, when civil war appeared possible. The *PCP*'s actions during this period were interpreted as an attempt at installing a *Communist* regime, in alliance with radical segments of the military. This hegemonic project was vigorously attacked by other relevant actors, notably the other parties – with the *PS* at the helm – their military allies and the Church, finally failing with the aborted coup of November 25th1975. Moreover, it eroded the capital of democratic legitimacy the *PCP* had earned as the main force of opposition to the *Estado Novo*, consigning it to an anti-system position.

4. The social anchoring of the Portuguese party system

Traditional cleavage strength has always been perceived to be weak in Portugal (see Gunther/Montero 2001). As Gunther and Montero point out, that neither class nor religion are particularly strong determinants of party voting is somewhat puzzling. Both class and religious cleavages are deeply-rooted in Portugal and, *ceteris paribus*, this should result in greater rooting of partisan preferences on social divisions than in fact does occur (see Gunther/Montero 2001: 96, 124). At the same time, the weakness of old cleavages has not been accompanied by a sustained growth of new, post-materialist orientations (see Jalali 2004).

This pattern is largely accounted by the context in which partisan support was encapsulated in democratic Portugal (see Jalali 2004). 1974 was, in a sense, the 'Year Zero' for political organisation in Portugal (Morlino 1998: 209-210; Jalali 2002: 19). All the parties – including the *PCP*, the only major party functioning in Portugal on the eve of the coup – emerged as legal political organisations seeking (mass) societal support for electoral purposes within the revolutionary context. Parties thus developed as organisations in a context where the most pressing issue was regime-choice, and this became the primary node of action for them, rather than establishing mass organisations designed to represent well-articulated social divisions.

With weak and unconsolidated organisations, the parties in favour of liberal democracy (*PS, PSD* and *CDS*) had one trump card to play against the *PCP*'s organisational solidity and Leninist strategy: that of their wide social support, signalling to the *PCP* and orbiting (but not always friendly) *groupuscules* the real risks of a forced take-over.[2] Thus, in the context of 1974/75, a broad and shallow support base was preferable to a deep but narrow one, and programmatic consistency a luxury the parties could ill-afford. While the *CDS*'s more obvious ties to the old regime placed it offside for much of the electorate, the *PS* and *PSD* successfully appealed on an interclassist line, facilitated by the weakness of class consciousness. At the same time, the centrist parties – and the *PS* in particular – allied themselves with the Church in order to halt the Red threat, and this reconciled Catholicism with voting for the *Socialists*, thus defusing the religious cleavage also.

After 1974/75 the main centrist parties also continued to avoid the consolidation of well-defined electoral bases: as Kirchheimer (1966) had predicted a decade earlier, shallow but wide support could win elections, deep but narrow could not. This, combined with the gradual settlement of the regime-choice question, has resulted in an increasingly *marais* electorate, whose vote is swayed by short-term political factors (notably, economic performance, political scandals and leader perceptions) rather than determined by established cleavage structures. This electorate thus becomes crucial for electoral success and winning government, providing the swing in the electoral wicket for *PS* and *PSD*.

The general party system patterns at the European and legislative levels are consistent with the predictions of the second-order model. While the strengthening of *PS* and *PSD* since the mid-1980s at the legislative level also occurs at the European election level – consistent with the existence of a large *marais* electorate (see Jalali 2004) – the main parties obtain a smaller share of the vote at the European level. However, as Figure 1 demonstrates, the European level increasingly resembles the legislative one in terms of the vote share of the main parties *vis-à-vis* other relevant parties.

Figure 1:   The evolution of party votes at Legislative and European Elections prior to 2004

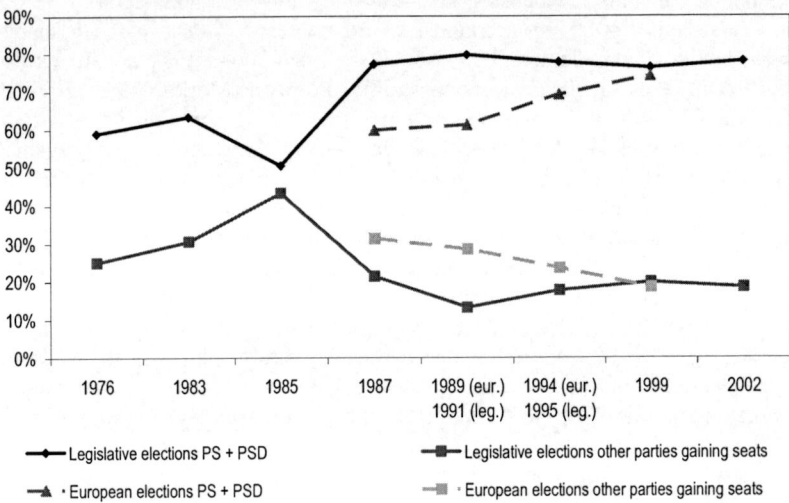

Source: Own calculations, based on data from the *Secretariado Técnico dos Assuntos para o Processo Eleitoral* (STAPE)
Note: Calculations for the 1979 and 1980 legislative elections are not possible because of the pre-electoral alliance between *PSD* and *CDS*. Those years are excluded from the figure.

5. The electoral system

The proximity between the Portuguese electoral system at legislative and European levels means that Reif and Schmitt's "equilibrium of measurement" (1980: 26) condition is amply met. Thus, both European and legislative elections use closed list one-tiered d'Hondt proportional representation. The one difference between the two levels is in terms of district magnitude. European deputies are elected at the national level, with 24 deputies being elected in 2004, whereas the legislative electoral system has 20 districts, corresponding to the administrative districts of Portugal as well as four deputies elected in two circles for Portuguese expatriates. Average district magnitude is thus lower for legislative elections than European elections, as Table 1 demonstrates.

Table 1: Proportional representation electoral systems with d'Hondt formula and single-tier districting, in increasing order of district magnitude

Electoral System	Av. District Magnitude	Number of Districts
France (1945-Nov. 1946)	5.19	102
France (1986)	5.79	96
Spain (1977-1989)	6.73	52
Norway (1945-9)	7.50	20
Switzerland (1947-1987)	8.20	23.91
Sweden (1948)	8.21	28
Portugal legislative level (with islands), 1991-1999	11.3	20
Portugal legislative level (with islands), 1975-1987	12.3	20
Finland (1945-1987)	13.21	15.15
Luxembourg (1945-1989)	14.02	4
Portugal, European level (1987-2004)	24.4	1
Holland (1946-1952)	100	1
Israel (1949)	120	1
Israel (1973-1988)	120	1
Holland (1956-1989)	150	1

Source: Adapted from Lijphart (1994: 22); Portugal data own calculations
Note: Average district magnitudes for Portugal's legislative electoral system were computed taking 250 as the size of parliament, with four seats going to the foreign constituencies, and 10 going to the islands. Note however that for the 1976 elections there were 263 deputies, with 4 for the foreign constituencies, and 12 for the islands. And for the 1975 there were only 3 foreign seats, and still 12 for the islands. These are minor differences, however, which would not produce any substantial difference in the indices obtained.

Potentially this difference might generate incentives for greater tactical voting at legislative elections, particularly in smaller, less proportional districts. However, there is little evidence of tactical voting between different sized districts in legislative elections, suggesting this is also unlikely to occur at the European election level (see Jalali 2002), especially given that the disparity between district sizes within the legislative level is greater than in relation to the European elections.[3]

Electoral rules are also basically identical. As law 14/87 of April 29th 1987 states in article 10, electoral campaigns for European elections are governed by the equivalent legislation for the election of the national parliament, the only exception being the reduction of the official campaign period to 12 days from the two weeks of the legislative campaigns.

6. The 2004 election campaign

In December 2001 António Guterres resigned as both Prime-Minister and as leader of the *Socialists* in the aftermath of poor local election results, in which his party lost control of several major towns, including Lisbon and Porto. The resulting March 17th 2002 general elections produced an alternation in government, with the centre-right *Social Democrats* replacing the *Socialists* as the most voted party. Yet the *PSD*'s 40.2 percent of the vote proved insufficient to deliver the parliamentary majority it had quietly sought during the campaign, leading to the first coalition government since 1985 as the *PSD* allied with the *CDS*.

The new right-wing government led by José Manuel Durão Barroso was however to enter office in a period of profound economic downturn, which saw the Portuguese economy diverge from the EU average, with negative real growth in 2003, and a very incipient recovery in 2004. At the same time, the Barroso government used the Euro-zone Stability and Growth Pact criterion of a 3 percent budget deficit to attempt a reduction in the weight of the public sector in the economy consistent with its neo-liberal stance. In a recessionary context and with rising unemployment (which reached 6.7 percent by the time of the European elections, a sharp rise from the approximately 4 percent at the end of 2001), the government was to face continued opposition and social action from a number of sectors, notably from public sector workers, hit by the restraints on public expenditure, and university students, dissatisfied with the rise in university fees.

Given the cohesiveness of the coalition and a recent history of alliances at second-order elections (as well as a more distant one of alliances at the legislative level), the governing parties chose to present a joint list to the European elections. The pre-electoral alliance was named *Força Portugal* – a name criticised by the opposition for its resemblance to the name of Berlusconi's party vehicle. The choice of name was not entirely innocent, trying to cash in on the football fervour of the Euro-2004 competition being held in Portugal and which began on the eve of the European elections. One *Força Portugal* billboard played up to the football imagery, with the candidates holding football scarves proclaiming "*Força Portugal*".

Meanwhile, the main opposition party faced troubles of a different kind due to the Casa Pia paedophilia affair, a sordid story of systematic abuse to children in a state-run care institution for minors. This rocked Portuguese society since its outbreak in late 2002, and a number of prominent public figures – including a top *Socialist* figure and former minister, Paulo Pedroso – were implicated in the affair. The *Socialist Party* leadership staunchly defended its former social security minister (against whom the charges were ultimately dropped, after initially being taken into custody). However, this defence often came across as haphazard and unreflective, and cost then *Socialist* leader Ferro Rodrigues popularity in the electorate and support within his party. The regular barometer survey by Marktest/DN/TSF found a consistent decline in the *Socialist* leader's popularity – from being the second most popular party leader in May 2003 (when Paulo Pedroso was taken into custody), Ferro Rodrigues was one year later the most unpopular party leader, closely followed by the incumbent prime-minister Barroso.[4]

The *Socialist* European campaign proved very good at overcoming the apparent handicap presented by the party leader, whilst maintaining the football overtones of its main rival. The *Socialist* campaign overtly sought to transform the elections into a second-order national contest. Thus, the agenda was squarely set on national issues, with the *Socialists* centring their campaign on the need for the electorate to show the incumbent coalition a "yellow card" – a clear translation of the second-order concept. The "yellow card" idea was thus amply and consistently exploited in political speeches, billboard advertising and party political broadcasts – and successful to such an extent that the *Communist Party* was during its campaign to ask the electorate to show a "red card" to the government.

Both pre- and post-electoral surveys confirm the electoral soundness of this *Socialist Party* campaign. As Eurobarometer 61 revealed, the Portuguese were considerably more preoccupied with national issues – and considerably less so about European ones – than their European counterparts when it came to deciding their vote at the June 2004 European election (see Figure 2).

Figure 2: Most important reasons for deciding who to vote for in 2004 European elections (percent; multiple answers possible)

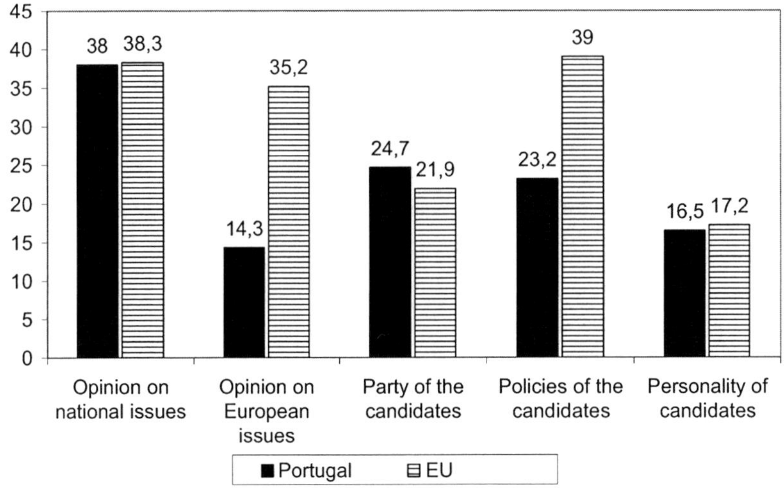

	Portugal	EU
Opinion on national issues	38	38,3
Opinion on European issues	14,3	35,2
Party of the candidates	24,7	21,9
Policies of the candidates	23,2	39
Personality of candidates	16,5	17,2

Source: Jalali et al. 2004: 47.

This pattern is inevitably reflected in the voters' preferences on campaign subjects. Inquired as to which themes the European election campaign should be centred on, unemployment ranked as the single most important issue (70 percent of respondents mentioning unemployment), with almost half of respondents identifying "specifically national issues" as their priority for the campaign (Jalali et al. 2004: 48). The *Força Portugal* also fought on its domestic record. First, it defended the necessity for the reforms it was undertaking; second, it endorsed the responsibility of the parlous economic situation in general, and of public finances in particular, to the inheritance it received from the previous Socialist administration. This second aspect of the coalition campaign had one particular target in mind: the leading *Socialist* candidate, António de Sousa Franco, who had served as finance minister under Guterres government.

The typical pleasantries that marked the early part of the campaign were dramatically curtailed by the death of the leading *Socialist* candidate on June 9th. While the cause of death was a sudden heart-attack, the death was indelibly associated with the campaign and with intra-*Socialist* party factionalism at the local level. Earlier that day the former finance minister had campaigned at a fish market in the Oporto suburb of Matosinhos. Press reports indicate that popular support in the market was regimented between the two estranged local party bosses, current mayor Narciso Miranda, and local party leader (and then vice-mayor), Manuel Seabra, who saw this as an opportunity to show their local support to national party bosses.[5] The television pictures of Sousa Franco's 15 minutes at this market were to become the abiding image of the campaign. The sixty-one year old former minister was literally pushed and pulled by supporters of the two factions, keen on having the candidate physically closer to their own local boss, with violence flaring up between the two sides in the background. Sousa Franco's first heart attack occurred five minutes after leaving the Matosinhos market; and little over an hour later, he was pronounced dead.[6]

The death of Sousa Franco led all parties to immediately halt their campaigns four days earlier than the official end of the campaign period. Its potential impact on voter perceptions is worth exploring. As Nunes (2005) points out, the death of Sousa Franco received an enormous amount of media coverage. As such, it may have contributed to increased interest in the European election campaign. Indeed, surveys suggest the 2004 election campaign had the greatest levels of public interest of those European elections for which data is available (see Lobo 2003; Nunes 2005). At the time it was suggested that Sousa Franco's death might contribute to both a greater turnout and to a bolstering of the *Socialist* vote. However, available data suggests such effect was at best marginal: practically 90 percent of valid responses in the 2004 European election survey stated that the death of Sousa Franco had no effect on their voter choice, with only 6 percent saying it impacted on their decision to vote or not, and 4 percent affirming it had impacted on their vote choice (see Nunes 2005).

7. The 2004 election results

The idea of a marginal Sousa Franco effect on electoral participation is reinforced by the turnout for the elections. The official abstention rate of 61 percent means that the 2004 European elections had the second-lowest turnout since democratisation (at any election level) – preceded only by the 1994 European elections, where abstention exceeded 64 percent. However, it must be noted that the official abstention data in Portugal was plagued by a significant portion 'phantom voters' – estimated to be in excess of one million – in the mid-1990s, with phantom voters accounting for almost 9 percent of abstention in the 1995 legislative elections (see Freire 2001: 20-21). As such, the 61 percent of the 2004 European election is likely to correspond to a higher level of real abstention than its 1994 counterpart. Such high abstention rates amply reaffirm the applicability of the second-order model to European elections in Portugal, and lend credence to Franklin's assertion of a likely continuation of decline in turnout at European elections in the absence of electoral reform in the European Union (see Franklin 2004).

The election results were to provide a strong victory for the *Socialist Party,* and a resounding defeat for the ruling coalition, as Table 2 demonstrates.

Table 2: Results of 2004 European election, Portugal

Parties	No. of Votes	% Votes	No. Seats	% Seats
PS	1.517.170	44.5	12	50
Força Portugal (PSD+CDS)	1.133.640	33.3	9	37.5
PCP+allies	309.406	9.1	2	8.3
BE	167.279	4.9	1	4.2
Other parties right total	90.625	2.7	-	-
Other parties left total	53.789	1.6	-	-

Total voters: 3.407.549 *(38.7 percent of registered voters)*
Registered voters: 8.812.081
Blank Ballots: 87.269 (2.6 percent)
Spoiled Ballots: 48.371 (1.4 percent)
Source: STAPE

The *Socialist Party* obtained its highest election result at any election level (though this result was subsequently marginally exceeded in the 2005 legislative elections). Meanwhile, the *Força Portugal* total of 33.3 percent represented the lowest ever share for the right since democratisation. There is little doubt that the elections were used to express discontent with government performance. Research at the legislative election level has shown the importance of short-term factors on voting behaviour, particularly in terms of distinguishing voters between the centre-right *PSD* and the centre-left *PS* (see Jalali 2004). A similar pattern is also apparent in the 2004 European elections, with the evaluation of government performance emerging as the strongest predictor of voting behaviour for both *Força Portugal* and *Socialist* voters (see Nunes 2005: 12). The *PSD*-led coalition was seemingly punished not only by centrist *marais* voters switching their support to the *Socialists*, but also by higher rates of abstention of 2002 *PSD* and *CDS* voters, with one-third of those inquired who had voted *PSD* and *CDS* in 2002 abstaining in the 2004 European elections (see Nunes 2005: 18).

The 2004 election result thus fits the predicted pattern of second-order election losses for incumbents. As Table 3 shows, this dynamic was already apparent in previous elections also. As such, the *Socialist Party*'s decision to firmly square the campaign on domestic matters by calling on a "yellow card vote" against the government proved to be perceptive of previous patterns.

Table 3: European elections and electoral cycles

European elections	Percentage change in incumbent party vote		
	Honeymoon period (first 12 months of government)	Mid-term (between 13th and 36th month of government)	End of term (between 37th and 48th month of government)
1987	-12.8		
1989		-17.5	
1994		-16.2	
1999			-0.6
2004		-15.6	

Source: Freire 2005.

8. Conclusion

The 2004 European election in Portugal provided a good example of how party campaigns can be used to "make European elections second-order national elections" (Marsh 1998: 607) confirming the second-order election theory not only on voter choices, but also on parties' campaign strategies. The party campaign strategies – notably of the opposition – actively sought to make the election 'about' the incumbent government's record; and the governing *Força Portugal* alliance used the campaign to defend its record. This in turn further excluded European issues from voters' minds, as confirmed by pre-electoral surveys. The proximity between the two main parties on Europe also serves to reinforce this demotion of European issues. European accession was for long a key goal (and source of cooperation between) of both main centrist parties, and no significant divisions over Europe have emerged since 1986. This further excludes European issues from centre-stage, be it at legislative or European elections.

References

Bruneau, Thomas (1997): Introduction. In: Bruneau, Thomas (Ed.): Political Parties and Democracy in Portugal. Boulder: Westview Press, 1-22.
Cabral, Manuel V. (2004): Confiança, mobilização e representação política em Portugal [Trust, mobilization and political representation in Portugal]. In: Freire, André/Lobo, Marina Costa/Magalhães, Pedro (Eds.): Portugal a Votos: As eleições legislativas de 2002 [Portugal at the Polls: the legislative

elections of 2002]. Lisbon: Imprensa de Ciências Sociais, 301-332 [Cabral: Trust, Mobilization and Political Representation in Portugal. In: Freire et al.: Portugal at the Polls: The Legislative Elections of 2002].

Charlot, Jean (1971): Les Partis Politiques [Political Parties]. Paris: Librarie Armand Colin [Political Parties].

Deutsch, Emeric/Lindon, Denis/Weil, Pierre (1966): Les familles politiques aujourd'hui en France [Political Families in Contemporary France]. Paris: Les Editions de Minuit [Political Families in Contemporary France].

Ferrara, Federico/Weishaupt, J. Timo (2004): Get Your Act Together: Party Performance in European Parliament Elections. In: European Union Politics Vol. 5, No. 3, 283-306.

Franklin, Mark N. (2004): Voter Turnout and the Dynamics of Electoral Competition in Established Democracies since 1945. Cambridge: Cambridge University Press.

Freire, André (2001): Mudança Eleitoral em Portugal: Clivagens, Economia e Voto em Eleições Legislativas, 1983-1999 [Electoral Change in Portugal: Cleavages, the Economy and Voting in Legislative Elections, 1983-1999]. Oeiras: Celta Editora [Electoral Change in Portugal: Cleavages, the Economy and Voting in Legislative Elections, 1983-1999].

Freire, André (2005): Portugal. In: Déloye, Yves (Ed.): Dictionnaire des Elections Européennes [Dictionary of European Elections]. Paris: Economica [Dictionary of European Elections].

Gunther, Richard/Montero, José R. (2001): The Anchors of Partisanship: A Comparative Analysis of Voting Behaviour in Four Southern European Democracies. In: Diamandouros, P. Nikiforos/Gunther, Richard (Eds.): Parties, Politics, and Democracy in the New Southern Europe. Baltimore: The Johns Hopkins University Press, 83-152.

Jalali, Carlos (2002): The Evolution of the Portuguese Party System in Comparative European Perspective since 1974. D.Phil. thesis, University of Oxford.

Jalali, Carlos (2004): As mesmas clivagens de sempre? Velhas clivagens e novos valores no comportamento eleitoral português [The Same Old Cleavages? Old cleavages and new values in Portuguese electoral behaviou]. In: Freire, André/Lobo, Marina Costa/Magalhães, Pedro (Eds.): Portugal a Votos: As eleições legislativas de 2002 [Portugal at the Polls: the legislative elections of 2002]. Lisbon: Imprensa de Ciências Sociais, 87-124 [Jalali: The Same Old Cleavages? Old Cleavages and New Values in Portuguese Electoral Behaviour. In: Freire et al.: Portugal at the Polls: The Legislative Elections of 2002].

Jalali, Carlos/Nunes, Filipe/Santo, Ana E. (2004): Eurobarometer 61: Public Opinion in the European Union, National Report Portugal, Spring 2004. European Opinion Research Group.

Katz, Richard/Mair, Peter (1995): Changing Models of Party Organisation: The Emergence of the Cartel Party. In: Party Politics, Vol. 1, No. 1, 5-28.

Kirchheimer, Otto (1966): The Transformation of the Western European Party Systems. In: LaPalombara, Joseph/Weiner, Myron (Eds.): Political Parties and Political Development. Princeton: Princeton University Press, 177-200.

Koole, Ruud (1994): The Vulnerability of the Modern Cadre Party in the Netherlands. In: Katz, Richard/Mair, Peter (Eds.): How Parties Organise: Change and Adaptation in Party Organisations in Western Democracies. London: Sage, 278-303.

Lijphart, Arend (1994): Electoral Systems and Party Systems: A Study of Twenty-Seven Democracies, 1945-1990. Oxford: Oxford University Press.

Lobo, Marina C. (2003): Legitimizing the EU? Elections to the European Parliament in Portugal, 1987-1999. In: Pinto, António Costa (Ed.): Contemporary Portugal: Politics, Society, and Culture. New York: Columbia University Press, 203-226.

Magalhães, Pedro (2004): Democratas, descontentes e desafectos: as atitudes dos portugueses em relação ao sistema político [Discontented and Disaffected Democrats: the attitudes of the Portuguese towards the political system]. In: Freire, Lobo/Magalhães, Pedro (Eds.): Portugal a Votos: As eleições legislativas de 2002 [Portugal at the Polls: the legislative elections of 2002]. Lisbon: Imprensa de Ciências Sociais, 333-362 [Magalhães: Discontented and Disaffected Democrats: The Attitudes of the Portuguese towards the Political System: In: Freire et al.: Portugal at the Polls: The Legislative Elections of 2002].

Mair, Peter (1997): Party System Change: Approaches and Interpretations. Oxford: Clarendon Press.

Manalvo, Nuno (2001): PSD: A marca dos líderes [PSD: the mark of the leaders]. Lisbon: Editorial Notícias [PSD: The Mark of the Leaders].

Marsh, Michael (1998): Testing the Second Order Elections Model after Four European Elections. In: British Journal of Political Science, Vol. 28, No. 4, 591-607.

Maxwell, Kenneth (1995): Democratisation in Portugal. Cambridge: Cambridge University Press.

Morlino, Leonardo (1998): Democracy Between Consolidation and Crisis: Parties, Groups and Citizens in Southern Europe. Oxford: Oxford University Press.

Nunes, Filipe (2005): Eleições de Segunda Ordem em Portugal: o Caso das Europeias de 2004. [Second Order Elections in Portugal: the Case of the 2004 European Elections]. Paper presented to the second Electoral Behaviour and Political Attitudes of the Portuguese Conference, ICS, Lisbon, January 2005 [Nunes: Second Order Elections in Portugal: The Case of the 2004 European Elections].

Reif, Karlheinz (1985): Ten Second-Order Elections. In: Reif, Karlheinz (Ed.): Ten European Elections. Aldershot: Gower, 1-36.

Reif, Karlheinz/Schmitt, Hermann (1980): Nine Second Order National Elections: A Conceptual Framework for the Analysis of European Election Results. In: European Journal of Political Research, Vol. 8, No. 1, 3-44.
Sousa, Marcelo Rebelo de (1983): Os Partidos Políticos no Direito Constitucional Português [Political Parties in Portuguese Constitutional Law]. Braga: Livraria Cruz [Political Parties in Portuguese Constitutional Law].
van der Eijk, Cees van der /Franklin, Mark (Eds.) (1996): Choosing Europe? The European Electorate and National Politics in the Face of Union. Ann Arbor: University of Michigan Press.

---

[1] The term is first used to categorize the French apolitical electorate (see Deutsch et al. 1966).
[2] For an account of the convoluted revolutionary period of 1974-5, and the risks of civil war it carried, see Maxwell (1995).
[3] The smallest district in the 2005 Portuguese legislative elections accounted for 2 deputies, against 48 in the largest district.
[4] "Imagem dos Políticos em Maio", Marktest database, http://www.marktest.com/wap/a/n/id~51b.aspx (25th June 2004).
[5] "Sousa Franco morreu após ataque cardíaco", Público online, http://dossiers.publico.pt/shownews.asp?id=1196045&idCanal=1324 (9th June 2004).
[6] Ibid.

…
Campaigning under the Shadow of the Annan Plan: The 2004 EP Elections in Cyprus[1]

*Athanassios N. Samaras & Giorgos Kentas**

1. Introduction

This paper deals with the European Parliament (EP) elections which took place in the Republic of Cyprus, a member state of the EU since the last enlargement of May 1st 2004. Since Turkey's invasion in 1974, the Republic of Cyprus is a semi-occupied state and its people, according to a number of judgments issued by the European Court of Human Rights, are victims of continuous, grave and mass scale human rights violations whose sole perpetrator is Turkey. The search for a solution of this conflict is the dominant issue in Cyprus political life. The EP elections took place almost two months after the April 24th referendum in which the Greek-Cypriot community rejected the Annan Plan. The "pro-anti Plan" split, which was primed into importance by the referendum campaign, posed a challenge to the "Right-Left" cleavage as the organizing element of the Greek-Cypriot party system. We are examining this challenge by analyzing political party strategies and campaign discourses.

In the first section, we present the Cyprus crisis. In the second section we portray Cyprus' route to EU accession, as well as the political attitudes and expectations toward that accession. In the third section, we examine the political context in which the June EP campaign and elections took place. In the fourth section the political campaign is presented. Finally, we describe and interpret the election's results.

2. The Cyprus crisis

The Republic of Cyprus, an independent state since 1960, has undergone internal clashes between its communities and suffered from foreign interventions through its so-called "guarantor powers" – Turkey, UK and Greece – that led to the ongoing political situation on the island (see Yiallourides/Tsakonas 1999). EU accession is considered as a means to overcome the ongoing status quo and to reach a comprehensive settlement of the Cyprus Problem (see Evriviades 2003).

---

* Athanassios N. Samaras, PhD. Senior Researcher at the Mediterranean Studies Foundation, Athens, Greece, email: ath.samaras@usa.net
Giorgos Kentas. *1976. PhD.-Candidate at the Vrije Universiteit, Brussels, Belgium, email: gkentas@yahoo.com

The Constitution of the Republic of Cyprus provides for a Greek Cypriot President and a Turkish Cypriot Vice-President, each elected by its own community. The Council of Ministers was to be divided 7:3 between Greek and Turkish Cypriots. Following a short period of peaceful, yet contrarious, coexistence, the Greek and the Turkish Cypriot communities quarreled over political and financial issues. Following a 1963 proposal for constitutional amendments by the President of Cyprus Archbishop Makarios, Turkish Cypriots abandoned their governmental, parliamentary, and juridical posts to seek a new state of affairs[2] in Cyprus (see Aimilianides 2003), and consequently the Greek Cypriot community was forced to run the Cypriot state as of 1964.

The Cyprus crisis culminated in 1974 when Turkey invaded the northern part of Cyprus and occupied 37 percent of the island's territory. Although Turkey claimed that it intervened in Cyprus to restore the status quo after a failed coup inspired by Greek Cypriots who supported the union of Cyprus with Greece, it maintained its forces in the northern part of the island, some 35.000 military troops. The United Nations General Assembly urged "the speedy withdrawal of all foreign armed forces and foreign military presence and personnel from the Republic of Cyprus and the cessation of all foreign interference in its affairs" (Resolution 3212/74). Since then, numerous resolutions repeated the terms of this resolution; however, Turkey refuses to obey.

The Government of the Republic of Cyprus, the only internationally recognized authority on the island (see UN Security Council Resolutions 541/83, 550/84), exercises control over the southern two thirds of the island, where about 730.000 Greek Cypriots live. In the northern occupied area there are about 80.000 Turkish Cypriots and some 115-120.000 Turkish settlers (see Laakso 2002). Although the Turkish Cypriots have set up some "administrative" mechanisms, Turkey exercises effective control over the occupied lands (see European Court of Human Rights 1998, 2001). In November 1983 the occupied territories unilaterally declared their "independence" via the "Turkish Republic of Northern Cyprus" (TRNC). The United Nations Security Council stated that this declaration was null and void, expressing its concern that "this attempt would contribute to a worsening of the situation in Cyprus" (UN Security Council Resolutions 541/83). Turkey is the only state that recognizes – and finances – the TRNC.

3. Cyprus' route to the EU

3.1 Toward EU accession

The majority of political forces, as well as the civil society, have warmly supported Cyprus' accession to the EU. Since 1973, Cyprus and the European Community have been linked by an Association Agreement which provided for the establishment of a customs union in two stages and within a period of ten years (see European Commission 1998). Following the first stage, an additional Protocol was signed in Luxembourg on October 19th 1987 for the implementation of the second stage. In accordance with the provisions of this Protocol, the final stage for the completion of the customs union, likewise in two phases, entered into force on January 1st 1988 (see European Commission 1998). In 1990, Cyprus filed an application for accession to the Union. Three years later, the European Commission responded positively. In its opinion, the Commission stated that, "in regard to economic aspects, the adoption of the *acquis communautaire* would pose no insurmountable problems". The opinion also stated "there would be a greater chance of narrowing the development gap between north and south in the event of Cyprus's integration with the Community". Thus, a new opportunity was born for Cyprus; its accession route would pave the way for reunification and prosperity for the island as a whole.

In Luxembourg, in December 1997, the European Council decided to open accession negotiations with Cyprus. In its conclusions, the EU Presidency stated that "the accession of Cyprus should benefit all communities and help to bring about civil peace and reconciliation. The accession negotiations will contribute positively to the search for a political solution to the Cyprus problem through the talks under the aegis of the United Nations which must continue with a view to creating a bi-community, bi-zonal federation. In this context, the European Council requests that the willingness of the Government of Cyprus to include representatives of the Turkish Cypriot community in the accession negotiating delegation be acted upon". However, the Turkish Cypriot leadership rejected the proposal inviting Turkish Cypriot representatives to participate in the accession negotiations (see European Commission 1998). The government of the Republic of Cyprus engaged in those negotiations, opened on March 31st 1998, without any Turkish Cypriot representatives.

On May 1st 2004, Cyprus joined the EU under the conditions spelled out in the Accession Treaty signed on April 16th 2003. Protocol No. 10 attached to the Accession Treaty which provides for the temporary suspension of the *acquis* in the areas of the country which are not under the effective control of the Government of Cyprus.[3] In the event of a solution to the Cyprus Problem, this suspension will be lifted. The European Union is ready to accommodate the terms of a settlement in line with the principles on which the EU is founded.

3.2 The EU and the Cyprus problem

Since 1977, the UN has sponsored bi-communal negotiations aimed at reaching an agreement between the Greek and the Turkish Cypriot leaders. Greek and Turkish Cypriot leaders, Makarios and R. Denktash, reached a high-level agreement as a basis for a settlement. In 1979, Kyprianou and Denktash reaffirmed the 1977 agreement, providing for the establishment of a bi-communal, bi-zonal federation. However, no agreement has been reached between the two sides, despite the repeated mediation efforts by the UN. The latest such initiative was launched in November 2002, when the UN Secretary General submitted a Plan entitled "Basis for Agreement on a Comprehensive Settlement of the Cyprus Problem", the so-called Annan Plan.[4] On April 24th 2004, the two communities held simultaneous referenda on the agreement. The Plan, as finalized by the UN Secretary General on March 31st 2004 was rejected by 76 percent of the Greek Cypriot electorate and endorsed by 65 percent of Turkish Cypriots and settlers.

The EU has taken on a constructive role in connection with the settlement of the Cyprus issue. In its Agenda 2000, in 1997, the EU reiterated that "the Union is determined to play a positive role in bringing about a just and lasting settlement in accordance with the relevant United Nations Resolutions. The status quo, which is at odds with international law, threatens the stability of the island, the region and has implications for security". Hence, Cyprus seeks to normalize its bilateral relations with Turkey, a candidate state that refuses to recognize the Government of the Republic of Cyprus, one of the 25 member states of the EU which it aspires to join. Cyprus has supported Turkey's accession prospects and requires the latter's change of attitude. The overall aim goes beyond "normalization" and incorporates three crucial issues: first, the withdrawal of the illegal presence of over 35.000 Turkish troops occupying 37 percent of the Republic's (and therefore EU's) territory; second, the unceasing flow of illegal Turkish settlers, whose number now exceeds 115.000; and third, the legally condemned exploitation of Greek Cypriot properties in the occupied "North". The Republic of Cyprus treats these issues as "the international aspects of the Cyprus problem", which have forced the European Court of Human Rights to condemn Turkey in such decisions as "Loizidou vs. Turkey", "Cyprus vs. Turkey", and "Aresti-Xenide vs. Turkey".

Although the Government of Cyprus recognizes the UN's role, it also seeks the EU's active intervention to the same end. The Government of Cyprus is eager that the EU plays a vital role in ascertaining the settlement's compatibility with the *acquis* and the EU's founding principles. The nomination of Mr. Jaako Blomberg, as Commissioner Olli Rehn's special advisor for Cyprus, was warmly welcomed by Nicosia. The EU can play a pivotal role in promoting Confidence Building Measures (CBMs) between Greek and Turkish Cypriots. By closely monitoring the ongoing Regulation 866/2004 and by cooperating with the Government of Cyprus, the EU can guarantee that Turkish Cypriots enjoy the benefits of accession. Clearly, the Union can ascertain that improving the Turkish Cypriots' socio-economic standards serves the end of Cypriot reunification and not the entrenchment of the illicit status quo.

4. The political context

4.1 The party system

In Cyprus there is a strict separation of power between the executive and the legislature. Members of the executive Council of Ministers cannot be Members of the House of Representatives. Elections are held at three levels: presidential, parliamentary, and municipal. Simple majority elects the President every five years, usually in two rounds. The elections for the House of Representatives are by simple proportional representation (1.79 percent). Elections have taken place under free and peaceful conditions in recent years.

In general, the institutions of the Republic of Cyprus function efficiently. There are nine political parties represented in the 56 seat House of Representatives: the communist *Progressive Party of the Working People* (*AKEL*) which is the oldest party in Cyprus currently holding 20 seats in Parliament, the rightwing *Democratic Rally* (*DISY*) founded by Glafcos Clerides holding 15 seats, the centrist *Democratic Party* (*DIKO*) founded by Spyros Kyprianou and led by Tassos Papadopoulos holding nine seats, the socialist *United Democratic Center Party* (*EDEK*) founded by Vassos Lyssarides holding four seats, and a few minor parties each of them holding one seat in the House of Representatives, namely the *Ecologists-Environmentalist Movement* founded by Yiorgos Perdikis, the *United Democrats* (*EDI*) founded by former President Georges Vassiliou, and the *Fighting Democratic Movement* (*ADIK*) founded by Dinos Michaelides. Finally, the *New Horizons* (*NEO*) founded by Nicos Koutsou has dissolved and joined forces with the newly established *European Democracy Party* (*EURO.DE*), founded by four MPs and leading ex-members of *DISY*, who left their party because of its favourable attitude toward the Annan Plan, which now holds four seats.

The political system in Cyprus is presidential with a strong presidency, and the parties nominate either party members or personalities with a wider appeal. In the last presidential elections (February 16th 2003) challenger Tassos Papadopoulos, leader of *DIKO* and supported by *AKEL, DIKO, EDEK*, and the *Ecologists-Environmentalist Movement*, won the elections in the first round with 51.5 percent of the popular vote. Incumbent President Clerides, supported by *DISY* and *EDI*, lost with 38.8 percent. The Attorney-General Alekos Markides, running as an independent candidate without any partisan support, took 6.6 percent, while *NEO* leader Koutsou took 2.2 percent.

4.2 The Annan Plan campaign

The continued inner struggle within the Greek Cypriot community between a) the desired but unattainable ideal – the Unitary State – and b) the painful but more realistic compromise (see Lordos 2004: 16) – the Federation – could explain the lack of enthusiasm with which the Greek Cypriot public opinion greeted the Plan. The Greek Cypriot have come to terms with the fact that any negotiated agreement that incorporates the "realities" created by the Turkish invasion of 1974 could not be fair to them and seem to have settled for an unfair but viable and workable solution. But, the new state of affairs that would emerge by the implementation of the Annan Plan did not seem as a viable solution to the Greek Cypriots. Moreover, their evaluation of the Plan was, from the very beginning, conditioned with fears that its outright rejection would block Cyprus' accession to the EU, would minimize the possibility of a new UN initiative, and would lead to a *de jure* partition of the island. These fears have led to the emergence of an attitude that accepts the Plan as a basis for negotiations but not as a basis towards the solution (see Samaras/Kentas 2005; Theophanous 2004). For many Greek Cypriots the construct of "negotiation" operated as a way to handle the cognitive dissonance emerging from having to deal with a highly disagreeable solution (see Mazou/Samaras 2002). Such expectations that the negotiations would lead to a better version of the Plan seized to exist when the Plan was finalized at Bürgenstock. As a consequence the Greek and Greek Cypriot public expressed their strong discontent towards the Plan. On April 24th 2004, the two simultaneous referenda took place among the Greek and Turkish Cypriot communities. Greek Cypriots rejected the Plan by a majority of 75.8 percent, while Turkish Cypriots and the settlers approved it by 64.9 percent. As a result, the Annan Plan as its own clauses prescribed became null and void, without any legal effect. Still, on May 1st 2004, the Republic of Cyprus joined the EU along with nine other European states.

A critical event in the campaign was President Papadopoulos' television address on April 7th. By calling on Greek Cypriots to reject the Annan Plan with a firm "No" in the upcoming referendum, Papadopoulos ended the period of introspection and commenced what was the final phase of the campaign. Papadopoulos explained the events at Bürgenstock, claimed that the current version of the Annan Plan was worse than the previous ones, and argued that the new state of affairs was neither viable nor functional, in the hope that this would make it easier for Greek Cypriots to vote "no" at the referendum. He concluded by requesting Greek Cypriots to "defend the Republic of Cyprus by voting 'No' to its dissolution", thus framing the Annan Plan as a threat rather than an opportunity (see Samaras/Kentas 2005).

The debate of the Annan Plan cut across partisan lines in Cyprus. The debate on previous plans and the interplay of such plans with party politics have led to the emergence of the bipolar "Rejectionists vs. Concessionists" (see Katsis 2002). This bipolarity cuts across the Right-Left bipolarity because the right-wing *DISY* and the left-wing *AKEL* both tend toward the "Concessionist" pole, whereas the centrist *DIKO*, the socialist *EDEK*, the *NEO*, and the *Ecologist Movement* tend toward the "Rejectionist" pole. The content of the Annan Plan was so much in discord with the wishes of the Greek Cypriots that it managed to turn the parties most likely to agree into contestants.

AKEL kept out of this trouble by gradually switching from a "yes" to a "yes and no" position, while it ended with a straightforward "no". In effect, it directly negotiated with the UN Secretary General and the former US Secretary of State, Mr. Powell, for a possible postponement of the referenda for a few months and decided to vote against the Plan only when this effort failed. *AKEL* synthesized tried to reconcile its traditional position with its current decision by claiming that it is "voting 'no' in order to cement the 'yes'" (Samaras/Kentas 2005:84). The final decision of *AKEL* induced commotion across the party lines. For the first time in its long history, *AKEL* passed through a period of serious retrospection in relation its position on the Cyprus issue. The solid cohesion of the party's leadership, however, did not permit public disputes or internal drifts.

4.3 The rift at DISY

As early as November 2002, when the first version of the Annan Plan appeared, a political culture study (via focus group) found two totally different attitudes towards the Plan among the *DISY* supporters. A number of them had adopted an actively concessionist stance, whereas others were insecure, frustrated, and partly agitated (see Mazou/Samaras 2002). Right from the beginning, the electoral basis of *DISY* was 'poles apart' in reference to the Annan Plan. During the presidential campaign, *DISY*'s MPs that opposed the plan supported the candidacy of the Attorney-General Alekos Markides[5] rather than the party ticket.

This rift was further widened during the campaign for the referendum. At *DISY* both Nicos Anastasiades, the current leader, and Glafkos Clerides, the founder and father figure of the party, have been ardent supporters of the Annan Plan. Thus, on April 7th, despite the disagreement of its supporters, the Political Office of *DISY* opted to support the Plan. The General Conference of the party confirmed this decision in a climate of intense intraparty conflict. Clerides' speech was highly emotional, its epitome being the statements: "The danger we are facing should we opt for the 'No' is the burial of our fatherland" and "I am 85 years old, I would rather die than see such an end to the struggle of the Cypriot people". A week later, Yiannakis Matsis, the ex-president of *DISY*, and a group of MPs of the party organized a rally against the Annan Plan. Matsis surrounded by Greek and Cypriot flags countered Clerides' statement by pointing out that: "by voting 'Yes' we shall transform our own country with our own vote into a *satrapy* (province) of Turkey". While both sides made public statements aiming to maintain party unity, the polarization between proponents and opponents of the Annan Plan within *DISY* kept being very strong.

Following their campaigning against the Plan, two members of the parliamentary team of *DISY*, Ricos Erotokritou and Prodromos Prodromou, were expelled from the party. Following this, another two MPs, Christodoulos Taramoundas and Dimitris Syllouris, quit *DISY* quit *DISY*. All supported the ex-president of *DISY*, Matsis' ticket for the European Parliament elections (named

"*For Europe*"). Matsis had previously declined *DISY*'s invitation to participate in the party's list since the party did not reverse its positive attitude towards the Annan Plan. The conflict between *DISY* and the coalition "*For Europe*" was one of the most prominent aspects of the EP campaign.

5. The European Parliament campaign

5.1 The general setting

In the period between the referendum of April 24th and the June 13th EP elections certain trends emerged:
- The UN Secretary along with high-ranking diplomats and technocrats from the EU, the U.S.A., and the U.K. worked hard in order to provide a comprehensive settlement for the Cyprus Problem. However, the Greek Cypriots considered the final form of the Annan Plan unfair and not viable for Cyprus as a whole. The "No" to the Annan Plan had a negative effect on Cyprus' international position and caused dissatisfaction across the international community (see Samaras/Kentas 2005: 89-91). This dissatisfaction led to a string of negative statements and measures which actually hijacked the news agenda.
- The fear appeals used by the proponents of the Annan Plan after the referendum interacted with the blame games and the "punishment strategies" of the UN, U.S.A., and U.K. to construct a "disaster bringing" discourse. The supporters of the Plan kept giving a symbolic fight aiming to control the meaning of the events while trying to "keep the plan alive".
- Greek Cypriot public opinion was crystallized in its decision to reject the Annan Plan. Despite international pressure and the 'disaster bringing' discourse produced by the supporters of the Annan Plan in Cyprus and abroad, only 9 percent of the voters claimed that they had regretted their vote in the referendum of April 24th. Posed with the possibility of a new referendum, with international guarantees but no substantial changes to the Plan, 61 percent of the electorate stated they would have voted against the Plan and 32 percent would have supported it.[6]

The EP elections took place less than two months after the referendum on the Annan Plan. Such a short time interval enhances the effect that one campaign had upon the other. Pre-persuasion, new circumstances and election fatigue are three kinds of effects that the referendum campaign may have had on the EP campaign. The most important effect was that the referendum campaign transformed the "rejectionist-concessionist" cleavage into a "pro-anti Annan Plan" cleavage. Prior to the Annan Plan referendum the "rejectionist-concessionist" cleavage – while present – could not displace the "Right-Left" cleavage and reorganize the party structure. However, the "pro-anti Plan" split, which was primed into importance by the referendum campaign, could pose an effective challenge to the "Right-Left" cleavage as the organizing element of the party system. The EP election campaign became important because it was the critical event through which the Cypriot party system would either absorb the pressures of the referendum or be reshaped by them.

The situation that each party faced after the referendum is better understood when the vote for the Plan is examined in relation to partisan preference in the last parliamentary elections. *DIKO* and *EDEK* traditionally tend towards the rejectionist pole; their supporters voted overwhelmingly for the party line and against the Plan (*DIKO* 89 percent against, *EDEK* 81 percent against). *AKEL* traditionally tends towards the concessionist pole, however it adopted a stance against the Plan. Of those that voted for *AKEL* in the last parliamentary campaign 80 percent voted against and 20 percent voted for the plan. *AKEL*'s difficulties were twofold. On the one hand, many of its supporters considered the party's attitude at the referendum to be in contradiction with its long-term policy of rapprochement (with the Turkish Cypriots); on the other hand, the opponents of the Plan were irritated by *AKEL*'s post-referendum statements concerning the terms and conditions under which the plan would be acceptable. Finally, of those who voted for *DISY* during the last parliamentary elections, 62 percent voted against the Plan and 38 percent in favour of it. The majority of the party supporters voted against the party line.

The challenge that the "pro-anti Plan" cleavage posed to the party system in the post-referendum era was twofold. The most obvious one was the challenge posed by the coalition *"For Europe"* on *DISY*, an intrablock conflict of two parties across the lines of the Annan Plan. The most important challenge, however, is the one that did not actually materialize. In relation to the "Cyprus issue" the Greek-Cypriot party system takes the form of an inverted U shape. The two large parties of the Right (*DISY*) and of the Left (*AKEL*) traditionally tend toward a "concessionist" stance, whereas the smaller centrist parties (*DIKO*, *EDEK*, *NEO*) tend toward a "rejectionist" stance. This peculiarity of the Cyprus party system leads to two alternative scenarios for the post-referendum era: either the smaller centrist parties merge into a single party and adopt a dominant position at the center of the party system or remain fragmented and most probably face a situation in which in the second round of the next presidential elections a "concessionist" of the Right would compete against a "concessionist" of the Left.

DIKO, *EDEK*, and *NEO* actually entered negotiations to form a single anti-Plan ticket during the EP elections, which failed because of *EDEK*. A joint ticket means a common election campaign, including coordinated communication and voters' mobilization processes. These common campaign processes during the EP campaign would integrate the apparatuses of the parties and pave the road for a new party. Moreover, a common message during the EP campaign would cement the sense of identity created by the campaign referendum. What happened instead is that the apparatus of the three parties had to actively compete against each other for the very same electorate.

5.2 The Annan Plan: position vs. valence issue

This process affected the campaign discourse of all three parties and turned the Annan Plan from a position into a valence issue. A position issue is one on which the rival parties reach out for the support of the electorate by taking different positions on a policy question in ways that divide the electorate, while valence issues are the issues used by parties and candidates to link themselves in the voters minds with conditions, goals, or symbols that are universally approved or disapproved by the electorate (see Stokes/Dilulio 1993: 6-7). During the referendum campaign the whole electorate discourse was organized around a central antithesis that treated the Annan Plan as a position issue. This situation would have maintained during the EP campaign if *DIKO*, *EDEK*, and *NEO* had appeared on a single ticket.

What actually happened is that the dominant antithesis that organized the referendum campaign (pro-anti Plan) was fragmented during the EP campaign into several antitheses. This in turn resulted to three different patterns of treatment of the Plan issue:

- The Plan was treated as a *position issue* in the conflict between *DISY* and "*For Europe*", the one party was for the Plan, while the other was against it.
- The Plan was treated as a *positive valence issue* by the minor party *EDI*, which focused its campaign on the ardent supporters of the Plan.
- The Plan was treated as a *negative valence issue* by *DIKO*, *EDEK*, *NEO*, and "*For Europe*" who focused their campaign to the opponents of the Plan. Turning the Plan into a negative valence issue implies that opposition to it was turned into a criterion for evaluation, and other parties were attacked for not complying adequately with this criterion. Thus, while all four parties supported Lyssarides' statement that: "the people should punish those politicians who urged them to vote for the Plan", instead of attacking the Plan proponents they attacked each other. For example, *EDEK* focused its attacks on the coalition "*For Europe*" with which they competed for the sixth seat in the European Parliament. *NEO* attacked *EDEK* for having "left the negotiation for a single ticket because of the pressure of (the Greek party) *PASOK* to join the Yes camp"[7], while it criticized "*For Europe*" for practicing opportunism[8]. Thus rather than unite and aim for political hegemony, each party attacked the other for a slice of the anti-Plan vote. Consequently, the campaigns of the anti-Plan parties constitute an exemplary case study of the victory of *petit-politics* and tacticism over strategic planning and structural transformation.

5.3 The rift at DISY, round two: DISY vs. "For Europe"

The conflict between *DISY* and "*For Europe*" was an intraparty conflict which turned into an intrablock conflict. The schism was due to the Annan Plan. The two parties contested for *DISY* supporters who voted against the party line at the referendum. They constituted 62 percent of the party's electorate. From this pool of voters one third (20 percent of the total) followed *"For Europe"*, while two thirds (42 percent of the total) went along with *DISY*. The latter benefited from a very strong party apparatus as well as from the traditional high levels of party loyalty of its followers (see Samaras 2005).

The conflict between the two parties was mainly fought out through a stealth campaign (canvassing, word of mouth, direct mail, push polling, and sms) which is difficult to account for. This inter-party/intra-block fight was conducted in the public via the following discourses:

- The *Plan-related discourse*. The Annan Plan was the main reason for the schism and was treated as a position issue, while *DISY*'s position on the Plan referendum was the focal point. The Plan-related discourse was functioning positive for '*For Europe*' since the majority of *DISY*'s electorate was opposing the party's stance on the Plan. *"For Europe"* portrayed the leadership of *DISY* as "unpatriotic" and "autocratic"; they were accused of using their control over the apparatus of the party in order to promote a solution that the majority of the party's electorate rejected. *DISY*'s reaction was to turn the focus away from the Plan both in terms of statements and in terms of persons. Party notables who had high visibility in the referendum campaign supporting the plan did not publicly participate in the EP campaign.

- The *discourse of party loyalty*. *"For Europe"* was formed by MPs, party notables and rank-and-file of *DISY*. Its members were considered as a part of the same partisan in-group by the *DISY* electorate. This increased the effectiveness of *"For Europe"*'s message. The latter's strategy was to facilitate this in-group mentality by presenting itself not as a party but as an electoral formation aiming to contest the EP elections but otherwise functioning within the context of *DISY*. This constituted the in-group or one-of-us rhetoric of *"For Europe"*. *DISY*, on the other hand, employed the rhetoric of splintering in order to deconstruct the one-of-us mentality. The rhetoric of splintering employed polarized communication; it was organized across the lines of "us (*DISY*) vs. them (*"For Europe"*)". It demonized the opponents and questioned their motivation and rationality by employing strategic framing and conspiratorial interpretations. The rhetoric of splintering aimed to create a fence around *DISY*. Interpretative schemata and tactics that had been employed in the past to mark off *DISY* from *NEO* were employed again. The interplay of the in-group rhetoric and of the rhetoric of splintering constituted the discourse of party loyalty.

Two major campaign events were related with the discourse of party loyalty. *"For Europe"* in order to maintain the in-group mentality with *DISY* used the term "Συναγερμός" (Rally) in the title ("Rally for Europe"). This term is part of the *DISY* name and constitutes the key word with which *DISY* supporters are traditionally identified. *DISY* contested the use of the term in court. The judiciary procedure was too time-consuming, the ballots could not be printed while the name of one of the parties was being legally contested, and it seemed that the whole affair would harm Cyprus Republic's international image because it gave the impression of not being able to organize an election. The deadlock ended when "*For Europe*" dropped the term 'Rally' from its title.

The differentiation strategy was also used when the application of "*For Europe*" to register as a party got in the hands of *DISY*, which informed its rank and file by massive mailings. This direct mail called into question 'For Europe's' claim that they were an electoral formation 'operating within the Rally's framework'.

- The *discourse of power*. *DISY* had the benefit of a strong party apparatus, while "*For Europe*" struggled to build the party infrastructure on the spot. *DISY* aimed to convey the image of strength that it would remain a party of power, while "*For Europe*" was presented as a party of protest. Within the context of the political culture of Cyprus where access to power is deemed as essential (see Samaras 2005) such images tend to function as self-fulfilling prophesies.

Both the discourse of party loyalty and the discourse of power primed partisan patriotism and long term access to power at the expense of Annan Plan considerations as criteria for electoral choice. Thus the overall potential of both discourses should be considered as positive for DISY.

5.4 The impact of the electoral system

In addition to the campaign discourses, the particularities of the electoral system affected campaigning. During the EP elections, Cyprus was a single constituency. The electoral system of proportional representation was employed, and voting was compulsory even though abstention did not result in penalties. The Cyprus EP elections involved a two-step vote: selection of a party and then up to two individual candidates from the chosen party list (see also Melakopides 2005). Thus, the list of candidate MPs for the European parliament was not a set list; the voter could make a choice by a preference mark. In effect, the party campaign co-existed alongside the individual campaigns of the candidate MEPs. In theory, set list supposedly strengthen the mobility of candidate MEPs towards the voters of the opponent party while the preference cross towards the voters of the same party. Therefore, with the preference cross system much of the campaign activity focused on party loyalists and did not enhance the party's general power-base; moreover, the focus on party loyalists might have weaken the overall party message aiming at floating voters. In the case of *DISY* and "*For Europe*", such disadvantages were turned into advantages since the apple of discord were party loyalists rather than floating voters.

The construction of the list with the candidate MEPs was an important image-making tool for every party. For some parties, like *EDH*, it represented a way to capitalize on the dynamics created by the referendum campaign by placing symbolic figures of the referendum as well as notables from other parties that disagreed with their party's position on the referendum on the list. On the other hand, the candidate list operated as an instrument to absorb the pressures created by the referendum campaign. This was the case for *DISY* which balanced its pro-Plan rhetoric by placing prominent members with a strong position against the Annan Plan on the candidate list. Such persons fulfilled a symbolic function by communicating to the *DISY* anti-Plan voters that the party wanted them, that there would be place for them in the party, and that they should not feel alienated by the referendum campaign. Moreover, the anti-Plan *DISY* candidate MPs had to campaign to get elected and thus actively compete with the "*For Europe*" candidates for the same anti-Plan *DISY* voters. Facing the experiences of the 2004 EP campaign it seems that the inclusion of both pro- and anti-Annan candidates in the lists of *DISY* and *AKEL* could be an on-going strategy for the party system to absorb the pressures created by the Plan in the forthcoming parliamentary elections as well.

5.5 The scanty of Eurocentric issues

Finally, an issue of concern in the analysis of every EP campaign is the degree that campaign discourse is centred on the EU. Successful European integration necessitates adequate processes of communication as well as the emergence of a public sphere that allows citizens to get involved in public discussions about European politics. However, this is very seldom the case in EP campaigns. Usually, the EU is treated as an image-making instrument rather than as the central issue of the political debate. More specifically, it is treated as a glittering generality: in order to associate a party with "modernity' and "effectiveness", as an instrument for supporting the credibility of policy proposal. Alternatively it can be employed as a name-calling device: a rhetorical tool used for demonization and for the transference of negative connotations, usually within the context of anti-globalization, anti-capitalism or economic populism discourses.

The process of using the EP election for domestic politics, also took place in Cyprus. Minimal reference was made to 'European issues'. Within the context of post-referendum politics, the construct 'Europe' fulfilled two main functions: since the date of accession to the EU the expectations of the Greek-Cypriot public were rising that a solution to the Cyprus issue could be found. Within this context, references to the EU and Europe functioned as a direct pledge to work for a European solution and an implicit rejection of the Annan Plan. This was evident even in the names of two tickets opposing the Plan: "*For Europe*" and "*European Coalition – NEO*". The second function had to do with the references to the bonds between Cypriot parties and EP parties. Such references were directly used as testimony to the parties' capacity to work for the interests of Cyprus within the EU, while they less directly supported the argument that a vote for a party not affiliated with a large European party was actually a lost vote. This argument was used by *DISY* at the expense of *"For Europe"* and by *EDEK* at the expense of both *DIKO* and *AKEL*.

6. EP elections' results

Cyprus was allocated six seats in the European parliament. On the basis of previous voter behaviour, it was expected that two seats would be allocated to *AKEL* and *DISY* – which was in fact the case – and one to *DIKO* leaving *EDEK* and *"For Europe"* to compete for the final seat. *"For Europe"* won by a narrow margin of 37 votes (see Table 1). The rise in support for *EDEK* from 6.5 percent in 2001 to 10.8 percent was unexpected. It cannot be explained by *EDEK*'s stance at the referendum,[9] since such a rise did not occur for the other anti-Plan parties. *NEO* actually had its percentages halved from the national parliamentary election 2001 compared to the EP election 2004, mainly due to the lost vote syndrome, whereas *DIKO*, President Papadopoulos' party, gained a mere 2.3 percent, which is attributed to the return of formerly alienated party figures.

Table 1: Turnout and Party results

Voters:	483.311	
Votes cast	350.387	72.5%
Valid votes	334.268	95.4%

Party	EU Elections			Parliament 2001	
	Votes	Percentage	Seats	Votes	Percentage
DISY	94.355	28.2	2	139.721	34.0
AKEL	93.212	27.9	2	142.648	34.7
DIKO	57.121	17.1	1	60.986	14.8
For Europe	36.112	10.8	1		
EDEK	36.075	10.8		26.767	6.5
EDI-European Cyprus	6.534	2.0		10.635	2.6
European Coalition-NEO	5.501	1.7		12.333	3.0
Ecologist Movement	2.872	0.9		8.121	2.0
ADHK				8.860	2.2

What was also unexpected was that *AKEL* came second to *DISY*. Media and politicians alike used the horse-race frame to evaluate results. This led to jubilations at *DISY* and blame games at *AKEL*. The horse-race frame, the evaluation of results according to who came first, is habitually used at parliamentary elections in Cyprus and is the most culturally relevant frame. In our opinion, however, it is not an appropriate instrument to assess the election outcome.

The results of the two parties are not comparable. For *DISY* the stakes were very high; they were involved in an intrablock fight with *"For Europe"*. This led to a strong 'first-order election' style of campaign which mobilized its remaining supporters. *AKEL*, on the other hand, was certain to win two seats but could not expect to gain a third one. Thus, with no actual stakes in the EP elections *AKEL* conducted a very loose "second-order election" style of campaign and failed to effectively mobilize its supporters. *AKEL*'s blame game identifies more reasons for the outcome:

- election fatigue,
- the expectation of the victory at the polls demobilised a part of *AKEL* voters resulting in a reverse bandwagon effect,
- disappointment of party members supporting the Plan with the party's stance prior to the referendum, and irritation of party members opposing the Plan with the party's stance after the referendum,
- tactical voting of *EDEK* by *AKEL* voters. It seems that the tactical support of *AKEL* voters to *EDEK* became evident in opinion polls and raised expectations to *EDEK* leadership leading the party to exit the negotiations with *DIKO* and *NEO* for forming a single anti-Plan ticket.

7. Conclusions

The post elections discourse in Cyprus, framed by the horse-race, masks the actual story of the EP campaign in Cyprus, which is the challenge that the "pro-anti Plan" cleavage poses to the "right-left" cleavage. In the post-referendum era the party system was given the opportunity for realignment, and the EP campaign was the critical incident for this to happen. However, what happened instead was that the party system absorbed the pressures created by the referendum without extensive restructuring occurring.

References

Aimilianides, Achilles (2003): Parliamentary Coexistence between Greek and Turkish Cypriots (1960-1963). Nicosia: Epiphaniou.
Coufoudakis, Van (1976), Essays on the Cyprus Conflict. New York: Pella Publishing Company.
European Commission (1998): Annual Regular Reports on the Progress of Cyprus towards Accession.
European Commission (2003): Comprehensive Monitoring Report on Cyprus's Preparations for Membership.
European Court of Human Rights (1998): Loizidou v. Turkey. Judgment 40/1193/435/514. Strasbourg, 28 July 1998.
European Court of Human Rights (2001): Cyprus v. Turkey. Application No. 25781/94. Judgment. Strasbourg, May 10th 2001).
Evriviades, Marios (2003): Europe in Cyprus: The Broader Security Implications. In: The Brown Journal of World Affairs, Vol. X, No. 1, 241-256.

Hatjikyriakos, Andreas/Christoforou, Christoforos (1996): Κοινοβουλευτικές Εκλογές. Nicosia: Intercollege Publications [Parliamentary Elections].
Katsis, Aristos (2002): Οι Προεδρικές Εκλογές στην Κύπρο 1959-1998. Nicosia: Argo Publications [The Presidential Elections in Cyprus 1959-1998].
Laakso, Jaako (2002): Colonization by Turkish Settlers of the Occupied Part of Cyprus. Memorandum, AS/mg, September 20th 2002, Council of Europe, Parliamentary Assembly.
Lordos, Alexandros (2004): Can the Cyprus Problem be Solved? Understanding the Greek Cypriot Response to the UN Peace Plan for Cyprus Nicosia. No publisher mentioned.
Mazou, Zeta/Samaras, Athanassios N. (2002): Political Culture and Attitudes towards the Annan Plan: A Focus Group Survey. Athens: IMM (unpublished report).
Melakopides, Costas (1996): Making Peace in Cyprus. Time for a Comprehensive Initiative. Toronto: Centre for International Relations, Queen's University.
Melakopides, Costas (2005): Cyprus. In: Lodge, Juliet (Ed.): The 2004 Elections to the European Parliament. Palgrave Macmillan, 81-88.
Samaras Athanassios N. (2005): Candidate Image In the 2003 Presidential Elections in Cyprus. Paper presented at the International Conference on Political Marketing (Kastoria, March 31st – April 3rd 2005). CD-Rom proceedings of the conference.
Samaras, Athanassios N./Kentas, Giorgos (2005): The Cypriot Referendum of April 24th. The Greek-Cypriot Perspective. European Association of Political Consultants (Ed.): Election Time: The European Yearbook of Political Campaigning 2004. Austria: Hartlinger Consulting, 67-91.
Stokes, Donald E./Dilulio, John J. (1993): The Setting: Valence Politics in Modern Elections. In: Nelson, Michael (Ed): The Elections of 1992. Washington DC: Congressional Quarterly, 1-20.
Theophanous, Andreas (2004): The Cyprus and the EU. The Challenge and the Promise. Nicosia: Intercollege Press.
Yiallourides, Christodoulos/Panayiotis, Tsakonas (1999): Greece and Turkey after the End of the Cold War. Athens: I. Sideris.

---

[1] The authors are grateful to Simos Aggelides and Zeta Mazou as well as to the editors of this volume for their comments.
[2] After the failure of the symbiotic model of 1960, the Turkish Cypriot community sought its own independent state in Cyprus. Some observers maintain that the Turkish Cypriot demand for the division of Cyprus into two homogeneous regions, one Greek and one Turkish, was the incarnation of the old demand for "taxim", traced back in the 1950s. For a succinct analysis of the 1960s situation in Cyprus see Cufoudakis (1976) and Melakopides (1996).
[3] See EU's Accession Treaty, April 16th 2003 (Protocol 10).

[4] The full text of the final version of the Annan Plan is found on the web: http://www.cyprus-un-plan.org, retrieval October 2004.
[5] Who actually turned out to be one of the most ardent supporters of the Annan Plan during the campaign for the referendum.
[6] Poll conducted by the Research and Development Center – Intercollege between October 6th and 11th 2004 for Simerini (Greek-Cypriot newspaper). Also Lordos (2004: 34).
[7] Statement made by party president Nicos Koutsou on the 5th of June.
[8] Statement made by Stelios Pnagides, party vice president on the 7th of June.
[9] For a different interpretation see Melakopides 2005: 79.

NATIONAL CASE STUDIES ON MEDIA COVERAGE

Game is the Name of the Frame: European Parliamentary Elections in Swedish Media 1995-2004

Lars W. Nord & Jesper Strömbäck[*]

1. Introduction

On the afternoon of May 26th 2004, the Swedish Prime Minister, Göran Persson, met *Social Democratic Party* workers at an internal meeting in Stockholm. He then stressed the importance of EU affairs, and encouraged campaign workers to better mobilize in order to improve voter turnout in the forthcoming European Parliamentary election. A few hours later the same day, the Prime Minister met a great number of Nordic Public Service News Editors and told them informally that the election was "as exciting as kissing your sister". Remarkably, this story did not leak out during the election campaign (see Holmkvist 2004).

The contradictory behaviour of the Prime Minister may, however, be explained by the experiences of EP elections in Sweden so far: Nobody seems to care about the campaigns, but everyone is surprised by the election results. In the three European Parliamentary elections conducted in Sweden – in 1995, 1999, and 2004 – voter turnout has decreased significantly from an already low level: from 41.6 percent in 1995 to 38.8 percent in 1999 and the "all-time low" in Swedish election history, 37.8 percent, in the elections held in 2004. This is rather sensational in a country where voter turnout in national elections has usually been around 80-90 percent (without compulsory voting) and among the highest in democratic states.

Perhaps as a consequence of the low level of voter participation and the electoral void, surprising results have been noted in every European Parliamentary election in Sweden. In 1995 two minor parties to the left, the *Left Party* and the *Green Party*, achieved their best voter support ever by receiving 12.9 percent and 17.2 percent respectively. In 1999 the *Liberal Party* almost tripled its voter support, moving from 4.8 percent to 13.9 percent. Finally, in 2004, a completely new and rather EU-sceptical political party, *Junilistan* (*The June List*), with almost no party organization and party workers, received 14.5 percent of the votes, thus becoming the third biggest Swedish party in the new European parliament. In the same election, the *Social Democrats* faced their worst electoral outcome ever – 24.6 percent.

---

[*] Lars W. Nord, PhD. *1958. Associate Professor at Mid Sweden University, email: lars.nord@miun.se
Jesper Strömbäck, PhD. *1971. Assistant Professor at Mid Sweden University, email: jesper.stromback@miun.se

Thus, the mixture of unexciting campaigns and dramatic electoral outcomes seems to be a distinctive feature of EP elections in Sweden, and the two trends are probably intertwined. However, the prospects of substantial and significant political changes have so far not mobilized the Swedish electorate. On the contrary, the lack of public debate and interest in the campaigns for the European Parliament seems to produce rather random electoral outcomes. In this chapter about Sweden, the EP election campaigns will be further examined in a political communication context, focusing on the nature of news coverage during the campaigns.

This chapter focuses on two questions. First, how did the leading national media in Sweden frame the elections to the European Parliament in 1995, 1999, and 2004 regarding the amount of news coverage, dominating aspects, and main actors in the news? Second, how can differences in framing, if any, be explained?

2. Setting the political stage

Historically, Sweden has always been somewhat sceptical and reluctant regarding European integration. When Sweden joined the EU in 1995 it was after a referendum in which only a bare majority, 52.3 percent, was in favour of membership in the union. Almost a decade later, in 2003, Sweden rejected the idea of joining the Euro by a significant margin in another referendum where 55.9 percent voted no and 42 percent voted yes. Furthermore, a majority of the political parties, among them the ruling *Social Democrats*, are divided in their opinions about the EU.

During the ten years that Sweden has been a member of the European Union the sceptical national feelings towards Brussels have remained. Together with the other two non-Euro-member countries, Denmark and Great Britain, Sweden must be regarded as one of the most critical and cautious members of the Union. The *Social Democratic* Government's EU policy can only be described as rather lukewarm, swinging between brief periods of sudden enthusiasm (as when Sweden was chair of the EU commission during the first six months of 2001) and longer periods of EU pessimism (as around EP elections generally and the Euro referendum in 2003).

Some further observations confirm obvious party uneasiness about the EP elections. Even if all parties officially emphasize the importance of the EP elections and the ideological majority in the European parliament, at the same time, they show only a modest interest in political marketing techniques in the election campaigns. Campaign budgets for the EP election in 2004 were about one-third of national election budgets for all parties. In 2002 the parties spent about 16 Million Euro in national election campaigning altogether, compared to 5 Million Euro in the EU election campaign in 2004 (see Abramsson/Strömbäck 2004).

Furthermore, in 2004 the parties once again nominated less known politicians to the European parliament. Campaign activities, such as town hall meetings and political debates, were less common than in national elections. Modern marketing practises, such as polls, focus groups, and voter segmentation, were only used to a small extent.

3. News and the EU

In most modern democracies, citizens receive information about current events mainly through the media (see Bennett/Entman 2001; Nord 2003). This is most evident in areas where personal experiences and knowledge are limited. The EU is such an area where citizens in general depend on media coverage of institutions and decisions (see Norris 2000: 209).

Theoretically, media coverage can influence public discourse and voting behaviour in different ways. A lot of media attention paid to campaign activities may increase awareness and the salience of the elections and mobilize the electorate. On the other hand, neglecting the campaigns or a media coverage focusing on negative news might contribute to a demobilization of the electorate (see Leighley 2004).

Media coverage of EP elections has generally been characterized by a focus on domestic issues and a more or less evident "absent-minded" attitude towards the EP election campaigns. A distinctive feature of the coverage is its low degree of newsworthiness. News about the campaign is sporadic, even during the last days before the elections. When EU affairs are on the media agenda, conflicts in the news appear to dominate (see de Vreese 2003; Siune 1991).

There is a classic point of departure in news research: All news is a construction of reality (see Schudson 2003; Shoemaker/Reese 1996; Tuchman 1978). Research of the construction of electoral campaign news generally focuses on two main questions: What is the substantive focus of election news, and what is the tone of the coverage?

International studies in the field indicate a growing importance of campaign-related reporting and less news focusing on issues (see Donsbach 1999; Norris et al. 1999; Patterson 1980; Strömbäck 2004). The campaign coverage thus overly focuses on probable winners and losers (the horse race), opinion polls, and televised debates between the candidates (see Just et al. 1996; Lewis 2001; Patterson 1993). The political game and its conflicts become one of the main themes in the news coverage of the campaigns, while policy positions are neglected.

The framing of election news as a game derives partly from its correlation with the conventions of the news process and reporters' norms and values (see Patterson 1993: 60). A driving force in all journalistic work is the need for a good story to tell. Many such stories can be told within the "game frame", including speculations about the electoral outcome, losses and gains, political strategies, media performances, and mixtures of facts and interpretations. "The game embodies the conflict that journalists prize in news" (Patterson 1993: 63). On the other hand, policy problems generally do not seem to meet journalistic criteria of newsworthiness.

Game-oriented stories are easier to report, as they usually require less knowledge and research than do issue stories. The often simple and stereotypical character of game-oriented news also seems to attract "softer" media formats outside the core of traditional political journalism, thus reaching other segments of the audience. Furthermore, the game-orientation provides commentators and political analysts with good opportunities to speculate about forthcoming events and electoral outcomes (see Gulati et al. 2004: 240). Compared to political news about policy orientation and party positions, game-oriented news is perceived as more in harmony with existing reporting norms, as more useful for new media formats, and as more useful for the growing number of pundits and commentators in the media.

The concept of framing is also relevant when discussing a possible bias in political news. Despite common wisdom, repeated analyses of election news coverage have found almost no evidence of systematic ideological bias in news reporting. On the contrary, they see the news product as remarkably conform in this aspect (see Bennett 2001; Hofstetter 1976; Just et al. 1996; Patterson 1993; Schudson 2003). On the other hand, some kind of "structural bias" in political reporting is widely acknowledged (see Gulati et al. 2004). From this perspective, election news is not biased because certain parties or candidates are systematically favoured, but because probable winners are always highly newsworthy, regardless of party affiliation: "Journalistic values, though, supposedly neutral, introduce an element of random partisanship into the campaign, which coincidentally works to the advantage of one side or another" (Patterson 1993: 52). Thus, measuring the media attention that parties or candidates get might be one indicator of bias in the coverage of campaigns.

In another study, Bennett identified four news biases in mainstream media that are more fundamental than ideology: personalized news focusing on personalities and emotions, dramatized news favouring melodramatic narrative stories, fragmented news without continuity, and authority-disorder news stereotyping and simplifying societal conflicts and public debate (see Bennett 2001). This is similar to what Schudson argues in his book "The Sociology of News" (2003: 48):

> "[...] media bias derives, not from intentional, ideological perversion, but from professional achievement under the constraints of organizational routines and pressures; news organizations and routines produce bias regardless of media ownership or the outlook of individual reporters."

Accordingly, too many event-centred newscasts, too much negative news, too detached journalists, too much emphasis on tactics, and too heavy reliance on official sources distort the norm of objectivity. Thus, framing politics as a strategic game and a news coverage heavily influenced by structural rather than ideological biases seem to be typical features of modern media coverage of election campaigns. There are, however, reasons to discuss the question under what conditions this kind of election coverage is encouraged. Which factors within the political communication system may influence the character of political reporting during the EP election campaigns?

4. Media market pressure and electoral void

The concept of framing has rapidly become more prominent in contemporary media research compared to the concept of bias. One reason is that framing shifts the analytical focus from the individual level to the structural level, thus stressing the importance of the marketplace, the nature of organisations, and the assumptions of professionals (see Schudson 2003).

The media system is undoubtedly an important factor in explaining all kinds of political news coverage (see Hallin/Mancini 2004), including EP election news. Like most EU countries Sweden has moved from a public monopoly to a dualistic television system with both private and public service channels (see Kelly et al. 2004). The question as to whether public service channels in this situation become more commercialized or whether the private ones become more public service-like is not clear. However, the general trend for public service channels to loose their audiences to commercial competitors in most parts of the EU indicates a smaller audience for informative programs. The diversity of commercial stations now existing in most member states has led to fragmented TV audiences (see McQuail 2000; Tracey 1998).

Studies of commercial media coverage of US elections show that this kind of media repeatedly decontextualizes campaigns, dramatizes campaign events, and trivializes campaign issues. A comparison with non-commercial media found that public service broadcasting organizations served democracy better than did similar commercial newscasts by providing the public with somewhat more detailed accounts of actors, conditions, and events (see Wasburn 1995). Or as Patterson (2002: 253) puts it (see also Strömbäck 2005b):

"Of the many effects of commercialism on news content, none is more consequential than the media's tendency to report politics not as an issue but as a game in which individual politicians view for power."

Media structure surely matters in explaining news coverage, but the electoral context is also important. In elections characterized by distinctive political predispositions among the electorate and a high level of party identification an intensive, issue-based or even partisan coverage of the elections is more likely. The politically aware audience would then probably demand facts about the political alternatives and accept that newspapers can adopt different party positions. In such an electoral context, the media would principally mirror political positions and standpoints.

Today, however, party identification, voter turnout, and confidence in political institutions are declining in most advanced democracies (see Dalton/Wattenberg 2000; Swanson 2004). Attachments to the political system are less likely for media organizations, especially in what Hallin and Mancini (2004) characterize as liberal and democratic corporatist models of media and political systems. At the same time, the media are dealing with a less politically articulated audience. Thus, political news tends to be more superficial and dramatic in order to maintain audience attraction. Well-informed segments of citizens turn to prestigious media, while an overwhelming majority stays with mainstream media and game-oriented political news.

To sum up, political news in electoral campaigns in media-centred democracies such as Sweden could normally be expected to be game-oriented and influenced by structural rather than ideological bias. These tendencies can be expected to be stronger the more commercial the media system is and the more an election is perceived as being of less interest in the minds of voters. That is, commercial media and less interested voters probably result in less ambitious media coverage of campaigns, but also in a coverage more game-oriented and influenced by structural bias. Thus, the commercialization of the media system and the public indifference to the election campaigns probably interact in explaining some of the news frames in EP elections.

5. The Swedish studies

The nationwide media examined in the study include the two largest tabloids during the period: *Aftonbladet* and *Expressen*, the commercial *TV4*'s news programme "*Nyheterna*", and the public service television's news programs "*Aktuellt*" and "*Rapport*". The newspapers are both evening papers and can be described as up-scale tabloids both in form and journalistic style. The editorial page of *Aftonbladet* is Social Democratic and the editorial page of *Expressen* is Liberal. All media companies in the study are based in the capital Stockholm.

News coverage during the last three weeks before the EP elections was analyzed: August 28th-September 17th 1995, May 25th-June 13th 1999 and May 24th-June 13th 2004. The study includes all newsjournalism media content including vignettes, headings, pictures/graphics, or words referring to the EP elections. In the case of newspapers, this includes news articles, news analyses, and special features on news pages by employees or freelances. It does not include editorials, polemic articles, and letters to the editor, as these cannot be classified as newsjournalism. It also excludes supplements. In the case of television news, the study includes all news journalism in the main news show each day that made explicit references to the EP elections.

The material was examined using quantitative content analysis. The same method of analysis and the same coding scheme with minor changes was used in all three elections. The units analyzed were each news article in the papers and each news story in television, defined as a 'semantic entity'. In total, 917 news items were coded.

6. Not much to tell about

The results from the content analysis confirm a general trend of decreasing media coverage of EP elections during the last three weeks before Election Day. Especially the tabloids gave EP election news considerably less space in 2004 (see Table 1).

Table 1: Number of news items about the EP elections in Sweden 1995, 1999 and 2004.

	Newspapers		TV News Programs			
	Expressen (T)	Aftonbladet (T)	Rapport (PS)	Aktuellt (PS)	TV4 Nyheterna (C)	N
1995	152	189	44	30	24	439
1999	100	153	30	25	18	326
2004	31	48	30	25	18	152
Sum	283	390	104	80	60	917

Note: T = Tabloid; PS = Public Service; C = Commercial

As shown in Table 1, the number of news items about the EP elections has decreased significantly from the first to the third EP election. In fact, slightly more than one-third of the news stories 'remain' after three elections. The results also support the assumption that media coverage was most extensive during the first election. All five news media analyzed here produced the most news in 1995. This is followed by a general slowdown in media interest, particularly in the tabloids where EP election news almost ceased to exist in 2004.

The number of news items about the EP elections can be compared to the number of news items about the general election in Sweden in 2002. During the last three weeks before election day in 2002, the same news media published 615 news items (see Strömbäck 2004: 162). That is, four times as many news items about the general election in 2002 than about the EP election in 2004. This clearly shows that the Swedish media view and treat EP elections as second-order elections.

When it comes to broadcast news, the tendency is more of status quo than of decline, and this is true for all three analyzed news programmes. The drop occurred between 1995 and 1999, while the number of news features remained the same between 1999 and 2004. However, the commercial channel still produces less EP election news than its main public service competitors.

The dramatic decline in tabloid coverage is notable and could be described as somewhat of a turning point in political print journalism in Sweden. Traditionally, links between the parties and newspapers have been well developed, and even in a contemporary 'post-party press era' most newspapers have covered political affairs extensively (see Strömbäck 2004; Stúr 2004). Tabloid journalism in Sweden is historically both connected with selling sensational news and, to some extent, with educating and informing the public about what is going on in society. Election news has often been front-page news so far, but in

2004 the EP elections almost disappeared from the tabloid news agenda. How could this happen in five years?

One explanation could be the increased commercialization of newspaper markets in Sweden (see Alström/Nord 2003). In recent years the biggest tabloids have faced problems with maintaining profitability and market-shares, due to changed media consumption patterns as well as to successful newcomers in the tabloid market, such as the freely distributed *Metro*. Competition has definitely increased and has probably affected the mix of news in the tabloids. In a situation where the battle for the audience becomes harder, it is relatively easy to understand why a "forgotten election" also becomes "forgotten news" in the tabloids.

The same increased market pressure does not seem to be as evident in television as in the newspapers. The more stable results regarding TV news coverage of the EP elections are plausible, as the most dramatic market changes in Swedish television occurred during the deregulation era of the 1990s, when public service media lost its former monopoly and was faced with commercial competitors. Since then, however, TV news seems to have settled into a rather stable dualistic broadcast media system, where converging trends are one distinctive feature. Public service news cannot be too boring as this will result in a reduction in its viewers, but at the same time commercial news cannot be too entertaining as this will then jeopardize its credibility among its viewers, who are used to watching serious and informational news (see McQuail/Siune 1998).

7. Horse races and dark horses

Regarding the character of the media coverage this chapter focuses on the extent to which the EP election news are game-oriented and the occurrence of structural bias in the news. Can the EP elections mainly be described as horse races with predestined winners and losers in the headlines? Does the number of game-oriented stories and winner stories correlate with the increased market orientation of the media system?

In the content analysis, news items have been categorized whether they are issue-oriented, game-oriented, or person-oriented. Issue-oriented news items are focused on the policies the parties have, the contents of different issues, or on actual issue-related problems in the "real world", and what solutions the parties suggest to solve these problems. In game-oriented news items, politics is framed as being all about winners and losers in the quest for voters and political power. Political power is framed as an end in itself, and not as a means to political reforms. Thus, game-oriented news items are focused on opinion polls, the campaigns and how they are conducted, the strategies behind the parties' actions, and what the parties are doing in order to win more votes. The language of war, horse race, battle, or sports is a salient feature in these news items. Finally, person-oriented news items are focused on politicians as individuals, what they stand for, battles and conflicts between individual politicians, or scandals involving individual politicians. Thus, these news items treat individual politicians as being more important than both the political parties and the substance of politics.

In the analysis, the dominating aspect of the whole news item was coded. The result confirms an increased share of game-oriented EP elections news in all media analyzed here (Table 2).

Table 2: Game-framed articles/news features (percentage of total EU coverage)

	Newspapers		TV News Programs			
	Expressen (T)	Aftonbladet (T)	Rapport (PS)	Aktuellt (PS)	TV4 Nyheterna (C)	All
1995	37	17	43	31	44	34
1999	44	43	43	62	67	52
2004	71	60	67	69	79	69
All	51	40	51	54	63	52

Note: T = Tabloid; PS = Public Service; C = Commercial. Percentages are rounded off. N = 917

The share of game-oriented election news has more than doubled between the first EP election in 1995 and the third election in 2004. The same trend can be observed in all media. Increasingly, game-oriented news coverage is most significant for the newspapers in the study, but the general level of game-oriented news is higher in television. Most game-oriented news items are to be found in the commercial channel. A majority of the overall EP election coverage could be described as game-framed, except for the tabloid *Aftonbladet,* where the relatively low figure can be explained by the overwhelming issue-oriented campaign coverage during the first election in 1995.

Obviously, game is the name of the frame when characterizing EP election news in the Swedish media studied here. Tabloids are giving less space to EP election news and are at the same time focusing more on the political game and the power play when covering the campaign. Thus, tabloid coverage becomes more fragmented, rhapsodic, and superficial. The same effect appears in TV news, even if the reduction of the coverage over time is less pronounced in the television news. Leaving aside different market pressures, both tabloids and TV news tend to focus on the election game with most attention being paid to opinion polls, electoral outcome speculations, and campaign strategies. Game-frames have become more common in the coverage for all media studied here, even though the tendency is slightly more pronounced in commercial media than in the public service media.

The third and final aspect of media coverage analyzed here regards the framing of probable winners in EP election news coverage. While ideological bias in political news is both easy to discover and incompatible with professional journalistic values, structural bias is in harmony with widespread perceptions among journalists and citizens about newsworthiness principles and story-telling practices. In other words: "The winner takes it all, and everybody likes to know the winner."

While well in touch with contemporary journalistic standards, such structural bias can distort the election debate in significant ways. One-sided media coverage undermines public discourse and the quality of the electoral campaign in terms of diversity and scrutiny. The risk is even more obvious when the quantity of the media coverage is low and mainly consists of opinion polls and speculations about the electoral outcome. Thus, it is interesting to study the coverage of the perceived winners in the three EP elections in Sweden. They can all be described as "dark horses" in the electoral horse race as they advanced in the polls from very modest positions at the beginning. In the first elections in 1995 both the *Left Party* and the *Green Party* were the final winners, in 1999 the *Liberal Party* played this role, and in 2004 the completely new party, *Junilistan*, surprised everyone by gaining around 15 percentage of the votes. Therefore, it is interesting to analyze the coverage of these winners in tabloids and broadcast news, as one operationalization of structural bias in the news. Table 3 shows the percentage of news items where the final winning parties in each election were the dominating actor.

Table 3: Structural bias in news items (percentage of coverage of final winning party)

	Newspapers		TV News Programs			
	Expressen (T)	*Aftonbladet (T)*	*Rapport (PS)*	*Aktuellt (PS)*	*TV4 Nyheterna (C)*	All
1995	14	5	20	20	19	16
1999	14	8	6	3	19	10
2004	19	22	20	27	37	25
All	16	12	15	17	25	17

Note: T = Tabloid; PS = Public Service; C = Commercial. Percentages are rounded off. N = 917

Of course, the question of balanced reporting is always delicate. As with the extent to which the news are game-oriented, there are no distinctive guidelines regarding how the media should report. If, for example, opinion polls are presented, then likely winners and losers have to be pointed out. An equal representation in news selection is also inappropriate, as it does not reflect political reality. On the other hand, news stories that frequently and repeatedly use the most common stereotypes about the political actors could certainly have negative effects on the quality of the public debate.

However, the overall pattern in Swedish EP election news coverage is contradictory in this regard. Slightly less than a fifth of the news is devoted to final election winners. This is not a very high figure. The *Liberal Party* in 1999 received particularly modest attention in the news coverage, and the two parties gaining large victories in 1995 were not generally favoured in the media.

Somewhat more alarming with regard to the coverage of likely winners is the coverage of the 2004 election. It is obvious from the content analysis that the new party *Junilistan* received a great deal of attention in all the media analyzed here. The increased coverage of a likely winner was most significant in the tabloid *Aftonbladet* and in the commercial TV channel. In *TV4 Nyheterna*, a completely new political party was the dominating actor in more than one-third of the total election news coverage.

The overall picture given here indicates that the coverage of winners in EP election news is not only a matter of election campaign context and the degree of market-orientation in the media system. More research is required within this area, but it is probably important to consider the character of the likely winner when possible structural bias is discussed. If the likely winner is a well-established party or candidate with a rather fixed position on the political scale, structural bias is less likely in the news. But if the likely winner is a political newcomer, who has populist perspectives and anti-establishment political attitudes, structural bias is more likely to occur in the news. This is equivalent to less examined voting theories suggesting the importance of voter's sense of curiosity or novelty in choosing a candidate or a party (see Newman/Perloff 2004: 20).

To sum up, the results confirm the decline in the number of articles and news features. There is also convincing evidence of an increasing game-orientation in election news coverage within all kinds of media. Both the reduced quantity of EP election news coverage and its increasing game-orientation can probably be explained by growing media commercialization, increasing media competition, and audience targeting. On the other hand, the focus on likely winners is not a general consequence of low-key elections and media commercialization but also depends on the perceived newsworthiness of different political actors. The horse race is undoubtedly a common theme in the news coverage, but the more black the "dark horse" running is, the more likely it is to really attract the news media.

8. The "evil circle" of communication in EU campaigns

The study of Swedish EP election news coverage in 1995, 1999, and 2004 shows that media interest in the elections is low, and the number of published news items tends to shrink for each election, especially in the tabloids. Media efforts to improve public discourse by producing more information and promoting discussions about political alternatives are rare. Journalistic values about monitoring, scrutinizing, and explaining seem to be less articulated in comparison to national elections (see Strömbäck 2004, 2005a).

On the other hand, media is just one important player in the political communication system. The shortcomings in the EP election news discussed here are probably the result of an "evil circle" where politicians play down EP campaigns as they know they do not attract media and voters, and the media frame EP campaigns in a certain way as the campaigns are marginalized by parties and candidates and do not attract the audience. Reciprocal perceptions among politicians and journalists thus seem to explain more about the low interest in the election campaigns than do oversimplifications about undemocratic media offering people too little information about the EP (see Abramsson/Strömbäck 2004). The framing of EP election news is basically grounded on market considerations and professional values, but is also affected by the missing public debate about the EU in general in Sweden.

Still, the tone of EP election news coverage is probably mostly due to specific media conditions. As already noted, less news is produced, but at the same time it becomes more game-oriented, focusing on winners and losers rather than on the issues at stake. Furthermore, a structural bias in EP election news seems to occur when a completely new political party enters the scene, in the sense that they tend to receive a disproportionate share of the news coverage.

These results should be seen in the light of the growing commercialization of the Swedish media system, where especially tabloids and commercial TV channels have become more market-driven. Thus, political news is often dramatized and personalized in order to attract a mainstream audience in a more competitive media environment.

The prospects for a revitalization of EP election campaigns in Sweden look gloomy. EU politicians and officials may continue to talk about the big project. That, however, will not make much of a difference as long as national politicians mainly regard EP elections as second- or third-order national elections rather than as true European affairs, as long as growing commercialization and preconceived ideas about their irrelevance form the media framing of the elections, or as long as a majority of the voters do not care about what is going on.

There may, however, be changes in public opinion in the future. Since fall 2004 the new EU commission has a new first deputy commissioner, Margot Wallström, who is responsible for promoting confidence in the EU project among citizens. She is from Sweden and a well-known political reformist and successful power player. But ironically she was actually appointed by the same Prime Minister who thinks EU elections are as exciting 'as kissing your sister'.

References

Abramsson, Erika/Strömbäck, Jesper (2004): EU-parlamentsvalet. En god eller dålig nyhet? Sundsvall: Centre for Political Communication Research? [The Election to the European Parliament. Good or Bad News?].
Alström, Börje/Nord, Lars W. (2003): Den skånska modellen. Sundsvall: Centre for Polical Communication Research [The South-Sweden Newspaper Model].
Bennett, W. Lance (2001): News. The Politics of Illusion. New York: Longman.
Bennett, W. Lance/Entman, Robert M. (2001): Mediated Politics. Communication in the Future of Democracy. Cambridge: Cambridge University Press.

Dalton, Russel J./Wattenberg, Martin P. (2000): Parties without Partisans. Political Change in Advanced Industrial Democracies. Oxford: Oxford University Press.
de Vreese, Claes H. (2003): Framing Europe. News Production, Content and Effects in a Cross-National Perspective. Amsterdam: Aksant.
Donsbach, Wolfgang (1999): Drehbücher und Inszenierungen. Die Union in der Defensive. Mediatisierung der Politik. In: Noelle-Neumann, Elisabeth/Kepplinger, Hans Mathias/Donsbach, Wolfgang (Eds.): Kampa. Meinungsklima und Medienwirkung im Bundestagswahlkampf 1998. München/Freiburg: Karl Alber, 40-77 [Donsbach: Screenplays and Stagings. The Union Party on the Defensive. Mediatization of Politics. In: Noelle-Neumann et al.: Kampa. Public Opinion and Media Effects in the National Election Campaign 1998].
Gulati, Girish J./Just, Marion R./Crigler, Ann N. (2004): News Coverage of Political Campaigns. In: Kaid, Lynda Lee (Ed.): Handbook of Political Communication Research. Mahwah: Lawrence Erlbaum, 237-256.
Hallin, Daniel C./Mancini, Paolo (2004): Comparing Media Systems. Three Models of Media and Politics. New York: Cambridge University Press.
Hofstetter, C. Richard (1976): Bias in the News: Network Television Coverage of the 1972 Election Campaign. Columbus: Ohio University Press.
Holmkvist, Leif (2004): Mediechefer höll tyst om Perssons utspel. In: Resumé, No. 27-33 [Newseditors Kept Quiet about Perssons' Comments].
Just, Marion R./Crigler, Ann N./Alger, Dean E./Cook, Timothy E./Kern, Montague/West, Darrell M. (1996): Crosstalk. Citizens, Candidates and the Media in A Presidential Campaign. Chicago: University of Chicago Press.
Kelly, Mary/Mazzoleni, Gianpietro/McQuail, Denis (2004): The Media in Europe. The Euromedia Handbook. London: Sage.
Leighley, Jan E. (2004): Mass Media and Politics. A Social Science Perspective. Boston: Houghton Mifflin Co.
Leroy, Pascale/Siune, Karen (1994): The Role of Television in European Elections. The Cases of Belgium and Denmark. In: European Journal of Communication, No. 9, 47-69.
Lewis, Justin (2001): Constructing Public Opinion. How Political Elites Do What They Like and Why We Seem to Go Along with It. New York: Columbia University Press.
McQuail, Denis/Siune, Karen (1998): Media Policy. Convergence, Concentration and Commerce. London: Sage.
McQuail, Denis (2000): Mass Communication Theory. London: Sage.
Newman, Bruce I./Perloff, Richard M. (2004): Political Marketing. Theory, Research and Applications. In: Kaid, Lynda Lee (Ed.): Handbook of Political Communication Research. Mahwah: Lawrence Erlbaum, 17-44.
Nord, Lars W. (2003): Dagstidningarna och demokratin. Stockholm: Tidningsutgivarna [Daily Newspapers and Democracy].

Nord, Lars W./Strömbäck, Jesper (2003): Valfeber och nyhetsfrossa. Politisk kommunikation i valrörelsen 2002. Stockholm: Sellin [Political Communication in the 2002 National Election].
Norris, Pippa/Curtice, John/Sanders, David/Scammell, Margaret/Semetko, Holli A. (1999): On Message. Communicating the Campaign. London: Sage.
Norris, Pippa (2000): A Virtuous Circle. Political Communication in Postindustrial Societies. Cambridge: Cambridge University Press.
Patterson, Thomas E. (1993): Out of Order. New York: Vintage Books.
Patterson, Thomas E. (2000): The United States: News in a Free-Market Society. In: Gunther, Richard/Mughan, Anthony (Eds.): Democracy and the Media. A Comparative Perspective. Cambridge: Cambridge University Press, 241-265.
Schudson, Michael (2003): The Sociology of News. New York: WW. Norton & Co.
Shoemaker, Pamela J./Reese, Stephen D. (1996): Mediating the Message. Theories of Influences on Mass Media Content. New York: Longman.
Siune, Karen (1991): EF på dagsordenen. Aarhus: Politica [EU on the Agenda].
Smith, Julie (1995): Voice of the People. The European Parliament in the 1990s. London: The Royal Institute of International Affairs.
Strömbäck, Jesper (2004): Den medialiserade demokratin. Om journalistikens ideal, verklighet och makt. Stockholm: SNS Förlag [The Mediated Democracy. On the Ideals, Practices and Power of Journalism].
Strömbäck, Jesper (2005a): In Search of a Standard. Four Models of Democracy and Their Normative Implications for Journalism. In: Journalism Studies, Vol. 6, No. 3, 331-345.
Strömbäck, Jesper (2005b): Commercialization and the Media Coverage of Swedish National Elections in 1998 and 2002. Paper presented at the American Political Science Association's Annual Conference. Washington, September 2005.
Stúr, Elisabeth (2004): Partier och val i pressen. Sundsvall: Centre for Political Communication Research [Parties and Elections in the Newspapers].
Swanson, David L. (2004): Transnational Trends in Political Communication. Conventional Views and New Realities. In: Esser, Frank/Pfetsch, Barbara (Eds.): Comparing Political Communication. Theories, Cases and Challenges. Cambridge: Cambridge University Press, 45-63.
Tracey, Michael (1998): The Decline and Fall of Public Service Broadcasting. Oxford: Oxford University Press.
Tuchman, Gaye (1978): Making News. A Study in the Construction of Reality. New York: The Free Press.
Wasburn, Philo C. (1995): Democracy and Media Ownership. A Comparison of Commercial, Public and Government Broadcast News. In: Media Culture & Society, Vol. 17, No. 4, 647-677.
Weaver, David/McCombs, Maxwell/Shaw, Donald L. (2004): Agenda-Setting Research: Issues, Attributes and Influences. In: Kaid, Lynda Lee (Ed.):

Handbook of Political Communication Research. Mahwah: Lawrence Erlbaum, 257-282.

Continuity and Change:
The 2004 European Elections in the Netherlands

Claes H. de Vreese[*]

1. Introduction

Dutch "euro-politics" is generally speaking predictable and stable. The elections for the European Parliament are considered unexciting, second-order events in which the incumbent government parties typically loose to the opposition parties, the political campaigns are low-key, and the media attention is minimal. However, though much of this still holds true, several things were different in the 2004 campaign for the European Parliament in the Netherlands. Most importantly public opinion and support for European integration is changing in the Netherlands, and reluctance and euro-scepticism is on the increase which was apparent in the June 2005 Dutch rejection of the European Constitutional Treaty. Moreover, during the European Parliamentary elections in June 2004, Dutch politics was recovering from one of its most tumultuous periods.

In this chapter these changes are first briefly discussed to set the scene for the 2004 European Parliamentary elections. The chapter then describes and analyses the turnout level and the election results. Next, the campaigns and the role of the media are discussed. The chapter concludes with a discussion of the Netherlands and European integration in the future. We begin with an outline of the context in which the elections took place.

2. The electoral context 2004

2.1 Changes in public opinion

The Netherlands is one of the founding fathers of what is today called the European Union. Public support for membership in the Netherlands is high and stable at 70 plus percent, which lies 15-20 percentage points above the overall EU average (see Eurobarometer 2004). However, recent polls suggest that the level of support is on the decline (see Eurobarometer 2004). Looking at *support for the common currency*, the euro consistently had an overall EU-wide approval rating of approximately 50 percent. Between 1998 and 2002 (when the currency was introduced) a considerable increase in the approval rating was matched by an

---

[*] Claes H. de Vreese, PhD. *1974. Professor and Chair of Political Communication and Scientific Director of The Amsterdam School of Communication at the University of Amsterdam, email: c.h.devreese@uva.nl

equal drop in the opposition to the currency so that the average was about 70 percent by the time the currency was introduced in the twelve countries (see Eurobarometer 2002). Dutch support for the euro was 71 percent in 2002. Turning to public *support for the 2004 enlargement of the Union*, the overall EU average was about 50 percent in 2002. Dutch support was roughly at the EU-average, with 58 percent favouring the enlargement. Several observers have noted that the debate about the EU and European integration has developed in a critical direction in the 1990s (see e.g. Harmsen 2004). There is increasing awareness that there could be a discrepancy between national interests and the current trajectory of the European Union. The fact that the Netherlands is the largest net contributor per capita to the EU budget has fuelled scepticism.

2.2 Changes in the political environment

The 2004 European elections took place in the aftermath of the dramatic general elections of 2002 and 2003. The 1998 re-elected 'Purple Cabinet' with the *Labour Party* (*PvdA*), the *Liberals* (*VVD*), and the *Center Democrats* (*D66*) fell prior to the dramatic May 2002 national elections. The rise and assassination of the populist Pim Fortuyn affected these elections profoundly. The three-party coalition government with the *Christian Democrats* (*CDA*), the *List Pim Fortuyn* (*LPF*), and the *Liberals* (*VVD*) that emerged out of the elections fell in October 2002. The new general elections in January 2003 again reshaped the political landscape. The *LPF* lost a lot of votes, and the *Labour party* made a recovery under a new party leader. The *PvdA* became the second largest party after the *Christian Democrats*. Lengthy coalition negotiations between the *PvdA* and the *CDA* ended in April 2003. A new coalition government was eventually formed between the *CDA*, the *VVD*, and the *D66* and took office in May 2003. The 2002 and 2003 general elections were the most dramatic elections in recent Dutch political history. They demonstrated dissatisfaction with previous consensus-driven governments, and the elections showed the volatility of a sizeable part of the Dutch electorate (for different interpretations of the *LPF* support see van der Burg 2003; Zwan 2004).

2.3 Changes in the media landscape and political reporting

The Dutch media landscape has changed significantly over the past two decades. As in most other European countries, there is increasing concentration and competition in both press and broadcasting. Moreover, ownership of television and cable is predominantly foreign, advertising revenue is stagnating, readership of newspapers is declining, and the audience size for public broadcasting is shrinking (see Brants 2004). While increased competition in the news market may lead to a marginalization of political content, the Dutch media, in particular television, have maintained high levels of political coverage, especially during national elections (see van Praag/Brants 2005). However, the share of television news during national elections that focuses on content and policy issues seems to be declining in favor of news focusing on polls and horse-race aspects of the campaign (see van Praag/Brants 2005: 83). Moreover, journalists' attitudes towards politicians are undergoing change. News organizations rely less on political actors for news and have attained more autonomy, and there is a higher degree of agenda-setting stemming from the news organizations (see de Vreese 2001).

In terms of media coverage of European affairs, Dutch news is characterized by a virtual absence of 'Europe' in the news (see de Vreese 2002). The de facto editorial policy to neglect European elections, despite initial plans to cover them more comprehensively, points toward a more pragmatic approach where elections news is evaluated on equal terms with other available news. While the absence of coverage of the European elections in the Netherlands may underline the fact that European elections are considered second-order elections, this is much less so the case in other countries. Important cross-national differences in the television news coverage of European elections emerge when looking at public broadcasters in other countries. In Britain and Denmark, for example, greater editorial effort is invested and more time is devoted to European elections despite a comparable competitive news environment (see de Vreese 2003).

3. Turnout

The participation rate in the 2004 elections rose for the first time since 1979 to 39.1 percent. This was an almost ten percentage point increase from the 29.8 percent turnout rate in 1999, but is still below the EU-wide turnout average. Dutch turnout at EP elections had dropped from 57.8 percent in 1979 to less than 30 percent in 1999, the second lowest turnout in the EU-15. Several factors help to understand the significant increase in turnout in 2004 (though it should still be noted that turnout is only about half as high as the general election turnout). These include the renewed interest in politics, the state of the economy, a greater differentiation between the political parties campaigning in the elections, and the emergence of anti-integrationist, populist parties.

First of all, the elections took place in the aftermath of the general elections discussed above. The incumbent government had a stronger ideological profile as a centrist-right government than the previous centrist coalition governments. The ideological cleavages were therefore more pronounced, and there was spillover effect from the relatively high levels of political interest that surrounded the national elections.

Second, the state of the Dutch economy affected turnout. After years of prosperity and economic growth, the Netherlands was hit comparatively hard by the recession between 2001 and 2004. This resulted in negligible GDP growth rates, strikes, and mass demonstration on issues of social security and welfare. Experience shows that such unfavourable economic conditions function as a motivation to vote and thus increase turnout (see e.g. Tufte 1978).

Third, turnout was up as a function of presenting more of a choice to the electorate. The 1999 and previous Dutch contests in European elections were characterized by a limited choice, with most political parties appealing to centrist voters and all parties campaigning with a rather pro-European message (see van der Eijk/Franklin 1996). In 2004, there were policy differences, and the liberal *VVD* party even offered a rather Euro-sceptic perspective, led in part by the Dutch Commissioner Bolkestein whose 2004 book 'The Borders of Europe' fuelled a discussion in the party and led to a campaign slogan saying 'The *VVD* is for Europe, but with borders/limitations' (same word in Dutch). On the other side of the political spectrum, the *Socialist Party (SP)* campaigned to increase transparency in the EU.

Fourth, along the same line of observations about the increased presence of choice, a number of 'critical' messages were available, most notably expressed in Paul van Buitenen's *Europa Transparent List*. Van Buitenen himself gained public awareness (and popularity) as the whistleblower who in 1998 contributed to the revelations about the financial improprieties in the Santer Commission, which led to the fall of the Commission in March 1999.

4. Results

The election outcome shows that in 2004 Dutch voters behaved as "they always do" in European elections, at least to some extent, but there were also some new developments. In short, the incumbent government parties were 'punished' by the electorate (as predicted by the second-order election perspective) (see Reif/ Schmitt 1980). The opposition won (relative to the last general election), and likewise smaller parties performed better, in particular the *Europa Transparent Party* that won 7 percent of the vote and 2 seats in the European Parliament.

Table 1 presents an overview of the 2004 election results as well as the results of the 1999 EP elections and the 2003 general election for the Parliament (Tweede Kamer) for the sake of comparison. The distribution of seats in 2004 was affected by the reduction in number of 'Dutch seats' in the EP from 31 to 27 due to the post-EU-enlargement. The seat distribution is based on proportional representation where seats are allocated according to the national average vote share. Voters could express a preference for an individual candidate on the party lists.

The incumbent *Christian Democrats (CDA)* suffered a small loss in the 2004 elections. Their vote share was down about 4 percent from the previous general elections and 2.5 percent from the 1999 European elections. The *CDA* was nonetheless the strongest party in the 2004 elections and suffered a much smaller defeat than their second largest coalition partner, the *VVD*. This was partly due to a

"Prime Minister Bonus" that ensures visibility of the party in the media. Given the overall reduction of Dutch seats in the EP, the *CDA*, however, lost two seats and now has seven seats in the EP.

Table 1: Election outcome of European elections 1999 and 2004 and National elections 2003.

Party	Label	EPE 2004	EPE 1999	National elections 2003	Seats in EP 2004
Christian Democratic Appeal CDA	Christian democrats	24.5	27.0	28.6	7
Partij van de Arbeid PvdA	Social democrats	23.6	20.1	27.3	7
Volkspartij Vrijheid en democratie VVD	Liberals	13.1	19.6	17.9	4
Groen-links	Green-left	7.4	11.9	5.1	2
ChristenUnie/ SGP	Calvinist	5.9	8.7	3.7	1
Democrats 1966 D66	Centrist progressive	4.2	5.8	4.1	1
Socialistisch Partij SP	Left-socialists	7.0	5.1	6.3	2
Europa Transparent	Van Buitenen	7.3	--	--	2
Lijst Pim Fortuyn LPF	List Pim Fortuyn	4.4	1.8	1.3	0
Other		4.4	1.8	1.3	--
Turnout		39.1	29.8	80.0	
Total seats					27

Source: Ministry of Domestic Affairs (Kiesraad).

The coalition partner, the liberal *VVD*-party, lost 6.5 percent compared to the 1999 European elections and 4.7 percent compared to the 2003 national elections. The number of seats in the EP went down from 6 to 4. Most of the loss was attributed to two internal party crises. The first involved former and current *VVD* leaders Dijkstal and van Artsen who fought over the *VVD* leadership style. The second involved the resignation of the Secretary of Education after a public row with the Minister. However, for a longer time already the *VVD* had been losing ground in the polls.

The smallest government coalition partner, the *Centrist Democrats (D66)* lost 1.6 percent of the vote and their representation in Parliament was reduced from two to one seat. This result follows a general decrease in support for the party, also in national politics, but was at the same level as the general elections in 2003.

The *Labour Party* (*PvdA*) was by far the strongest opposition party. It did less well (by about 4 percent) than in the previous general elections, but it increased its vote share by 3.5 percent compared to the 1999 European elections. The 2004 result was a continuation of the success of the new party leader, Wouter Bos, who increased the party's vote share in the general elections in

2003 to 27.3 percent, up from the all-time low in 2002 where the *PvdA* merely received 15 percent.

The *Green Party* (*GroenLinks*) lost significantly going down from 11.9 percent in 1999 to 7.4 percent in 2004. Despite this loss that cost the party two of the four seats, the 2004 elections brought the first electoral increase after three consecutive domestic election losses. *Europa Transparent* was, with its 7.3 percent of the vote, a de facto winner of the elections. The list was headed by Paul van Buitenen, a former employee of the European Commission and known for uncovering fraud in the Commission. The magnitude of the party's gain was rather unexpected and was interpreted as a voters' expression of dissatisfaction with the political establishment and their reluctance to increase European integration.

The *Socialist Party* (*SP*) received 7 percent of the vote, up from 5.1 percent in 1999 and 6.3 percent in the general elections in 2003. The party thus continued the positive trend from recent national and European elections. The *Christian Union/ Political Reformed Party* experienced a decline in support from 8.8 percent in 1999 to 5.9 percent in 2004. This reduced their share of seats from three to two. Finally, the *List Pim Fortuyn* continued its freefall after the height of popularity in the general elections of 2002. The *LPF* gained 2.6 percent of the vote and received no seat in the Parliament.

5. The campaigns and the media

The level of political and campaign activity was higher in 2004 than in 1999 (see de Vreese 2005). During the 2004 campaign the miserable turnout record of 1999 was often recalled. As mentioned above, the low level of media attention for the European elections in the Netherlands has been a reflection of the virtual absence of engaged political campaigning. However, media coverage of European elections has been comparatively modest in the Netherlands ever since the first elections in 1979 (see Siune 1983). In 1999, The Amsterdam School of Communications Research conducted an analysis of the most widely watched television news programs in the – at that time – 15 EU member states during the two weeks leading up to the 1999 European elections. The results showed that the average time spent on the election on national television news for all EU member states was 8 percent. Belgium, Britain, Germany, Ireland, and Spain devoted even less than 5 percent of the news to the elections. Austria, Denmark, Finland, France, Greece, Italy, and Sweden were somewhat above average, devoting 8 percent to 13 percent of the news on European elections, while television news in Portugal outdid all other countries with 27 percent of the news dealing with the elections (see de Vreese et al. 2005).

In 1999, Dutch news media stood out for their lack of coverage of the elections. The two main national television news shows (*"NOS Journaal"* and *"RTL Nieuws"*) both carried one story on the evening before the elections reminding the electorate of the elections and the predictions of a low turnout. In 2004 the Dutch television news programs increased their coverage of the European elections substantially (see Figure 1).

Figure 1:   Visibility of European elections on national television news 1999 and 2004

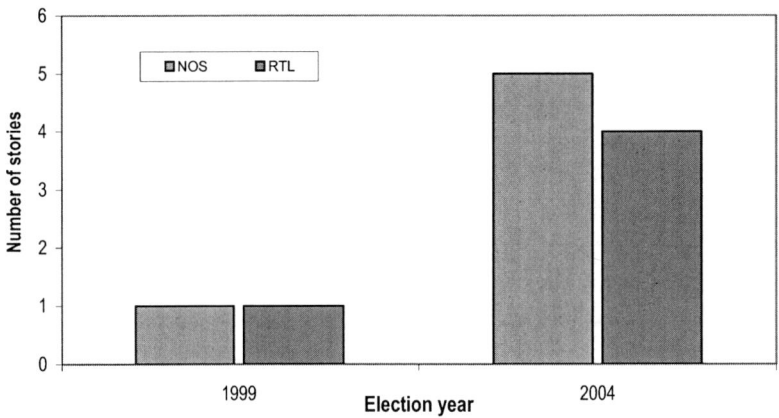

Note: Number of stories about the European elections in the main evening television news in the two weeks leading up to the elections. Source: European election media study.

"NOS Journaal" carried five election stories and *"RTL Nieuws four"*. These numbers represent a significant increase compared to 1999. The Netherlands remains, however, a country with comparatively low levels of media attention – measured as main television evening news – for European elections (see de Vreese et al. 2005). The Head of the Political Unit at *"NOS Journaal"* said about the 2004 elections:

"We still have the problem of explaining why this is important. In that sense the challenge is the same as in 1999 and earlier. Again, the elections fell in a very 'news rich' period. [...] In hindsight we should have done more about what happens in other European countries and what the elections mean there. But such stories take a lot of explanation. This was easier when reporting the enlargement where there were clear events and developments."

An indication of the relative importance of the elections in 2004 compared to 1999 was the fact that the elections made the front page of most national dailies on June 11th, which was one day after the elections (see Figure 2).

The Dutch media coverage in 2004 was often idiosyncratic to the national context – and focused on themes such as voter apathy and disinterest and the emergence of euro-scepticism. Previous elections have led broadcasters in Europe to pursue one of two strategies in relation to European elections (see de Vreese 2003). News organizations either neglected the elections (like the Dutch news in 1999), providing minimal coverage, or they set an individual agenda driven, for example, by self-commissioned polls (such as e.g. Danish news organizations in 1999). In 2004 these dynamics were still at work, but the absence of readily defined and contestable political issues resulted in voter disinterest in the election, which in turn became one of the key election stories. The media attention to the 2004 elections was in part sparked by the emergence of lukewarm or anti-integrationist parties and movements. As argued elsewhere, such activities and the presence of conflict are well-known and well-established prerequisites for issues and events to become news (see de Vreese et al. 2005).

Figure 2: Front pages of national newspapers June 11th

As part of an on-going research project on the 2004 European elections at The Amsterdam School of Communications Research, journalists and campaign managers were interviewed about the particular challenges inherent to campaigning and covering European elections. A Dutch journalist summarized the difficulty in covering the elections: "There is a lack of themes to address, the politicians are not high-profile, and domestic politicians often neglect 'Europe' as a topic."

The campaign managers of the political parties highlighted different aspects with regard to how they had organized the campaign. However, they spoke with one voice about several factors that determine the success of political campaigning in European elections in the Netherlands. Most campaign managers felt that the elections did not receive top priority from the political party. This was expressed by rather modest campaign budgets and difficulties in mobilizing the local party organizations for canvassing and campaign activities. This problem was accentuated by the perception of a moderately interested electorate (see de Vreese 2005). The campaign managers agreed on the difficulty in getting access to the news, in particular national television news, with stories about the election and candidates. Finally, several campaign managers pointed out that they felt challenged to deal with a rather EU-sceptic attitude of journalists.

6. Conclusion

The 2004 European elections in the Netherlands continued the long-standing tradition of low-key, second-order elections. However, the campaign and the election results were interesting for a number of reasons: First, turnout was up almost ten percentage points to 39 percent, second, parties campaigning with anti-integration and EU-skeptic messages gained a substantial share of the vote, and third, media attention for the campaign increased significantly compared to the 1999 European elections.

The turnout increase from 29.8 percent to 39.1 percent was the outcome of several factors. First of all, *politics* was a societal concern in the aftermath of the dramatic 2002 and 2003 general elections. This sparked an increased awareness in politics (however, also increased cynicism, according to some observers). Second, there appeared to be more of a *choice* for the electorate. A number of traditional pro-European parties, such as the *VVD*, included EU-sceptic messages in their campaigns and the socialist *SP* along with the *Europa Transparent* movement campaigned with EU-critical messages, too. This arguably increased turnout and also led to a different election outcome in which the 'critical' parties and movements obtained a substantial share of the vote and several of the 'Dutch' seats in the European Parliament. The election outcome, however, was by no means a landslide election. The pattern of European elections as second-order elections was continued. The governing parties (*CDA-VVD-D66*) were 'punished' by the electorate, whereas the opposition parties improved their performance relative to the last general elections.

The campaigns by the political parties were more vigorous than in 1999, and the increased campaign engagement – in addition to the factors discussed above – resulted in an increase in visibility of the elections in the media. The two main evening Dutch television news programs devoted nine stories to the European elections in the last two weeks leading up to the elections which is a noteworthy jump from the two stories broadcast in 1999 (see de Vreese et al. 2005). This increase was in part a function of a more exciting election (compared to 1999), in part a response to the absence of coverage of the European elections in 1999 which then resulted in disagreement about the importance of 'Europe' as a theme in news and current affairs. However, some of this 'new' news attention went to topics such as the lack of public interest and critical, anti-integrationist standpoints. While Europhiles are likely to be worried by news focussing on apathy and EU-resistance, this coverage is still both potentially more mobilizing and more democratic than either a uniform pro-European coverage or a complete neglect of a cornerstone of democracy, namely elections. In sum, the 2004 European elections, while continuing a number of well-known features of these elections, also had more characteristics of a *real* election than some of its predecessors.

In the aftermath of the 2004 elections, the issue of European integration was given a more central position on the Dutch political and media agenda. The Dutch Presidency of the EU in fall 2004 culminated in the December summit in which a compromise was reached to initiate negotiations about Turkish EU membership in 2005. In 2005 the Dutch government took on the challenge of holding a national referendum on the ratification of the EU Constitutional Treaty. Public opinion on this issue was divided and the referendum ended in a No vote. In addition to key predictors of support for European integration, such as economic evaluations, assessments of the government's performance, and anti-immigration sentiments (de Vreese/Boomgaarden 2005), the campaign and the media's coverage of the referendum issue were crucial to understand the dynamics of the referendum and the No outcome.

References

Blumler, Jay G. (1983): Communicating to Voters. Television in the First European Parliamentary Elections. London: Sage.

Brants, Kees (2004): The Netherlands. In: Kelly, Mary/Mazzoleni, Gianpietro/ McQuail, Denis (Eds.): The Media in Europe. The Euromedia Handbook. London: Sage, 156-156.

Brug, Wouter van der (2003): How the LPF Fuelled Discontent. Empirical Tests of Explanations of LPF Support. In: Acta Politica. International Journal of Political Science, No. 38, 79-83.

de Vreese, Claes H./Boomgaarden, Hajo G. (2005): Projecting EU Referendums. Fear of Immigration and Support for European Integration. In: European Union Politics, No. 6, 59-82.

de Vreese, Claes H. (2001): Election Coverage – New Directions for Public Broadcasting: The Netherlands and Beyond. In: European Journal of Communication, No. 16, 2, 155-179.

de Vreese, Claes H. (2002): Framing Europe. Television News and European Integration. Amsterdam: Aksant Academic Publishers.

de Vreese, Claes H. (2003): Television Reporting of Second-Order Elections. In: Journalism Studies, Vol. 4, No. 2, 183-198.

de Vreese, Claes H. (2005): Campaign Styles in the 2004 European Elections. Paper Presented at the Conference 'European Governance: Challenges for the Future'. Emory University, Atlanta, GA, April 10th–12th 2005.

de Vreese, Claes H./Lauf, Edmund/Peter, Jochen (2005, in press): The Media and European Parliament Elections. Second-Rate Coverage of a Second-Order Event? In: van der Brug, Wouter/van der Eijk, Cees (Eds.). European Elections and Domestic Politics. Lessons from the Past and Scenarios for the Future. University of Notre Dame Press.

de Vreese, Claes/Banducci, Susan/Semetko, Holli A./Boomgaarden, Hajo G. (2005): "Offline". The 2004 EP Elections on Television News in the Enlarged Europe. Manuscript accepted for publication in Information Polity.

Eijk, Cees van der/Franklin, Mark (1996): Choosing Europe. The European Electorate and National Politics in the Face of Union. Michigan: University of Michigan Press.

European Commission (2004). Standard Eurobarometer: First Results. (Report No. 62) Brussels, Belgium: Directorate-General X.

Harmsen, Robert (2004): Euroscepticism in the Netherlands: Stirring of Dissent. In: Harmsen, Robert/Spiering, Menno (Eds.): Euroscepticism: Party Politics, National Identity and European Integration. Amsterdam: Rodopi.

Reif, Karl-Heinz/Schmitt, Hermann (1980): Nine Second Order National Elections. A Conceptual Framework for the Analysis of European Election Results. In: European Journal of Political Research, No. 8, 3-44.

Siune, Karen (1983): The Campaign on Television. What Was Said and Who Said It? In: Blumler, Jay G. (Ed.): Communicating to Voters. Television in the First European Parliamentary Elections. London: Sage, 223-240.

Tufte, Edward R (1978): Political Control of the Economy. Princeton: Princeton University Press.

van Praag, Philip/Brants, Kees (2005): Gefascineerd door horse race. In: Brants, Kees/van Praag, Philip (Eds.): Politiek en media in verwarring. De verkiezingscampagnes in het lange jaar 2002. Amsterdam: Het Spinhuis, 66-91 [van Praag/Brants: Fascinated by Horse Race. In: Brants/van Praag: Politics and Media on the Drift. The Election Campaign of the Long Year 2002].

Zwan, Arie van der (2004): How the LPF Fuelled Discontent. A Comment. In: Acta Politica. International Journal of Political Science, No. 39, 79-83.

More or Less Europe: Media Coverage of European Parliamentary Elections in the Czech Republic[1]

*Petr Kopáček**

1. Introduction

Only several weeks after Czech's EU-accession at the May 1st 2004 together with nine other new members of the EU, the European parliamentary elections were held in the Czech Republic in June. The primary focus of this paper is on how (printed) media covered this campaign, more specifically, which topics linked to EP elections attracted the attention of the media, for which parties and politicians space was provided, whether there were any significant differences among dailies and also political parties, to which extent Czech EP elections were virtually "European" elections, and to which extent they centred on domestic political issues, which role political figures played, etc. The method of quantitative content analysis was used to investigate these issues and questions.

The political campaign preceding the European Parliamentary Elections in the ČR was overshadowed by the EU accession of the Czech Republic on May 1st. After this historical event had taken place, approximately from mid-May, the Czech printed media began to inform more about issues linked to the EP elections. Although the European parliamentary campaign had actually started several months before when the list of candidates was formed by the major parties, it was officially launched on May 26th – in accordance with legislation – 16 days before election day. From this time on, the political campaign also started on public TV and national radio.

This paper mainly focuses on those political powers in the ČR, which had a realistic chance to be successful and win some seats in the EP. These parties and movements were the *Czech Social Democratic Party* (*ČSSD*), the *Civic Democratic Party* (*ODS*), the *Christian Democrats-Czechoslovak People's Party* (*KDU-ČSL*), the *Union of Liberty-Democratic Union* (*US-DEU*, which was united with several other small factions in a political group called *Union of Liberal Democrats*), the *Communist Party of Bohemia and Moravia* (*KSČM*), the *Association of Independents and European Democrats* (*SNK-ED*), the *Movement of Independents* (*Nezávislí*), and the *Green Party* (*Strana zelených*).

As the title of this paper indicates, the attitude toward European integration and its character is a source of major political cleavage among major parties.

---

* Petr Kopáček, PhD. *1979. Charles University in Prague, Institute of Political Science, email: Kopacek.Petr@seznam.cz

The par-ties of the governing coalition (leftist *ČSSD*, conservative and catholic *KDU-ČSL*, liberal *US-DEU*)[2] declared their "pro-Europeanism" and consequently support activities to promote European integration. In contrast, the major opposition party *ODS* often argued against the EU and criticize diverse aspects of European integration or the EU.[3] Similarly leaders of the second strongest opposition party – *KSČM* – often raised questions concerning national interests in relation to the EU and the necessity to ensure the sovereignty of the ČR.[4]

Interestingly, two political movements called "Independents", which both succeeded in gaining seats in Strasbourg, had almost completely different views on the EU. The first one, *"Nezávislí"*, stressed – similar to the *ODS* – national interests and unfavourable accession conditions for the ČR. The leader of this movement even admitted that in the referendum he opposed the joining of the ČR to the EU. In contrast, the *Movement of Independents and European Democrats* had the opposite attitude to the EU, and leaders of this political camp used arguments of federalism to justify their conviction.

In contrast to some other European states, the political sphere in the ČR was lacking clear consensus about the attitude to European integration and its future. While in other states " [...] issues linked with EU and Europe are vanishing as one of division in politics" (Dürr et al. 2004: 84), in the ČR the attitude to the EU has become more and more a battlefield among political parties, which stress the differences among them concerning this issue and use it as a political instrument.

In summary, the European election campaign was also the duel between "the Euro-optimistic political camp" and the "Eurosceptic political camp". Paradoxically, according to many public election polls, the electorate of the anti-European *ODS* had a much stronger Euro-optimistic orientation than the electorate of the traditionally Euro-optimistic *ČSSD*, whose supporters often declared their fear of the social consequences of the accession to the EU (e.g. an increase of the unemployment rate.)[5] Consequently, it also illustrated the positions of the Czech voters and the fact that issues connected with the EU and European integration were not so significant for the electorate in the ČR as it was in "old member states". People voted *ODS* not because of its attitudes and opinions linked to the EU, but in spite of them.

2. Electoral system and results

2.1 Electoral system

The Czech electoral system to the European elections (which is very similar to the system of elections to the Czech national parliament) is a system of proportional representation using the d'Hondt electoral formula. But in contrast to national elections, only one constituency for the whole state exists in EP elections. Preferential voting is also practiced in the ČR, even the candidate from the bottom of the list can become a member of the EP if he or she gains more than five percent preferential votes of all valid votes gained by his or her party.

Despite this, the Czech electoral system is unique in one aspect. The ČR was the only member state of the EU which held EP elections on two consecutive days: Friday the 11th and Saturday the 12th.[6] Many politicians were motivated to run for office in these elections because the personal costs for running in the elections were minimal, anybody willing to run in the nationwide EP elections only had to pay 15.000 crowns (roughly 500 Euro). The threshold for gaining a seat in the EP is 5 percent of all votes. Any citizen of the ČR or another state of the EU who is at least 18 years old is entitled to vote and is eligible for political office if he or she is at least 21 years of age. Participation in European elections is not compulsory in the ČR, and a person may not simultaneously hold both a mandate in the EP and one in the national parliament.

The legislation concerning the conduction of European elections does not differ much from the regulations for elections to the Czech national parliament. The campaigns, which start 16 days before polling day (in comparison with other member states, this is relatively short, Brandová/Šaradín 2004: 181), "must be run honestly and fairly, it is strictly forbidden to publish any false information about candidates, political parties, movements, or coalitions which participate in elections".[7] It is also prohibited to publish any results of public election polls starting three days before election day until the end of elections. During the official campaign, each political group running has the right to equal broadcasting time for its advertising on public TV and national radio. The total time for free political propaganda is 28 hours.[8] Also, there are restrictions concerning the propaganda activities of candidates in a certain distance from the polling station on election day.

2.2 Results of EP elections

The number of parties and movements participating in the European election reached 31 (which was the highest number in the entire EU except for Spain), and they struggled to obtain one or more of the 24 seats reserved in the EP for the ČR. According to many public pre-election polls, it had been clear long before elections that coalition parties (*ČSSD, KDU-ČSL, US-DEU*) would encounter total defeat. Especially the strongest social democratic party (*ČSSD*) expected a steep decline of public support, and preference of the *US-DEU* even dropped to a mere 1-2 percent. In contrast, the strongest opposition party *ODS* looked forward to an obvious victory, extreme leftist *KSČM* to its political reinforcement, and two political groups of *Independents* also had a realistic chance to gain some seats in the EP (see Šaradín 2004: 238).[9]

The 24 seats in the EP allotted to the ČR were divided among six political parties and movements. The results of the elections corresponded with public election polls, and similiarly to most of the European states, the governing parties were defeated by the political opposition, in case of the ČR by Eurosceptic right-wing *ODS* and extreme leftist *KSČM*. Finally, the *ODS* gained 30 percent votes and nine seats in the EP, the KSČM 20 percent votes and six seats.

The elections can be characterized as a total "political funeral" for the governing parties, even worse than what happened in other states. Almost scandalous, the strongest party *ČSSD* gained less than 9 percent of the votes and only two seats (this party, which had won the Parliament elections in 2002 with 30 percent votes, received even less of the ballot than the *Association of Independents and European Democrats*, which was considered to be marginal up to this time.). The *KDU-ČSL* gained 9.6 percent and two seats, the *SNK-ED* got 11 percent and three seats in the EP, and almost the same number of votes was gained by the Independents with 8.1 percent and two seats.[10] As generally expected, the threshold of 5 percent was too high for the governing *US-DEU*. The *Union of Liberal Democrats*, which consisted of several small political groups including the *US-DEU* (it was surely the big marketing mistake), gained only 1.7 percent. This was even less than in the case of the *Green Party* (3.1 percent).

The media played the key role in this total defeat of the *ČSSD*, because longtime internal tensions inside the *ČSSD* and arguments among party wings leaked through to the media. Shortly before elections, the new minister of health and member of the *ČSSD* publicly stated his intention to sue his predecessor and also a member of the *ČSSD* for disadvantageous contracts and wasting public funds. Moreover, some well-known persons such as former Minister of Foreign Affairs and President of the General Assembly of the UN, Jan Kavan, or the leading social democratic expert on foreign policy, Jan Laštůvka, gave up their candidacy because their position on the list of candidates was too low. Paradoxically, as it will be shown below, social democrats could not complain about a lack of space in the media.

The frustration of the people with politics and the current political elite was also demonstrated by their great and unexpected support for two political groups of "Independents", which previously had no representation in Parliament but with only fractional political power. As a result, voters elected a charismatic populist and extremely egoistic man, Vladimír Železný; his colleague on the same list, Jana Bobošíková, former moderator of a political talk show, also became a new member of the EP.[11]

On the other hand, the second political group of Independents, the "*SNK-ED*", who was also not represented in central legislative bodies, got even more votes than Železny. Unlike Železny's *Independents*, this political group found support among more educated and higher income social groups with an optimistic attitude toward European integration. Both Josef Zieleniec, former minister of foreign affairs in Václav Klaus's governments and former ambassador in the Near East, Jana Hybášková, were elected to the EP on the list of the *SNK-ED*.

It is really interesting (but typical for the Czech socio-political and cultural context 1) that some parties participating in the European elections in the ČR were virtually meant as a joke, e.g. "Balbínova poetická strana", which was in fact a group of artist-friends, another peculiar group running was "Helax-Ostrava se baví" (formed by employees of a local radio station with the same name.). It is remarkable that both groups together gained over 17.000 votes, more than 0.7 percent of all valid votes and almost half of the votes gained by a "serious" party, namely the *Union of Liberal Democrats*.

The dissatisfaction of the Czech people with the political situation was demonstrated by very low turnout, which fell below the record level of 30 percent (28.3 percent). Only three new member states had even lower voter activity. Czech turnout dropped more than 17 percent below the average turnout in the entire EU (45.5 percent). Several reasons for such a low turnout in the ČR were found: EP elections were generally considered to be dominated by domestic issues and to be less important than national elections, where the results directly affect the executive formation. People also felt frustrated with politics and had a growing distrust of politicians. It is clear that a positive or negative attitude to European integration did not play the crucial role in people's decisions whether vote or not (see Linek 2004: 304).

3. The EP campaign in printed media

3.1 Methodical approach

This paper centres on quantitative content analysis and interpretations of mined data. The sample of this research includes five major Czech dailies which cover the whole ideological (right-left) political spectrum and also represent different reader target groups: *"Lidové noviny"* (*LN*) is a right-wing oriented daily, *"Mladá fronta"* (*MfD*) is a right and central wing oriented newspaper, *"Hospodářské noviny"* (*HN*) is considered to be a very prestigious daily without any clear ideological preferences and with a particular focus on the economy, and *"Právo"* is the biggest left-wing oriented daily. Finally, a tabloid called *"Blesk"*, is the biggest daily in the Czech Republic with more than 522.000 sold copies per day.[12]

Copies of roughly three weeks created the sample of this analysis. The five mentioned printed newspapers were analyzed from Monday May 17th 2004 to Saturday May 22nd 2004, from Tuesday June 1st 2004 to Saturday June 5th 2004, and finally from Monday June 7th to Saturday June 12th 2004. The basic unit of this content analysis, was a selected article, which was often divided into smaller parts to facilitate quantification (the space included photographs and tables but no political cartoons). The space devoted to specific categories representing several indicators which were chosen for this analysis was measured.

3.2 Media coverage and issues

The most space (in absolute numbers) for news and commentaries linked to EP elections and political campaigns was provided by *Lidové noviny*. However, the economic newspaper *Hospodářské noviny* reached top place in reference to space devoted to EP elections in relation to total space reserved for domestic reporting and commentaries (pages with foreign news, economy, sports etc. were excluded), namely 18.2 percent. In comparison, the portion of the space reserved for the EP elections on the domestic-news and commentary pages of all five dailies was 13.5 percent of the total space reserved for domestic news and commentaries.[13]

Table 1: Genres used for reporting about EP elections in major dailies (percent of coded space)

Genre	Právo	Mladá fronta Dnes	Lidové noviny	Hospodářské noviny	Blesk	Total (relative numbers in %)	Total (absolute numbers in mm²)
Reporting about EP elections	56.3	59.2	78.9	65	65.4	67.1	519.798
Commentary about EP elections	28.8	19.4	18.8	14.8	9.2	18.9	146.062
Interview about EP elections	14.9	21.4	2.2	20.1	25.4	14	108.777

Focusing only on the analyzed contents of the selected dailies, it is obvious that the greater part was reserved for reporting (average of 67.1 percent), almost 19 percent of the space was filled with commentaries, and the remaining 14 percent contained interviews about EP elections (see Table 1). For instance, the leftist daily *Právo* published many commentaries about EP elections, on the other hand, the tabloid *Blesk* preferred interviews much more. In contrast, this genre was almost completely absent in the contents of *Lidové noviny*.

Which topics linked to EP elections attracted the attention of the newspapers? This survey basically confirmed the widespread feeling of experts (and even journalists) that media coverage was almost completely limited to non-program questions[14] and topics linked to EP elections, such as specific candidates, speculations about the results, prediction of turnout etc.

Roughly 12.5 percent of the space in the newspapers devoted to EP elections appears to deal with program questions (if such categories such as attitudes concerning the future of European integration, social matters, national interests, etc. are included). Surprisingly, the tabloid *Blesk* had the highest portion of program issues, namely more than one fifth (see Table 2). The reason is probably its critical judgement of the Czech accession conditions for joining EU. This survey also confirmed the position of *Hospodářské noviny* (*HN*) as a respected economic daily in many aspects in contrast to the tabloid *Blesk*. *HN* also devoted more than one-fifth of its space linked to EP elections to program topics, and unlike *Blesk* also paid great attention to questions connected with the future of Europe. According to this survey, *LN* showed only minimal interest in party programs.

Table 2: Space devoted to specific topics in major dailies (percent of coded space)

Topics	Právo	Mladá fronta Dnes	Lidové noviny	Hospodářské noviny	Blesk	Total (relative numbers in %)	Total (absolute numbers in mm²)
Political agitation and propaganda [without any reference to program]	17.2	13	4.5	9.3	2,6	10.5	81 538
List of candidates [forming, personal information about candidates etc.]	1.1	26.3	33.3	19.8	3.1	21.7	168 383
Prediction of the results [public opinion polls etc.]	19.7	11.3	6.3	1.9	1.2	8	61 772
Prediction of turnout	2.8	0.7	5.3	7.1	0.4	4.1	31 826
Speculations about consequences of election results	2.2	8.1	5.2	4.1	0	4.7	36 862
Competition among parties	6.3	3.4	0.2	1	12.5	2.8	21 452
Conflicts inside parties	2.5	3.1	1.8	0.4	5.3	2.1	16 166
Technical and administrative issues related to elections and voting act	7.4	3.2	3	3.5	1	3.7	28 683
Scandals and corruption	6.3	7.6	3.3	4.4	23.4	6.2	48 100
Curiosities closely linked to elections	2.7	1.8	1.4	0	2.6	1.4	10 983
EP elections abroad [including references to European parties]	3.8	0.4	15.3	17.6	0	10	77 686
Information about EP [its role, competences etc]	0.1	5.3	7.4	5.5	2	5	39 256
Political program for EP elections	0.5	1.5	2.9	6.9	10.5	3.8	28 881
Social Europe, solidarity	5.3	0	0	5	11.3	2.7	21 276
The future of EU and form of European integration	2.8	4.6	0.7	7.3	0	3.4	26 404
National interests	6.5	3.3	1.9	2.4	0	2.8	22 185
Voting act [run of elections]	8	6.3	2.8	0	1.6	3.6	27 534
Others	4.7	0	4.5	3.6	3.6	3.4	25 650

The rest of the space in dailies was occupied by topics linked to the list of candidates (e.g. presentation of candidates, their knowledge and competencies – almost 22 percent); the printed media frequently covered the political campaign of the parties and many forms of their agitation activities, e.g. rallies (10.5 percent), but without any mention of the political programs.

This situation was also the result of the efforts of the parties themselves, whose free political agitation on public TV and national radio was often criticized in printed media and called dull, lacking any new ideas, and with little influence on voter mobilization (LN 27.5.2004: 3). Only the TV spots prepared by the *Green Party*, which ironically attacked President Klaus (and former long-time leader of the *ODS*) and also the leader of the *Independents*, Železný (MfD 20.5.2004: A/2), were held in high regard by the printed media.

Nevertheless, the media actively criticized not only TV spots but the whole way how the EP campaign was run and called the campaign slogans uninspired. Journalists directly (or indirectly through the mouths of interviewed experts) accused all political parties of neglecting the European dimension of these elections, noted the absence of acceptable candidates, the lack of clear ideas and political inspiration for ordinary citizens (MfD 11.6.2004: A/2, 4.6.2004: A/9).

Other frequent issues covered in the media were predictions of turnout, speculations about possible consequences of these results on the stability of the government (e.g. headlines such as "Coalition is heading for Euro-disgrace" Právo 21.5.2004: 8), and in particular the prediction of the election results.

Due to the fact that a clear victory of the opposition *ODS* and reinforcement of the *KSČM* were generally expected because of the political disaster of the governing parties, the media speculated with pleasure about possible scenarios of political development after the expected election failure of the government. Because of permanent tensions inside the government and even inside the strongest party *ČSSD*, there were even predictions of the fall of the government.[15]

In this context, the confident *ODS* called the EP elections a "referendum about current government and its legitimacy", which representatives of the governing parties including Prime Minister Špidla strictly refuted and declared the continuance of the current coalition regardless of election outcome. However, a short time before elections, the government celebrated its two year anniversary of its empowerment, which was a great opportunity for the media to analyze its activities in detail. And this evaluation was not very favourable for the government (see HN 10.6.2004: 3; LN 10.6.2004: 3).

In the EP campaign, the governing parties faced strong critique from the opposition parties, especially the *ODS* (*Independents*, *KSČM* as well), which blamed them for neglecting national interests and declared that the conditions of EU accession were unfavourable. Especially the *Social Democrats* (*ČSSD*) and *Christian Democrats* (*KDU-ČSL*) opposed in European terms. During the campaign they emphasized their political positions in the European political sphere, proclaimed their exclusive relationships with political "friends" in the EP (*Social-Democrats – PES*) etc. The leaders of the *ČSSD* used this political card very often not only against the *ODS*, but also against the *KSČM* and *Independents*. They were accused of having no "political allies" in the EP and no contacts with existing political powers in the European sphere (see Právo 11.6.2004: 1, 5). The *KDU-ČSL* even made reference to its future membership in the EP fraction of the *Christian-Conservative Party* group *EPP-ED* through its major slogan for their campaign: "*Christian Democrats* are the strongest negotiators." Despite these serious political tensions, however, it is surprising how little space was reserved for topics linked to "national interests" in the dailies.

Besides the fact that program issues took up only a small amount of the space reserved for the EP elections in printed media and the fact that the media paid much more attention to the election contest itself (and many forms of political agitation), the media coverage of political programs linked to EP elections also lacked the "European dimension". The character of the campaign was based on domestic problems, which had no clear link to European matters and the future influence of Czech EP members (see Brandová/Šaradín 2004: 179.). Furthermore, the opposition ODS chose the critique of domestic policy as practised by the current government as the "pillar" of its EP election campaign.

This can be blamed on both the media (by focusing mostly on non-program issues and curiosities linked to elections) and politicians who often gave up actively informing about their program (they gave their opinions about "European questions" almost entirely in interviews with the media). Such topics as the "European constitution", "EU membership of Turkey", or "common security and foreign policy" were almost totally ignored by both media and politicians.

Nevertheless, according to some analyses, several "European topics" – such as social and employment policy, the budget policy of the EU, or the advantages of European cohesion policy – appeared in the Czech EP campaign.[16] However, this survey showed that these topics were almost completely ignored by printed media.

3.3 Media coverage and actors

In the case of the EP elections, it is obvious that the actors (initiators of an action) of the political campaign were mostly politicians or political figures (81.2 percent). In addition to that, voters appeared regularly as actors in the context of repeated opinion polls. The most variable from this point of view was coverage of *Hospodářské noviny*, which also provided relatively much (above-average) space to experts (see Table 3).

It is also typical that the attention of the media was highly attracted by former Czech president, Václav Havel, who became a "political celebrity". His recommendation of the *Green Party* and some candidates from the list of candidates of the *Union of Liberal Democrats* was seriously analyzed and often commented on the pages of the dailies (see MfD 10.6.2004: 1).

If the type of actor is limited to only the political figures (relevant political parties and leaders of their list of candidates, see Table 4), it is clear that except for the category of politicians in general (44 percent), the largest space in the dailies was devoted to the social democratic *ČSSD* (9.6 percent). Of course, leftist daily *Právo* paid special attention to *ČSSD* as well. The space of other parties in relative numbers correspond with their support among the people (at least according to public election polls) and their relative position in state administration or parliament (the second biggest party, the *Civic Democratic Party – ODS*, was given 7 percent of the space).

Table 3: Space allotted to different types of actors in major dailies (percent of coded space)

Type of actor	Právo	Mladá fronta Dnes	Lidové noviny	Hospodářské noviny	Blesk	Total (relative numbers in %)	Total (absolute numbers in mm²)
Politician, political figure	78.9	86.7	84.2	71.3	93.8	81.4	630 281
Voters*	8.6	2.2	4	12.6	0.4	6.2	47 929
Citizens**	0.5	4	6.8	6.8	0	4.9	37 666
Representatives of institutions, administration or offices	5.2	3.2	2	3.4	0.6	3	22 929
Celebrities***	0.8	1.5	2.7	0.4	1.9	1.5	12 068
Czech experts	1.2	0	0	2.6	0	0.8	6 463
Foreign experts	0	0	0	1.3	0	0.3	2 426
Government, governing coalition	1.8	1.2	0	1	0	0.8	6 144
Firm	3	0	0	0.5	3.2	0.8	6 005
Others	0	1.2	0.3	0	0	0.4	2 726

* The people who strongly support any party or who are decided to participate in elections, e.g. visitors of a campaign rally.
** The people in a more general meaning, e.g. respondents in public election polls.
*** Including former Czech president Václav Havel, who publicly expressed his political preferences for these elections.

But one striking exception existed: "*The Independents*", led by Vladimír Železný, former owner of the biggest private TV station in Central Europe (*TV NOVA*). Due to his controversial personality and his scandals,[17] more was written about this political group in the dailies than about much better known and respected parties. The vice leader of the *Independents*, Jana Bobošíková, made clever use of her previous experiences as a TV star and was also very visible in the media (for instance, a report about her visit in a coal mine).

Moreover, from the figures of Table 4 it is possible to estimate the role which leaders of different political camp were assigned to play within media's coverage. Especially in the case of Železný and his camp of "Independents" it is obvious that articles dealing exclusively with him take up the majority of the newspaper space reporting about his political party. A similar case is Zieleniec's movement "*SNK and ED*". In contrast, the leader of the *ČSSD*, Rouček, did not belong to frequently mentioned persons by the media, which is also an indication of his weak leadership.

Finally, it is interesting that references to the *SNK* and Zieleniec were linked to negative evaluations, the same as in the case of the Independents and controversial Železný. In contrast, the *Green Party* and its leader Patočka can be regarded as favourites of printed media with above-average positive evaluation.

Through inquiries and interviews, the dailies examined leaders' knowledge of the EU, EP, their language skills, etc. (see e.g. MfD 10.6.2004: 3).[18] However, their opinions on the future of the EU and European questions, such as common foreign and security policy, were demanded by the media very rarely (see Table 5). The majority of space devoted to these interviews was not related to the program and European problems; questions were usually limited to speculations about the results, about the form of the political campaign, etc. (with some exceptions in interviews with Zieleniec).

Table 4: Space devoted to specific political actors
(percent of coded space and their evaluation in major dailies)

Name of actor	Právo	Mladá fronta Dnes	Lidové noviny	Hospodář-ské noviny	Blesk	Total (relative numbers in %)	Total (absolute numbers in mm^2)**	Evaluation of actor		
								positive	negative	neutral
ČSSD	21.9	13.4	2.2	6.3	21.9	9.6	59.983	7.9	25.9	66.2
References to the leader of the ČSSD Rouček	5	6.7	0	1.3	6.7	3	18.970	0	13.5	86.5
ODS	5.1	6.3	2.7	11.3	19.6	7	43.847	0	20.4	79.6
References to the leader of the ODS Zahradil	2.2	3.7	0.6	1.3	3.8	1.9	12.066	0	0	100
KSČM	10	7.4	1.3	9.8	4	5.8	36.582	6	36.1	57.8
References to the leader of the KSČM Ransdorf	4.9	0	0	2.3	4	1.5	9.307	0	0	100
KDU-ČSL	6	8.8	2.6	9	5.2	6	38.122	0	20.1	79.9
References to the leader of the KDU-ČSL Roithová	4.4	3.9	0	1.3	2.8	2	12.564	0	0	100
Union of Liberal Democrats	2.8	5.1	3.8	4.7	6.6	4.4	27.591	0	17.9	82.1
References to the leader of the ULD Rögnerová	1.6	4.1	0	4.1	6.6	2.5	15.993	0	0	100
SNK and ED	1.3	1	1	8	14.1	3.5	22.166	0	46.2	53.8
References to the leader of the SNK and ED Zieleniec	1.3	0.7	0.7	2	14.1	2%	12.856	0	48.7	51.3
Independents	6.1	11.8	5.3	5.5	10	7.4	46.047	0	56	44
Reference to the leader of the Independents Železný	4	9.2	5	3	10	5.8	36.286	0	63.4	32.9
The Green Party	9.2	4	2	2.1	0	3.4	21.011	10.3	0.8	88.9
Reference to the leader of The Green Party Patočka	4.5	1.2	0.7	1.3	0	1.4	8.990	0	32	68
Politicians in general*	32	26.5	71.2	41	7.2	44.5	278.087	0.6	24.6	74.8
Other political actors	6.3	15.4	7.7	2	11.3	8.3	52.036	4.7	29.8	65.5

* Meaning politicians in general, as the whole social group, or in those cases where it was impossible to distinguish between individual politicians or parties inside one single article.
** The sample is smaller than in other indexes because of the fact that non-political actors were not counted.

The attention of the printed media was also attracted by the likelihood of the election success of extreme leftist *KSČM*, which in the last parliament elections got more than 18 percent of the votes.[19] In this context, the *MfD* chose a unique solution: the chief editor publicly declared that his daily would not seek an interview with the leader of the *KSČM* and would also provide no space for their paid advertisements (see MfD 1.6.2004: 10), but would publish this information for the leaders of the other major parties.[20]

Table 5: Topics linked to major political actors in five analysed dailies (percent of coded space)

Topics	The percentage of space devoted to major political actors									
	ČSSD	ODS	KSČM	KDU-ČSL	Union of I.D.	SNK and ED	Independents	The Green Party	Politicians in general meaning*	Others	Total
Political agitation and propaganda [without any reference to program]	16.3	18.2	20.9	21	14.2	0.5	7.6	27.9	5.2	22.2	10.5
List of candidates [forming, personal information about candidates]	20.9	3.4	5.6	26.2	27.4	4	14.7	16.4	37.8	24.8	21.7
Prediction of the election results [public opinion polls etc.]	1.,8	8.8	5.5	15.4	4	4.5	5.3	0	13.6	1.3	8
Speculations about consequences of election results	13	3.5	21.6	0	20	0	0	0	4.3	0	4.7
Contest among parties	2.4	10.7	0	0	1.5	22.2	3.3	16.8	1	0	2.8
Conflicts inside parties	6.9	0	0	25.6	0	0	0	4	0.5	0	2.1
Scandals and corruption	6.6	3.6	0.5	1.8	1.8	25	46.1	0.8	1	1	6.2
Political program for EP elections	4.5	21.5	6.5	6.8	1	8.5	3	16.2	1.5	1.4	3.8
Social Europe, solidarity	6.9	0	31.6	0	11	0	5.5	0	0	0	2.7
The future of EU and form of European integration	1.5	2	2.4	3.3	3.2	4	5.4	17.9	4.2	1.7	3.4
National interests	7.3	12.5	0	0	6.1	0	0	0	0.5	5	2.8
EP elections abroad [including references to European parties]	0.5	4.9	0	0	0	0	0	0	16.4	21.8	10
Others	11.5	10.9	5.5	0	9.6	31.3	8.9	0	14	20.6	21.2

* Meaning politicians in general, as the whole social group, or in those cases where it was impossible to distinguish between individual politicians or parties inside one single article

It is not surprising that the printed media also reflected the strong focus of the *ODS* on national interests, but the dailies also paid great attention to the program of the *ODS*. The political program of the *Green Party* also attracted the attention of the media, especially its (optimistic) view of the future of the EU. However, the political programs of the major parties were rather vague, too declarative, without any new ideas and clear message, they contained more promises (often unrealistic ones) than clear positions and conceptions. The parties relied much more on mobilizing supporters through their campaign and through political agitation than trying to convince voters on the basis of their program (see Buchal 2004: 232).

The issue "competition among parties" was often connected with the *SNK* and also the *Green Party*. The EP election campaign avoided any serious clashes among political actors, maybe with the exception of the rare attacks by representatives of established "old" parties, especially the *ODS*, against independent political powers (who were regarded as politically inexperienced, without any clear political profile). Because of the similarity in names, there also existed permanent tensions between two political camps which declared their independency from "old" political powers: the *SNK* and the *Independents* (MfD 22.5.2004: A/1). But what appeared even more regularly in the dailies was the *KDU-ČSL* with its inner-party conflicts.[21]

In the case of the *KSČM* and *Union of Liberal Democrats*, the media focused especially on the speculations about the consequences of election results. The *KSČM* was often considered a possible member of the future governing coalition. In contrast, the *Union of Liberty* was generally expected to be thrown out of the government after the probable election failure of the governing parties. Because of a controversial politician, Vladimír Železný, it is not surprising that almost half of the space reserved for his *Movement of Independents* was filled with scandals.

The printed media informed very often about issues and events with controversial (one could also say "marginal") informational value and social importance, e.g. about different kinds of promotional activities of parties, such as the election of Miss *KDU-ČSL* ("Miss dvacítky", MfD 11.6.2004: A/2) or the visit of a retirement home by Dolly Buster. In addition, what is striking is the extent to which the media informed about political activities of such "respected" political persons as former porno star and leader of a so-called "*Independent Erotic Initiative*" – Dolly Buster. The media devoted more space to such events as low-classed printing of small portion of ballots than many other much more important issues. The political campaign in the analysed dailies was reduced to speculations about the election results and their possible consequences.

Journalists were more interested in the political contest and the salary of future European members of parliament than in the role and competences of the European parliament. Since the EP elections were held in the ČR for the first time, it was really remarkable that the Czech printed media paid so little attention to the role and future of the EP (perhaps with the exception of *Hospodářské noviny*).[22]

Paradoxically, as mentioned above in reference to TV promotions, the media often criticized the form of the campaign and referred to the lack of program issues and European topics in the campaign. Candidates were also very often criticized in dailies and blamed for promising things which they could not hold – due to the competences of the European parliament (see Hn 7.6.2004: 2; Právo 31.5.2004: 5). From all analysed dailies, Hospodářské noviny did the most serious reporting about EP elections. It published many analyses and articles with information about a broad range of issues connected with the EP elections, it published more information about the EP itself and its role, it regularly published reports about other EU countries, and journalists interviewed politicians about their visions for the EU.

4. Conclusion

Paradoxically, the first European elections in the ČR also led to the reinforcement of Eurosceptic forces, besides the *ODS* the *KSČM* and Independents were also successful so that most of the new Czech members of the EP were surely not very enthusiastic about the EU (17 of a total of 24, that makes 81 percent). The results of the election as a whole could be summarized as a historical victory of (Eurosceptic) opposition parties and a total defeat of (Euro-optimistic) governing parties.

The European elections in the ČR were unique in one respect. Unlike the rest of the EU, where many governmental parties were also defeated, the catastrophic defeat of the coalition parties and the total triumph of the conservative-liberal opposition in the ČR consequently led to the fall of the government, because Prime Minister Vladimír Špidla was forced to resign after losing his support inside his party – the *ČSSD*. In this "political disaster" the media played more an indirect than a direct role, especially in the sense of reflecting long-term internal tensions in the *ČSSD*, underlining the fact that the *Social Democrats* lacked a charismatic, generally recognized and well-known leader on its list of candidates, that their political campaign had no clear message etc.[23]

In all of Europe, there were two phenomena that were also characteristic of former EP-campaigns: "The different election campaigns remain very much dominated by national specificities and the respective domestic situation" and the fact that "even campaign themes that directly relate to the EU often have little to do with the European Parliament and its core competence" (Preview of the 2004 European Parliament Elections results of an Epin survey of national experts: 2). Similar to the rest of Europe, the Czech EP election campaign was also dominated by domestic issues, problems, and perceptions – from the point of view of media, politicians, and also voters. In other words, instead of a contest among parties with different views on the character and tasks of European integration, the role of the ČR in Europe etc., the EP election campaigns were virtually confined to the political competition among political powers and their leaders, promising almost everything in order to gain any support. It resulted in a campaign without European themes and with very limited program content.

It is certainly justified to describe the way the media reported about the campaign as horse race reporting, characterized by focusing on the leaders, forms of political agitations, and the predictions of the results accompanied by many photographs and graphs, but without any in-depth analytic articles. Even interviews with leaders mostly concerned the personalities of politicians or were about the form of the campaign, and usually ignored the theme of EP and EU. In my view, the reason for this situation is predominantly rooted in the specific character of the media and their routine of convenience without making any effort to penetrate "under the surface".

References

Brandová, Eva/Šaradín, Pavel (2004): Volební kampaň. In: Šaradín, Pavel et al. (Eds.): Volby do Evropského parlamentu v České republice. Olomouc: Periplum, 179-207 [Brandová: Election Campaign. In: Šaradín et al.: EP Elections in the Czech Republic].
Buchal, Petr (2004): Analýza volebních programů. In: Šaradín, Pavel et al. (Eds.): Volby do Evropského parlamentu v České republice. Olomouc: Periplum, 209-235 [Buchal: The Analysis of EP Election Programs. In: Šaradín et al.: EP Elections in the Czech Republic].
Dočekalová, Pavla/Tunkrová (2004): Evropský parlament.. Vývoj, funkce, struktura a politické skupiny. In: Šaradín, Pavel et al. (Eds.): Volby do Evropského parlamentu v České republice. Olomouc: Periplum, 11-77 [Dočekalová/Tunkrová: European Parliament. Its Development, Functions, Structure and Political Groups. In: Šaradín et al.: EP Elections in the Czech Republic].
Dürr, Jakub et al. (2004): Europeizace české politické scény. Politické strany a referendum o přistoupení k EU. In: Šaradín, Pavel et al. (Eds.): Volby do Evropského parlamentu v České republice. Olomouc: Periplum, 79-116 [Dürr: Europeanization of the Czech Political Scene and the Referendum on Joining the EU. In: Šaradín et al.: EP Elections in the Czech Republic].
Fiala, Petr/ Pitrová, Markéta (2003): Evropská unie. Brno: Centrum pro studium demokracie a kultury [European Union].
Linek, Lukáš (2004): Volební účast. In: Šaradín, Pavel et al. (Eds.): Volby do Evropského parlamentu v České republice. Olomouc: Periplum, 267-305 [Linek: Turnout. In: Šaradín et al.: EP Elections in the Czech Republic].
Linek, Lukáš/Outlý,Jan (2004): Výběr kandidátů do Evropského parlamentu v hlavních politických stranách. In: Šaradín, Pavel et al. (Eds.): Volby do Evropského parlamentu v České republice. Olomouc: Periplum, 143-177 [Linek/Outlý: Selection of the Candidates to the European Parliament within Major Political Parties. In: Šaradín et al.: EP Elections in the Czech Republic].
Marsh, Michael: The Results of the 2004 European Parliament Elections and the Second-Order Model. At: http://www.ees-homepage.net/Papers.htm, retrieval Feb. 17th 2005.
Outlý, Jan (2004): Vybrané otázky volebního systému pro volby do Evropského parlamentu. In: Šaradín, Pavel et al. (Eds.): Volby do Evropského parlamentu v České republice. Olomouc: Periplum, 117-142 [Outlý: Some Questions on the Electoral System to the EP. In: Šaradín et al.: EP Elections in the Czech Republic].
Preview of the 2004 European Parliament Elections Results of an Epin Survey of Sational Experts. Epin Working Paper No. 11/May 2004. At: http://www.epin.org/convention/index.html, retrieval Jan. 13th 2005.

Šaradín, Pavel (2004): Analýza volebních výsledků. In: Šaradín et al. (Eds.): Volby do Evropského parlamentu v České republice. Olomouc: Periplum, 237-265 [Šaradín: The Analysis of the EP Election Results. In: Šaradín et al.: EP Elections in the Czech Republic].
Schmitt, Hermann: The European Parliament of June 2004: Still Second-Order? (Version of February 13, 2005). At: http://www.ees-homepage.net/Papers. htm, retrieval Feb. 17th 2005.
Schulz, Winfried et al. (1998): Analýza obsahu mediálních sdělení. Praha: Karolinum [Content Analysis of Media Messages].
Stöver, Philip/Wüst, Andreas M.: Electoral Systems. At: http://www.ees-homepage.net/Papers.htm, retrieval: Feb. 21st 2005.

---

[1] I would like to give many thanks to my colleagues from Charles University, especially to Dr. Trampota, because the quantitative content analysis method I used was in fact inspired by them. My code book and its categories and variables were created on the basis of previous studies, in which I cooperated with them.

[2] The strongest party was the *ČSSD*, which got more than 30 percent of all votes in parliamentary elections in 2002, *KDU-ČSL* and *US-DEU* joined together for elections and got more than 14 percent.

[3] Apparatus of the EU was often blamed by representatives of the *ODS* for being too bureaucratic, European integration was said to endanger the sovereignty of member states and nations and their national interests etc. The *ODS* warned against the creation of a "super-state" called EU, the accession conditions of the ČR to the EU were called unfavourable by the *ODS*, and some leaders of this party including vice-chairman Ivan Langer even publicly proclaimed that because of this they had voted against the accession of the ČR to the EU (see Dürr et al. 2004: 96).

[4] Officially the *KSČM* was not very keen about European integration, maybe with the exception of some younger and less traditionalistic communist leaders including the lead candidate for the EP, Miroslav Randsdorf, who often expressed his confidence in the process of European integration and federalist tendencies.

[5] According to surveys, in the referendum about the accession of the ČR to the EU voted yes: 92 percent voters of the *US-DEU*, 86 percent voters of the *ODS*, 84 percent voters of the *KDU-ČSL*, 82 percent voters of the *ČSSD* and merely 37 percent voters of the *KSČM* (see Dürr et al. 2004: 107).

[6] In the Czech Republic, the polling stations were open from 2 pm to 10 pm on Friday and from 8 am to 2 pm on Saturday.

[7] Quotations and other regulations stem from the Legislation Act Number 62/2003, §59 (Zákon ze dne 18. února 2003 o volbách do Evropského parlamentu a o změně některých zákonů, č. 62/2003 Sb., §59).

[8] This solution is very generous in comparison to other member states where media are often not required to broadcast or the amount of time devoted to election agitation of political parties is not as large as in the ČR (see Brandová/Šaradín 2004: 181-187).

[9] According to public election polls of agency *CVVM*, which was published in June 4th 2004, *ODS* would gain 25.5 percent, *KSČM* 11.5 percent, *ČSSD* 9.5 percent, *KDU-ČSL* 7.5 percent. Other parties including the governing *US-DEU* had no chance to obtain a seat in the EP. http://www.euroskop.cz/cze/article.asp?id=43630&cat=5081&ts=5ec58, retrieval: Feb. 1st 2005.

10 See total results in http://www.volby.cz/pls/ep2004/ep11?xjazyk=CZ, retrieval: Jan. 10th 2005. 19 of 24 new members of the EP were men and only 5 women, the Czech member of the EP is almost 49 years old on average. Only one of member of the EP who had been elected in the ČR was not a citizen of the ČR.
11 Both were leaders of the *"Independents"* and their political program was called by Petr Buchal to be only a "populist school essay" without any new ideas (see Buchal 2004: 232). Železný stressed national interests, and even more than the *ODS* he talked about danger coming from the EU.
12 The second biggest daily *MfD* exceeded 312.000 copies, followed by leftist *Právo* with more than 182.000, right-wing *Lidové noviny* with more than 72.000, and finally *Hospodářské noviny* with 66.500 copies. (Ověřované náklady periodik ABC ČR, http://mam.ihned.cz/1-20004085-15021710-102000_d-44, retrieval: Mar. 16th 2005).
13 *LN* reserved for EP election reporting and comments 16.4 percent of the total space of domestic news and commentaries, *Právo*: 8.2 percent, *MfD*: 11.6 percent, *LN*: 16.4 percent, *HN*: 18.2 percent, *Blesk*: 15.8 percent, but the last mentioned figure is distorted by the small data-base. In absolute numbers, *MfD*, *Právo*, and *LN* had roughly the same space devoted to domestic news and commentaries, the economic paper *HN* had about 1/3 less space, and finally the tabloid *Blesk* had only 1/5 of the total space of *LN*, because specific features such as reports about celebrities, crimes, etc., were excluded. But also in this case, the distortion is high because the advertisements, which often occupy 1/5 of the total space of any page, were counted in the total space. The share of the five analysed dailies going into the whole data-package,-in other words their data-relevance for the whole content, was: *Právo* – 15 percent, *MfD* – 21 percent, *LN* – 33 percent, *HN* – 24.5 percent, *Blesk* – 6.4 percent. *LN* was the only daily in the analysed time period which devoted a supplement to the topic of the EP elections and did this even twice – on July 7th and July 10th.
14 Non-program questions can be characterized as issues that are not closely linked to the content of politics but only to its form. Politicians or media do not say *what* but are concerned about *how*.
15 See e.g. MfD 29.4.; Hn 11.6.: 3. Headlines were published such as "The Government would be destroyed not by a victory of the *ODS* but by internal conflicts" or "EP elections are the game between Špidla and Mareš" – leaders of governing parties in: LN 11.6.: 2.
16 www.epin.org/EPsurvey2004.xls, retrieval: Mar. 7th 2005.
17 A short time before the elections, during the campaign, Železný was charged with tax fraud. He also played the key role in other "scandals", which started through his statement that the ballot boxes were not stored properly and also proclaimed his fear of manipulation with the ballot-boxes in time from the end of voting to the scrutiny.
18 Instead of leaders *HN* interviewed interesting persons on the list of candidates, tabloid *Blesk* provided space to "ordinary" people, who were allowed to interview politicians, instead of journalists.
19 For instance, the centrist *MfD* devoted a whole page to the phenomenon of the *KSČM* and communist parties in the EU in general. One article was entitled "Communists are heading for 'the club of capitalists'", and it was pointed out that "unreformed" Czech communists would probably make up the biggest share of the extreme leftist political camp in the new member states (see MFD 10.6.2004: 7).
20 The reason given was "to not give the communists space for their propaganda" (MfD 8.6.2004: 9).
21 Some candidates from the bottom of the list of this party started separate campaigns and appealed to people to give them preferential votes. Therefore, the leader of the *KDU-ČSL*, Roithová, expressed her worries in the media about the loss of her top list position (see commentary in LN 9.6.2004: 10).

²² But political parties also did not inform very much about their attitude to the EP, and their programs were based upon domestic problems and expected benefits from structural policy (see Buchal 2004: 217).
²³ The *ČSSD* also paid for the dissatisfaction of the majority of the people with the government's policy in the middle of the electoral cycle and also the frustration of ordinary people with politics as a whole, supporters of the *ČSSD* were also less disciplined than voters of the *ODS* or *KSČM* (more in Marsh 2005: 144, 146, 158; also Schmitt 2005: 3).

Two Hungaries?
European Parliamentary Elections and Their Media Coverage in Hungary

*Ágnes Simon**

1. Introduction

Since the 2002 general elections Hungary has been a politically deeply divided country. There are currently four parties present in the Hungarian Parliament: the leftist *Hungarian Socialist Party* (*MSZP*), the liberal *Alliance of Free Democrats* (*SZDSZ*), the centre-right *Hungarian Democratic Forum* (*MDF*), and the *Fidesz–Hungarian Civic Alliance* (*Fidesz-MPSZ*). The two big parties – the *MSZP* and the *Fidesz-MPSZ* – together possess the support of about 80 percent of the electorate, while the other two parliamentary parties are fighting for survival hardly passing the 5 percent threshold.[1] The Hungarian political landscape of the EP elections was determined by the result of the 2002 general elections that ended with a narrow left-liberal, *MSZP-SZDSZ*, victory. Péter Medgyessy, who was not a member of any of the coalition parties, headed the cabinet. The leading party of the opposition has been *Fidesz-MPSZ*, while in the past two national elections the survival of the smaller opposition party, *MDF*, has depended on its election alliance with *Fidesz*.

Ever since the 2002 general elections both government and opposition parties tried to prove that they were morally better suited to govern than their opponents. Instead of a productive political dispute, a clear demarcation line emerged between the two camps. Each side had its own set of values, vision of Hungary, and the support of roughly half of the population. Under these circumstances, it was not surprising that Hungarian parties took the 2004 EP elections rather seriously and engaged in a long campaign. Indeed, campaigning started months before Election Day and prior even to the beginning of the official campaign period. Yet, the two big parties announced the official opening of their campaign and intensified their campaign activities only about a month before Election Day on June 13th.[2] It is this last month of campaigning that this chapter focuses on.

The left-right cleavage that divides the political elite and the electorate is also present in the media. The socialist and liberal domination of the media is a consequence of the regime change: while Socialist journalists preserved most of their positions, the *Liberal* intellectuals of the Democratic Opposition gained significant influence. However, between 1998 and 2002 the centre-right gov-

---

* Ágnes Simon, MA. *1977. Central European University, Department of International Relations and European Studies, currently Doctoral Student, University of Missouri-Columbia, email: agi_simon@yahoo.com

ernment of Viktor Orbán changed the very uneven balance of the media by establishing a solid rightist faction with the use of governmental funds. Nonetheless, the claim that 90 percent of the media supports the left-liberal side remains a common topic of discussion amongst rightist politicians and journalists (see Csontos 2004: 16). Indeed, pointing out the unbalanced structure of the media became one of the, albeit less important, campaign issues. Rightist parties accused the public service and commercial TV channels with left-liberal bias in their reporting of campaign events (see Nagy 2004b: 3). Indeed, a bias in favour of the government was detected by a content analysis of the news programs of the electronic media (see Gidró 2004: 1). The centre-right *MDF* claimed that it had difficulties in getting publicity in both the written and the electronic press, but especially in the rightist ones (see Buják 2004: 11). Parties running in the EP elections, but not represented in the Hungarian Parliament, complained that the press was biased in favour of the parliamentary parties and neglected reporting on their campaigns (N.a. 2004d: 2). The left accused the Hungarian news channel, *Hír-TV,* and the state radio channels of having rightist bias (Papp 2004: 14; N.a. 2004e: 6). This dispute, however, focused primarily on the electronic media.

The political division in the written press is somewhat different. Daily newspapers are political enterprises and the same is true, or believed to be true, for most of the political weeklies. Indeed, there is a common belief that certain papers support the left and others support the right. Namely, the daily of *Magyar Nemzet* and weeklies of *Heti Válasz* and *Magyar Demokrata* are supposed to be the leading rightist, and the daily of *Népszabadság* and the weeklies of *HVG* and *168 Óra* the main leftist papers. It is this general belief that this chapter would like to examine. More precisely, we were interested in not only whether the papers favoured any of the parties, but also the extent and nature of their bias: i.e. if they remained neutral in their articles or if they adopted the rhetoric of the politicians of the favoured parties. Initially we planned to proceed with discourse analysis; however, while conducting the research it became obvious that augmenting it with a quantitative approach could be beneficial. It proved especially useful in understanding such questions as whether the complaints of extra-parliamentary parties were justified.

Table 1: Sales records of the papers analyzed, April-June 2004 (mean value)

Title	Numbers printed	Numbers sold
Magyar Nemzet	100.116	77.789
Népszabadság	187.058	163.535
Heti Válasz	28.722	14.837
HVG	118.558	97.117
Magyar Demokrata	59.335	40.911
168 Óra	46.970	33.174

Source: MATESZ 2004

After describing the legal setting of the EP elections, the political landscape of Hungary, and the major issues of the pre-May 10th campaign period, this analysis presents the coverage of the EP election campaign between May 10th and June 13th 2004. It concludes that the three rightist papers were heavily biased towards the leading opposition party, while it disproves some of the common wisdom concerning the partisanship of the papers associated with the left. An interesting correlation was also found between the extent of bias and the sale records of the six papers in the examined period.

2. Legal setting

In Hungary the system of European parliamentary elections differs from the two-round, mixed formula of national parliamentary elections. Time constraints and the highly divided Hungarian political culture resulted in a law that contains only the minimal regulations necessary to hold the EP elections. The passing of the Act CXIII on the Election to the European Parliament by the Hungarian Parliamentary Assembly on December 15th 2003 meant a modification of Act C of 1997 on Election Procedures so as to harmonize Hungarian election rules with European standards.

Hungary sends twenty-four deputies to the European Parliament. The country forms a single electoral district, and all political parties are free to participate through either individual or joint national party lists. Each party list, including the names of the candidates, had to be submitted to the National Election Committee (OVB) together with at least twenty thousand recommendations from the electorate 30 days before Election Day at the latest. These closed party lists may include up to 72 candidates. However, only parties that receive at least 5 percent of the votes cast may win mandates. Mandates are conferred by the d'Hondt method.

All Hungarian and European citizens living in Hungary and desiring to vote in this country can cast their votes in the Republic of Hungary. A voter may only recommend one party list and vote only for a single list. They cast their votes in 10.871 voting districts. However, unlike the national elections, Hungarian citizens who are abroad on Election Day are also eligible to vote; they constitute one single voting district.

Similar to national elections, it is the National Election Committee that is responsible for the organization and administration of the elections.[3] The OVB announces the official results of the elections that – along with other decisions of the OVB – can be challenged at the Supreme Court. During the 2004 EP elections it had 13 members: five independent members and eight delegated by the political parties participating in the elections.

The first modification of the Act on the Election to the EP already occurred before the elections. On May 24th 2004 the costly solution to send a four-member committee consisting of the representatives of the parliamentary parties to each country in which Hungarian citizens expressed their wish to vote was abolished. Instead, a new regulation was drawn up according to which ballot boxes are to be closed by embassy workers and sent to the OVB. Votes are to be counted by a three-member committee elected from the members of the OVB (Act XLIII of 2004). Moreover, it was only after the election that the Hungarian Parliament regulated the legal status of the Hungarian members of the European Parliament (Act LVII of 2004). It must also be noted that there are no provisions concerning the financing of the EP election campaign, and thus, parties may spend as much as they can afford and have no obligation to report on their campaign spending.

The President of the Republic is required to set the polling date 72 days before the election at the latest. The official election campaign begins on the day when the President calls the election. Similar to national elections, campaigning must end at the beginning of the day prior to voting day, and until the closing of the ballot boxes the election moratorium must be observed by the parties and the media alike.

3. The Hungarian political landscape in 2004 and EP election results

Initially sixteen parties declared their intention to compete in the European Parliamentary elections. However, only nine party lists were submitted for registration to the OVB, eight of which were registered between April 29th and May 17th 2004: in addition to the four parliamentary parties, the *Social Democratic Party* (*SZDP*), the rightist *Hungarian National Alliance* (*MNSZ*), the extreme-left *Worker's Party* (*MP*), and the extreme-right *Party of Hungarian Justice and Life* (*MIÉP*) also entered the election contest. During the process of collecting recommendations for the joint list of the *Green Party* and the *Hungarian Countryside and Civic Party*, a violation of the regulations of the election procedures occurred, and the list was, therefore, rejected by the OVB (see OVB 2004a).

Each party had different, but domestic stakes in the elections. *Fidesz-MPSZ* longed for a revenge for its defeat in the general and local elections in 2002. Victory was necessary to assure their supporters that they were still able to win, a first step in their preparation for the 2006 national elections. The *MDF* that used to cooperate closely with *Fidesz* decided to run independently and to demonstrate that it was capable of passing the 5 percent threshold on its own right. For party leader Ibolya Dávid, it was also a test of leadership. She had to find a means to translate her personal popularity into votes for her party. Only by winning a seat in the EP was she expected to calm down inner-party opposition that favoured maintaining the close ties with the larger opposition party. The timing of the election was rather unfavourable to the coalition parties since it took place at the middle of their term. Consequently, it was essential for the *MSZP* to minimize the extent of defeat, while the *SZDSZ*, similar to the *MDF*, tried to establish itself as an independent political force.

Table 2: Pre-election public opinion polls, European Elections 2004 (in percent)

	Capital Research	Gallup	Medián	Szonda Ipsos	Tárki-Századvég
Fidesz-Hungarian Civic Alliance	44	47	47	49	44
Hungarian Socialist Party	36	41	37	39	45
Alliance of Free Democrats	10	7	9	6	6
Hungarian Democratic Forum	8	3	4	3	3
Others	2	2	3	3	2

Source: N.a. 2004c: 16; Capital Research 2004

Political analysts anticipated a fierce campaign between the two big parties in their struggle to obtain most of the 24 seats. Public opinion polls forecasted a clear *Fidesz* victory, whereas the *MDF*, at best, was expected to win one, and the *SZDSZ* one or two seats in the EP. None of the extra-parliamentary parties were thought to pass the five-percent threshold – for them being able to register their party lists and thus having the opportunity to present their views during the campaign were already significant achievements (see N.a. 2004a).

The campaign and the results confirmed European trends: voter turnout was low (38.5 percent), opposition centre-right parties won the majority of seats, the campaign overwhelmingly focused on domestic issues, and the electorate learned little about the role and tasks of the European Parliament.

Table 3: EP election results in Hungary, June 13th, 2004

Parties	Number of votes	Percent of votes	Number of seats
Fidesz–Hungarian Civic Alliance	1.457.750	47.40	12
Hungarian Socialist Party	1.054.921	34.30	9
Alliance of Free Democrats	237.908	7.74	2
Hungarian Democratic Forum	164.025	5.33	1
Hungarian Justice and Life	72.203	2.35	0
Worker's Party	56.221	1.83	0
Hungarian National Alliance	20.226	0.66	0
Social Democratic Party	12.196	0.40	0
Total	3.075.450	100.00	24

Source: OVB 2004b

The results also matched some of the expectations of most political analysts: *Fidesz-MPSZ* defeated the *MSZP* by three seats, and none of the extra-parliamentary parties could even come close to passing the 5 percent threshold. The smaller parliamentary parties did better than expected on the basis of their performance at national elections: both comfortably passed the threshold, and the *SZDSZ* won not one, but two mandates. Finally, in late August, as a consequence of the election results, the incumbent Prime Minister, Péter Medgyessy, was forced to resign.

4. The early stage of campaigning

Campaigning started in mid-January, that is, about two months before the calling of the election on March 18th 2004, and the beginning of the official campaign period. This was possible because the official starting date of the campaign signifies the beginning of campaigning via means of political commercials, campaign rallies, and election posters, while there are no restrictions on presenting a party's program. Furthermore, the OVB could only enforce the Act on Election Procedures after the registration of the party lists, which could take place anytime between March 18th and May 14th 2004 (see L. K. 2004: 5).

Sensing the desire of average voters to ease the confrontation between the politicians of the left and the right, governmental and opposition parties came forward with symbolic, consensus-oriented proposals in the early period of the campaign. In his annual State of the Country speech, Prime Minister Medgyessy suggested that parliamentary parties run on a single list approved by the President of the Republic. However, this idea was denounced not only by the *Fidesz-MPSZ* and the *MDF*, but also by the junior coalition party and the European Union which saw the logic of democratic party competition at stake. *Fidesz* published a nine-point initiative to protect the 'common interest' of the nation. Meanwhile, the *Hungarian Democratic Forum* put forward its 'Monok Manifesto' that called for national dialogue and partnership in order to establish long-term national objectives (see Bozóki/Simon 2006).

Nevertheless, the *SZDSZ* utilized the opportunity present in early campaigning the best. It tried to get its message to the electorate before the big parties entered the competition. Its program focused on the liberal identity of the party for the first time and targeted only the *SZDSZ*'s small, but stable voting base as well as young voters (see Tóth 2004). On the one hand, they "educated" the public about the differences between socialism, liberalism, and conservatism. On the other hand, they had an issue-oriented approach that concentrated on both domestic and European themes: tax reduction, free speech, and more subsidies for cities and towns from the EU budget (see Tamás 2004). Mayor Gábor Demszky of Budapest, being the leader of their party list, helped put emphasis on the latter point. Once the campaign got officially underway, forceful and imaginative posters and TV commercials augmented the program.

In contrast to the positive message of the *Free Democrats*, the *Democratic Forum* ran a value-based, mainly negative campaign with the slogan 'For a Normal Hungary'. It accused both the *MSZP* and *Fidesz* with corruption and stressed the moral superiority of the *MDF*. The *Democratic Forum* built on their opposition to the war in Iraq and Hungary's participation in it. Although two smaller non-contending parties, the *Independent Smallholders' Party* and the *Hungarian Democratic People's Party*, endorsed its campaign, the greatest asset of the *MDF* was its party leader, Ibolya Dávid. In order to exploit her personal popularity, she was selected as the leader of the party's EP list, although she had no intention to move to Strasbourg.

The two big parties pursued very hostile campaigns from the very beginning. Ironically, each committed itself to positive campaigning and accused the other of having a confrontational strategy. Domestic symbolic issues and a competition for determining the campaign themes of the European election as an important issue dominated their campaign activities. On March 29th, President Viktor Orbán of the *Fidesz-MPSZ* launched the 'National Petition' that focused on security in everyday life. Although it practically was a party program, *Fidesz* presented it as a quasi-popular initiative and collected the signatures of the citizens in its support. In addition, they questioned the honesty and sincerity of *Socialist* cabinet members and argued that the country was in deep economic crisis. The leader of their list Pál Schmitt – a former Olympic champion, President of the Hungarian Olympic Committee, and *Fidesz*'s 2002 candidate for the post of the Mayor of Budapest – was responsible for the positive image of the party.

In contrast, the *Socialists* suffered from the lack of a charismatic figure: their two leading candidates, Foreign Minister and President of the Party László Kovács and ex-Prime Minister Gyula Horn, were respected figures in Europe, but too old and "out-dated" to attract votes in Hungary. They also declared that they would resign their seats if elected (Bátory 2004: 6). In addition, the *MSZP* ran a very negative campaign against *Fidesz*, which was more than unusual from a party in power. The issues focused on by the *MSZP* were quite revealing: both the claim of EP-candidate Magda Kósáné Kovács that the Vatican wanted to dominate the European Union as well as the information-leak about the training that advisor Ron Werber held for *MSZP* campaign activists led to public outrage.

5. The media and the last month of the election campaign

The last month of the campaign differed from the previous period in that both the *Fidesz-MPSZ* and the *Socialist Party* limited their official campaign offensive to this period holding their campaign opening rallies on May 9th and May 15th respectively. Negative campaigning remained not only dominant, but gradually became more belligerent with the nearing of Election Day, in spite of the four parliamentary parties' signing of the 'Ethical Code of the EP Elections' on May 13th. Although the Code was unable to ensure the civilized nature of the campaign, it offered an excellent collection of the unwelcome symptoms of the EP campaign: irresponsible demagogy, appropriating national symbols, discrediting political rivals, and accusing each others' candidates of committing various crimes (see H.Z. 2004: 7; Mátyás 2004 12). Indeed, political analysts saw the Ethical Code as an effort by the parties to respond to average voters' wish for less harshness in political confrontations (see Tábori/Kis 2004: 3; Nagy 2004a: 3).

While substantive debates were rather rare, the tradition of delegitimizing each other – that is, to prove that the opponent was morally unfit to govern –

continued. The *MDF*, whose interest was to gain the support of the voters of both big parties, accused both *Socialist* and *Fidesz* politicians with corruption. The delegitimizing efforts of the *Fidesz-MPSZ* and the *MSZP* were twofold. First, they tried to associate their opponents with questionable aims or historical figures and eras. Viktor Orbán of *Fidesz* claimed that the incumbent 'banker's cabinet' wished to exploit the citizens, their accusation of Mayor Kósa of Debrecen was similar to the Communist techniques of the 1950s, and it was stated that those who abstain from voting "support the former ally of the Soviet Union" (Dombi 2004: 2; Nagy 2004d: 3). When the governing parties voted against discussing the details of the 'National Petition' in the Parliamentary Assembly, *Fidesz* considered it as the evidence for their earlier allegations that the *Socialists* wanted to introduce an austerity package that would lead to declining living standards. In addition, Orbán used the same occasion to question the democratic intentions of the government stating on several occasions that "in a democratic country the government could not neglect the request of one million people"[4] (Czirják 2004: 1). On the other hand, the *MSZP* focused on exposing and 'stopping the lie-factory of *Fidesz*.' Cabinet member Ferenc Gyurcsány asserted that "on the right, ideology and values are changing while [...] populist rhetoric is eternal" (N. SZ. 2004: 6). *Fidesz* was also associated with social and political turmoil in the country and accused of intentionally campaigning in churches.

Second, both *Socialists* and Conservatives used corruption as a means of delegitimizing their rivals and bringing the election campaign to the agenda. For example, the *MSZP* accused the Mayor of Debrecen of misappropriating public funds, while the *Fidesz-MPSZ* accused the company owners, namely the sons of the Prime Minister and a Cabinet member, of exploiting their fathers' position for their personal benefit. For several days, new details were published daily in order to keep the 'scandals' on the agenda. Most of the papers joined this delegitimization campaign to a smaller or greater extent.

The rightist daily, *Magyar Nemzet*, published any allegations about *Socialist* corruption that were put forward by *Fidesz* politicians on prominent pages – often on the cover. Although *Socialist* denials were duly reported, the truth value of the sensational revelations by the *Fidesz-MPSZ* was never questioned by the journalists of *Magyar Nemzet*. It was, however, not the news section that was of real concern. In each issue journalists and other right-wing public figures often put forward their views in two or three different articles on the issues that were covered in the news section. In these, leftist politicians accused of corruption were condemned without reservation, while politicians of *Fidesz* were defended against the *MSZP*'s accusations. A certain amount of bias was also present in the leftist *Népszabadság*: it covered the allegations of the *MSZP* in more detail than those of *Fidesz*. Yet, it tried to remain as objective in its rhetoric and presentation as possible and often expressed reservations about the *Socialists*' charges. Articles dealing with the alleged corruption of *Fidesz*'s politicians slightly outnumbered the articles dedicated to the supposed wrongdoings of the government. Yet, it is important to stress that the paper did not refrain from criticizing the government. For example, it questioned the conduct of the Medgyessy and Baráth sons as well as the Prime Minister's passionate defence of his son (see Debreczeni 2004: 12).

The serious bias of *Magyar Nemzet* was not surprising for Hungarians: this paper was the one purchased by the Orbán-government to challenge the supremacy of the left-liberal media. The paper also identifies itself in its headline as 'civic', using the same expression which is used by parties on the right side of the political spectrum to describe themselves. Furthermore, it did not simply have a rightist bias, but favoured the *Fidesz-MPSZ* over any other party. Firstly, *Magyar Nemzet*'s hostility towards an independent *Hungarian Democratic Forum* was occasionally harsher than towards the government (see L. Tóth 2004: 6). Secondly, any party – including the *SZDP*, *MIÉP*, and the *MDF* – could get covered by *Magyar Nemzet* if they denounced the coalition. Indeed, there were no articles giving an objective report on the campaign and the program of the coalition parties or a single interview with *Liberal* and *Socialist* politicians, though it must be added that many *Socialist* politicians were reluctant to talk to journalists of *Magyar Nemzet* because of its rightist bias. Indeed, the paper seemed to be a part of the *Fidesz*'s campaign rather than to objectively cover the EP elections. There were no more than five references to the liberal identity of the *SZDSZ*, but these were either linked to loose ethics, or – mistakenly – mixed up with libertarianism (see Bayer 2004: 7). In these commentaries it was frequently made clear that 'true Hungarians' would vote for *Fidesz*. Moreover, in the 'EU elections 2004' section, which was introduced ten days prior to election day, such 'quasi-news' appeared as the calls by rightist organizations to vote for *Fidesz* (see N.a. 2004b: 3). With maps and directions, the article on the upcoming *Fidesz*'s rally in support of the 'National Petition' looked more like a guide to showing citizens how to get to the meeting (see Kis 2004: 3). Finally, in the days preceding Election Day full-page advertisements appeared with centre-right symbols and members of the editorial board of the paper or its prominent right-wing publicists urging people to vote.

Yet, the most partial of all the analyzed rightist papers was *Magyar Demokrata*. Its only objective articles were public opinion polls. It devoted much space to cover the campaign of *Fidesz* with special focus on Viktor Orbán and Pál Schmitt. In addition, it duly reported where voters might personally meet the leader of the *Fidesz* list. The other three parliamentary parties got very little but hostile coverage. Moreover, the style of *Magyar Demokrata*'s reports was strikingly similar to the rhetoric of right-wing radicals. Euro-scepticism was not foreign to this weekly, either.

The least prejudiced of the rightist papers was *Heti Válasz*. Although it did endorse the *Fidesz-MPSZ*, rightist voters could read about other parties' views as well. Interviews with politicians of the *MDF*, *SZDSZ,* and the *MSZP* also appeared. Yet, with the nearing of Election Day its rightist bias became more straightforward.

The attitude of the leftist *168 Óra* could be likened to *Heti Válasz*. Curiously, however, *168 Óra* proved to be the most biased of the three leftist papers. Some of its articles did denounce the *Fidesz-MPSZ*'s conduct and defended *Socialist* politicians against rightist accusation with great zeal. Although prominent politicians of the *MDF* and *Fidesz-MPSZ* were also interviewed, interviews with *Socialist* politicians dominated. Furthermore, the two pages of readers' opinions in each issue were heavily pro-*MSZP*. The *Socialist Party* also placed some party advertisements in this medium so as to reach out to its voters.

Even though readers of *Népszabadság* were subjects of leftist bias, they could become well-informed about the elections and the positions of the parliamentary parties. While commentaries favoured the coalition, any of the governmental and opposition parties could put forward their opinions in form of either an interview or a lengthy essay. Former Foreign Secretary János Martonyi of *Fidesz*, Mayor of Budapest Gábor Demszky of *SZDSZ*, Ibolya Dávid and her vice-president Sándor Lezsák (*MDF*) all grasped the latter opportunity. Meanwhile President Gábor Kuncze of *SZDSZ*, Prime Minister Medgyessy, and Pál Schmitt of *Fidesz-MPSZ* expressed their opinions about campaign issues in long interviews. Indeed, there was only one article published in *Népszabadság* that urged readers to participate in the elections and refrain from voting for the *MIÉP* or *Fidesz*, however, it was a response to a declaration of leftist intellectuals who called upon centre-left sympathizers to punish the *Socialist Party* for its negative campaign by their abstention on voting day (see Hegyi 2004: 14). In the last ten days before Election Day, the *MSZP* invested significant amounts of money into political advertisements in *Népszabadság*: on eight occasions *MSZP* ads appeared at the bottom of the cover (June 1-2, 4-5, 7 and 9-11),[5] four times they occupied a full page with rather negative messages (June 4-5, 9, and 11),[6] and two ads invited people to attend *MSZP* campaign meetings (June 8 and 10). The *SZDSZ* also tried to reach out to voters through *Népszabadság*: the party placed four half-page advertisements (June 3, 9, 10), and an essay by Demszky was published as a political ad (see Demszky 2004: 14).

Finally, our analysis found *HVG* to be a balanced and neutral economic and political weekly. It did not publish many articles on the elections, yet it devoted a two-page interview to the leaders of each parliamentary party. Although it reported on campaign events as well, its coverage remained objective. In addition, it was the only newspaper that carried a neutral ad that called attention to the importance of voting on June 13th.

6. Conclusion

In Hungary, parties took the European Parliamentary elections seriously and engaged in notable and fierce campaigns. They considered it a test of domestic popularity and the preparation for the 2006 national elections. As a consequence, domestic issues dominated, whereas European topics were rarely mentioned, and the electorate received almost no education on the competences of and political divisions within the European Parliament from the elite. Indeed, candidates overwhelmingly stressed that they were best qualified to represent Hungarian national interests in the EP. The negative campaigns of the *MSZP* and the *Fidesz-MPSZ* dominated the written press during the last month of the campaign. In this period the two small parliamentary parties could not successfully compete with the two big parties for the attention of the media – therefore, it seemed a wise decision that they started campaigning early. The campaigns of the four extra-parliamentary parties together were not mentioned more than 30 times in all the papers examined, while articles covering the campaigns of the parliamentary parties exceeded that number at least three times in any week of the analyzed period. Moreover, articles on extra-parliamentary parties were usually not longer than one or two sentences. Yet, the *MNSZ*'s attempt to challenge the results of the elections and get the election repeated due to unequal (i.e. unfair) media attention went beyond the realities of multi-party election competition. All in all, readers of the six papers could not get full information on the campaigns of all eight parties. However, in the written press some efforts were made to inform people about the European Parliament and EP elections in other European countries.

The common wisdom in relation to the political sympathy of the examined two dailies and four weeklies was not fully confirmed. The bias of the papers associated with the political right, namely *Magyar Nemzet*, *Heti Válasz*, and *Magyar Demokrata*, was established. However, these proved not simply rightist, but solely pro-*Fidesz*-MPSZ. All three, to a lesser or greater extent, acted as part of or an auxiliary to the campaign of the bigger opposition party. Thus, it seemed that the right-wing press tried to balance what they believed to be the overwhelming superiority of the left-liberal media (90 vs. 10 percent) by increasing its bias in favour of the right (see Csontos 2004: 16). It may also serve as an explanation for their low sales records compared to the other three papers. Both *Magyar Nemzet* and *Magyar Demokrata* may appeal only to committed centre-right voters (and the latter probably to right-wing radicals as well), but are not informative or balanced enough to help uncommitted voters to make up their minds. Meanwhile, *Heti Válasz* is probably still too biased for undecided voters, but too neutral for die-hard rightist readers.

The analysis of the supposedly left-liberal papers led to a more complex conclusion. The general belief of *HVG* having leftist sympathies was disproved in relation to its coverage of the European Parliamentary elections. It gave a neutral and well-balanced account of the elections. While a clear left-liberal bias was established in relation to *Népszabadság*, this daily did exercise criticism towards the government, even if to a smaller degree than to the opposition. Although its reports dealt with *Socialist* campaign events in more depth, an effort was made to supply information on all parliamentary parties. Therefore, we concluded that not only *HVG*, but also *Népszabadság* could appeal to many citizens – and not only to leftist and liberal sympathizers. *168 Óra* is comparable to the above mentioned right-wing papers because of its open bias in favour of the coalition parties and against the centre-right, which was confirmed by its sales record. To sum up, despite the popular belief regarding the nature of the political commitment of the written media, the deep and rigid division in the society between the supporters of the left and the right, that is the 'two Hungaries', was not fully mirrored at the level of the leading political dailies and weekly papers.

References

Act CXIII of 2003 on the Election to the European Parliament. In: http://www.complex.hu/kzldat/t0300113.htm/t0300113.htm, retrieval Nov. 5th 2004.

Act XLIII of 2004 on the Modification of Act C of 1997 on the Election Process. In: http://www.complex.hu/kzldat/t0400043.htm/t0400043.htm, retrieval Nov. 5th 2004.

Act LVII of 2004 on the Legal Standing of the Hungarian Members of the European Parliament. In: http://www.complex.hu/kzldat/t0400057.htm/t0400057.htm, retrieval Nov. 5th 2004.

Bátory, Ágnes (2004): 2004 European Parliamentary Election Briefing No. 8: The European Parliamentary Elections in Hungary, June 13th 2004. In: http://www.sussex.ac.uk/sei/documents/epernep2004hungary.pdf, retrieval Nov. 5th 2004.

Bayer, Zsolt (2004): Ha szül a csajom... In: Magyar Nemzet, Vol. 67, No. 134, 7. [If My Girlfriend Is Pregnant...].

Bozóki, András/Simon, Ágnes (2006): European Parliamentary Elections in Hungary in 2004. In: Déloye, Yves (Ed.): Encyclopaedia of European Elections. Palgrave: MacMillan (forthcoming).

Buják, Attila (2004): Kóbor lovagok. Boross Péterrel a kétpártrendszer veszélyeiről. In: 168 Óra, Vol. 16, No. 21, 10-11 [Knight-Errant. Péter Boross on the Dangers of a Two-Party System].

Capital Research (2004): A Fidesz nyerné az EP választást, biztos befutók a kispártok. In: http://www.capitalresearch.hu/sajtoanyag/politikai_kutatas_capital_research_20040601.pdf, retrieval Nov. 5th 2004 [Fidesz Is to Win, Small Parties Are Sure to Win Mandates].

Czirják, Imre (2004): Orbán: válaszút előtt az ország. In: Magyar Nemzet, Vol. 67, No. 124, 1 and 3 [Orbán: The Country Is at a Crossroad].

Csontos, János (2004): Sajtódiszkrimináció egy 'normális' országban. In: Magyar Nemzet, Vol. 67, No. 121, 6 [Media Discrimination in a 'Normal' Country].

Debreczeni, József (2004): Apák és fiúk. In Népszabadság, Vol. 62, No. 124, 12 [Fathers and Sons].

Demszky, Gábor (2004): A tisztább Budapestért. In: Népszabadság, Vol. 62, No. 130, 14 [For a Cleaner Budapest].

Dombi, Margit (2004): Vadásznak Kósára. In: Magyar Nemzet, Vol. 67, No. 147, 2 [Kósa Wanted].
Gidró, Krisztina (2004): Baloldali médiatúlsúly. In: Magyar Nemzet, Vol. 67, No. 138, 1 [Leftist Media Domination].
H. Z. (2004): Ígéretet tettek egymásnak a pártok. In Népszabadság, Vol. 62, No. 112, 7 [Parties Made Promises to Each Other].
Hegyi, Gyula (2004): Búcsú a józan baloldaltól? In: Népszabadság, Vol. 62, No. 130, 14 [Good-bye to the Sane Left?].
Kis, Ferenc (2004): Fidesz nagygyűlés a Műegytemnél. In: Magyar Nemzet, Vol. 67, No. 142, 3 [Fidesz Rally at the Technical University].
L. K. (2004): Idő előtti választási start? In: Népszabadság, Vol. 62, No. 23, 5 [Premature Start of the Election?].
MATESZ (2004): 2004/I. In: http://www.matesz.hu/download/GYORS204.zip, retrieval Nov. 5th 2004.
Mátyás, Győző (2004): Szó, szó, szó. In: 168 Óra, Vol. 16, No. 20, 12 [Word, Word, Word].
N.a. (2004a): Közel a döntetlenhez. In: www.mno.hu, retrieval Nov. 5th 2004.
N.a. (2004b): Nemzeti felkérés. In: Magyar Nemzet, Vol. 67, No. 140, 3 [National Request].
N.a. (2004c): EP voks. Szoros verseny ígérkezik. In: Népszabadság, Vol. 62, No. 129, 1/6 [EP Elections. Close Race for Mandates].
N.a. (2004d): Tiltakoznak a kispártok. In: Magyar Nemzet, Vol. 67. No. 147, 2 [Small Parties Protest].
N.a. (2004e): Vizsgálatot kérnek a közráadió hírműsoraira. In: Népszabadság, Vol. 62, No. 133, 6 [Request to Monitor the News Sections of the Public Service Radio].
Nagy, Péter N. (2004a): Lövészárok barátkozás. In: Népszabadság, Vol. 62, No. 113, 3 [Trench Friendship].
Nagy, Péter N. (2004b): Háború nélküli hadüzenet. In: Népszabadság, Vol. 62, No. 131, 3 [Declaration of War without War].
Nagy, Péter N. (2004c): Újra számlálás. In: Népszabadság, Vol. 62, No. 135, 3 [Counting Again].
N. SZ. (2004): 'Autószerelők' a taton. In Népszabadság, Vol. 62, No. 117, 6 ['Car-Mechanics' at the Wheel].
OVB (2004a): Resolution 54/2004 (May 17). In: http://www.valasztas.hu/ep 2004/04/hu/04/4_2.html, retrieval Nov. 5th 2004.
OVB (2004b): The Aggregated Results of the European Parliamentary Elections. In: www.valasztas.hu/ep2004/04/en/10/10_0.html, retrieval Nov. 5th 2004.
Papp, László Tamás (2004): A pártossági ráta. In: Népszabadság, Vol. 62, No. 121. 14 [Rate of Partisanship].
Tamás, Tibor (2004): SZDSZ. Igazi kampány. In: www.nol.hu, retrieval Nov. 5th 2004 [SZDSZ. Real Campaign].

Tábori, Gabriella/Kis, Ferenc (2004): Kampányfogás az etikai kódex? In: Magyar Nemzet, Vol. 67, No. 122, 3 [Is the Ethical Codex a Campaign Trick?].

Tóth, Csaba (2004): Az SZDSZ kampánya és választási szereplése. Paper presented at 10th Congress of the Hungarian Political Science Association, Siófok, June 25-26, 2004 [The Campaign and Election Result of the SZDSZ].

Tóth, László Gy. (2004): Dávid Ibolya Fóruma. In: Magyar Nemzet, Vol. 67, No. 138, 6 [The Forum of Ibolya Dávid].

---

[1] In the general elections 152 of the 386 seats in the Parliamentary Assembly are distributed through regional party lists, but – similar to EP election regulations – only those parties may win seats whose list passes the 5 percent threshold.

[2] The *Fidesz-MPSZ* officially launched its campaign on May 9th and the *MSZP* on May 15th.

[3] The OVB is the organ which parties must notify if they wish to participate in the elections, that verifies whether they fulfill the legal requirements of taking part in the elections and draws the order in which party lists appear on the ballot. It also investigates any wrongdoings in relation to the election and the campaign.

[4] The number of people that signed the petition by that time, according to *Fidesz*. The *Socialists* disputed the number of signatures, arguing that many of them were faked.

[5] On the first 7 occasions the advertisements acclaimed the successful governing of the *MSZP* since 2002, while the last two advertisements encouraged voters to vote on June 13th, 2004.

[6] The central slogan of these ads called on voters to 'Stop the lie-factory of *Fidesz*'.

Europe Stays Distant: Media Coverage and Voting in the European Parliamentary Elections in Slovakia

Radoslava Brhlíková, Mária Kočnerová & Tatiana Tökölyová*

1. Introduction

The Slovak Republic (SR), as the nine other new member states of the EU, has started a new period of its existence. It has to get itself and its citizens prepared for the new political situation and acquire the know-how needed to access all important information and resources offered by the EU.

Elections to the EU parliament were held in Slovakia for the first time in 2004. Five political parties which had passed the five percent hurdle competed in the EU elections, in which 16.96 percent of all eligible Slovak voters participated. The first opportunity to exercise the right of a full member of the EU – with its duties and legal obligations – arose immediately after accession. However, the first election to the European Parliament in Slovakia failed to mobilise a big majority of the electorate. What was the reason for this?

The main objective of this paper is to present an in-depth analysis of the electoral process, the results, the behaviour of individual political subjects, and the pre-election campaign in the Slovak Republic. In pursuing this goal, the authors use comparative and statistical methods, analyses, and explanations to provide information not only to experts but also to all EU citizens.

In examining these issues the authors uncover particularities of the party system and electoral system, including the electoral law for EU elections, and specific characteristics of the media system and electoral campaign. The authors look at the role of the government and the role of political parties and the media in campaign design.

One important basis of this paper is the Constitution of the SR as the main legislative, political, and theoretical framework for all Slovaks. Its examination helps to understand the role of all political subjects involved in the EU elections.

---

* Radoslava Brhlíková, PhD. *1972. Associated lecturer at the Constantine the Philosopher University in Nitra, email: rbrhlikova@ukf.sk
Mária Kočnerová, PhD. *1977. Junior lecturer at the Constantine the Philosopher University in Nitra, email: marush@pobox.sk
Tatiana Tökölyová. *1978. PhD student at the Constantine the Philosopher University in Nitra and University of Matej Bel in Banská Bystrica, email: t.tokolyova@orange mail.sk

2. Short overview of the political, electoral, and party system in Slovakia

The present Constitution, ratified on September 1st 1992, and entered into force on January 1st 1993, established a parliamentary democracy. It was amended in 1999 to allow the direct election of the president, who is elected by a direct popular vote for a term of five years. The president has the power to appoint and remove the Prime Minister and other members of the government and also to negotiate and ratify international agreements. The president is the commander-in chief of the armed forces as well. The office of the President and the Office of the Government of the SR represent the executive power. The consent of more than one-half of the deputies present is required to pass a resolution. The committees, any member of the national parliament (*Národná rada Slovenskej republiky*, NRSR), and the Government may introduce bills to the NRSR. The President of the NRSR, the President of the SR, and the Prime Minister have the power to sign laws passed by the NRSR. The President has a right of veto.

The members of the NRSR are elected on the basis of a proportional representation for a term of four years. The elections usually take place over two days – Friday and Saturday. Each party gets seats in the NRSR according to the percentage of votes they received. Contesting political parties must either submit a declaration of the party's member base of at least 10.000 or if membership is below that number, a petition must be submitted with the missing number of signatures. This does not apply to those parties with at least 100.000 votes in the last elections. The threshold for entering the NRSR is 5 percent of the votes. Parties, which do not clear this hurdle, do not get a seat, and their votes are divided among those parties who have made it into parliament in the so-called second scrutiny. The President entrusts the formation of a new government to the leader of the winning party. This government must have a majority in the NRSR, which usually means forming a coalition with other parties.

Although political parties play an important role in the Slovak political scene, the party system is rather unstable. It is characterised by cleavage and fusion of parties into coalitions and by quite fast emergence of new ones. Such processes of rapid "party-building" usually take place within the Parliament and shortly after the national elections (the latest example was the registration of the *Party of Minorities* on February 2005, established by a former member of the *Communist Party* and MEP Herman Arvay). All newly founded parties must be registered at the Ministry of the Interior, and to date there are about 120 registered political parties.

Party and national electoral politics in Slovakia have so far rather focused on top leaders and their personalities than on political programmes. It is quite difficult to make a clear distinction between left and right party orientation in the sense of "old European democracies". In the SR, moderate or gradual reformers are viewed as "left" oriented and radical reformers as "right" (the case of the present governing coalition).

Slovakia also can be characterised by a new model of political party, a cartel party, which is the fourth stage of party development (see Katz/Mair 1995). Thus, the political parties are primarily characterized by clear ideological differences expressed at their parties' programmes. In addition to that, most of the Slovakians have not developed an affiliation to the slowly emerging political parties after 1993. Political parties and other interest groups are simply perceived as unimportant and unsuccessful forces within the realm of national politics (see Klíma 1998).

Besides elections, there are almost no ways for Slovakians to participate at the political process. The elector, an organised party member as well as a voter, usually stays passive. Parties do not play the role of an effective mediator between the civic society and the state anymore. The citizens do not see any sense in being involved in their structures and refuse to support them financially (see Krno 2000; Srb 2001). This trend is confirmed by several public opinion surveys which show that in Slovakia only eight percent of the respondents trust the political parties, 17 percent of the respondents trust the government, and 19 percent of the respondents trust the Parliament (Eurobarometer 61a 2004; Brhlíková 2004a).

Political parties have become dependent on the state financing and sponsorship by lobbyists. Parties have lost dramatically in membership-sizes. The ties between the parties' elites and the parties' bases have been weakening. Instead, party politics predominantly follow the interests of economic lobby groups, international institutions, and the egoistic desires of its elites (see Srb 2001; Lysý 2002).

3. European Parliament elections in Slovakia

On Sunday, June 13th 2004, the first elections to the European Parliament in Slovakia took place. Of a total of 17 parties competing for seats, only five cleared the five percent hurdle and entered the European Parliament: *SDKÚ* (*Slovak Democratic Christian Union*) with 17.1 percent, *KDH* (*Christian Democratic Movement*) 17 percent, *SMER* (*Direction*) 16.9 percent, *ĽÚ-HZDS* (*Popular Union – Movement for Democratic Society*) 16.2 percent, and *SMK* (*Party of Hungarian Coalition*) 13.2 percent. Fourteen candidates – *SDKÚ* – three candidates (*Peter Šťastný, Milan Gaľa, Zita Pleštinská*), *KDH* – three candidates (Anna Záborská, Miroslav Mikolášik, Vladimír Hudacký), *SMER* – three candidates (Monika Beňová, Miloš Koterec, Vladimír Maňka), *ĽÚ-HZDS* – three candidates (Peter Baco, Sergej Kozlík, Irena Belohorská), and *SMK* – two candidates (Edit Bauer, Árpád Duka-Zólyomi), altogether five women and nine men, were elected to the European Parliament (EP) for a term of five years (see Table 1).

Table 1: European Parliament Elections 2004

Party	Votes	Official results according to the Central Election Committee	Number of seats	EP Parliament Faction
SDKÚ	119.954	17.1%	3	EPP-ED
KDH	119.582	17.0%	3	EPP-ED
SMER	118.535	16.9%	3	PES
ĽÚ-HZDS	113.665	16.2%	3	Non-attached
SMK-MKP	92.927	13.2%	2	EPP-ED

Source: Pravda, June 21st 2004: 3.

However, Slovakia had the highest abstention rate among all EU member countries – 83.2 percent, which is a surprisingly high figure, especially in comparison with turnout in national elections. There are enormous differences between turnout in the EU elections (16.69 percent) and in the last national elections (70 percent) (see Table 2) and the accession referendum (52 percent). On Election Day only 714.508 of 4.210.463 eligible voters came to the polls.

Table 2: Comparison of turnout – national elections vs. European elections

National Elections 1994	National Elections 1998	National Elections 2002	EP Elections 2004
75.4	84.3	70.0	16.96

Source: Flash Eurobarometer 162, July 2004: 6.

According to the European Parliament Election Act No. 331/2003, the election results are determined by the principle of proportionality. The whole country forms a single constituency. The elections took place only on one day, on Sunday from 7 a.m. to 10 p.m. (see §4/2, 3 of the European Parliament Election Act No. 331/2003). Traditionally in Slovakia, national elections are held two days – Friday and Saturday. Only political parties are allowed to submit candidate lists on which the party can place either its own member or a person without political affiliation (see §13/ 4 of the European Parliament Election Act No. 331/2003). The list consists of no more than 14 candidates (see §13/5). Slovak election law contains a provision that a political party willing to run in an election must pay an electoral deposit of 50.000 Slovak crowns (ca. 1.000 Euro, see §13/3e, 6). According to §23/5, voters can choose only one candidate list of a single political party and can give a preferential vote to one candidate of the fourteen he or she prefers. Interviews made with several voters showed that this provision was generally criticised because voters would prefer to choose all 14 candidates (see Brhlíková 2004b). Public opinion surveys, conducted before the elections showed that voters' decisions depended heavily on which leading political figures were on the list.

Thus, Slovak voters expected to be able to choose more than one candidate and to see the names of established and well-known political leaders or at least former observers to the EP, who already had some experience with European Parliament work, on the candidate lists. As public opinion surveys showed, for

Slovak voters (69 percent) it was not very important which particular party gained the most seats in the EP (see Flash Eurobarometer 162, 2004: 26; Brhlíková 2004b).

The candidate lists consisted of subaltern politicians, second-rate politicians, and vice-presidents of the parties, for whom it was a kind of reward (namely: *SMER* – Beňová, *SNS* – Súlovsky, *SMK* – Duka-Zólyomi, *SF* – Šimko, *KSS* – Fajnor, Ondriaš). There were no eminent personalities, popular figures, actors, or celebrities from the world of sports (*SDKÚ* is an exception, because ice-hockey player P. Šťastný became an electoral leader). Young candidates and women did not get any promising ranks on the candidate lists.

The last issue we would like to address in reference to the European Parliament Election Act No. 331/2003 is §19, which deals with media and political advertising. According to the law, not only state-owned media but also private media can broadcast political advertising during the electoral campaign, which is not the case in national parliamentary elections. Also, the law makes no mention of the allocation of free broadcasting time so that, above all, less known political parties whose budgets do not allow paid political advertising can not present their political programmes and visions.

In the Czech Republic, for example, the state-owned public *Czech Television* (*ČT*) is obliged by law to allocate as many as 14 hours of broadcasting time for the campaign. Czech Television provides broadcasting time for the election spots for free. The state-owned public *Slovak Television STV* can allocate a maximum of five hours, but only for paid political advertising, which, in effect, gives each of the parties almost 30 minutes (see §19/1,3); but that is not the case in national parliamentary elections. Moreover, it would be misleading to apply the same regulations that pertain to the broadcasting of normal commercials to paid political advertisements (i.e. limited to three percent of the total daily broadcast time, as in the case of commercial advertising), which would result in spots lasting only 20 seconds with design of a not very high quality. This fact has been criticised by a number of political parties, and many of them including parliamentary parties *KDH, ANO, SMK,* or *ĽS-HZDS* did not show any interest in producing such spots.

Czech Television prepared special news programmes related to the EP elections and even commissioned its own exclusive survey; this channel had special election broadcasts. In contrast, the Slovak public media did not pay any attention to the EP elections in their broadcasts, with the exception of paid electoral spots. The *Slovak Television* spokesperson said that the low turnout was a result of "the overall climate in society that is tired of politics" (www.infovolby.sk). Moreover, there is no fixed ceiling for campaign expenditures, which is not the case for national parliamentary elections. The parties themselves financed their own EP election campaigns.

4. The media system, media coverage, and European electoral campaign

The press and broadcasting media play an important role in the country's identity. There are six national dailies in Slovakia and several magazines and journals. Slovakia is divided into eight counties, and each county has at least one own newspaper. The biggest Hungarian minority publishes its own newspapers. Besides print media, there are four national TV channels: the state-owned public *Slovak TV* (*STV*) and private *TV Markíza*, *TA3*, and *TV Joj*. Several regional TV channels also exist. There are also a state-owned public broadcasting radio *Slovak Radio* and more than 30 private radio stations of which the most important or widespread are *Radio Expres*, *Radio Twist*, *Fun Radio* and *Radio Okey*.

Concerning the electoral campaign, the media mostly devoted their time to the respective parties as well as the tone in which these parties and their members were portrayed. According to our own observations, we can note that:
- The topic of the European Parliament elections was generally outside of the media focus, as it ranked among the top five only on *Slovak Radio*.
- In the context of the EP elections, it was the *ANO* party that received the most coverage of all the monitored media stations (*TV Markíza*, *TA3*, *STV*, and *Radio Twist*), with a total media time of 16 minutes and 52 seconds.
- The monitored media differed quite strongly in reference to which candidate they devoted most of the time. Mr. Šťastný (*SDKÚ*) got the most time of all candidates on *TV Joj* and *Radio Okey*, Mr. Heriban (*ANO*) on *TV Markíza* and *TA3*, Mr. Fajnor (*KSS*) on *Slovak Radio* and *Radio Twist*, Mr. Kozlík (*ĽU-HZDS*) on *STV*, and Mr. Súlovský (*SNS*) on *Radio Expres*.
- The campaign's information quality was poor even after its official beginning, due to the legal framework of *STV*.
- The media devoted the most time to the coalition member *ANO* party – altogether 16 minutes and 52 seconds. Four of the examined media gave this party the greatest attention (*STV*, *TV Markíza*, *TA3*, and *Radio Twist*), with *TV Markíza* devoting to the party the largest absolute part (49.6 percent, i.e. 6 minutes 10 seconds). One reason for this was the fact that the *ANO* was amongst the first to announce its list of candidates for the upcoming elections, and above that, this list became a subject of intra-party rows that attracted wide media attention.

The second most often presented political party was the coalition *SNS – PSNS* that received 10 minutes 33 seconds of the total media time. The *Slovak Radio* and *Radio Expres*, however, gave the greatest attention to *SNS – PSNS*.

Third place in reference to broadcasting time was the governmental SDKÚ, receiving 6 minutes 26 seconds of total media time. It was given more attention on TV Joj and Radio Okey than any other party. SMER, the party with the highest rankings in public opinion polls, was offered no more than 2 minutes 22 seconds of the media time, coming in eighth place. Among the seventeen political parties, the media did not make a single mention of six of them – *Hungarian Federalist Party* (*MSF*), *Živnostenská Party of Slovakia* (*ŽSSR*), Democratic

Union of Slovakia (DÚ), Active Women – Axis of Slovakia (AŽ-OS), Civic Conservative Party (OKS), and Roma Christian Democratic Movement in Slovakia (RKDH).

There was not a single negative statement made about any of the EP election candidates. The media portrayed the parties and coalitions in an almost purely neutral manner, with only SDKU (five), SNS-PSNS (three), and KDH (two) receiving some positive coverage. Still, particular candidates for MEP posts received only scant attention, mostly due to the "battle for Presidency", namely the second round of the presidential elections in mid-April. Although none of the EP candidates played a direct role in the presidential electoral campaign, the media as well as the majority of the political parties were focusing on it, and as a result the EP elections remained almost fully outside of their sphere of interest.

Pre-election activities of EP candidates were hardly visible. The media paid attention to only a few leaders. The most media time was given to the SDKU candidate Peter Šťastný – 4 minutes 12 seconds He was the most covered of all candidates on TV Joj and Radio Okey. TV Joj gave Mr. Šťastný the largest portion of time of all media – 1 minute and 12 seconds. At the same time, the SDKU candidate was the only candidate who received a considerable number of positive mentions – five positive mentions versus zero negative mentions. Other leaders got mostly neutral mentions, and no negative mentions were made in connection with any EP candidate.

Another leader who got somewhat more media attention was Mr. Heriban (ANO party candidate) – 2 minutes 37 seconds of airtime. TA3 and TV Markíza gave him the most coverage of all candidates. The media devoted a considerable amount of time to other top party leaders: Mr. Kozlík (ĽS-HZDS), Mr. Súlovský (SNS-PSNS), and Mr. Fajnor (KSS) – 1 minute 50 seconds. These leaders also ranked among those who were given most of the broadcast time in some of the media: Mr. Fajnor was the most covered candidate on Slovak Radio and Radio Twist, Mr. Kozlík on STV, and Mr. Súlovský on Radio Expres.

Almost half of the EP candidates (eight) did not receive any time in any of the media newscasts, namely Mr. Nagy (MFS), Mr. Sirotka (ŽSSR), Mr. Šlachta (DÚ), Mr. Šimko (SF), Mr. Trnovec (SĽS), Ms. Bartošová (AŽ-OS), Mr. Osuský (OKS), and Mr. Miľo (RKDH).

Overall it can be said that the Slovak public suffered from a "syndrome of electoral fatigue" as the voters, after two rounds of presidential elections and a referendum, were expected to go to the polls for the third time in 2004. The citizens were hardly aware of the importance of the EP elections. After a poor EU entry pre-referendum campaign under governmental "leadership" (of the Vice Premier Pál Csáky, in particular), which showed a blatant lack of discussion on the advantages and disadvantages of Slovakia's entry into the EU, this time the incumbent government decided not to allocate any funds for the EP pre-election campaign and left all the communication to the contesting political parties.

The whole campaign did not inform adequately and was almost hidden from the electorate. As a public opinion survey showed, almost 90 percent of the respondents indicated that neither a political party nor a single candidate contacted them. They were neither approached on the street by the political parties or candidates or their representatives nor were they confronted with any other non-party campaign or advertisement (see Flash Eurobarometer 162 2004: 32, 34, 38, 52). On the other hand, 65 percent of respondents indicated that they received leaflets concerning European elections, 80 percent saw advertisements of parties or candidates, 67 percent read about it in the newspapers, and 88 percent saw or heard about it on TV or radio (see Flash Eurobarometer 162 2004: 36, 40, 42, 44).

The topic of EP elections and related issues was only of marginal interest for both the media and political parties. Total media time devoted to the topic can hardly be compared to the time given to presentations of candidates in the presidential race nor is it comparable to the time devoted to the general topic of "Slovakia's EU integration". Of all the media, *Slovak Radio* broadcasted the most about the topic of the EP elections – over 31 minutes in total, while *Radio Expres* gave the least coverage – just slightly over four minutes.

Moreover, the whole electoral campaign did not even correspond with the topics the voters were interested in. Pre-election public opinion surveys indicated that 48 percent of voters had decided to go to the polls. Voters indicated that they would decide more on the basis of the candidate's policy (39 percent) than according to his or her affiliation to a particular political party (22 percent). Moreover, Slovak voters (70 percent) preferred well-known personalities on the candidate lists (see Brhlíková 2004b).

Concerning the specific topics, the issue of unemployment – or better employment – became the most dominant topic. Other relevant topics the voters indicated they would like to discuss were the rights of EU citizens, some specific problems of the country, agriculture, crime etc. (see Table 3).

Table 3: Topics expected by Slovak citizens to be addressed in the electoral campaign

Employment	79%
Rights of citizens as EU citizens	63%
Specific problems of the country	59%

Source: Eurobarometer 61a 2004

The salary and incomes of the Slovak EP members became the "topic of the day" among the politicians and voters before and during the electoral campaign indirectly and somehow automatically, although an official survey on this topic was not conducted, in private interviews with several respondents this was given as the main reason for abstention.

5. Reasons for abstention

Concerning the reasons for abstention, 40 percent of the Slovak respondents stated distrust with politics in general, and 26 percent indicated that they were not interested in politics as such. Too busy or at work were reported by 15 percent of the respondents, and on holiday or away from home were mentioned by six percent. About 23 percent of the respondents believed that their "vote does not change much or does not change anything", and 13 percent of them stated that they did not know anything or just a little about the EU. Almost 76 percent of the respondents declared their dissatisfaction with and criticism of domestic policy (see Brhlíková 2004b). In general it can be said that the high abstention rate supports the hypothesis of the "punishment" of the present government and policy.

To sum up and conclude the most important reasons for the abstention of Slovak voters are listed:

- The EU has been treated by the political representatives of Slovakia as an image-making instrument rather than an issue of political debate. The EU has been used in an abstract and symbolic manner. In relation to the EU, the Slovak representation/government has almost behaved like a little child, who just wants to test how far he or she can go. A professional approach is lacking.
- The electorate in Slovakia distrusts political parties and their candidates (only eight percent of Slovak citizens trust political parties, and 17 percent of the citizens trust the Slovak government). Considering this, it was ridiculous and childish to present the election results as a victory of the government party, as the governing *SDKÚ* had done.
- The actual significance of the European elections was lost, and the citizens were not allowed to feel as being a part of a larger community. A referendum about the accession was held shortly before the elections, and perhaps the voters got the impression that they had already voted and nothing important was at "stake" anymore.
- The campaign itself went more or less unnoticed. It seemed that the pre-election campaign centred on a discussion of the salary and income of the EP members. Topics expected to be addressed by the voters were more or less not covered.
- An important change in traditional voting practice had occurred. In national elections there are two election days, but European electoral law allows only one day to cast a vote, which contrasted sharply with the voting habits of Slovak citizens. Moreover, the voting process appeared problematic for voters. Only political parties were allowed to nominate candidates. In most cases, these parties set up lists with second-rate candidates. In any case, there was a distinct lack of well-known personalities on the lists. Voters stated that they would have preferred party-independent candidate lists.

6. Conclusion

European elections are considered as second-order national elections recognised by government, political parties as well as the mass media only as a test for national politics. Both the European and other minor campaigns and elections are to be thought as single appointments of a continuing political competition. Consequently, the case of Slovakia seems to be a perfect verification of the above-mentioned hypothesis. The European elections in Slovakia 2004 were understood not only by voters but also by the government, politicians, political parties, and the mass media primarily as a second-order election where nothing important was at "stake" and through which nothing important would happen or change.

References

Bárány, Eduard/Brhlikova, Radoslava/Colotka, Peter (2001): Slovakia. In: Auer, Andreas/Bützer, Michael (Eds.): Direct Democracy: The Eastern and Central European Experience. Aldershot: Ashgate, 170-192.

Brhlíková, Radoslava (2004a): EÚ a jej rozšírenie očami jej občanov. In: Politický vývoj v krajinách V4. UKF Nitra, 136 -144 [EU and Its Enlargement Seen by Its Citizens].

Brhlíková, Radoslava (2004b): Volebná účasť v eurovoľbách 2004 na Slovensku. In: Formovanie európskej občianskej spoločnosti. Prešov 2005, 143-150 [Voter Turnout in European Elections 2004 in Slovakia].

Comparative Highlights. Eurobarometer 61 – CC-EB 2004. May 1st 2004.

Eurobarometer 61a 2004. May 1st 2004.

European Parliament Elections Act, Law No.: 330/2003, Slovak Republic.

Kahn, Kim F./Kenney, Patrick J. (1999): Do Negative Campaigns Mobilize or Suppress Turnout? Clarifying the Relationship between Negativity and Participation. In: American Political Science Review, No. 93, 877-889.

Katz, Richard S./Mair, Peter (1995): Changing Models of Party Organization and Party Democracy. The Emergence of the "Cartel Party". In: Party Politics, Vol. 1, No. 1, 5-28.

Klíma, Michal (1998): Volby a politické strany v moderních demokraciích. Radix: Praha [Elections and Political Parties in Modern Democracies].

Krno, Svetozar (2000): Politické strany krajín východnej Európy. Univerzita Konštantína Filozofa Nitra [Political Parties of East European Countries].

Lysý, Jozef (2002): Korupcia ako politický system. In: Centrum pre hospodársky rozvoj (Eds.): Čo by mal vedieť občan o korupcii. Transparency international Slovensko, Bratislava, 51-68 [Corruption as a Political System].

Post European Election 2004 Survey, Flash Eurobarometer 162, July 2004.

Srb, Vladimír (2002): Volby mezi Nitrou a Tatrami. In: Mezinárodní politika, No. 8, 22-23 [Elections between Nitra and Tatras].

The Influence of the March 11th Madrid Bombings on the 2004 European Campaign in Spain: An Analysis of Television News

*Rosa Berganza & Javier Beroiz**

1. Interpreting the 2004 European election context

The Madrid bombings on March 11th 2004[1] and media coverage during this day and the following three days had quite significant political repercussions on domestic and foreign policy in Spain. Effects were also visible in citizen involvement and interest in foreign affairs, specifically regarding Spanish relations with the United States and the European Union.

The attacks brought on an increase in the turnout in the general elections that took place three days later (March 14th). It went up from 68.7 percent in 2000 to 77.2 percent in 2004. The higher turnout and government and media management of information following the attacks contributed to an unexpected change of the Prime Minister that most published public opinion polls had not indicated, because they had been carried out before the bombings. José Luis Rodríguez Zapatero from the *Socialist Party* (*PSOE*) won the general elections. José María Aznar (from the *Popular Party – PP*) had been in power eight years and had an absolute majority of seats in the Parliament (183 out of 350). His policy regarding Iraq, close to the position of President Bush, had been very unpopular.

One of the consequences of the *PSOE*'s victory in the general elections was the reinforcement of Spanish relationships with France and Germany and a "cooling off" of US-Spain bilateral relations. This generated a new frame of issues under discussion in public opinion and in the media and provoked a change of strategies adopted by the parties for the 2004 European campaign. The *PSOE* slogan during these European elections ('We return to Europe' implying that they felt closer to the European Union than to the United States) and the first decision taken by the new government (the withdrawal of Spanish troops from Iraq) are two indications of this change.

The European campaign was interpreted by the *PP* as a means to confirm their theory that the *PSOE* had won the general elections using lies and because of the effect the terrorist attacks had on voting behaviour (a part of the electorate saw a connection between the bombings and Spanish policy on Iraq). According to *El País,* Manuel Fraga, President of the *Autonomous Community of Galicia*

---

* Rosa Berganza, PhD. *1971. Professor at the Department of Communication II, University Rey Juan Carlos (Spain), email: rosa.berganza@urjc.es
Javier Beroiz. *1975. PhD student at Sheffield University (United Kingdom), email: jberoizgorosquieta@yahoo.es

and *PP* founder, explicitly stated at a European campaign rally that the general election results were "tricked and forced by the circumstances". He went on to add that "the elections were not normal" and urged citizens to vote for their "lives and futures" in the European elections in order to "restore the natural majority in Spain and Galicia". Fraga had already accused the Socialists of not acting fairly after the terrorist massacre of March 11th (see *El País*, May 31st 2004).

On the other side, the *PSOE* argued that their victory was due to three main reasons. In the first place, according to all major polls, Aznar's policy regarding Iraq, was contrary to the views held by the majority of the Spanish population. Secondly, there were demands of the general public for a new style of politics. Thirdly, there was dissatisfaction with government information given to citizens and the media immediately following the tragedy of March 11th, especially the delay in recognising that it was not the Basque terrorist separatist organisation *ETA* – as claimed during the first few days – who was responsible for the crimes, but actually a fundamentalist Muslim group. These were also the chief reasons given by the three most widely circulated Spanish news dailies to explain the upward swing in votes in the 14th March elections, and they predicted these factors would also lead to a victory for the *PSOE* in the European elections.

The online edition of *The Guardian* neatly sums up the attitude of the Spanish press in light of the general election results:

"(In an editorial entitled 'Of Lies') El País delivers Aznar and his government a bitter rebuke, putting its defeat down largely to 'inevitable sense of manipulation and deception the electorate felt' over its reaction to the Madrid bombings. 'But as if that was not serious enough, the worst mistake which accompanies Aznar's farewell is his dogged insistence in converting his particular obsessions and questionable ideas about Spain, the Spanish, and the way which they are governed into dogma', the paper says, before concluding that it was 'the manipulation, the lies, the offensive use of the argument of the war against terror to justify just about any policy, the blatant opportunism and puerile arrogance that caused those in power to lose it yesterday. Under the banner headline 'Spain castigates the PP and puts its trust in Zapatero', the centre-right El Mundo said that voters had 'fiercely chastised the PP for its management of the crisis and had presented [the government] with the overdue bill for the war in Iraq'. 'Aznar signed the invoice [at pre-war summit with Bush and Blair] in the Azores, and [his successor] Rajoy is paying now', the paper noted in an analysis similar if less fiercely critical than that of El País. In an editorial entitled 'Three days that changed Spain' the right-leaning ABC noted that 'in the end, the debate over manifestos, the merits of the personalities involved, the state of parties, was all substituted by a vote which let off steam over the March 11 attacks and castigated the government".[2]

As already mentioned above, *PSOE* won the general elections on March 14th. It was the first time in the history of Spanish democracy that a party having an absolute majority of seats in Parliament lost the elections. The results in the 2000 and 2004 general elections for the *PP* and *PSOE* were as follows (see Table 1):

Table 1: Results in 2000 and 2004 general elections

Total seats in Spanish Parliament: 350	Seats 2000 general elections	Percentage of votes in 2000	Seats 2004 general elections	Percentage of votes in 2004
Popular Party (*PP*)	183	45.2	148	37.6
Socialist Party (*PSOE*)	125	34.7	164	42.6
CIU	15	4.3	10	3.2
IU	8	5.5	5	5
PNV	7	1.6	7	1.6
CC	4	1.1	3	0.9
BNG	3	1.3	2	0.8
PA	1	0.9		0.7
ERC	1	0.9	8	2.5
IC-V	1	0.5		
EA	1	0.4	1	0.3
CHA	1	0.3	1	0.4
Na-Bai			1	0.2

Source: Congreso de los Diputados (Spanish Congress, House of Representatives, http://www.congreso.es)

The scarce interest of Spanish voters in the 2004 European campaign, which we will explore later, is reflected in the high level of abstention registered, the highest in Spain for a European Parliament election. The turnout was 45.1 percent, lower than the European average (45.7 percent). Turnout in 1999 was 63.0 percent (regional and local elections took place at the same time) and 59.1 percent in 1994, as shown in Figure 1. In both cases, Spanish turnout was higher than the European average.

Figure 1: Development of turnout during European elections in Spain and in EU countries (percentages)

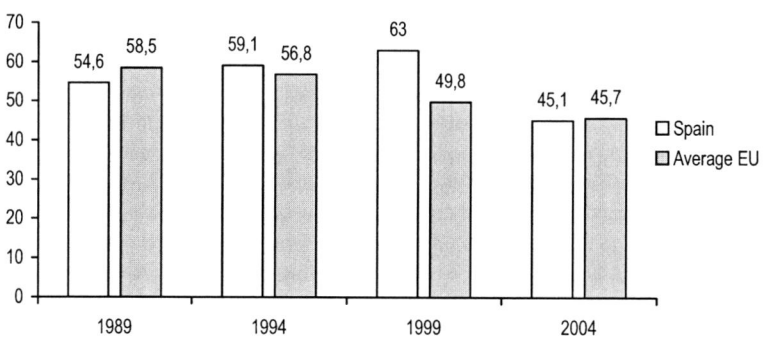

Source: http://www.elections2004.eu.int

Thirty-two candidacies were put forward in the 2004 elections. As shown in Table 2, the 2004 European elections led to a new victory for the *PSOE* (after having won the Spanish general elections three months before), although this time with a narrow lead over the *PP*. The nationalist parties' demands were certainly important in these elections, as will be shown in the media content analysis later in this chapter. The nationalist forces formed three coalitions.[3]

Table 2: Results of European elections 1999 and 2004

Parties	Seats (1999)	Percentage of votes (1999)	Seats (2004)	Percentage of votes (2004)
Popular Party PP	27	39.8	24	41.2
Socialist Party PSOE	24	35.2	25	43.5
IU	4	5.8	2	4.1
Galeusca	4	6.1	2	5.1
Europa de los Pueblos	2	2.9	1	2.5
C. Europea	2	3.2	0	
Others	1	7.0	0	3.6
Total	64[4]	100	54	100

Source: European Parliament (http://www.elections2004.eu.int)

The European election campaign in Spain lasted 15 days and ended 24 hours before the polling stations opened, the moment from which no further electoral messages were allowed to be broadcasted. Furthermore, poll results were not allowed to be published during the final week of the campaign (see Canel/Berganza 2001).

Canel and Berganza also point out that the law imposes a set of "objectivity criteria" for public broadcasting channels. *TVE1* is the first channel of the Spanish national public broadcasting network *Radio Televisión Española* (*RTVE*). Both the General Statute of *RTVE* and the internal document "Basic Principles and Programming Guidelines" formulate the policy that information must be objective, accurate, and impartial. This not only requires an explicit separation of information and opinion, but also that the different trade unions and political, cultural, and religious forces receive a balanced and equitable treatment. The application of this principle during the election campaign is regulated through what is called a "mathematical equilibrium": Each party has a right to an airtime that is directly proportional to the votes received in the previous election. The specific distribution of this airtime is agreed on by the Administrative Council of the public broadcaster. The law does not, however, make any reference to private networks, so these are not obligated to allocate airtime to political parties during the campaign in any particular way. Neither is there any specific definition or conception of journalistic objectivity for broadcasters following commercial criteria (see Canel/Berganza 2001).

2. Methodology and hypotheses

In order to analyse the 2004 European Parliament campaign, the news coverage offered by two of the television channels with the largest audiences[5] in Spain, *TVE1* (public) and *Tele 5* (private), during the last week of the campaign (from June 4th to June 11th) was examined. Elections took place in Spain on June 13th. For our study we used the methodology of quantitative and qualitative content analysis.

The frame and salience of European issues in political and media discourse resulting from the events that took place between the March 11th bombings and the March 14th general elections have been analyzed. It is interesting to compare it to 1999 European elections in order to see more clearly the change in framing European topics that took place between the two campaigns. The following five points were examined:

1. The Madrid bombings drastically altered the political parties' agenda in the European Elections. The 2004 European campaign was conceived by parties and the media as a second round of general elections (see Reif 1985). It was part of a permanent campaign, and domestic affairs and ratification of the popularity of politicians were central issues (see Marini 2001: 23; Kevin 2003: 79-80; Leroy/Siune 1994).
2. The agenda of political actors strongly influenced the media agenda in terms of the issues under discussion and framing of topics (see McCombs/ Shaw 1972; Kevin 2003: 175).
3. As a consequence of the new political context, the relations between Spain and the EU versus the relations between Spain and the USA were a core issue in the campaign (both for politicians and the media). This can be measured in terms of the time the media devoted to European issues compared to the 1999 campaign, as well as in terms of how relevant the European frame of news was.
4. Each of the analysed television channels "framed" the European issues following its own political interests, newsroom routines and style of coverage. This hypothesis would confirm the framing paradigm (see Reese et al. 2001; Shoemaker/Reese 1991; Goffman 1974).
5. Television coverage did not significantly increase public knowledge and information levels about European issues, as was also the case in the 1999 European campaign in Spain (see Canel/Berganza 2001) and as found in other national case studies (see Kevin 2003: 122-125).

3. Parties, leaders, and slogans: The EU on the political agenda

The main actors in the campaign were the two larger parties (*PP* and *PSOE*). The candidate lists for these parties were headed by Josep Borrell (*PSOE*), who is the current President of the European Parliament, and Jaime Mayor Oreja

(*PP*). We shall refer to them in the following as the candidates. An interesting phenomenon during the campaign was that the leaders of the three main political parties played a more active role than the candidates themselves. The recently elected Prime Minister José Luis Rodríguez Zapatero enjoyed considerable more airtime in television news than the *PSOE* candidate (Josep Borrell). The same is applicable to Mariano Rajoy, the new leader of the *PP*, who had recently replaced former Prime Minister José María Aznar (he appeared more often than Jaime Mayor Oreja), and to *Izquierda Unida* (*IU*), a coalition of left wing parties gathered around the *Communist Party*.

Table 3: Airtime in television news

Party leaders and candidates	Time on air in the news
Borrell (PSOE candidate)	3 minutes 17 seconds
Zapatero (PSOE leader)	10 minutes
Mayor (PP candidate)	6 minutes 14 seconds
Rajoy (PP leader)	10 minutes 38 seconds
Meyer (IU candidate)	1 minute 13 seconds
Llamazares (IU leader)	2 minutes 4 seconds

The slogans used by the different parties during the campaign were also an indication of their respective strategies to gain votes. The *PP*'s main slogan was "With you we are strong in Europe". The term 'strong' made reference to the core *PP* policy presented to the electorate in these elections as benefits from a party (*PSOE* was often characterised by them as 'weak') that had governed for eight years. The *PP*'s electoral manifesto revolved around four main ideas. Firstly, the fight against international terrorism. Secondly, the necessity of furthering and maintaining economic and social cohesion as one of the basic pillars of European solidarity. Thirdly, education and research modernization, two core issues in order to achieve a system that respects the environment while maintaining the public's standard of living, that can face the challenge of ageing European populations and that guarantees social benefits. Finally, a firm bet on a common foreign and security policy based on the reinforcement of transatlantic bonds, dialogue with the Islamic world and the assignation of 0.7 percent of General National Product to development aid (see *El País*, May 27th 2004).

The *PSOE*'s slogan, on the other hand, was "We return to Europe", alluding to their foreign affairs policy (closer to the EU than the USA), as clearly illustrated by the fact that the new government's first action in this area was the withdrawal of Spanish troops from Iraq. The referendum and signing of the European Constitution, European enlargement (including Turkey), and preventive diplomacy (instead of preventive war) were the three main topics reflected in their electoral manifesto. *IU* based its program on "the transformation of Europe into a more social, more ecological, more democratic, more feminist, and more united space, and on a stronger compromise with peace" (see *El País*, May 27th 2004). To this end, they proposed a EU that is more autonomous of the

USA, the dissolution of the NATO, and banning of all nuclear and mass destruction weaponry. It demanded a referendum on the European Constitution, towards which it maintained a very critical attitude.[6]

The manifestos of the nationalist coalitions reflected the main objections coming from different regions of Spain regarding the EU. *Galeusca*, with candidate Ignasi Guardans (*CiU*) at its head, mainly demanded to have more direct representation in European institutions: participation of peoples and regions in equal footing with states; the inclusion of representatives of Catalonia, Basque Country, and Galicia in the EU Ministerial council; participation in Spanish governmental delegations in European institutions; the right to manage and control European funds; and the acceptance and international recognition of their national sport teams.

Europa de los Pueblos proposed the following in their program: a greater participation of peoples and regions in the EU; the creation of a Senate of the people in the EU as a chamber where states, nations without a state, people, and regions are represented; official recognition of all European languages by the Union; and the right to manage and control structural funds by the regions.

Finally, *Coalición Europea* centred on: measures to stop the growing economic, cultural, and social differences between the people and regions of the EU; a voice and a right to vote for the Autonomous Communities in whatever administrative bodies were to shape the future of Europe; acceptance of Spanish as one of the "working languages" of the EU; the fight for full employment; defence of European cohesion funds conceded to Spain; the creation of a European Senate and a European army; the fight against international terrorism and a common foreign policy (see *El País*, May 27th 2004). The main demands of the nationalist coalitions were well reflected by their campaign slogans: "We want to be there to decide" (*Coalición Canaria-Coalición Europea*) or *"Galicia, a European nation"* (*BNG-Galeusca*) are two examples.

4. The European campaign on television

At least 46 percent of the Spanish public claimed to have heard or seen EP election candidates on television. This confirms the generally acknowledged importance of television during election campaigns (see Eurobarometer 2004). Furthermore, according to the same poll, when the public was asked how they got information relating to the EU, 60 percent said they used television, 30 percent radio, and 10 percent internet.

Television channels designed a specific block of news (with its own logo and music at the beginning and at the end) to cover the campaign as part of their news programs.

The two channels in this analysis, furthermore, increased the amount of time dedicated to the 2004 elections relative to the previous ones in 1999 (see Table 4). For example, during the second week of the campaign in 1999, *TVE1* dedicated a daily average of 4.2 minutes (see Canel/Bergánza 2001: 91-121), whereas in 2004 they dedicated an average of 7.3 minutes each day to the campaign in the news (which is 18 percent of the time of the news program). The amount of time they gave each party depended on their representation in the European Parliament. *Tele 5* dedicated much less time to the campaign: a daily average of 1.5 minutes – 4.5 percent of the television news program. In 1999, the channel dedicated an average of 0.2 minutes (see Canel/Bergánza 2001: 91-121).

Table 4: Time reserved by *TVE1* and *Tele 5* in the 1999 and 2004 European campaigns (daily average in the second campaign week)

	TVE1	Tele 5
1999	4.2 minutes	0.2 minutes
2004	7.3 minutes	1.5 minutes

The number of news items on the European election 2004 was also much smaller in *Tele 5* than in *TVE1*: 79.7 percent of the items analyzed (55) came from *TVE1*, whereas 20.3 percent (14 items) were from *Tele 5*.

The two television channels followed the elections very differently in reference to their style of coverage. *TVE1* gave little critical coverage to candidates except for one instance in which the following phrase, which incidentally describes the campaign very succinctly, could be heard:

"*Today, Saturday, we have heard many accusations between candidates but also other messages concerning the problem with water, television debates, or the environment. They have always paid more attention to domestic affairs than to the new Europe that we are about to build.*"

What they wanted to say is that, in general terms, the campaign was based more on attacks between candidates and debates on national issues (for example, about how to better distribute the water resources between the different Spanish regions, or new governmental measures concerning the environment) than on European ones.

TVE1's tone of coverage was merely descriptive. Most of the time the public channel reduced the coverage of the two main parties to live broadcasts of their rallies lasting for an average of two minutes. For the other parties *TVE1* offered a summary of the electoral events they organised during the day and some candidates' statements.

Tele 5 also designed a specific block of European campaign news, which was supported by the European Commission and the European Parliament. The "frames" of the news in *Tele 5* were much more critical than in *TVE1*, and they introduced more journalists' comments. They not only reported on rallies (35.7 percent of the items) but also tried to offer more general information in an attempt to increase the Spanish public's knowledge about the EU. They aired reports, for example, on *MEP*'s work and wage, religion in Europe, or a discussion on whether there should be a reference to Christianity in the European Constitution. They broadcasted not only news (as *TVE1*) but also some features (28.6 percent of items). The majority of the images they offered were recorded (71.4 percent) instead of live.

The analysed channels scarcely considered EU matters as very relevant in their newscasts. During the period under study, a piece on the European elections was used as an "opener" (first news item in the program) only twice, both times in *Tele 5*, and it only made the headlines once (on *TVE1*).

Topics receiving most coverage (in terms of time) in TV news show a campaign more focused on domestic issues than on European ones. Disagreements and attacks between candidates were the issues to which the analysed media dedicated more time. They referred mainly to the manipulation or "spinning" of information given during the Madrid bombings, about USA and EU relations with Spain, the Iraq war, and the signing of European Constitution.[7] The topics covered, listed in decreasing order of amount of airtime, were: the March 14th general elections; potential reforms of the Spanish Constitution; nationalist claims; weight of Spain in EU institutions; need of direct representation of Spanish regions in EU institutions; Spanish position on Iraq war; tone of the campaign (which nationalist coalitions described as boring and too centred on the debate between the two main parties); foreign and security policy of the EU; and agriculture policy of the EU.

Despite domestic issues occupying a central spot in the media agenda, Spain-EU relations were a subject that implicitly appears in the main debate issues. It is, in fact, the crucial question on which the two major parties centred most of their reproaches, especially regarding the afore-mentioned topics of the Iraq War, the signing of the European Constitution, and the demands of the nationalist coalitions. Some of them demanded a stronger direct representation in the Union's institutions at the same time as demanding more independence from the Spanish state. Some even demanded total independence from Spain.

Table 5: Frames of discourse (main issue) (N=69)

Frame	TVE1 (n=55)	Tele 5 (n=14)	Total (N=69)
Domestic	50.9%	21.4%	39.0%
European	5.5%	64.4%	36.0%
Nationalist	34.6%	7.1%	17.4%
Other/Not clear	9%	7.1%	7.6%

This European "tone", in which many of the debated issues were framed, can be seen in the focus from which they are observed. Although, as far as the Spanish media context is concerned, the national focus has a slight lead[8] (see Table 5), the European focus is also significant (36 percent), as is the nationalist one (17.4 percent). Apart from this, the main issues aired on *Tele 5* were focused more strongly on Europe than on *TVE1*, probably because European institutions financed the European block in the *Tele 5* newscast, as well as the fact that *Tele 5* covered not only rallies but gave more general information on the EU.

5. Public reception of information, European involvement, and knowledge

A key question in democracy is whether information given during the campaign was useful to citizens for their decision for whom to vote. According to the results of a survey by the Centro de Investigaciones Sociológicas (Center for Sociological Research – CIS) in a post-electoral poll from June 2004, the answer is negative. 72.2 percent of the respondents considered the information received during the campaign little useful or not useful at all in order to be informed about different parties' proposals and manifestos. 67.7 percent of the respondents felt the information received about different candidates was little useful or not useful at all, and 71.1 percent said the same about the information given for distinguishing between different parties in reference to their ideas concerning European policies.

The same poll shows that 47.7 percent of the Spanish people based their votes mainly on issues related to domestic policy.[9] Only for 17,0 percent European issues were the main concern when choosing which party to vote. These data can be interpreted as a confirmation of these elections as second-order ones and as the conception of these elections as a second turn of general ones.

Having completed this analysis of the political and media agenda and the focus of the main issues under discussion, we consider it necessary to briefly review Europeanism of Spanish citizens in order to paint a full picture of the political and media context in which 2004 European elections were held. We would also like to point out some Spanish problems related to the deficit of information given by the media concerning the EU as well as the missing political and public debate. This has led to significant effects on the knowledge of and interest in European issues by Spanish citizens (see Berganza 2005).

Recent public opinion polls reflect an increase of European involvement in Spain after March 11th Madrid bombings. Elcano Institute public opinion polls showed in February 2004 that Spain's best friend was considered to be the USA (42.0 percent), followed by France (12.7 percent), Great Britain (7.1 percent), and Germany (5.4 percent). In contrast, in May 2004 respondents considered France to be the best friend of Spain (28.5 percent), followed by the USA (16.2 percent), and Germany (15.5 percent). CIS Institute confirmed these results: In May 2004, 84.0 percent of the interviewees felt close or very close to the European Union, whereas a mere 27.4 percent felt the same towards the USA.

In contrast, the knowledge of the population concerning European issues continues to be very low. According to the CIS, only 42.0 percent of 2,488 people interviewed could name one of the ten countries that entered the EU on May 1st 2004. The poll was carried out between May 7th and May 12th, that is to say, several days after the enlargement. In the same study, 56.0 percent admitted they did not know about the work of the European Convention (who was preparing the European Constitution).

Figure 2: Development of number of citizens feeling little informed or not informed at all about EU issues (percentages)

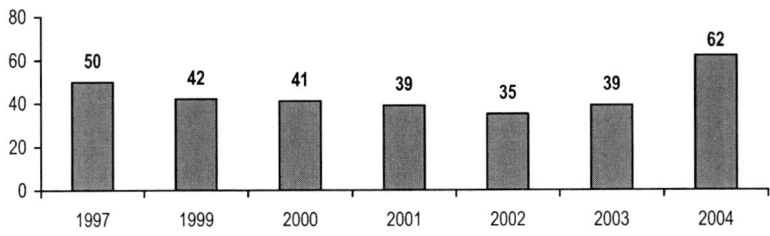

Source: CIS (http://www.cis.es)

Part of this lack of knowledge of Spanish citizens regarding European issues can be explained by the little interest of politicians in talking about their positions regarding European issues and the low quality of news information related to EU affairs, a repetition of what happened in the 1999 European elections (see Berganza 2005). In 1997, half of the sample interviewed by the CIS felt to be "scarcely informed" or "not informed at all" about European issues. In 2004 the percentage went up to 62 percent. The biggest increase was between 2003 and 2004. These data are illustrated in Figure 2. The fact that the Spain-EU relations was a key issue of the campaign could have provoked more interest in European issues and the recognition in the public of having a deficit of knowledge on those matters.

Figure 3: Development of number of people feeling very interested or quite interested in EU news (percentages)

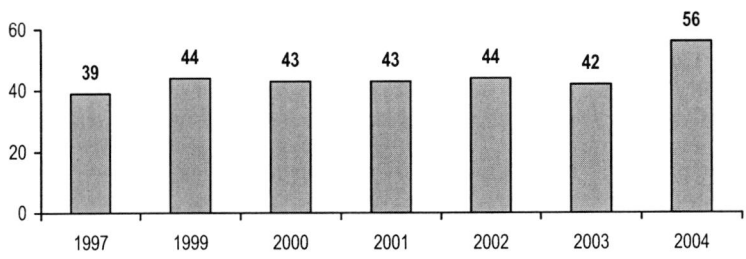

Source: CIS (http://www.cis.es)

Also, during the period from 1997 to 2004 an increase in the population's interest regarding EU news (from 39 percent to 56 percent) was observed. It was also between 2003 and 2004 when the development was especially significant (it went up from 42 percent to 56 percent) as we can see in Figure 3.

An Elcano public opinion poll, however, showed little interest on the part of Spanish voters for the European elections: 49 percent of the sample admitted in February 2004 they were "not very interested" or "not interested at all".

Perhaps Spanish citizens' interest in European elections would have been higher if their concerns had been better considered in the political and media agenda. The Eurobarometer No. 61/2004 data (spring) shows that according to Spanish citizens the most important problems facing Spain were firstly, terrorism (58 percent), followed by unemployment and immigration (20 percent). Interesting is a comparison of these Spanish data with results for European citizens in general: It was found that Europeans believed the most prominent topics in the 2004 European campaign should have been unemployment and immigration (45 percent), the fight against crime (45 percent), country-specific issues (35 percent), and the environment (34 percent).

6. Conclusions

The March 11th bombings and the results of the general elections on March 14th changed the parties' agenda in European elections completely. Both of these topics became the central questions debated in the political and media agenda. They also influenced European involvement in Spain. Recent public opinion polls reflect an increase of this feeling after March 2004.

Parties designed the 2004 European Parliament campaign as a second turn of the general elections. Through these elections the *PP* hoped to recover the absolute majority that it had lost in the previous elections. Its main aim was to confirm the hypothesis that the *PSOE* victory was caused by attacks to government during the last days of the campaign and the effect of the terrorist attacks on voters. On the other hand, the *PSOE* tried to legitimise its victory in the general elections by seeking a clear victory in the European Parliament elections.

The political agenda influenced the television news agenda, especially on *TVE1*, which limited its agenda practically to covering the rallies and press meetings with the political parties. The two television channels followed the elections very differently in reference to their style of coverage. *TVE1*'s was merely descriptive. Because they see themselves as a public service, their task is to be neutral and 'objective'. For this reason they allocated time for each party dependent on its respective representation in the European Parliament (as they had done in the 1999 European campaign). *Tele 5* dedicated so little time to the campaign that it is difficult to perceive a clear European agenda during these elections. Nevertheless, their 'frames' of news were much more critical, and the news contained more journalists' comments.

European issues did appear prominently on the television channels during the campaign, but normally within a national and international context. The Iraq war and the relations both with European institutions and the more powerful countries in Europe were core issues in the campaign. The European frame of discourse was also relevant in the context of Spanish media, as was the nationalist one. Nevertheless, topics discussed show a campaign more focused on domestic issues than on European ones. This campaign was also very conflictive as it was rift by the attacks between the two leading political parties, mainly because of the alleged news manipulation in the aftermath of March 11th bombings, the Iraq war, and the unfreezing of the European Constitution signing.

The 2004 European campaign was more relevant for the television newscasts than the 1999 one. The fact that the latter took place during the same period as the regional and local ones could have been a contributing factor. Newscasters also designed a specific block of news (with its own logotype and music at the beginning and at the end) to cover the campaign as part of their news programs.

Spaniards did not consider the campaign very relevant. Neither the media nor the parties promoted citizens' interest. As public opinion polls show, they still feel uninformed about European issues, and they believe that they did not have the necessary information to differentiate between candidates and parties' agendas during the campaign. Also there is a divergence between the media agenda regarding both European elections and integration and citizens' concerns.

References

Berganza, María R. (2005): Periodismo Especializado e información de la Unión Europea. Madrid: Ediciones Internacionales Universitarias [Specialised Journalism and Information about the European Union].

Canel, M. J./Berganza, María R.(2001): La campagna in Spagna. Localizzatione mediatica o discorso político europeo? In: Marini, Rolando (Ed.): L'Europa dell'euro e della guerra. La campagna elettorale 1999 in Italia e in sette paesi dell'Unione. Roma: RAI, VQPT, 91-121 [Canel/Berganza: The Campaign in Spain. Domestic Media Focus or European Political Discourse? In: Marini: The Europe of the Euro and of the War. The 1999 Campaign in Italy and in Seven EU Countries].

Fundesco (1996): La Unión Europea en los medios de comunicación. Madrid [The European Union in the Mass Media].

El País (2004): Fraga dice que los comicios del 14-M estuvieron 'trucados'. At: http://www.elpais.es, retrieval May 31st 2004 [Fraga Says that March 14th Elections Were „Tricked"].

El País (2004): Con la vista puesta en la nueva Europa. At: http://www.elpais.es, retrieval May 27th 2004 [Regarding the New Europe].

Goffman, Erwin (1974): Frame Analysis. Boston: Northeastern University Press.
Kevin, Deirdre. (2003): Europe in the Media. London: Erlbaum.
Leroy, Pascale/Siune, Karen (1994): The Role of Television in European Elections. The Cases of Belgium and Denmark. In: European Journal of Communication, Vol. 9, 47-69.
Marini, Rolando (2001): L'Europa dell'euro e della guerra. La campagna elettorale 1999 in Italia e in sette paesi dell'Unione. Roma: RAI, VQPT [The Europe of the Euro and of the War. The 1999 Campaign in Italy and in Seven EU Countries].
McCombs, Maxwell/Shaw, Donald (1972): The Agenda-Setting Function of the Mass Media. In: Public Opinion Quarterly, Vol. 36, 176-187.
Reese, Steven/Gandy, Oscar H./Grant, August. E. (2001): Framing Public Life. London: Erlbaum Associates.
Reif, Karlheinz (1985): The Second-Order National Elections. In: Reif, Karlheinz (Ed.): Ten European Elections. Gorver: Aldershot, 1-36.
Shoemaker, Pamela/Reese, Steven (1991): Mediating the Message. Theories of Influences on Mass Media Content. New York: Longman.
Torreblanca, José Ignacio (2004): Keys to Understanding Abstention in the European Elections. In: ARI (Análisis del Real Instituto Elcano), Vol. 112 (http://www.realinstitutoelcano.org).

---

[1]   192 people were killed by a number of bomb blasts on Madrid suburban trains.
[2]   http://www.guardian.co.uk/spain/article/0,,1169810,00.html, retrieval March 15th 2004.
[3]   First, *Galeusca*, formed by Catalan *Convergencia i Unió*, Basque *Partido Nacionalista Vasco*, Galician *Bloque Nacionalista Galego* and *Bloc Nacionalista Valencià*. Second, *Europa de los Pueblos* formed by nationalist parties from different Autonomous Communities: *Esquerra Republicana de Catalunya, Euko Alkartasuna, Chunta Aragonesista, Partido Socialista de Andalucía, Andecha Astur, Conceju Nacionaliegu Cántabro, Iniciativa Ciudadana de La Rioja*. Finally, *Coalición Europea* was composed of *Coalición Canaria, Partido Andalucista, Partido Aragonés Regionalista, Unión Valenciana, Covergencia de Demócratas de Navarra, Extremadura Unida, Unió Mallorquina* and *Partido Asturianista*. The latter did not obtain any seats.
[4]   Due to EU enlargement in May 2004 the number of seats allocated to Spain in 2004 (54) decreased in comparison to 1999 (64).
[5]   From June 4th to June 11th 2004 the *Tele 5* newscast at 20.30h (the one which was analysed) had a daily average of 1.588.586 viewers, with 18.3 percent of the share. During the same period, *TVE1* 21h newscast had a daily average of 2.282.700 viewers (18.8 percent of the share). Source: http://www.laguiatv.com/audiencias.php.
[6]   During the Spanish referendum on the European Constitution (February 20th 2005) *IU* was the only national party asking for the No.
[7]   Aznar, while he was Prime Minister, refused to sign the European Constitution, something which Rodríguez Zapatero did directly after forming his Government. The main reason given by Aznar for his refusal to sign was that Spain allegedly lost influence and power in EU institutions, in comparison to the Nice Treaty.

[8] A report released by Fundesco in 1996 quantified the European focus in Spanish media as 32.8 percent, compared to the 41.3 percent in the press of the rest of the Union.
[9] This result is very similar to the one reflected in Eurobarometer 61/2004. Forty percent of polled Spaniards stated they would vote on the basis of their opinions on national issues and topics.

Europe on the Agenda? The Greek Case

*Nicolas Demertzis**

1. Introduction

Given the indeterminacy as far as geographical and cultural delineations are concerned, it would be quite correct to say that Greece is a European country in the Balkans. Greece (*Ellas*) has gone its own way to modernity through an antinomic blend of traditions and innovations, a decisive instance of which was its accession to the EC/EU. As a full member state, Greece joined the European Union in 1980. Nevertheless, the adjustment to the European economic, political, and cultural environment has not been an easy task for the country. On December 5th, 1991, the French newspaper *Le Figaro* mentioned that the Greek elite no longer believed in their own country, pointing to various fears concerning the future and viability of social dynamics that were permeated by long-standing inflexibilities that prevented adjustment to the changing international environment (see Vergopoulos 1995). As late as the beginning of the 1990s there were still social, economic, and cultural inertial forces at work against the "Europeanization" of the country.

Since then, however, a multitude of socio-economic changes have taken place making it easier for the country to adjust better to European integration processes and institutions. It is not a coincidence that Greece has been member of the Euro zone since 2002. Recently (January to June 2003), Greece held the rotating European Presidency and all the more seems to feel itself at home with EU policies. Of course, there are still discrepancies regarding regional development, fiscal deficit, and identification with Europe. It's not too much to say, though, that nowadays frictions with the EU are not so much of economic as of political-cultural character. On the one hand, Greece has received considerable amounts of subsidiary funds, such as the Mediterranean Integrated Programs and the three Support Community Frames, which contributed greatly to its socio-economic take-off. On the other hand, it is far from participating in what we would call a "nascent European public sphere" where new political-cultural topics are raised beyond the confinements of the national state. Thus, topics such as enlargement and integration, the European Constitution, and citizenship were hardly brought up for discussion and deliberation in and through the media during the last elections to the European Parliament, where Greece nominated twenty-four delegates. In general, as in other member states (see Reif 1985; Kevin 2003: 118ff.), the media in Greece pay little attention to Europe and

---

* Nicolas Demertzis, PhD. *1958. Professor of Political Sociology, University of Athens, Faculty of Communication and Media Studies, email: ndemert@media.uoa.gr

European politics. This paper presents the research results of a content analysis of the Greek media coverage of the 2004 European Election. As demonstrated below, this coverage did not contribute to a possible construction of a European public sphere.

Before addressing this, however, some preliminary remarks are needed as to the overall institutional context, in which the European election took place, and on three political-cultural issues absolutely vital for the understanding of the research results.

2. The context of the competition

As in Belgium and Luxemburg, in Greece voting for the European election is compulsory; in spite of its "second order" nature, this has been conducive to high electoral turnout in all six elections for the European Parliament. The electoral system is based on proportional representation with a nationwide constituency and provides a 3 percent clause; i.e. a party is allowed to participate in the distribution of the 24 seats as long as it gets a minimum of 3 percent of the votes on a national basis.

In Greece, the European elections of June 13th 2004 were not held simultaneously with national or local elections, as was the case in other EU countries. On March 7th 2004 a general national election took place in Greece in which *PASOK* stepped down after eleven consecutive years in office. Naturally, such a short period between the two competitions did not leave room for any protest voting against the new incumbents of power (*Nea Democratia*). As a consequence, the governing party won the election with 43.1 percent, while the *Socialists* (*PASOK*) fared with a much smaller percentage of the votes. Table 1 depicts the electoral percentages and seats won by each party that bet the threshold of 3 percent.

Table 1: Results of the 2004 European elections

Party	% of vote	Seats in European Parliament
Nea Democratia (N.D.)	43.1	11
Panhellenic Socialist Movement (PASOK)	34.0	8
Communist Party of Greece (KKE)	9.4	3
Left Coalition (Synaspismos)	4.1	1
Popular-Orthodox Alarm	4.1	1

Unlike all other EU countries, a TV debate between the party leaders was organized in Greece for the European elections. The debate took place five days before the election day, i.e. on June 8th 2004, and it was transmitted by seven nationwide TV channels. It lasted 81 minutes, and according to the Television Audience Measurement System used by *AGB Hellas*, its TV share of audience was

25.6 percent, a rather poor rate. In the meantime, between May 18th and June 11th 2004, a governmental decree regulated the television and radio coverage of the campaign. All party leaders were given 60 minutes free time for an interview by the public channel *ERT* and 60 more minutes of free time for a televised press conference which the commercial TV and radio stations should transmit either live or pre-recorded video. They should also cover four round tables and one pre-electoral rally for each party. Besides that, the parties were given free television and radio time for their political ads in both public and private channels according to their electoral rate in the previous European election. The advertising time share shouldn't exceed four minutes per hour, and the total cost of 5.2 Million Euro was paid for by the state. Accordingly, 33 percent of public and private channels' news bulletins duration of news were granted to the parties' activities. Unlike *KKE* and *Synaspismos,* the other three parties made use of political advertising in newspapers and magazines the total cost of which, according to Media Services,[1] was 3.1 Million Euro.

3. Attitudes towards the EU

Attitudes towards European affairs depend both on short-term socio-economic fluctuations and longitudinal political-cultural factors (see Demertzis 1997). At the outset, Greeks had a rather negative attitude towards accession to the EC: According to Eurobarometer surveys, in 1981 only 38 percent believed that accession would be a good thing; in 1983, 44 percent stated that Greece had benefited from the EC membership. In the early 1980s accession to the EC entailed a great number of structural changes at different economic and social levels, which came up against the inertia of Greek society. At that time, known as the "populist decade", a number of socio-psychological defence mechanisms were activated against the "thread" of Europe. The populist responses to 'Europeanization' were mostly voiced by Andrea Papandreou's *PASOK* and *KKE.* For middle class layers, which were and still are the backbone of Greek society, full-fledged accession to the EC would contradict state corporatist regulations and state protectionism, which offered them many advantages for several decades before and after the Second World War.

Yet, political rhetoric succumbed to the "iron laws of economy"; EC subsidiary policies helped Greece to bridge long-standing financial deficiencies when compared with other member states. In a few years, the Community's financial support improved living standards and increased household consumption. Since 1985 Greeks' attitude toward the EC has shifted drastically, and the financial and political importance of the European Union membership is acknowledged by political elites and the public. In 1985 the governing party of *PASOK* abandoned its negative stance toward the EC and promulgated a clearly pro-European policy, meeting the country's obligations to the Community/ Union. Consequently, in 1993 the view that accession to the EC was a good thing was expressed by 74 percent of the Greek respondents; also, that year 70 percent stated that Greece benefited from EC membership, one of the highest scores among all European countries (see Eurobarometer 1994). Quite recently, almost three-quarters of the Greeks (71 percent) expressed the view that 'EU membership is a good thing', the second highest score in the entire EU (see Eurobarometer 2004). In a survey just after the 2004 European Elections, this score increased even more: 83 percent of the Greek public believed that membership was a good thing (see Flash Eurobarometer 2004).

Although there are fluctuations between each European public opinion measurement, the tendency is clear: Greeks have learned to trust the EU and its political institutions to a great extent.[2] Namely, 68 percent state they trust the EU, the highest rate in the entire Union of the 25 (see Eurobarometer 61),[3] also, Greeks trust the European Parliament the most (70 percent) and say that it takes into consideration the concerns of European citizens (see Flash Eurobarometer 2004).

4. European identity

Identification with the EU is one of the most complicated issues in the process of European integration. The creation of a common European identity is considered an indispensable political-cultural prerequisite for the legitimacy of the current and far-reaching goals of the European decision-making institutions. Although European identity would by no means entail cultural homogenization, it certainly should be buttressed by some common emotional basis, a particular feeling of belonging, empathy, enabling active participation in European politics. It is difficult, however, to develop such empathy due to historical memories of past conflicts and a variety of resistances that set tight limits to its actualization. Arguments concerning the erosion of national identity are rather sweeping in character, tending to gloss over local variations and over-generalize the impact of globalization. Consider for example the statement: "there is an underlying crisis of national identity in most European states expressed in different forms of popular disillusionment with established institutions and elites" (Wallace 1994: 74). As Smith (1991: 152) remarks, "there is little prospect of a European 'super-nation' until the majority of each European nation's population becomes infused with a genuinely European consciousness". Even if one can sense an "identity panic", its source should better be looked for in local and regional centrifugal trends and multicultural configurations rather than in an assumed overarching process of Europeanization. Therefore, much needs to be done for the emergence of a 'genuinely' European consciousness based on a set of relevant sentiments and not just on cognitions and information about Europe and the EU.

Inevitably, as 'Europeanness' remains to be built up, identification with the EU is fluctuating and rather limited. Like the people of other member states,

Greeks see themselves primarily in terms of their own nationality and as Europeans at the same time and far less as Europeans alone. At the beginning of the 1990s Greeks presented a highly pro-European profile, as 55 percent said that they regarded themselves both as Greek and Europeans (see Eurobarometer 1992). Table 2 shows Greeks' fluctuating identification with Europe, as expressed in their answers to a recurring question of the Eurobarometer.

Table 2: European and national identity

In the near future, do you see yourself as...	Trends from 1992 to 2004 (%)					
	EB 37 Spring 1992	EB 43 Atumn 1995	EB 49 Spring 1998	EB 54 Autumn 2000	EB 58 Autumn 2002	EB 61 Spring 2004
(1) Greek only	38	52	56	50	52	55
(2) Greek & European	55	41	39	42	42	39
(3) European & Greek	4	4	3	3	4	3
(4) European only	2	2	2	2	2	2

The difference between (1), (2), (3) and (4) and 100 is the percentage of "don't know" (not shown).

At the beginning of the 1990s the percentage of those who considered themselves only Greek was much lower than the percentage 15 years later. Also, by the end of the 1990s, apart from the attachment felt for their country, the people in Greece felt very attached (81 percent) and fairly attached (13 percent) to their town or village and much less attached to Europe (see Eurobarometer 1999). Currently, almost 64 percent of the Greeks feel as citizens of the EU, and they do feel attached to Europe. Yet, as far as both feelings are concerned, Greece ranks last and second to last in the EU 15 and the EU 25 (see Flash Eurobarometer 2004).[4] This is connected to the fact that 34 percent of the Greek respondents do not feel proud as Europeans (see Eurobarometer 2003), and 46 percent would feel indifferent if the EU would be dissolved (see Eurobarometer 2003).

5. Electoral turnout

Ten years ago, although Greeks ranked second last before the British as far as satisfaction with democracy in the EU was concerned, they were first (87 percent) in electoral turnout at the 1994 European Elections (see Eurobarometer 1994). Five years later, in 1999, their satisfaction with democracy in the EU had increased to 41 percent (with the mean EU15 percentage being 42 percent) (see Eurobarometer 1999).

As far as interest in EC/EU politics is concerned, since 1982 the percentage of those who are not interested ('not much' and/or 'not at all') has decreased fairly steadily, and currently Greeks rank quite highly regarding their interest in European politics. According to the standard (see Eurobarometer 2004), Greeks were the most likely to vote in the 2004 EP elections – though they came in fourth at the end of election day (76 percent). They did participate strongly in spite of the widespread climate of apathy and indifference throughout most member states. This high voting turnout is partly due to the compulsory voting demanded by the Greek electoral law, and partly to the fact that Greeks are in the habit of participating in elections due to their political culture. In practice, however, since ten years the pressure to go out and vote has diminished, since there are no legal consequences for not voting anymore.

6. A short appraisal

Research has shown that acknowledgement of the beneficiary role of the EU in the country's socio-economic development and trust in the European institutions do not lead to a weakening of national identity, nor is it conducive to a robust double political-cultural identity, i.e. to a Greek-European identity. At the same time, although they feel little attachment to the EU, Greeks have been participating strongly in all elections for the European Parliament since 1983. These ambiguities can be explained by three interrelated factors: first, by a widespread instrumentalist and utilitarian stance towards the EU due to its funding and subsidiary policies. For more than a whole decade the EU's financial support was absorbed in unproductive activities and a gray economy hindering Greece from meeting European standards. That setback still affects public financing and modernization processes today.

Second, it is also explained by the deep-rooted ethno-nationalist political culture of the country. Greek nationalism is more 'cultural' than 'political' in the sense that national identity is constructed selectively on the basis of the religious and historical past, according to the so-called 'Hellenic-Christian' tradition. Among others, this conception of the nation explains the ambivalence of the Greek public towards the 'West' in general, expressed as a socio-psychological oscillation between attraction and repulsion (see Demertzis 1997).

Third, the 'over-politicization' of the post-authoritarian Greek public sphere expressed in terms of a solid partytocratic democracy. Evidently, issues concerned with European politics could not but get absorbed by the dynamics of the domestic political and party system. It is not accidental that (together with the Portuguese and the Irish) the Greeks' opinion about European issues counts much less as a reason for deciding to vote for the European Parliament (22 percent). Thus, when 86 percent of the Greek respondents state that the EP elections are important, their statement is based on national criteria rather than on European ones (see Eurobarometer 2004). Although it is true that citizens' opinion about national issues is the main reason for casting their ballot in the European elections for all EU 15, for Greeks this reason is considerably stronger. So, since 1983 Greeks have dealt with elections to the European Parliament in terms of domestic policy priorities. For instance, even though elections to the EP are regarded as 'second-order elections', 58 percent of the Greek respondents say that it is very important for them which particular party gains the most seats in the EP elections, whereas the average score for this variable in the EU 15 is 49 percent (see Flash Eurobarometer 2004).

This 'domestic' stance towards European elections is sustained by the news media which pay little attention to international news and news about the EU for that matter. Certainly, this is not a Greek peculiarity; research shows that there is more supply than demand for international news and that national and/or local criteria prevail in the news rooms (see Papathanassopoulos 2002: 164-187). To the extent that 1) the public is dependent on the media for the examination and understanding of such an unobtrusive issue as the structure and the role of the EP; 2) Europe and the EU appear infrequently on the media agenda; and 3) European affairs are quite relevant to most of the people, it follows that the public feels uncertain with regard to its knowledge and information about the EU. This uncertainty fuels a rather strong need for orientation. It is not accidental, therefore, that there has been a remarkable discrepancy between the affective and cognitive component of the Greek attitude towards the EU. That is, although Greeks are positively and confidently disposed towards EU affairs, they appear to know little about them. Ten years ago three-quarters of the Greek respondents (76 percent) described themselves as 'not very well' and 'not at all well' informed about the EU (see Eurobarometer 1994). This perceived information deficit was also shared by other Europeans. Although smaller today, this deficit still exists: 42 percent of the Greek respondents think that their national media report too little about the EU (see Eurobarometer 2003). In addition, half of them do not understand the way the EU works, and 80 percent believe that the media should provide more information on the European Convention and its preparatory work on the European Constitution (see Eurobarometer 2003).

When people consider an issue relevant, but know little about it, making it difficult for them to understand it, they turn to the media in order to satisfy their need for orientation (see McCombs/Bell 1996). Yet, as long as the media do not actually meet this need, precisely because – as in our case – they stick to national rather than European news, a vicious circle emerges. As far as the impact of the news media is concerned, we could claim that, in spite of their interest in EU affairs and trust in European institutions, Greeks approach EP elections with domestic criteria in mind because, among other things, they lack alternative cognitive resources; and they lack alternative cognitive resources as long as the news media do not provide them with ample information about the EU. To put it in another way: Journalists might say that they cover EU affairs and EP elections not extensively and only according to national criteria because the public expects them to do so; the public, however, might say that they prioritize national issues because they know little about the European ones due to the insufficient news media outputs. Hence, a double self-fulfilling prophecy comes into effect. To a considerable extent, either as a vicious circle and/or a self-fulfilling prophecy, the way the Greek media covered the 2004 EP elections did not meet the public's need for orientation.

7. Researching European elections news coverage

As the European Parliament is the only directly elected body of the EU it is essential to know the premises under which the electorate casts its ballot. One of these is the relative importance of political issues for EP elections; for Greeks "employment" was the most important one (70 percent) as it was for all EU 15 respondents (see Eurobarometer 2004). A second crucial premise is the timing of the decision to vote.

A third premise, equally important as the two mentioned above, is the media coverage of the elections as it frames and sets the agenda of the public debate influencing, thus, public perceptions of the EU. In tandem with a number of studies on European news (see Leroy/Siune 1994; Semetko/Valkenburg 2000; Kevin 2003), I conducted a content analysis of the media coverage of the 2004 European election campaign. The research extends over the last two weeks of the campaign (June 1st to June 13th 2004).

The unit of analysis was every single principal publication and/or video (news item, opinionated article etc.) referring to the European elections (either the previous or the imminent one), to the EU, European integration, and EU governance with regard to both European and national political institutions. With regard to the newspapers, as a 'principal' publication was counted every main reference in main headlines, the short headlines, the leading paragraph, and the main body of the news items concerned with 'European' context. As for the TV channels the criteria for selection were analogous to those of newspapers: introductory announcement, superimposed title, video footing, and the main body of the news item were analyzed.

The research material was selected from twelve news media: six nationwide newspapers, two regional papers, three commercial, and one public service television channels, all representative for the Greek media system. We selected 1.357 cases from 102 copies of the eight newspapers and 245 cases (units of analysis) from fifty-two prime time television news bulletins. Apart from the director, one supervisor and seven assistants comprised the research team.

Before starting the actual analysis, pilot research was done on the publications and the news bulletins of the first week of the campaign in order to conclude to the final coding sheet and research variables. For the categorical variables intercoder reliability was 0.84; for the numeric variables it was 0.93 (Pearson's correlation coefficient).

For the newspapers the research units were examined with respect to their number and size, their type (editorial, report, opinionated article or interview), their position within the newspaper (political section, international section, financial section, other), page of publication, position of page of publication (right or left), attached photos, their issue content (forty-six different categories were provided), their focus (twenty-two different categories), their tone, their framing, and communicator type. The television news bulletins were inspected likewise as far as issue content, focus, tone, framing, and communicator type were concerned. Further, European news items in television bulletins were coded according to their order of appearance, their duration, and whether they were autonomous or embedded in another news video. In the following the main findings of this research is presented.

7.1 Coverage

Apart from one regional paper (*Peloponnessos*), all seven newspapers, which comprise approximately 90 percent of the total circulation and the largest part of the political spectrum, covered the European elections quite similarly (see Figure 1, grey bars). Usually regional newspapers in Greece keep a more or less local repertoire in their news as most of their readers also buy a 'national' paper in which they can read international news. In reference to the *Public News Channel* (*NET*), the picture was more diverse: Here the European election received much more coverage than in the three commercial channels (see Figure 1, white bars).

Figure 1: Press and TV coverage of EP elections

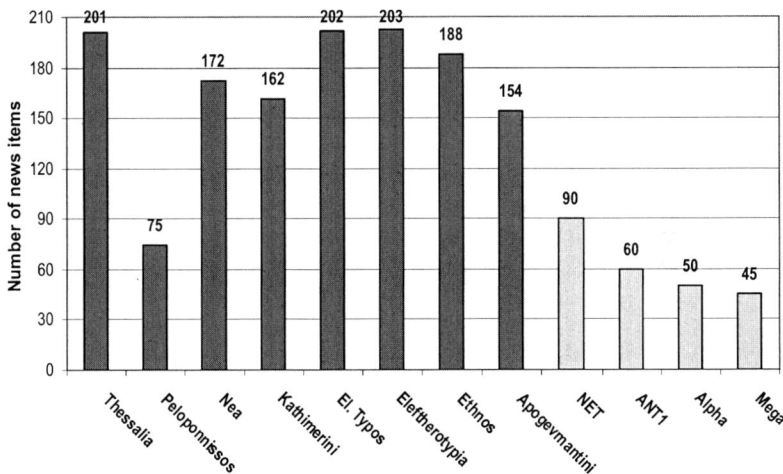

Yet, in the end, the mere number of news outlets does not say much about the weight given to the news story by the respective medium; here, other variables must be considered. Thus, a "visibility index" was constructed for both media; for the newspapers this index was based on the size of the publication, its type, position, page, the position of the particular page in the paper, and the photos (if any) accompanying the article. The calculated mean value was 14.4 (min. 5, max. 37 and standard deviation 5.1). For television news, "visibility" of each news outlet was based on its order of appearance in the bulletin, its duration, and on its being autonomous or embedded in another news story. The mean value here was 6.7 (min. 2, max. 16 and standard deviation 3.3). These findings clearly show that EP elections were not endowed with a high news value for both media types.

Figure 2: Visibility of press output

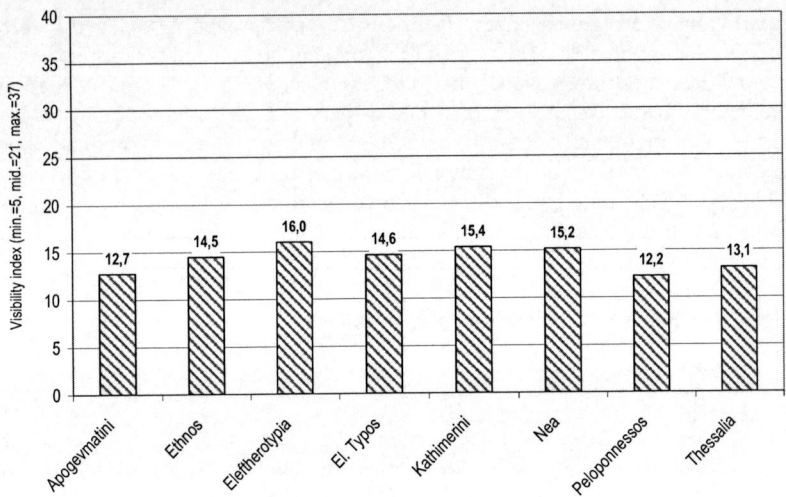

Figure 3: Visibility of television outlets

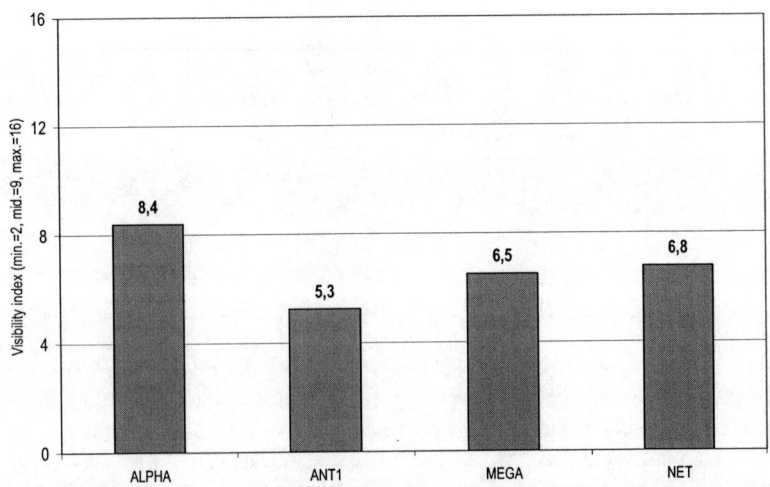

Compared with the number of news items in both media, one can see the following: 1) apart from the regional *Thessalia* the classification of the amount and the visibility of the news items in all seven newspapers is proportional, though to a lesser degree in *El. Typos* and *Kathimerini* (see Figure 2). Although *Thessalia* publishes a great number of news about the EP elections, this paper gives them little news value. 2) A striking difference was found for the visibility index of the television outlets. Although the output of the commercial channel *ALPHA* is limited in terms of quantity, it is characterized by high news value (see Figure 3); the opposite tendency was found for the commercial channel *ANT1* and the public *NET*.

7.2 Contents

As mentioned above, forty-six different categories were constructed for the assignment of the contents of the European Elections news prior to starting the study. Unfortunately, it was found that for both media the variation was quite poor; so that these categories were grouped into five classes of topics: a) activities of the Greek political parties, b) the modus operandi of the EU, c) activities of the political parties in the European parliament, d) social and economic issues, and e) miscellaneous issues. In both media, the majority of news items were coded in category (a). For the most part, a 'European' news story dealt with Greek political parties, and this was the case not only during the last two weeks of the campaign but almost during a forty-day period before Election Day. Yet, as shown in Table 3, there is a significant difference between television and press. With the broadsheets leading the way, newspapers pay much more attention to the procedures, the workings, the structure, and the function of the EU than television channels. It should be noted, however, that in comparison to the other three channels the public *NET* reports more extensively on the EU: 21.0 percent as compared to 6.7 percent (*MEGA*), 11.7 percent (*ANT1*), and 6.0 percent (*ALPHA*).

Table 3: Results of content analysis

Medium	Press		Television	
Issues	absolute number of articles	per cent	absolute number of articles	per cent
Activities of the Greek political parties	729	53.7	176	71.8
EU modus operandi	395	29.1	32	13.1
Social and economic issues	251	18.5	32	13.1
Activities of the European political parties	69	5.1	14	5.7
Miscellaneous	92	6.8	33	13.5
Total	1,536	113.2	287	117.2

7.3 Focus

In addition to the particular issues covered by the media, in this research project we measured the focus by the news items upon specific 'agents' of the stories, i.e., the prime minister, the government, the leader of the opposition, members of parliament, Greek and European political parties, and the institutions of the EU (Committee, ECOFIN, Council, EP etc.).

For both media European elections were treated in terms of domestic politics; in Figure 4 it is clearly shown that they favour bipartism at the expense of the European institutions. This is hardly a surprise because the Greek public has always seen European elections as another stage for national political controversies. It is true that the newspapers did focus somehow on the European parties and the European institutions as they published stories on the EU enlargement, the common foreign and defence policy, the prospect of Turkey's accession to the Union, and the European Constitution. But these stories were scattered and presented unsystematically.

Figure 4: Focus of press and TV news items

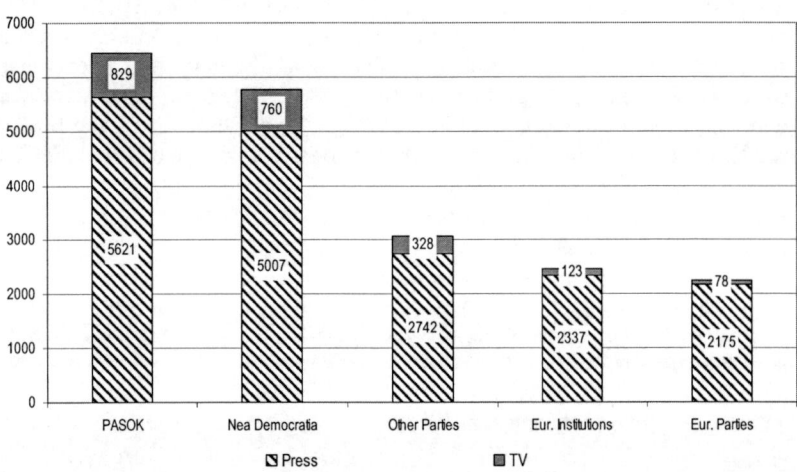

To the extent that the Eurobarometer measurements before the EP elections are sufficiently valid, one could maintain that the Greek media, and especially the television channels, did not meet the informational needs of their consumers precisely because Greece is the country most in favour of enlargement (66 percent) and common foreign policy (78 percent). Also, it ranks third (80 percent) regarding its support of common defence and security policy (see Eurobarometer 2004). On the other hand, however, one should bear in mind that Greeks, along with all European people, put great emphasis (70 percent) on employment as the most important issue for them in the 2004 EP elections. Even in this respect the Greek media did not offer much; for the most part they referred to inter-party skirmishes and electoral tactics rather than to an important domestic (as well as European) issue such as employment.

7.4 The tone

Irrespective of the content and the focus of the news items, the tone the media adopted was overtly ethnocentric; that is to say, they approached the European news events according to a "Greek" angle and to the extent they fitted to the national priorities of the country. Yet, there is a great difference between press and television: The latter's tone was almost totally ethnocentric (214 out of 245 cases), whereas the former leaves sizeable space for Eurocentric (352 out of 1,357 cases) as well mixed approaches (132 out of 1,357 cases).

Another difference between the two media appears in reference to the tone in which they covered European issues. Even if it was about the election to the EP, activities of the Greek political parties or even social and economic issues were treated with an ethnocentric tone. Nevertheless, if not bizarre, it is certainly atypical to approach the workings of the EU with a completely ethnocentric tone. This is the case with the Greek television channels in contrast to the Greek newspapers: They approached EU issues ethnocentrically as much as in 56.3 percent the cases, unlike the newspapers whose ethnocentric tone in covering EU issues was found in only 25.3 percent of the cases. Thus, if the newspapers would give some more weight to Eurocentric perspectives, they could stimulate discussions of European issues and further promote the idea of a European public sphere.

7.5 Framing

As in most 25 EU member states the campaign of the 2004 EP elections was rather cool and apathetic. No big rallies, no political fervour, no heated debates took place. Usually this is not the climate electoral campaigns are run in Greece, but this time there were two particular factors that contributed to the relaxed atmosphere of the elections. First, three months before, Greeks voted in the general national elections where the winner was the centre-right party of *Nea Democratia*. Second, the then new leader of *PASOK*, George Papandreou, adopted a calm style of opposition because his party was undergoing a phase of recovery after a painful defeat at that time. So in one way or another, the electoral milieu was peaceful; only during the last week of the campaign it started to get somewhat harsher due to *PASOK*'s efforts to increase voting turnout. The media too covered the campaign in a non-conflictive way. In this research, the news framing in two different kinds of stories was appraised: those concerned with issues (either European or national) and those referring to party strategies. As shown in

Table 4 both media mainly adopted a non-conflictive framing. With reference to specific types of issues, only stories about the activities of European and Greek political parties were framed to some extent in a conflictive style, which is only something natural enough (see Tables 5a and 5b.).

Table 4: Media framing

Medium	Press		Television	
Frame	absolute number of articles	per cent	absolute number of articles	per cent
Non-conflictive – strategic	364	26.8	91	37.1
Non-conflictive – thematic	623	45.9	76	31.0
Conflictive – strategic	168	12.4	41	16.7
Conflictive – thematic	202	14.9	37	15.1
Total	1.357	100.0	245	100

Table 5a: Issue framing in the Press

Issues/Framing		EU Procedures	Socio-Economic	EU Parties Activities	Greek Parties Activities	Other
Conflictive – thematic	Total	22	7	42	297	28
	Issue %	5.6	2.8	60.0	40.7	30.4
Conflictive – strategic	Total	301	199	18	159	56
	Issue %	76.2	79.3	25.7	21.8	60.9
Non-Conflictive – thematic	Total	6	2	7	158	1
	Issue %	1.5	0.8	10.0	21.7	1.1
Non-Conflictive – strategic	Total	66	43	3	115	7
	Issue %	16.7	17.1	4.3	15.8	30.4
Total	Total	395	251	70	729	92
	Issue %	100	100	100	100	100

Table 5b: Issue framing in television

Issues/Framing		EU Procedures	Socio-Economic	EU Parties Activities	Greek Parties Activities	Other
Conflictive – thematic	Total	2	10	0	30	7
	Issue %	6.3	31.3	0	17.0	21.3
Conflictive – strategic	Total	1	0	3	34	1
	Issue %	3.1	0.0	21.4	19.3	3.0
Non-Conflictive – thematic	Total	26	21	4	28	17
	Issue %	81.3	65.6	28.6	15.9	51.5
Non-Conflictive – strategic	Total	3	1	7	84	8
	Issue %	9.4	3.1	50.0	47.7	24.2
Total	Total	32	32	14	176	33
	Issue %	100	100	100	100	100

7.6 Types of communicators

A remarkable difference was found between the two media with regard to the types of communicators they employ. Communicators are opinion makers and issue claimers (experts, journalists, scientists, intellectuals etc.) who mediate the information about an issue to the public. In the newspapers, the only legitimate communicators for European matters and electoral coverage were the journalists (see Figure 5).

Figure 5:   Types of communicators in television and the press

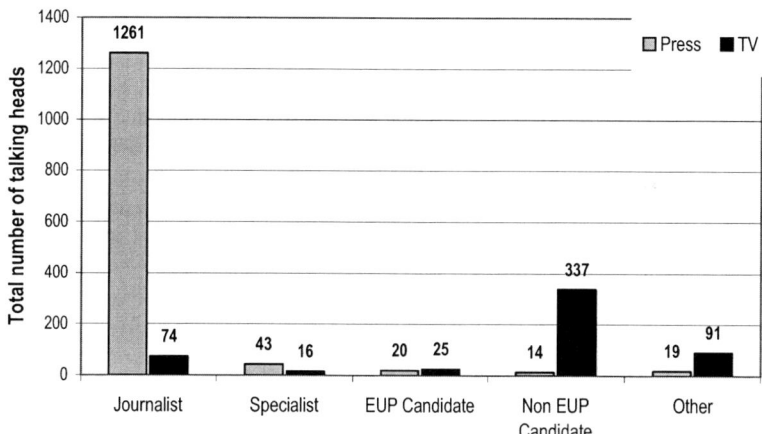

This is surprising because during electoral campaigns Greek newspapers usually make use of independent analysts, experts, and intellectuals to publish their views. In contrast, the proportion of journalists in the 'talking heads' in the television broadcasts is quite small. It should be noted, however, that a decree regulating the March 2004 national election campaign activities and spending, which was operative for the European election as well, allowed just a few appearances of the candidates in both commercial and public television channels. That is why the vast majority of 'talking heads' are politicians from the two bigger parties who did not run for a European seat (see Figure 5).

8. Conclusion

Among other things, this research established that: a) most of the news about the European elections referred to the Greek political parties and domestic public issues rather than to European issues; b) for the most part, the tone of the European news was highly ethnocentric; c) in television channels the politicians were the main communicators, whereas in newspapers journalists and experts were the major sources of various European news; d) most of the news items were framed in a non-conflictive way. Irrespective of these findings, a question arises as to whether the media coverage of the 2004 European elections contributed to the formation of a European public sphere by disseminating the appropriate information. The answer is negative; the way the Greek media covered the recent European Elections did not bridge the gap between Europe and the Greek citizens nor did they contribute to the establishment of a European public sphere. On the contrary, it seems that it (the media) upheld the legitimacy deficit of the European polity. As a matter of fact, however, this practice is common in many national communication systems throughout the EU 25. To many citizens the European Union is still an important but remote and non-comprehensible political entity; the more they know about it, the more they will find their way in the integration processes. This presents a great challenge for the national media.

References

Demertzis, Nicolas (1997): Greece. In: Eatwell, Roger (Ed.): European Political Cultures. Conflict or Convergence? London: Routledge, 107-121.
Eurobarometer No. 37 (1992).
Eurobarometer No. 41 (1994).
Eurobarometer No. 42 (1994).
Eurobarometer No. 51 (1999).
Eurobarometer No.59.1 (2003).
Eurobarometer No. 60.1 (2003).
Eurobarometer No. 61 (2004).
Eurobarometer No. 163 (2004).
Kevin, Deirdre (2003): Europe in the Media. A Comparison of Reporting, Representation, and Rhetoric in National Media Systems in Europe. London: Lawrence Erlbaum Associates.
Leroy, Pascale/Siune, Karen (1994): The Role of Television in European Elections. The Cases of Belgium and Denmark. In: European Journal of Communication, Vol. 9, No. 1, 47-69.
McCombs, Maxwell/Bell, Tamara (1996): The Agenda-Setting Role of Mass Communication. In: Michale, Salwen/Don, Stacks (Eds.): An Integrated Approach to Communication Theory and Research. New Jersey: Lawrence Erlbaum Associates, 93-110.
Panagiotopoulou, Roy (1997): Greeks in Europe. Antinomies in National Identities. In: Journal of Modern Greek Studies, Vol. 15, 349-370.
Papathanassopoulos, Stylianos (2002): European Television in the Digital Age. London: Polity Press.
Reif, Karlheinz (1985): The Second Order National Elections. In: Reif, Karlheinz (Ed.): Ten European Elections. Grover: Aldershot, 1-36.

Semetko, Holli/Valkenburg, Patti (2000): Framing European Politics. A Content Analysis of Press and Television News. In: Journal of Communication, Vol. 50, No. 2, 93-109.
Smith, Anthony (1991): National Identity. London: Penguin Books.
Vergopoulos, Kostas (1995): Regionalism and Stabilization. The Case of Greece in the EC. In: Constas, Dimitri/Stavrou, Theofanis (Eds.): Greece Prepares for the Twenty-First Century. Baltimore: The John Hopkins University Press, 124-145.
Wallace, William (1994): Rescue or Retreat? The Nation State in Western Europe, 1945-1993. In: Political Studies, Vol. 17, 72-87.

---

[1] A Greek agency which monitors the advertising revenues and expenses in print and electronic media.
[2] 60 percent say they trust the "EU institutions" (see Flash Eurobarometer 2004).
[3] Yet, they rank last with 40 percent as far as trust in the UN is concerned.
[4] UK ranks last with 44 percent concerning the attachment to Europe.

Media Framing of the European Parliamentary Elections: A View from the United States

Andrew Paul Williams & Lynda Lee Kaid[*]

1. Introduction

In May of 2004, the European Union (EU) became a much larger entity, accessioning ten new countries. This expansion of the fifteen existing members to twenty five brought into the EU many countries that only fifteen years earlier were under the domination of the former Soviet Union-countries for which democracy itself was quite a new and evolving concept. For the accessioning countries, as well as the 15 current members of the EU, the 2004 elections marked the first opportunity for the selection of representatives to the new and enlarged European Parliament. These elections, held from June 10th– 13th of 2004, provided an important opportunity to study how the political parties and candidates in each of the countries would present their arguments and market themselves to their electorates.

The purpose of this chapter is to determine how the United States news media covered and framed the 2004 EU Parliamentary Elections. Additionally, the research examined related broad and issue-specific topics (e.g., proportional representation, long-term EU plans, and basic election results) in the news media's EU election coverage; and assessed if such coverage was positive (pro-EU), negative (EU-skeptic), or neutral.

2. Framing and the EU elections

Framing theory suggests that the media have the power to select not only what is covered, but also how items are covered. One of the clearest, and most frequently cited, definitions of news framing explains that a media frame is the "central organizing idea for news content that supplies a context and suggests what the issue is using selection, emphasis, exclusion, and elaboration" (Tankard et al. 1991: 3). Similarly, Gamson and Modigliani (1987: 143) define framing as "the central organizing idea or story line that provides meaning to an unfolding strip of events".

---

[*] Andrew Paul Williams, PhD. *1967. Assistant Professor in the Department of Communication, Virginia Tech University, email: apwilliams@vt.edu
Lynda Lee Kaid, PhD. *1948. Professor in the Department of Telecommunication, University of Florida, email lkaid@jou.ufl.edu.

Entman (1993: 52) states that, "to frame is to select some aspects of a perceived reality and make them more salient in a communicating text". According to Gitlin (1980), "media frames" organize the world both for journalists who report it and, in some important degree, for consumers who rely on their reports.

De Vreese (2003: 4) argues "that frames have inherent valence by suggesting, for example, positive or negative aspects, solutions, or treatments. Given this valence, news frames can be expected to influence public support for various policy measures."

Iyengar (1991) suggests that network news frames can be classified as being either episodic or thematic: Episodic frames focus only on specific events and incidents, and thematic frames emphasize abstract ideas and provide more general, broad information.

In an analysis of framing European politics in both print and broadcast news, Semetko and Valkenburg (2000) identified five frames that categorized the media content: 1) conflict frames; 2) human interest frames; 3) economic consequences frames; 4) morality frames; and 5) responsibility frames.

De Vreese (2004a) asserts that analyzing generic news frames in different cultures can also link such broad frames with ones that are culturally specific. For example, in a comparison of the results of previous comparative content analyses of United States and European news coverage, de Vreese (2004b) noted that the economic consequences and conflict frames were manifest.

Scholars have been warned to avoid what is considered to be *ad hoc* framing: "By *ad hoc* we mean frames defined specifically for a single study with little or no attention to explicating either their basic characteristics or theoretical context" (McCombs/Ghanem 2003: 79).

However, in building on prior research about the use of frames in political news, it is acknowledged that scholars may benefit by evaluating both issue-specific and generic media frames (see de Vreese, 1999; de Vreese et al. 2001). Additionally, in support of continued analyses of issue-specific frames, de Vreese (2001: 286f.) states that a focused examination of key events in studies about European integration are crucial, "because they constitute some of the few moments when the EU is visible in mainstream news that attracts a large audience".

Framing, however, has been a theoretical construct with varying interpretations in the communication discipline. For example, researchers have expanded their original definition of agenda setting to include the concept of framing, stating that, "Both the selection of objects for attention and the selection of frames for thinking about these objects are powerful agenda-setting roles [...] [that may] direct attention toward certain attributes and away from others" (McCombs/ Shaw 1993: 62).

This chapter seeks to advance framing research by analyzing both United States print and broadcast media coverage of the 2004 EU expansion and Parliamentary elections. By focusing on this historic political event, the research aims to compare both previously established generic and issue-specific frames, in terms of frequency and dominance.

3. Method

This research employed a quantitative content analysis of print (daily newspapers and weekly news magazines) and broadcast media (television and radio) coverage in the United States of the 2004 EU Parliamentary Elections. News stories from three months – May, June, and July – were collected and evaluated.

Through the use of the Lexis-Nexis electronic database, transcripts of the universe of United States media stories directly relating to the 2004 EU Parliamentary Elections and the EU expansion during this time period were collected and coded. Both, frequency and length of the stories were measured to assess the prioritization of EU election coverage.

Stories from eleven newspapers were gathered for the newspaper sample. The newspapers selected represent the leading national and regional dailies: *The New York Times*; *The Washington Post; The Christian Science Monitor; USA Today; The Boston Globe; The Atlanta Journal-Constitution*; *St. Petersburg Times*; *The Houston Chronicle*; *Chicago Sun-Times*; *Los Angeles Times*; and *The Seattle Times*. Stories from all three weekly news magazines – *Newsweek; Time; and US News & World Report* – comprise that sample. The television news network coverage sample is based on story transcripts from *ABC*; *CBS*; *NBC*; *FOX* and *CNN* (a search of *Public Broadcasting* (*PBS*) *Newshour with Jim Lehrer* did not yield one story pertaining to the EU). Transcripts of stories from *National Public Radio* (*NPR*) constitute the radio sample.

A codesheet and codebook were developed, and two coders went through several training sessions. Ten articles were randomly selected, coded, and compared; and intercoder reliability was assessed at .89 using Holsti's formula (Holsti 1969).[1] Based upon the definition provided by Tankard et al. (1991) of framing as "a central organizing idea" and the argument by de Vreese (1999) analyzing both issue-specific and generic media frames, as well as other previous research on the use of the framing of political events and elections and of European issues, the chapter was guided by the following broad research questions:
1. What was the extent of United States news media coverage of the 2004 European Union expansion and Parliamentary Elections?
2. How did the United States news media frame the 2004 European Union expansion and Parliamentary Elections?
3. To what extent did the United States news media cover broad and issue-specific topics (e.g., political issues, parties, and figures) in their coverage of the 2004 European Union expansion and Parliamentary Elections?

4. Results

The first research question asked what was the extent of United States news media coverage of the 2004 European Union Elections, and if there were cross-media differences. The total number of stories for this time period was only 79 – with 52 originating from daily newspapers, four from weekly news magazines, 17 from televised news broadcasts, and six from radio news broadcasts.

As per story length, aggregate United States news content totalled only 79 stories with a mean length of 583 words. Comparisons of the amount of coverage per story by media channel found the mean word length to be 682 for print newspapers, 521 for news magazines, 428 for televised news broadcasts, and 704 for radio news broadcasts.

The second research question asked how the United States news media framed the 2004 European Union elections. The most frequently present and prevalent frames relied upon by the media were: 1) EU Expansion in General, 2) European Integration, 3) Political Consequences, 4) Societal Impact/National Identity, 5) Economic Consequences, 6) Conflict, 7) Voter Backlash/Payback, 8) EU Expansion Celebratory, and 9): Low Voter Turnout/Apathy.

Table 1: Frames in EU expansion and election coverage by U. S. media

Frame	Number of Stories			
	Newspapers	Magazines	TV	Radio
EU Expansion	45	4	7	5
EU Expansion/Celebratory	15	1	4	0
Low Voter Turnout/Apathy	8	0	5	2
Voter Backlash/Payback	12	0	10	1
Economic Consequences	19	3	3	1
Political Consequences	21	2	10	2
Conflict	19	3	3	0
European Integration	34	3	6	5
Societal Impact/National Identity	22	0	3	3

Additionally, the overall story slant/tone of the U.S. media coverage of the EU expansion and elections was evaluated. Each story was coded as being either positive (Pro-EU), negative (EU-Skeptic), or neutral. We found that of the 79 stories, 30 were negative, 26 were neutral, and 23 were positive. These close results indicate fairly balanced coverage; differences were not statistically significant.

Frame dominance was also evaluated. The two frames that tied as the most frequent were the EU Expansion Celebratory and the Voter Backlash/Payback; the third most dominant was the EU Expansion in General; in fourth place was Economic Consequences; ranking fifth was Political Consequences; tying in sixth place were European Integration and Conflict; followed by Low Voter

Turnout/Apathy as the eighth most frequent story frame; and in the ninth and least dominant position was Societal Impact/National Identity.

Also, each of the dominant frames was evaluated in terms of positive, negative, or neutral news coverage slant. The dominant frames that were characterized as positive were: EU Expansion Celebratory, EU Expansion in General, and European Integration. The dominant frames that were characterized as negative were: Voter Backlash/Payback, Low Voter Turnout/Apathy, Societal Impact/National Identity, and Political Consequences. The dominant frames that were characterized as neutral were: Economic Consequences and Conflict.

The third and final research question asked to what extent did the United States news media cover broad and issue-specific topics in the 2004 European Union Elections. The most frequently covered broad and issue-specific topics were: 1) War/Terrorism, 2) Long-term EU Plans/EU Evolution, 3) Basic Election Results, 4) Polls and Polling Data, 5) Language Issues/Translation, 6) the Cyprus – Greece/Turkey Issue, 7) the EURO, 8) Rallies/Protests, 9) Proportional Representation, and 10) Fraud/Corruption.

5. Discussion

As expected, the amount of United States news media coverage of the EU Parliamentary elections was not extensive, but it was notably low during the three months analyzed for this study. Aggregate United States news media content totalled only 79 stories with a mean length of 639 words. An interpretation of these data indicates either a blatant neglect or general avoidance of specific EU election coverage.

This neglect was not, of course, uniform among the media types. For instance, the *New York Times* had twelve stories, the *Los Angeles Times* had ten stories, and the *Washington Post* published eight stories on EU election or expansion issues. At the other end of the spectrum, three papers, the *Atlanta Journal-Constitution*, the *St. Petersburg Times*, and the *Seattle Times* posted only one story each.

As disappointing as these totals might be for newspaper coverage, the U.S. television networks were even more neglectful of the EU in their reporting. Over the three month period, the five television networks monitored gave only twelve stories to the EU issues. *ABC*, *CBS*, and *FOX* news devoted only a single news story to the EU expansion and elections during the entire period analyzed here. *NBC* had two stories. The majority of the coverage on television was available on *CNN* which aired twelve stories, which is still a very small number for a network that counts international news as one of its major missions.

An American seeking news about the EU would also have found little information in the top three U.S. news magazines, which might have been expected to provide more in-depth coverage of the EU. Instead, such a reader would have found only two stories each in *Time* and in *U.S. News and World Report*. For a

Newsweek reader, the EU expansion and election were invisible, since the magazine did not feature a single major story on the topic.

Possible explanations for this minimal amount of EU election content could be attributed to a focus of the United States news media on stories about the EU relating to the Iraqi war and terrorism and perhaps to a lack of understanding on the part of the United States news media in general about the EU, the impact of the accessioning of the ten new EU members, the continuing process of EU integration, and the complexity of the cross-national EU voting system and proportional representation. This is somewhat perplexing, however, considering the reality of the global economy and prior research that suggests Europe, in general, can be considered an important news topic for the United States. However it supports assertions in prior research of media frames having a strong ethnocentric bias, whereas a lack of issue importance or geographical proximity can equate to a lack of content (see Shoemaker/Reese 1991).

In terms of the prominence and patterns of United States news media framing of the EU elections, the event-specific frames ranged from broad to narrow coverage patterns. A notable and frequent frame was the EU expansion frame, which provided little to no contextual information (political, economic, social, or otherwise) about this historic event. Nonetheless, 45 stories (83 percent of all newspaper stories about the EU) noted the expansion as part of the coverage. Similarly, an EU expansion/celebratory frame emerged in which the media vaguely emphasized the excitement and possibilities of a new EU that now included post-Soviet countries as members.

Two other noteworthy and salient political implication frames also emerged, and both were negative: The first was the low-voter-turnout/apathy frame, which painted a picture of a disengaged European citizens; and the second was the voter backlash/payback frame, which focused on voters getting even with established parties or political leaders by voting them out. This frame was particularly evident in the television coverage, where *CNN* included these concerns of voter disenchantment and its political consequences in 10 of its 12 stories on the EU during this period. Magazine readers and radio listeners got to know much less about these concerns.

Finally, in contrast with prior scholarship regarding the framing of Europe, two frames – economic consequences and conflict – had lower prominence, which was an unexpected finding, due to the obvious economic issues affecting the continued EU integration and the conflict surrounding the exclusion of Turkey into the EU, an issue exacerbated by the division of Cyprus.

It was somewhat surprising that the main political topic and issue emphasized was War/Terrorism, but this is perhaps due to the American media's preoccupation with its own country's major issue at the time of the EU expansion and elections. The emergence of long-term EU Plans/EU Evolution as the second-most prevalent topic indicates an effort on the part of the United States news media to inform the public about both, the history and the continuing development of the EU.

However, the overall coverage of these topics and issues was often cursory and not a detailed analysis of newsworthy stories. For example, coverage about a critical issue such as the division of Cyprus and exactly how the EU functions, in regard to proportional representation and the specific social and political ramification of accessioning former communist countries into this democratic body, were mentioned; but only superficially (see e.g. Stein 2004).

Political party coverage was dominated by that of the leading parties in the United Kingdom, France, and Germany. The nature of such coverage primarily dealt with political unrest and the opposition of Euroskeptic parties to the established ones. The overall United States coverage of these adversarial European political parties is noteworthy, as it indicates that previously marginalized, anti-EU political parties were able to market successfully their ideological stances to voters, which translated into increased media coverage and understanding as well. Additionally, this finding suggests that United States media coverage of a major international political event is similar to the coverage of its own elections, in that prior research indicates a strong tendency of the media to cover issues either very little or to emphasize the negative in a given election (see Lichter et al. 1999).

In terms of political figures emphasized, the UK's Tony Blair was by far the most visible politician in the U.S. media coverage of the EU expansion and 2004 elections. Of course, it is not surprising that the leader of Great Britain would be the most visible foreign leader in American coverage, given the fact that Blair was an outspoken supporter of U.S. policy in Iraq at that time as well. He was followed closely by Germany's Gerhard Schröder and France's Jacques Chirac. Another frequent mention was Ireland's Bertie Ahern, who was leading the EU expansion celebrations in early May.

The view from the United States of the European Union Parliamentary elections was indeed one that provided an ethnocentric and quite limited perspective. This was evidenced not only by the minimal EU expansion and election coverage overall, but also by the way in which the United States media inserted its country's views into its coverage of an international event.

For example, George W. Bush and the U.S. war with Iraq were frequently mentioned as reasons for conflict and political upheaval in Europe. This was the specific reason the U.S. media repeatedly offered for British Labour Party's "punishment" in the election. The U.S. media also often reported that Chirac and Schröder and their respective parties faced negative consequences at the polls, emphasizing that these poor election outcomes were despite the fact that these leading European political figures had opposed Bush and the U.S. war against Iraq.

Another interesting example of such ethnocentric bias was credit given for the labelling of the expanding European Union as "A New Europe" by U.S. Secretary of Defense Donald Rumsfeld. The theme of "A New Europe" was so prevalent in the United States media coverage that it could be considered to have emerged as an issue-specific frame. Similarly, the European expansion and elections were frequently heralded as the "Largest Exercise in Democracy" and praised by the U.S. news media.

6. Conclusions

This chapter provides a broad overview of the United States media coverage of the 2004 European Union expansion and Parliamentary elections. As with any research, there are limitations, and the current research is no exception. Due to the scant EU coverage across all U.S. media channels, the chapter is very limited in its number of cross-media analyzes – beyond that of the volume of coverage. Also, similar to the media coverage itself, the research is limited in detailed examinations of the coverage of the leading European political parties and figures.

Despite these constraints, the research has several noteworthy implications about the framing of an unprecedented international event. First, the finding that issue-specific frames and common trends emerged – which may be largely due to a need for journalists to simplify information – reinforces prior scholarship (see, e.g., de Vreese 1999) that argues that an examination of these detailed frames offers greater insight into what becomes salient to the media in a given situation. Also, the results that indicate generic frames appear to be prevalent – perhaps because such content can be broad/vague and lack in-depth analyzes of seemingly complex subject matter – support previous research that argues for a continued examination of both issue-specific and generic news frames.

While frames are characterized as central organizing themes, the presence of a frame does not necessarily mean that the frame is filled with information. Perhaps the noteworthy finding, and advance in framing theory in this research, is what we found in terms of the identification of two new media frame categories: ambiguous and substantive.

The ambiguous news frame is vague and indistinct, providing little to no context or clear information. Such frames are in essence considered empty or lacking, if the story did not provide any details to help to inform the audience in some educative way. For example, if coverage offers generic news frames such as political or economic consequences, these frames would be considered ambiguous – incomplete and insufficient – if they fail to inform the audience and do not advance understanding about specific facts about the political or economic consequences, instead just merely acknowledge these issues.

Conversely, a substantive news frame is detailed and informative, offering context and detailed information. For example, if a story presented an issue-specific news frame such as the EU expansion celebratory or EU integration frames, these frames would be considered substantive – complete and sufficient – if they inform the audience and advance understanding about the facts involved in the EU expansion or integration, instead of just merely acknowledging the event.

The argument for the emergence of these two new classifications of frame is different from Iyengar's (1991) classification of frames as being episodic or thematic. Both characterizations of frames help to describe how the frames actually function within the context of the news coverage. The classification of episodic and thematic frames deals with how the coverage is framed – and distinguishes frames as being either specific or broad in nature. Ambiguous and substantive frames consider what is framed – and distinguish frames as being either empty or full in nature.

The findings reported in this chapter represent an ongoing effort to analyze the 2004 European Parliamentary elections that will continue to be expanded by teasing out a number of key variables, as mentioned above and by adding Web coverage to the U.S. media content analyzed. It is especially important to measure the presence or absence of ambiguous and substantive frames and to determine if certain issue-specific or generic frames tend to fall into these classifications. The United States media coverage will also be included in comparisons with international media coverage of the 2004 EU expansion and Parliamentary elections. Additionally, the researchers intend to conduct ongoing content analyses of both European party and political figures' controlled media collected during the elections (e.g., web sites and political advertisements) with international mass media coverage. Such comparisons will provide opportunities to examine if there is evidence of intermedia agenda setting.

References

de Vreese, Claes H. (1999): News and European Integration. News Content and Effects in Cross-National Comparative Perspective. In: Research Report. Amsterdam School of Communications Research, University of Amsterdam.

de Vreese, Claes H. (2001): 'Europe' in the News. A Cross-National Comparative Study of News Coverage of Key EU Events. In: European Union Politics, Vol. 2, No. 3, 283-307.

de Vreese, Claes H. (2003): Valence News Frames and Public Support for the EU. Paper presented at the International Communication Association Annual Convention, San Diego, CA.

de Vreese, Claes H. (2004a): Framing Europe. Television News and European Integration. Amsterdam: Aksant Academic Publishers.

de Vreese, Claes H. (2004b): The Effects of Frames in Political Television News on Audience Perceptions of Routine Political News. In: Journalism and Mass Communication Quarterly, Vol. 81, No. 1, 36-52.

de Vreese, Claes H./Peter, Jochen/Semetko, Holli A. (2001): Framing Politics at the Launch of the Euro. A Cross-National Comparative Study of Frames in the News. In: Political Communication, Vol. 18, No. 2, 107-122.

Entman, Robert M. (1993): Framing. Toward a Clarification of a Fractured Paradigm. In: Journal of Communication, Vol. 43, No. 4, 51-58.

Gamson, William A./Modigliani, Andre (1987): The Changing Culture of Affirmative Action. In: Frontiers in Social Movement Theory. Greenwich, CT: JAI Press, Vol. 3, 137-177.
Gitlin, Todd (1980): The Whole World is Watching: Mass Media in the Making and Unmaking of the New Left. Berkeley, CA: University of California Press.
Iyengar, Shanto (1991): Is Anyone Responsible? Chicago: University of Chicago Press.
Lichter, S. Robert/Noyes, Richard E./Kaid, Lynda Lee (1999): No News or Negative News: How the Networks Nixed the '96 Campaign. In: Kaid, Lynda Lee/Bystrom, Dianne (Eds.): The Electronic Election. Mahwah, NJ: Lawrence Erlbaum Associates, 3-13.
McCombs, Maxwell/Ghanem, Salma (2003): The Convergence of Agenda Setting and Framing. In: Reese, Stephen D./Gandy, Oscar H. Jr./Grant, August E. (Eds.): Framing Public Life. Perspectives on Media and Our Understanding of the Social World. Mahwah, NJ, 67-81.
McCombs, Maxwell/Llamas, Juan P./Lopez-Escobar, Esteban/Rey, Federico (1997): Candidate Images in Spanish Elections. Second-Level Agenda-Setting Effects. In: Journalism and Mass Communication Quarterly, Vol. 74, No. 4, 703-717.
McCombs, Maxwell/Shaw Donald L. (1993): The Evolution of Agenda-Setting Research: Twenty-Five Years in the Marketplace of Ideas. In: Journal of Communication, Vol. 43, No. 2, 58-67.
North, Robert C./Holsti, Ole/Zaninovich, M. George/Zinnes, Dina A. (1963): Content Analysis: A Handbook with Applications for the Study of International Crisis. Evanston, IL: Northwestern University Press.
Semetko, Holli. A./Valkenburg, Patti. M. (2000): Framing European Politics. A Content Analysis of Press and Television News. In: Journal of Communication, Vol. 50, No. 2, 93-109.
Shoemaker, Pamela J./Reese, Stephen D. (1991): Mediating the Message: Theories of Influence on Mass Media Content. New York, NY: Longman Publishing Group.
Stein, Lisa (2004): The New EU. In: U.S. News & World Report, Vol. 135, No. 16, 14.
Tankard, James W./Handerson, Laura/Silberman, Jackie/Bliss, Kriss/Ghanem, Salma (1991): Media Frames. Approaches to Conceptualization and Measurement. Paper presented at the Association for Education in Journalism and Mass Communication Annual Convention. Boston, MA.

---

[1] The formula used to compute reliability is a formula given by North et al. (1963). It is given for two coders and can be modified for any number of coders. R = 2 (C1,2) / C1 + C2 . C1,2 = # of category assignments both coders agree on $C\underline{1}$ + $C\underline{2}$ = total category assignments made by both coders.

NATIONAL CASE STUDIES ON CAMPAIGN EFFECTS

The 2004 European Elections in Belgium: An Election That Went by Unnoticed

*Pascal Delwit**

1. Introduction

On June 13th 2004, Belgians voted in a European election for the sixth time. On that day, Belgium stood out from the majority of other European states on three points.

First of all, voting was compulsory. Whereas most analysts concentrated on the issue of turnout before (see Delwit 2000) and during the days following June 13th (see IDEA 2004), the Belgian state was spared the grumbles and worries about low voter turnout.

Secondly, against the tide and not at all like the state of affairs in the United Kingdom or Poland, where everything was blown out of proportion, the agenda of European issues was not the reason for any conflict or any appreciable split in the Belgian political arena (see Delwit 2004).

Lastly, beyond this observation, the European election took a backseat to the regional elections with which it was connected from that point onward. The regional elections of June 2004 were very important and virtually overshadowed their European counterpart.

The following analysis is divided into three parts. First of all, data dealing with the electoral context will be analyzed. We then break down the results according to the different institutional levels concerned. In the third and final part, we consider the impact of the European parliamentary vote on the Belgian political scene.

2. The election context

2.1 The changing legal and administrative framework for elections

Following the example of national and regional elections, the ballot system used in the Belgian European elections was proportional, organized on the basis of a D'Hondt model. The country was divided into three linguistic regions, namely Flemish, French-speaking, and German-speaking, and into four electoral districts, Wallonia, the German-speaking district, Flanders (minus the Hal-Vilvorde constituencies), and Brussels-Hal-Vilvorde. The voters from Brussels and those

---

* Pascal Delwit, PhD. *1961. Professor for Political Science at the Université libre de Bruxelles, email: pdelwit@ulb.ac.be

from the Hal-Vilvorde constituencies were able to vote for a list of French-speaking candidates or for a list of Flemish candidates. The division of seats was as follows: thirteen MEP's to be elected in the Flemish region, nine in the French-speaking and one in the German-speaking district.

In the European election, just as in other Belgian elections, voters made their decision within the system of semi-open lists. There were two options available for casting a valid ballot. First, electors could opt for the entire list as such (list ballot). Second, they could select one or several candidates from the same list (preference vote). The allocation of seats inside the list was then done on the basis of an eligibility threshold, starting from the leader on the list all the way down to the last name. If, with his/her preferential votes, a candidate did not reach the eligibility threshold, he/she "took" votes from the "top of the list", at least if there were any or if any remained. Indeed, increasingly fewer Belgians voted for the lists as such, preferring to vote for a specific candidate (see Wauters et al. 2004). In addition, the legislature halved the impact of list redistribution (see Cadranel/Delcor 2001). In other words, "block list voting" was reduced to the percent before the redistribution of seats inside the list was carried out.

Besides cutting the list partitioning effect in half, the Parliament introduced new restrictions for the creation of lists. According to this new regulation, lists had to include an equal number of males and females. In the event of an odd number of candidates, the number of individuals of one sex could only exceed the number of individuals of the other sex by one. In addition, in the future the two top spots on the list had to be filled by a member of each gender.

Finally, after having eliminated it in 2000, the Parliament reintroduced the principle of substitutes: each list contained a series of titular candidates and a series of substitute candidates. A substitute candidate becomes a MEP in case the titular candidate resigns.

2.2 The June 13th European elections: an issue of personalities

The Belgian run-up to the June 13th 2004 European elections was unquestionably marked by the decision of political parties to place their leading mentors at the top of their lists, who were not (necessarily) meant to take the seat: Prime Minister Guy Verhofstadt for the *Flemish Liberal Party* (*Vlaamse Liberalen en Democraten – VLD*), former Prime Minister Jean-Luc Dehaene for the coalition of the *Flemish Christian Democratic Party* and the *Flemish Nationalist Party* (*Christen Democratisch & Vlaams-Nieuwe Vlaams Alliantie – CD&V-N-VA*), the chairman of the French-speaking *Christian Democratic Party* (*Centre démocrate humaniste – CDH*) Joëlle Milquet, the leader of the *Socialist Party* (*Parti socialiste, PS*) Elio Di Rupo, and Vice Prime Minister and Minister of Foreign Affairs Louis Michel for the French-speaking *Liberal Party* (*Mouvement réformateur – MR*). For good measure, the coalition between the Flemish

Socialist Party (Socialistische Partij.anders, SP.A) and Spirit put forward the chairmwoman of the *Socialist Trade Union (Fédération générale du travail de Belgique – FGTB-ABVV)* Mia De Vits. Only the two *Green* parties and the far-right party *Flemish Bloc (Vlaams Blok)* selected outgoing MEPs: Pierre Jonckheer *(Ecolo)*, Bart Staes *(Groen!)*, and Frank Van Hecke *(Vlaams Blok – Vl.Blok)*. Nevertheless, it should be stressed that Van Hecke was the leader of the extreme right-wing *Flemish Party* and that *Ecolo* and *Groen!* had "surrounded" these lesser-known list leaders by personalities better known in the media: Isabelle Durant (Vice-Prime Minister between 1999 and 2003, *Ecolo*) and José Daras (Walloon Vice-Prime Minister in office at the time of the elections, *Ecolo*), Vera Dua (President of the party, Flemish regional Minister between 1999 and 2003, *Groen!*), Jos Geysel (political secretary between 1998 and 2003, *Groen!*), and Eddy Boutmans (Secretary of State for Development and Cooperation between 1999 and 2003, *Groen!*).

Strictly speaking, this was nothing new, but it was practiced on a much broader scale than before. It was a process that took place under two perspectives. The first aimed at maximizing party results as much as possible. The presence of a political *heavyweight* at the head of the list clearly increased party visibility within the context of an election that was not creating much attention or interest and was overpowered by regional elections. The second concerned the continual need to assess a person's popularity in order to highlight it in the many negotiations taking place in Belgian political life. Politicians with a high number of personal votes at elections are stronger in the daily political decision-making process. From this standpoint, there were two major contests:
1. In the Flemish political scene, the current Prime Minister competing against his predecessor, with the implicit expectation, for one or the other, to be named Commission President.
2. In the French-speaking political arena, the two most enigmatic personalities, namely the *Socialist Party* leader and the *Liberal Party* strongman, were contesting against each other.

2.3 The socio-political context

As mentioned above, the 2004 European elections were held simultaneously with the regional elections. In the latter, far more attention was logically paid to all those involved: parties, media, social organizations, and voters. The regional election issues were crucial, especially on the Flemish side. The following questions were at stake:
- If the parties so desired, to what extent could the symmetry of coalitions between the federal government and the executive branches of the federal bodies be upheld?
- Which would be the number one Flemish party – and consequently of Belgium, in principle – after Election Day?

- What results would the *Vlaams Blok* obtain, which had not lost an election since the 1988 local elections?
- Which party affiliation would the Minister-President of the Brussels Region have considering the harsh struggle between *Socialists* and *Liberals* and the ambitions of the two list leaders – Jacques Simonet (*MR*) and Charles Picqué (*PS*) – to hold this office?
- Did the *Socialist Party* intend to continue the coalition with the *Liberals* (and *Greens*) in the Walloon and Brussels regions and in the French-speaking community?

The regional and European elections took place in a complex political context. From the very start of the new federal government, in September 2003, two major factors paralyzed government activity. The first was linked to the calendar. As it was an election year, it was clear that no major activities would be undertaken during the election run-up period. At the same time, the governmental partners were starting off the new year in a different mindset. The *Socialists*, the big winner of the May 2003 Federal elections (27.9 per cent), clearly wanted to mark the occasion and convey an image of *division between their party and* the top executive branch led by Guy Verhofstadt (*VLD*). As for the *Liberals* (who came in second place with 26.8 per cent, they wanted to keep the old dynamics, in which they were the key political family and determined the way business was conducted. Under such conditions, the legislature period had a difficult start, and the coalition parties were at each other's throats on several occasions. In short, a weakened ruling majority was running in the different elections.

In addition, several issues had a certain communitarian dimension (in the Belgian context, meaning relations between linguistic communities). Just shortly before the election, there was an outburst of community agitation over the subject of dissolvement of the electoral constituency of Brussels-Hal-Vilvorde. The election constituency permitted French-speaking voters in several urban districts around Brussels (the Hal-Vilvorde districts) to vote for the same lists for the elections to the House of Representatives as the French-speaking voters in Brussels and also let Flemish voters in Brussels have their votes counted with those from the Hal-Vilvorde districts. In addition, on the occasion of the senatorial and European elections, voters had the choice between a vote for the French-speaking or Flemish-speaking list. This situation was no longer accepted by any of the Flemish parties. Arguing on the basis of a decision by the Constitutional Court (see Delwit/Pilet 2004), they demanded the dissolution of this district and the inclusion of the Hal-Vilvorde districts in the Flemish-Brabant electoral constituency. However, in so doing, they omitted to include the fact that its very creation had been the price for dealing with the demands of French-speakers for the expansion of the Brussels region.

On the day before the elections, several mayors of district communities threatened to boycott the elections and were backed by a demonstration of 10.000 to 15.000 people in favor of this demand. To ward off the threat of an election boycott, a warning was issued by the Minister of the Interior and, above all, the Flemish parties of the ruling majority pledged that they would settle the issue immediately after the election, although the demand as such was not acceptable to any French-speaking party.

2.4 A relatively weak European cleavage

Belgium is reputed to be a Europhile country, if not a Euro-enthusiastic one (see Delwit 2004a). Even though this general statement needs to be qualified, it does hold true that for fifty years there has been a kind of cross-party consensus on European issues. The study of EU-related treaty ratifications shows that approvals generally had a broader base than simple parliamentary majorities. For example, the treaties that established the Common Market and Euratom or the Single European Act were overwhelmingly approved by members of the House of Representatives (see Table 1).

Table 1: Ratification of European treaties in Belgium

	House of Representatives			Senate		
	Yes	No	Abstention	Yes	No	Abstention
European Coal and Steel Community	165	13	13	102	4	58
European Defense Community	148	49	3	125	49	3
Common Market / Euratom	179	4	2	134	2	2
European Single Act	180	0	0	148	0	0
Maastricht Treaty	146	33	3	115	26	1
Amsterdam Treaty	105	23	0	49	13	0
Nice Treaty	106	24	7	46	11	2

From the citizens' point of view, the European Union is largely viewed as a good thing for the country. However, a small number think oppositely (see Table 2).

For the past fifteen years or so, the relationship to the European construction has become a bit more complex in Belgium, in particular by the emergence and expansion of an increasingly more powerful extreme right-wing party: the *Vlaams Blok*. The *Vlaams Blok* was the only Belgian parliamentary party, which not only adopted a favourable position to the construction of a federal Europe, but which even supported the concept of a confederal Europe. The *Vlaams Blok* MP's objected to any institutional development by the European Community towards a political union. Their line of argument was based on a Flemish nationalist discourse (see Swyngedouw 1998). The Flemish extreme right wing felt that people should be able to choose their own destinies without being subject to restrictions of the EU, so they called for a clear division of tasks between the European Union and Member States.

Table 2: Belgians' judgment concerning Belgium's membership in the European Union (1991-2004) (in percentages)

	A good thing	A bad thing	Neither good nor bad	No answer	A good thing (European average)	A bad thing (European average)
1991	70	4	21	5	69	8
1992	59	9	27	5	58	12
1993	59	9	26	6	57	13
1994	56	10	27	7	55	12
1995	67	9	22	2	57	12
1996	48	15	31	6	45	17
1997	42	18	31	9	42	14
1998	47	9	36	8	54	12
1999	54	6	34	6	51	12
2000	62	10	23	5	49	14
2001	57	9	28	6	54	12
2002	58	4	30	8	53	11
2003	67	7	20	6	54	14
2004	57	10	29	5	48	17

Question: "Generally speaking, do you think that Belgium's membership in the European Community is ...?"
Source: Eurobarometer

Although the *Vlaams Blok* played a rather exceptional role in the Belgian party landscape, we should, however, point out that European issues were far from occupying the forefront of its 2004 election propaganda or political message. From this angle, the party can be considered as Eurosceptic in the view given by Peter Mair (2000), but even more so in the one given by Paul Taggart (1998). Nonetheless, we should mention that the *Vlaams Blok* was in favour of the European single market concept and recognized the peace-making role that European construction has played and the historical moment connected to Central and Eastern European enlargement.

In addition to that, some extreme left-wing parties, hostile to the European Union and to the adoption of a European *Constitution*, have hardly had any success, including the European elections, which are nevertheless better suited for tactical voting.

Another factor that complicated the relationship of political and social actors in face of the European construction was related to the reluctance that might be expressed (and sometimes translated into parliamentary votes) of Pro-Europe parties which were dissatisfied by the institutional route or hostile or reserved towards the course of the European Union which was considered neo-liberal.

In reference to reluctance expressed by federalist parties, an example would be the attitude of the *Christian Democrats* – in the opposition at the time – towards the Nice Treaty. Judging this treaty to be incomprehensible and considerably short of the developing needs of the European Union, the French-speaking, and to some extent the Flemish, *Christian Democrats* took the decision not to back it, which was quite a novel event for this political party.

Further, it has to be mentioned that the *Belgian Greens – Ecolo* and *Agalev* – rejected the Maastricht Treaty on the basis of the treaty contents and the timetable provided for the creation of the Economic and Monetary Union. However, the refusal to ratify the treaty did not denote an anti-European or anti-Community feeling. Amongst the ecologist parties (see Bomberg 1998; Van de Walle 2003), the *Belgian Greens* thus combined Europeanism and criticism towards the economic, monetary, and social route being taken by the European Union.

For two years, the *Socialists* in Flanders and in the French-speaking part have shown themselves to be especially critical towards the European Union's development, and this party has communicated its concerns about the effects of the on-going enlargement process. At the end of 2002, the *SP.A* formally expressed these concerns and criticized the non-parallel paths of enlargement and consolidation: "We can not rally behind the European project such as it has developed to date. Our position is therefore: No to Europe, unless it changes" (Le Soir, October 4th 2002).

In short, these positions of political actors and citizens towards the European Union explain the lack of issues in the European campaign in Belgium. Obviously, a number of issues touched the debate – the European Constitution, Presidency of the European Commission, the hypothetical membership of Turkey in the European Union, the Bolkestein directive[1] relating to the liberalization of services, etc. – but they never became a (major) topic in the political debate, let alone a cornerstone of the discussion.

3. The results

Since the works of Reif and Schmitt (see Reif/Schmitt 1980; Reif 1985; Marsh 1998), the study of the results of European elections has been carried out mainly from the angle of "second order" elections. However, this perspective is only partially applicable in Belgium. In the first place, this is due to institutional reasons. The low turnout linked to the mediocre interest of citizens and social actors could only be checked since voting is compulsory in Belgium. It is also difficult due to political reasons. In Belgium governments are formed by a number of parties, sometimes without any one political party being dominant. Then, it is difficult for a voter to sanction the government through protest voting.

3.1 Voter turnout

Due to compulsory voting, participation rates are very high. In all European elections, the voter turnout rate has always been higher than 90 percent. The

June 2004 European elections confirmed this trend, since nearly 91 percent of the electorate went to the polls (see Table 3).

Table 3: Electoral turnout at European elections in Belgium (in percentages)

	1979	1984	1989	1994	1999	2004
Turnout	91.3	92.1	90.7	90.7	90.9	90.8
Blanks and invalids	14.1	10.9	8.4	8.7	6.8	5.2

Source: Ministry of Interior

On the other hand, one factor distinguishes countries with compulsory voting: the significance of a proportionately higher number of blank and invalid ballots. In contrast to what was seen for voter turnout, the 5.2 percent blank and invalid ballots cast in 2004 was very high compared to the percentages recorded in other EU states. At the same time, we should note that there is a trend toward a continuous decrease in the percentage of blanks and invalid ballots. It is possible that with the introduction and development of computerized voting (see Delwit et al. 2004), which reduced potential mechanical errors – while still allowing a blank ballot – might have contributed to this reduction.

3.2 Breakdown of results

Considering the linguistic basis of Belgian political parties, it is not very informative to present the results at a national level, if not from the perspective of individual political parties. The 2004 European elections confirmed the analyses carried out since 1984: there is no longer any dominant *political family* in Belgium.[2] The three main historical political families – *Liberal*, *Socialist* and *Christian Democrat* – have always achieved relatively similar results, with each obtaining less than a quarter of the votes (see Table 4). The second point concerns the relative loss of the *Christian Democrats*. Despite an alliance in Flanders with the *Nieuw-Vlaamse Alliantie* and a recovery compared to 1999, the *Christian Democratic* family slipped to third place in the Kingdom, even though it had been the leading family for a very long time.

As for the *Liberals*, they obtained their best results in a European election in 2004. Nonetheless, they had to give up the place of number one political family which they had reached in 1999. This time the leading position went to the *Socialist* family, a rather seldom occurrence in Belgium.[3]

The results of the extreme right wing meant that from now on, Belgium was amongst the nations with the highest proportion of voters who voted for an extreme right-wing party.

Finally, the disastrous results of the *Greens* in the national elections (see Delwit/Hellings 2004; Rihoux/ Hooghe 2003) was confirmed, but in a less clearcut manner. At least each of the two *Green* parties was able to save its hides, i.e. to retain one MEP each, which was not foreseeable.

Table 4: Belgian political families in European elections (in percentages)

	1979	1984	1989	1994	1999	2004	Seats/2004
Liberals	16.3	18.1	17.8	20.6	23.8	24.0	6
Christian Democrats	37.7	27.4	29.2	24.2	18.8	23.4	6
Socialists	23.4	30.4	26.9	22.4	18.5	24.7	7
Right Wing	0.6	1.3	4.1	11.4	10.9	17.6	3
Greens	3.4	8.2	13.9	11.6	16.0	8.7	2
Far Left	4.2	2.7	1.2	1.9	1.5	1.0	0
Volksunie	6.0	8.5	5.4	4.4	7.6		0
FDF-RW	7.6	2.5	1.5	0.0	0.0		

Source: Ministry of Interior

Distinguishing between language communities, the election results show the perpetuation of distinct political landscapes. Without it coming to a clash, the competition in the French-speaking political arena mainly had *Socialists* (*PS*) and *Liberals* (*MR*) grappling with one another. Contrary to 1999, the *Socialist Party* (clearly) gained the upper hand by winning nearly 900.000 votes against 672.000 for the *Liberals* (see Table 5). This turnaround was mainly due to the excellent *Socialist* results. Indeed, although outdistanced, the French-speaking *Liberals* had their best ever result in a European election (27.6 percent in the French-speaking constituency).

Table 5: Electoral results in the French-speaking community

	Votes	Percentage	Seats
PS	878.577	36.1	4
MR	671.422	27.6	3
CDH	368.753	15.2	1
Ecolo	239.687	9.8	1
FN	181.351	7.5	0
RWF	23.090	0.9	0
CDF	19.718	0.8	0
PTB	19.645	0.8	0
MAS	5.675	0.2	0
FNB	26.775	1.1	0

Source: Ministry of Interior

For their part, the Christian Democrats (CDH) obtained respectable results but remained well below the results they got in the seventies and eighties. As for the Greens, they lost 60 percent of their voters of the 1999 European election and suffered the loss of two of their three MEPs.

Although it did not succeed in winning any seat, the *Front national* (*FN*) made remarkable gains compared to previous elections. One should add that together with the 27.000 votes obtained by its rival, the *Front nouveau de Bel-*

gique (*FNB*), this resulted in almost 210.000 voters (8.55 percent) of the French-speaking electorate opting for the extreme right wing. The position of the Belgian *Front national* was very different from its Dutch-speaking counterpart, the *Vlaams Blok*. It was a party without visibility and without party membership, and had a very poor ideological background. Plus, it had the greatest difficulty in promoting a national(ist) dimension: Belgian, French-speaking, Walloon, or Brussels do not make much sense. But in terms of elections, its results could be compared to a *soufflé*: notable rises (1994-1995 and 2003-2004), with a remarkable collapse (between 1999 and 2000), due to the lack of a political base and because of identity and organizational reasons.

Unlike the configuration that prevailed in the French-speaking spectrum, the Flemish political landscape is an extremely fragmented one. No party won more than 30 percent of the votes (see Table 6). We should add that on the occasion of this election date, the three traditional political families were off campaigning within the framework of an electoral coalition: the *Christian Democrats* (*CD&V*) with the "main" parties stemming from the former *Volksunie* (the Flemish nationalist party), *New Flemish Alliance* (*N-VA*); *Socialists* (*SP.A*) with the libertarian wing of the former *Volksunie*, *Spirit*; and the *Liberals* (*VLD*) with a small ultra-liberal party advocating the elimination of income tax, *Vivant*.

Table 6: Electoral results in Flanders

	Votes	Percentage	Seats	Percentage
VLD-Vivant	880.279	21.9	3	21.43
SP.A-Spirit	716.317	17.8	3	21.43
CD&V-N-VA	1.131.119	28.1	4	28.57
Vlaams Blok	930.731	23.2	3	21.43
Groen!	320.874	8.0	1	7.14
PVDA	24.807	0.6	0	0
LSP	14.166	0.4	0	0

Source: Ministry of Interior

The results of the European elections were basically in line with the results of the regional ballots obtained the same day, with a few fine differences. The two parties of the federal government (and in the outgoing regional executive) recorded appreciable losses compared to the May 2003 Federal elections. The trend was especially obvious for the Socialists, well below the 20 percent level. Admittedly, the list leader, the outgoing president of the Socialist trade union, did not have the same charisma or level of popularity as the Prime Minister in office, Guy Verhofstadt, or as Jean-Luc Dehaene, Vice-President of the European Convention and Prime Minister until 1999. Even so, the fragility of the 2003 election victory was underlined by this result and that, hardly better, of the regional elections.

The situation of the Prime Minister's party was hardly more enviable. It was very far away indeed from its hope of pulling ahead of the *CD&V* and emerging as *"the"* party of the centre-right in Flanders. Worse yet, not only did they lose what had won in 2003, but the *VLD* emerged from this election more divided than ever.

The *Christian Democrats* did not win the elections. At the regional level and at the European to a somewhat lesser extent, the *CD&V-N-VA* coalition was very far from reaching the percentage that some polls had predicted (29.6 per cent, *Le Soir*, March 29th 2004). More fundamentally, the electoral coalition's result did not reflect the combined results of the *CD&V* and *N-VA* in 2003, even though those results had been considered very poor for each party. In another example, in 1999 the combined result of *Christian Democrats* and *Volksunie* reached 34 percent. Even if at the European level Jean-Luc Dehaene did contribute just a bit *more*, this contribution certainly did not allow *Flemish Christian Democracy* to quietly contemplate the future, after fifteen years of a downward spiral.

The real winner of the election was the *Vlaams Blok*. Led by Frank Vanhecke, the extreme right-wing Flemish nationalist confirmed his *Iron Law* practiced since the October 1988 local elections: the party has not lost any election since. Compared with the European elections in June 1999, it gained eight additional percentage points. And if one takes the May 2003 Federal elections as a reference, the results are up again by six percentage points. The *Vlaams Blok* came in ahead of the two parties of the federal executive and matched the results of the *CD&V*.

Finally, *Groen!*, the Flemish Green Party, succeeded in passing the 5 percent threshold and therefore held onto a seat, which had been unimaginable a few months before the elections.

As mentioned above, the election in the German-speaking district was an electoral contest in name only. From the outset, the seat has gone to the *Christlich Soziale Partei* (the German-speaking branch of the *CDH, CSP*). 2004 was no different. The German-speaking *Christian Democrats* triumphed over the *Liberals* with ease (leading with 20 percentage points!). We should note that this election confirmed the difficulty that left-wing parties have in gaining a foothold among German-speaking Belgians. *Ecolo* and the *Sozialistische Partei* (the German-speaking branch of the *PS, SP*), who nonetheless hold the Minister-Presidency of the German-speaking Community, only got 25 percent of votes.

3.3 A leadership struggle unfavourable to the Liberals

The proportional voting system with semi-open lists, combined with an increased personalization of the political contest, has led political actors to examine the preferential votes submitted for candidates with almost equal scrutiny as the results themselves, if not even more so at times. In this game of daily struggles for power, inherent in coalition governments, the *Liberals* turned out to be the losers.

In the French-speaking constituency, the *Socialist party* leader, Elio Di Rupo (483.644 votes) was ahead of the outgoing Foreign Affairs Minister, Louis Michel (327.374 votes), the leader of the *Centre démocrate humaniste*, Joëlle Milquet (191.900 votes), Secretary of State for European Affairs, Frédérique Ries (*MR* – 123.000 votes), outgoing European Commissioner Philippe Busquin (*PS* –114.503) votes), Finance Minister Didier Reynders (*MR* – 95.475 votes), and former Vice Prime Minister from *Ecolo*, Isabelle Durant (73.597 votes).

In the Flemish political arena, on this sensitive area of preferential votes, Guy Verhofstadt was overtaken by his predecessor. With 651.345 preferential votes, the former *CD&V* and Belgian strongman completely outdistanced Guy Verhofstadt (*VLD* – 388.011 votes). Winning third place, the leader of the *Vlaams Blok*, Frank Vanhecke (260.430 votes) arrived in front of the head of the *Socialist* list, Mia De Vits (202.402 votes) and the strongman of the Flemish extreme right wing, Filip De Winter (193.525 votes).

What was the impact of the candidature of well-known personalities without any ambition to sit? As expected, a certain number of those elected on June 13th quickly announced their resignation. In total, eight of twenty-four elected MEPs decided not to assume their office: Geert Bourgeois (*N-VA*), Michel Daerden (*PS*), Karel De Gucht (*VLD*), Filip De Winter (*Vlaams Blok*), Elio Di Rupo (*PS*), Louis Michel (*MR*), Joëlle Milquet (*CDH*), and Guy Verhofstadt (*VLD*). However, in anticipation of this event, several parties had lined up the necessary substitutes for the leading candidates: for example, Philippe Busquin, former *PS* president and outgoing European Commissioner, Antoine Duquesne, outgoing leader of *MR*, Raymond Langendries, former President of the House of Representatives, and Dirk Sterkx, outgoing leader of the *VLD*.

4. The impact of the European elections on national politics

The Belgian political system was greatly affected by the results of June 13th 2004. But to tell the truth, it wasn't so much the European elections as the outcome of the regional elections, namely the fact that in Flanders one out of every four voters voted for an extreme right-wing party. This new extreme right-wing upsurge, the defeat of the Flemish government parties, the victory of the *Socialist Party* in the Brussels Region, and the good showing by the *Centre démocrate humaniste* were important topics addressed by the analysis and made the European election results all the more *invisible*, with the exception of the two *battles of the leaders:* between Jean-Luc Dehaene and Guy Verhofstadt on the one hand and Elio Di Rupo and Louis Michel on the other.

Generally speaking, the European elections had no impact on national politics, except perhaps on the *Greens,* who had feared being politically marginalized at the national level and in *Green* European organizations (*European Green*

Party and the *Green-EFA group* in the European Parliament) on the supposition that they would not have been able to partially redress the 2003 election disaster.

In fact, the European issue only (re)appeared at the political and media forefront on the occasions of the European Council June 17th-18th 2004, the ratification of the European Constitution, and the negotiations regarding the appointment of the European Commission President.[4]

Backed by the German and French delegations, Guy Verhofstadt came up against the opposition from several other delegations, including British and Italian. This failure enabled his Minister of Foreign Affairs, Louis Michel, to walk off with the minor role of Belgian European Commissioner insofar as José-Manuel Barroso was preferred to Jean-Luc Dehaene inside the EPP and the EPP-ED group and was nominated on June the 29th by the Council meeting of Heads of State or Government.

5. Conclusion

In the end, the European elections hardly gathered any attention or actors. Paradoxically, the campaign only attracted public attention on the issue concerning the splitting of the Brussels-Hal-Vilvorde district and the threat of boycott by a number of mayors from the Flemish outskirts of Brussels, in short, Belgo-Belgian issues.

The absence of any focus on European issues among political parties (with the exception, in part, of the *Vlaams Blok*) and in particular the contemporaneousness of these elections and regional elections – perhaps the most important elections in Belgium from now on – contributed to this low visibility, if not to say invisibility. Of course, one should consider the relative unfamiliarity with the mechanisms of the European decision-making process and its machinery in the European Parliament.

Most of the attention was focused on peripheral aspects (without being trivial) of the elections: the battle, not for seats but for preferential votes, oddly between Jean-Luc Dehaene and Guy Verhofstadt, on the one hand, and Elio Di Rupo and Louis Michel, on the other.

All the same, because voting is compulsory, the Belgians did go and vote. This obligation to vote distorted the outcome of the Belgian vote compared to other European countries, and logically had an effect on general statements concerning large-scale abstention. On the other hand, the punishment mechanism for the government was demonstrated to some degree: three of the four Federal government parties (the *VLD*, *MR*, and *SP.A-Spirit*) suffered a setback compared with the 2003 national result. The *PS* was the exception in this picture.

Paradoxically, however, it is not certain if the election outcomes serve as confirmation for assumptions concerning theories about second-order elections. Indeed, two facts qualify our last remark. The first is that for two of the three parties concerned (*VLD* and *MR*), the outcome was less harsh than at the regional level, which was supposedly a first-order election with a greater amount of tactical voting. Only the *Flemish Socialists* obtained worse results in the European elections than in the regional one. The second has to do with the terms of comparison. If one takes the May 2003 national elections as a reference point, the remark is unambiguous, but we have to stress that the *Liberals* of the *VLD* and *MR* had achieved their best result ever since the introduction of universal suffrage at this election. Then, it was difficult to improve this electoral result. On the other hand, if we look at things from the perspective of *European elections* in Belgium, it must be noted that the *Liberals*, who were presented as the losers of the June 13th 2004 elections, achieved in the 2004 European elections the best results ever obtained in this type of election.

References

Bomberg, Elizabeth (1998): Green Parties and Politics in the European Union. London: Routledge.
Cadranel, Benjamin/Delcor, Frédéric (2001): La réduction de moitié de l'effet dévolutif de la case de tête. In: Actes du Colloque (Eds.): Les élections dans tous leurs états organize. Brussels: Bruylant, 121-144 [Cadranel/Delcor: Reducing by Half the Effect of List Voting].
Delwit, Pascal (2000): Electoral Participation and European Polls: A Limited Legitimacy. In: Grunberg, Gérard/Perrineau, Pascal/Ysmal, Colette (Eds.): Europe at the Polls. The European Elections of 1999, London-New York: Palgrave-Macmillan, 207-222.
Delwit, Pascal (2004): La Belgique, l'Union européenne et les élections européennes. Brussels: Bureau belge auprès du Parlement européen [Belgium, the European Union and the European Elections].
Delwit, Pascal (2004a): Belgique et Union européenne: une histoire d'amour et de raison. In: Dulphy, Anne/Manigand Christian (Eds.): Les opinions publiques face à l'Europe communautaire. Entre cultures nationales et horizon européen. Brussels-Bern-Berlin: Peter Lang, 79-102 [Delwit: Belgium and the European Union. A Love Story and a Marriage of Convenience. In: Dulphy/Manigand: Public Opinion on the European Union. Between National Cultures and a European Horizon].
Delwit, Pascal/Hellings, Benoit (2004): Ecolo et les élections du 18 mai 2003. Du paradis au purgatoire ou à l'enfer? In: L'année sociale 2003, No. 1, 38-49 [Ecolo and the 18th of May 2003 Elections. From Paradise to Purgatory or to Hell?].
Delwit, Pascal/Kulahci, Erol/Pilet Jean-Benoit (2004): Le vote électronique en Belgique. Un choix légitime? Ghent: Academia Press [Electronic Voting in Belgium. A legitimate Choice?].
Delwit, Pascal/Pilet Jean-Benoit (2004): Fédéralisme, institutions et vie politique. Stabilité, instabilité et retour. In: Coenen, Marie-Thérèse/Govaert, Serge

(Eds.): L'état de la Belgique? 1989-2004. Quinze années à la charnière du siècle, Brussels: De Boeck, 43-79 [Delwit/Pilet: Federalism, Institutions, and Political Life. Stability, Instability and Return. In: Coenen/Govaert: The State of Belgium? 1989-2004. Fifteen Years at the turn of the century].

Deschouwer, Kris (1999): From Consociationalism to Federalism: How the Belgian Parties Won. In: Deschouwer, Kris/Luther, Kurt R. (Eds): Party Elites in Divided Societies. Political Parties in Consociational Democracies. London: Routledge, 74-107.

IDEA (2004): Europe Expands, Turnout Falls. The Significance of the 2004 European Parliament Elections. Stockholm: International Institute for Democracy and Electoral Assistance.

Mair, Peter (2000): The Limited Impact of Europe on National Party Systems. In: West European Politics, Vol. 23, No. 4, 26-51.

Marsh, Michael (1998): Testing the Second-Order Election Theory after Four European Elections. In: British Journal of Political Science, Vol. 28, 591-607.

Reif, Karlheinz (1985): Ten Second-Order National Elections. In: Reif, Karlheinz (Ed.): Ten European Elections. London: Gower, 1-36.

Reif, Karlheinz/Schmitt, Herman (1980): Nine Second-Order National Elections. A Conceptual Framework for the Analysis of European Election Results. In: European Journal of Political Research, Vol. 8, No. 1, 3-44.

Rihoux, Benoît/Hooghe, Marc (2003): The Harder the Fall... The Greens in the Belgian General Elections of 18 May 2003. In: Environmental Politics, Vol. 12, No. 4, 120-126.

Swyngedouw, Marc (1998): L'idéologie du Vlaams Blok. L'offre identitaire. In: Revue internationale de politique comparée, Vol. 5, No. 1, 189-202 [The Flemish Bloc Ideology. The Identity's Proposal].

Taggart, Paul (1998): A Touchstone of Dissent. Euroscepticism in Contemporary Western European Party Systems. In: European Journal of Political Research, Vol. 33, No. 3, 363-388.

Van de Walle, Cédric (2003): Le rôle de la Fédération européenne des partis verts. Etude de la coopération multilatérale entre partis verts à l'échelle européenne. Brussels: Thèse de doctorat en science politique de l'ULB [The Role of the European Federation of Green Parties. Research on the Multilateral Cooperation between Green Parties at the European Level].

Wauters, Bram/Weekers, Karolien/Pilet, Jean-Benoit (2004): Het gebruik van de voorkeurstem bij de regionale en Europese parlementsverkiezingen van 13 juni 2004. In: Res Publica, Vol. XLVI, No. 2-3, 377-412 [The Use of Personal Votes at the June 2004 Regional and European Elections].

[1] In Belgium too there is opposition to the Bolkestein Directive. It is led by leftist and green organisations and parties. For example, the French-speaking *Socialist Party* has launched a petition against this directive on its website: http://www.stopbolkestein.org/

[2] Aggregate results of *Christian Democratic Parties* and *Socialist Parties* give evidence of this situation: 78.5 percent in 1954, 62.6 percent in 1965, 58.0 in 1987, and 48.0 in the 2004 European elections.

[3] After World War II, this only occurred in the 1987 and 1991 national elections and in the 1984 European election.

[4] For example in two important newspapers *Le Soir* and *De Staandard*: "Chirac en Schröder pokeren met Verhofstadt", *De Staandard*, June 17th 2004; "Verhofstadt jette l'éponge étoilée", *Le Soir*, June 19th 2004; "Dehaene ziet zich niet als kandidaat-voorzitter", *De Staandard*, June 19th 2004; "L'histoire du Belge qui se rêvait Président", *Le Soir*, June 21st 2004; "Angleterre-Belgique: 2-0. Dehaene-Verhofstadt: ?", *Le Soir*, June 21st 2004; "Verhofstadt: retour à la case 16", *Le Soir*, June 21st 2004; "Waarom Guy Verhofstadt geen voorzitter van de Commissie kon worden", De Staandard, June 21st 2004; "Quelle perle pour l'Europe?", *Le Soir*, June 26th 2004; "Verhofstadt en Michel wilden Dehaene lanceren voor Commissie", *De Staandard*, June 26th 2004; "Barroso donné grand favori", *Le Soir*, June 28th 2004.

Campaigning and Media in Austria: Lessons to be Learned from the "HPM Phenomenon" in the European Parliamentary Elections

*Peter Filzmaier**

1. Introduction

For political scientists and communication experts it seems to be common knowledge that campaigns on a national level are either won or lost through air wars on mass media, which, however, must be supported by a solid ground war with get-out-the-vote-drives (GOTV, Green 2004) in order to mobilize the base of a party. Impressed by the example of the United States, we usually further argue that media-centred democracies are dominated by television, whereas newspapers have less influence on campaigning and/or have to adapt sound bites and TV-style pictures to the print medium (see Altendorfer 2004: 346-349; Althaus 2003: 295; Filzmaier 2004b).

On June 13th 2004, a new party list in Austria that had never competed in any campaign before and was founded less than two months before election day finished in third place leaving the *Liberal Party* (*Freiheitliche Partei Österreichs/FPOE*), formerly led by the well-known right-wing populist Jörg Haider, as well as the *Green Party* far behind. The *Social Democrats* (*Sozialdemokratische Partei Österreichs/SPOE*) and the conservative *Peoples Party* (*Österreichische Volkspartei/OEVP*) gained some additional votes because of the *FPOE* disaster, but both clearly failed to obtain results comparable to those in the national parliamentary elections in 2002. Responsible for all this was the list of *Hans-Peter Martin* („*HPM*") although

- as a founder of a totally new list *HPM* had no conception for conducting get-out-the-vote drives at all,
- his platform suffered from a total lack of money, and
- Austrian television widely ignored him.

How could this happen against all odds and against almost all theories of campaigning? The only strong supporter of *HPM* was the daily paper *Neue Kronen Zeitung* (*NKZ*) followed by a kind of a *hype* in other printed media. For this reason, it seems worthwhile to discuss the idea that – at least under certain circumstances – print media are underestimated by campaigns and how we can profit from this knowledge in the future. This contribution will further analyze results

---

* Peter Filzmaier, PhD. *1967. Professor for Political Science and Head of Department for Political Communication at the University of Krems, email: peter.filzmaier@donau-uni.ac.at

and turnout of the European parliamentary elections in Austria with regard to the party system and the electoral system as well as to the campaigns and the strategies behind them, while focussing on:
- results by socio-demographic groups like gender, age, occupation etc. and by categories of EU support and EU scepticism,
- reasons for a voter turnout that was 40 (!) percent points lower than in the last national parliamentary elections, and
- voting behaviour.

The following analysis is empirically based on a series of pre-election day interviews and exit polls that were carried out by the *Austrian Society for Marketing* (*OGM*) and commissioned by the *Austrian Broadcasting Corporation* (*ORF*) (see OGM 2004; Filzmaier/Hajek 2004a). Various data of other surveys on the European parliamentary elections in Austria will also be considered (Plasser/Ulram 2004b, SORA 2004).

2. Austria elects Europe

Every analysis must take into consideration the critical view which Austrians hold against the European Union. The EU is often associated with negative issues, such as:
- The conflict with the Czech Republic about the atomic power plant Temelin and the Benes Decretes which led to the expulsion and expropriation of the Sudeten- and Carpats Germans and Hungarians without any compensation after Second World War.
- The EU-enlargement which is often seen as a danger instead of an opportunity.
- The failed negotiations for a new transit treaty between Austria and the EU.
- The budget stabilization pact of the EU which de facto has been declared invalid.
- The negotiations for a new EU-Constitution which failed on first attempt.

Only about half of the Austrians (49 percent) saw an advantage in EU-membership in the election year 2004. Forty-two percent feared disadvantages (OGM 2004). Furthermore, the EU still is underestimated in the minds of the Austrian population (see Plasser/Ulram 2002: 174): in 2002 71 percent of the Austrian population stated that their national citizenship was more attractive than being a EU citizen. Only 8 percent stressed that they were a citizen of Europe and 21 percent felt as both Austrians and Europeans. In comparison to the year of accession (1995) when only 4 percent felt as European citizens, an increase of a European identity is evident, however, this seems to be limited to groups with a very high educational level.

Furthermore, 40 percent of the Austrian population have the feeling that the EU permanently fails to deal successfully with important issues (see Plasser/Ulram 2002: 180). Since 1996 the number of supporters of the accession to the EU has been increasing, because previously undecided voters now agree with the statement that joining the EU was the right decision. Nevertheless, the proportion of EU opponents (approximately 35 percent) stayed constant for a long time until the end of the year 2000. Then there was a decrease to 26 percent in 2004, but most of the EU opponents strongly supported HPM: 24 percent of his total votes came from this group (see Plasser/Ulram 2004b: 8, 19).

2.1 Overview of results

On June 13th 2004, 6.049.129 Austrians were eligible to vote in the elections to the European Parliament. Of the only 2.566.639 votes cast, 2.500.610 (97.4 percent) were valid and 66.029 (2.6 percent) were invalid. These figures result in a voter turnout of only 42.4 percent, which is the lowest result ever obtained in nationwide elections in Austria. Compared with 1999, this means a decrease of 7 percent. In comparison to the Austrian presidential election which was held on April 25, 2004 (see OGM 2004), turnout was almost 30 percent lower. The percentage of voting for the national parliamentary elections in 2002 was twice as high as for Europe in 2004.

Table 1: Results of the European Parliamentary elections in Austria, 2004 (in percentages)

Name of Party	Short Form	Votes	Percent	Seats
Sozialdemokratische Partei Österreichs (Social Democratic Party of Austria)	SPOE	833.517	33.33 (+1.6)	7 (+/-0)
Österreichische Volkspartei (Austrian People's Party)	OEVP	817.716	32.7 (+2.0)	6 (-1)
Freiheitliche Partei Österreichs (Liberal Party of Austria)	FPOE	157.722	6.31 (-17.1)	1 (-4)
Die Grünen – Die Grüne Alternative (The Greens)	Gruene	322.429	12.89 (+3.6)	2 (+/-0)
Opposition für ein solidarisches Europa – Europäische Linke, KPÖ, Unabhängige (Opposition for a Europe of Solidarity – European Left, Communist Party of Austria, Independents)	LINKE	19.530	0.78*	-*
Liste Dr. Hans-Peter Martin – für echte Kontrolle in Brüssel (List Dr. Hans Peter Martin – for real control in Brussels)	MARTIN („HPM")	349.696	13.98*	2*

Source: Ministry of the Interior, Republic of Austria.
* No candidature in 1999.

The SPOE got 33.3 percent of the nationwide votes and – based on an electoral system of proportional representation with party lists on the ballot – seven of 18 possible seats. The *OEVP* gained 32.7 percent and six seats, followed by the *Greens* with 12.9 percent and two seats. The list "*Dr. Hans Peter Martin – for a true control in Brussels*" (*HPM*) obtained with its first-time candidature 14 percent of the votes and two seats (see Table 1). The list was led by *HPM* as a former *SPOE* representative who had focused on the abuses within the European parliament and had been strongly supported by the *NKZ* as the leading Austrian daily newspaper.

Tail ender of the political parties who made it into the EU parliament was the *FPOE* with 6.3 percent. The only seat of the *FPOE* was not given to Hans Kronberger, who was first place on the party list, but to Andreas Mölzer who was number three and got 21.980 personal votes. He gained 13.9 percent of all votes for the *FPOE* and therefore was able to reach the number one position (in accordance with the European Parliamentary election law in Austria which provides for an upgrade within the list when 7 percent of all party votes are personal ones). The left platform "*Opposition for a Europe of Solidarity*" by communists and others got 0.8 percent.

Because of the enlargement of the EU through ten new members in May 2004, Austria was faced with a reduction of representatives from 21 to 18. Therefore, it is quite difficult to make references to the election result of 1999 in reference to number of seats. However, in comparison to 1999, the election outcome shows an increase of 1.6 percentage points for the *Social Democratic Party,* while the *OEVP* gained 2 points. With 17.1 percentage points the *FPOE* had to face the biggest loss of votes ever seen in a nationwide election. The *Greens* gained 3.6 points. Looking at the number of seats, the *SPOE* and the *Greens* were able to hold their results of 1999. The *OEVP* lost one of their seven seats, the *FPOE* lost four of their five representatives. The lists *HPM* and the left platform did not participate in the elections of 1999, therefore no comparison can be drawn.

2.2 Voter transition

Compared to 1999 the analysis of voter transition of the European Parliamentary elections in Austria 2004 shows the following results (see Table 2 and SORA 2004): as for all elections in Austria since 2002 with the exception of Carinthia 2004 the most dramatic change was the decline of the *FPOE*: 60 percent of the *FPOE* voters of 1999 (over 400.000 votes) did not participate in the election 2004.

The decrease in voter turnout seems to be strongly related to the abstention of former *FPOE* supporters: these voters are now available for all political parties. In national parliamentary elections 2002 they voted for the *OEVP*, in various regional elections 2003/04 they showed a slight tendency toward electing the *SPOE* (see Filzmaier 2004a: 7-10). In the European parliamentary elections

2004 they mainly voted for the list of *HPM* whose supporters were strongly protest orientated.

Table 2: Voter transition in the European Parliamentary elections in Austria, 2004

	SPOE 2004	OEVP 2004	FPOE 2004	Greens 2004	HPM 2004	Left Wing 2004	Non-Voters 2004	Total 1999
SPOE 1999	76	1	0	1	9	0	13	100
OEVP 1999	2	80	1	3	6	0	8	100
FPOE 1999	3	2	16	3	15	0	60	100
Greens 1999	5	1	2	71	8	1	13	100
Others 1999	17	19	11	18	16	7	12	100
Non-Voters 1999	2	2	0	1	2	0	93	100

All data in percent.
Example: 76 percent of the *SPOE* voters in 1999 voted for their party again in 2004, 1 percent voted for the *OEVP* and the *Greens*, nearly none voted for the *FPOE*, 9 percent voted for *HPM*, 13 percent did not vote at all, etc.
Source: SORA 2004.

The *FPOE* lost 15 percent of its voters to the list of *HPM*. Beside these 100.000 votes, the list *HPM* gained 81.000 votes from the *SPOE*, 65.000 votes from 1999 non-voters, and 54.000 votes from the *OEVP*. With a rate of party-aligned voters of 80 percent the *OEVP* was most successful in bringing its voters from the year 1999 to the polls again. The *SPOE* (76 percent) and the *Greens* (71 percent) were nearly as successful in party alignment. The *SPOE* was also able to gain voters from voter transition from the *OEVP*, the *Greens*, and the *FPOE*. In other words: its loss of voters was smaller than what it gained from the other parties. A clear win of the *SPOE* was prevented by the success of the list *HPM* and the connected loss of *SPOE*-voters to this list.

2.3 Motives for voting and party preferences

The gathering of a great number of disappointed and disillusioned voters combined with the sudden fall of the *FPOE* was the reason for *HPM*'s success (see Table 3; OGM 2004; Filzmaier/Hajek 2005; Filzmaier 2005b). The protest vote reflects citizens' annoyance with the EU and is less an expression of domestic political criticism. *HPM* managed to exploit the EU parliament scandal ("expense account fiddling" and lack of control) and make it an election issue resulting in a landslide of votes for his list. As could be expected, 97 percent of his voters supported his accusation of scandalous behaviour by EU representatives and declared it as their most important voting motive.

Table 3: Motives for voting a political party, European Parliamentary elections in Austria 2004 (in percentages, multiple responses allowed)

Voter Motives	All Parties	SPOE	OEVP	FPOE	Greens	HPM
Control of abuses in the European Parliament	85	85	89	99	73	97
Chosen party is the best representative for Austria	78	83	86	84	70	73
EU-critical party	60	60	38	75	58	79
Traditional/Accustomed Voters	58	76	70	73	42	0
Pro-EU Party	54	59	70	32	63	28
Against the accession of Turkey to the EU	54	52	56	63	34	76
Role of the SPOE during the EU sanctions against Austria	36	48	36	66	19	51
Protest against the national government	26	43	13	23	32	26
Josef Broukal-Statement*	24	18	29	48	15	34

* In a speech to the Austrian Parliament Representative Josef Broukal alleged that the *OEVP* and the *FPOE* mourn the loss of National Socialism times.
Source: OGM 2004.

On the other hand, a very high percentage of *HPM* voters identified themselves with critical opinions which had not been voiced by *HPM*. The following issues were very important for *HPM* voters, although they were put on the agenda by the *FPOE*: general critique of the EU (important for 79 percent), opposition against the accession of Turkey to the EU (51 percent), and even disapproval of the role of the *SPOE* during the so-called EU sanctions against Austria in 2000, when the governments of the 14 other EU member states restricted their official contacts because Jörg Haider's far right *FPOE* became a coalition partner of the *OEVP*.

The obvious conclusion that the *FPOE* gathered votes for *HPM* with its critique points can be explained by various factors:

- Since the *FPOE* is part of the government, it has lost its ability to skim off the protest potential. The recovery of the *FPOE* after its crash in 2002 is confined to Carinthia where Haider won regional elections in 2004. If this party aggressively addresses critical issues, it will benefit *HPM* and other oppositional parties.
- In general it appears that voters are becoming increasingly mobilized by e-motions Annoyance with current politics in parts of the voting population may have led to more votes for *HPM*.
- Two-thirds of the EU-critics did not go to the polls. The other third voted for the list *HPM* and the *FPOE* more often than the general electorate did. These data show that in particular *HPM* and also the *FPOE* to a lesser extent would have profited if more EU-critics would have gone to the polls. The higher proportion of pro-Europeans among the *OEVP, Greens,* and *SPOE* voters was no surprise.

The remedy of abuses and control of the EU was the most important voting motive of Austrian voters which was independent of party preferences (and indicated by 85 percent of all interviewees in an exit poll, see Table 3). The representation of Austrian interests in Brussels through the elected party (78 percent) came in second. For 58 percent of the electorate their habitual voting behaviour was a very important reason for choosing their accustomed party. Furthermore, the European Parliamentary elections cannot be seen as a "reminder lesson" for the government, because only 26 percent of the voters stated that as a very important reason for voting.

Distinguishing between political parties, the following interesting aspects were found:

- Only voters of the *SPOE* were strongly mobilized through the call for a "reminder lesson" for the national government (43 percent). Furthermore, this group of voters was mobilized through the debate about the role of the *SPOE* during the sanctions of the EU member states against the Austrian *OEVP/FPOE* government 2000. Tradition – important for 58 percent of the total electorate – was seen as the main reason for *SPOE* voters to vote for "their" party (76 percent).

- The voters of the *OEVP* were strongly attracted by the clear Pro-European position of their party. The voting motive "Pro-EU Party" (54 percent overall) was extraordinarily strong among *OEVP* voters (70 percent), whereas the issue about the EU sanctions was of secondary importance.

- Besides the voters of the list *HPM*, the voters of the *FPOE* were mostly attracted by the remedy of abuses and increased control in the EP. The voting motive "Critical EU-party" (60 percent overall) was a main motive among *FPOE* and *HPM* voters (75 percent respectively 79 percent). Also important for this group was the "Broukal-statement" as well as the role of the *SPOE* during the EU sanctions.

- The voters of the *Green Party*, who were very critical of the EU in former times, have changed their attitude very clearly over the last years. For this group the pro-EU attitude of the *Greens* was extremely important for voting. Recent affairs (EU sanctions and Broukal) did not really impress these voters. With its development to a middle-sized party, the *Greens* have become the driving force of European integration, and its electorate has changed accordingly: 63 percent mentioned "Pro EU" as their main motive for voting the party.

- The voters of *HPM* were the strongest EU–critics. As most important motive they mentioned the control of abuses in the EU, followed by criticism against the EU, and opposition to the accession of Turkey as a member state of the EU. Furthermore, the role of the *SPOE* during the EU sanctions and the Broukal-statement played an important role. Noteworthy is the already mentioned overlapping of traditional agenda points of the *FPOE* with motives of the *HPM* voters. This was a further indication of how strong *HPM* broke into the *FPOE* voters segment.

3. The *NKZ* and the *HPM* phenomenon

3.1 Media and political campaigns in Austria

The Austrian media system is characterized
- by the dominance of one public broadcasting corporation, ORF (private television stations in Austria have only a very small percentage of the market and also must compete against other foreign cable and satellite programmes) – the ORF television station has a market share of 52 percent, and the ORF radio station 75.2 percent (see ORF 2004) – and
- by a concentration of a small number of press publishing houses with a high share of German co-owners. To put it clearly: Austria is the only country within Western democracies with such a high media and – in particular – press concentration (see Plasser/Ulram 2004a: 43).

The most widely read daily newspaper in Austria is the *Neue Kronen Zeitung* (*NKZ*) with a range of nearly three million readers. Its range increased from 5.4 percent to 43.8 percent of the adult population between the years 1965 to 2003 (see Table 4). The market share increased to nearly two-thirds of the total number of readers. In relation to the number of inhabitants of a country, the *NKZ* is by far the most widely read daily newspaper of the world and despite the fact that Austria is a relatively small country, even in absolute numbers among the 20 leading newspapers.

Table 4: Readership of selected print media in Austria

Medium	Readership (viewers/listeners) in thousands*	Range in per cent*	Share of readers who are interested in domestic and foreign politics (in per cent)	HPM-Factor in reporting**
NKZ	2.925	43.8	~25	+++
Kleine Zeitung	829	12.4	~29	++
Kurier	745	11.2	~42	+
Der Standard	390	5.8	~48	+
Die Presse	339	5.1	~50	o
Total of daily newspapers	5.019	75.2		++
ORF-television station	4.095	60.0	-	+
ORF-radio station	~5.000	74.9	-	+

* Adult Population (over 12 respectively 14 years).
** "+(++)" stands for intensity of positive reporting on *HPM* based on a quantitative and qualitative content analysis.
Sources: ORF 2004, Media-Analysis 2004 and own research

In 2003/04 the market leader *NKZ* had more readers than all daily newspapers ranked from second to sixth place taken together.[1] It was followed by the *Kleine*

Zeitung and the *Kurier* with 830.000 respectively 740.000 readers daily. The numerical difference between these yellow press papers, characterized by positive reports on *HPM*, and the so-called quality papers *Die Presse* and *Der Standard* that reported on *HPM* less positively or partly even ignored him but only have around 350.000 readers each is quite evident. The readership statistics of weekly newspapers is led by the tabloid *Die Ganze Woche* (approximately 1.5 million readers), followed by the magazine News (1.25 million readers), and normally the television magazine *tv-media*, which has almost one million readers despite the competition with the television supplements in the Thursday and Friday issues of the major daily newspapers. Especially the magazine "News" covered the candidature of *HPM* in a very positive way.

The media power of the *NKZ* had been demonstrated repeatedly before the European parliamentary elections 2004 (see Pelinka et al. 1992), e.g. 1984 in a campaign against the construction of the Danube power plant in Hainburg and 2002 concerning the *FPOE* organized referendum "Veto against Temelin" (for an Austrian veto against the accession of the Czech Republic to the EU if the Czechs put their nuclear power plant Temelin near the Upper Austrian border in operation). In the latter case, 25 percent of the *NKZ* readers signed up for this referendum, but only 10 percent of the readers of other daily newspapers did the same (see Plasser/Ulram 2002: 185).

Table 5: Importance and (subjective) reliability of various sources of political information in Austria, 2003/04
(in percentages, multiple answers allowed)

	Seen as primary source for political information (multiple answers possible)		Think it is very reliable	
	For politics in 2003	For the campaign of EP elections in 2004*	For politics in 2003	For the campaign of EP elections in 2004*
Television	75	56	51	37
Daily Newspapers	49	51	14	19
Radio	38	17	8	4
Magazines	n.a.	4	2	1
Discussions	8	12	n.a.	10
Internet	4	8	2	4

* Remaining answers are "others" or "no comment".
Sources: Opinion polls of Fessel+GFK-Institutes (see Plasser/Ulram 2004a: 73) and OGM 2004.

In the case of the European parliamentary elections, the extraordinary position of the *NKZ* even reduced the influence of the *ORF* television station. In general, 75 percent of the Austrians say that they get their political information mainly from television (see Table 5). Although multiple responses are possible, newspapers (49 percent) and radio stations (38 percent) follow with a clear distance: this trend of decreasing importance has gotten considerably stronger during the last decades. Further, television is also seen as a very credible and reliable source of information (stated by 51 percent) compared to newspapers (with only 14 percent) (see Plasser/Ulram 2004a: 73; Filzmaier 2004b: 10).

In contrast to these data from 2003, in an exit poll on election day on June 13th 2004, only 56 percent of the actual voters (!) mentioned television as a primary source for political information during the European parliamentary election campaign. Fifty-one percent stated this for newspapers. Only 37 percent indicated television as the most reliable source during the campaign. In spite of a large number of refusals to answer newspapers reached nearly 20 percent (OGM 2004). In connection with the market leadership of the *NKZ*, this is a definite indicator for its power to influence election outcomes.

3.2 Detailed analysis of the *HPM* results in connection with the *NKZ*

Compared to the total electorate, *HPM* voters tended to be older (as *NKZ* readers are). Furthermore, *HPM* results showed a higher share of female voters (in contrast to *NKZ* readers), of male and female pensioners (the same as *NKZ* readers), and less educated workers (as *NKZ* readers are, too) (see Table 6). So we can summarize: in comparing the socio-demographic profile of the *HPM* voters with the readers of the *NKZ*, there is a strong correspondence of age and occupational level, which indirectly indicates a correlation with the level of education. Only the gender of *HPM* voters seems to deviate from the profile of the *NKZ* readers. Middle-aged voters with a lower educational level and a low or middle occupational status voted for *HPM* and read the *NKZ*.

Table 6: Profile of HPM-voters, European Parliamentary elections in Austria 2004 (in percentages)

Category	Share of *HPM* voters	Share of all of voters
Male	43	48
Female	57	52
Under 30 years	12	18
30–44 years	24	25
45–60 years	33	27
60 years and older	31	30
Self-employed	9	11
White collar workers	32	35
Blue collar workers	12	7
Unemployed	15	18
Pensioners	32	29

Source: Plasser/Ulram 2004b: 21.

Who else voted for *HPM*? The majority of his supporters were critical of the EU (only *FPOE* voters are even more distant and sceptical. 86 percent of the *HPM* voters were annoyed with the EU lately, two-thirds feared disadvantages by the

EU-enlargement, which took place on May 1st 2004 (see Table 7). In any case, the *NKZ* is very reserved about the EU. It has always been a traditional position of the *NKZ* to criticize the EU. Furthermore, in former elections a significant number of *NKZ* readers were government-critical protest voters, which corresponds to the motives of nearly all *HPM* voters who stressed their disappointment with and resentments about domestic and European politics. 77 percent of the *HPM* voters are regular readers of the *NKZ*. Of those *NKZ* readers who participated in the European parliamentary election in Austria on June 13th 2004, 21 percent voted for the list of *HPM* (see Table 6 above).

Table 7: Political opinions of HPM-voters, European Parliamentary elections in Austria 2004 (in percentages)

	HPM-voters	FPOE-voters
EU-entry of Austria		
Right decision	47	31
Wrong decision	49	69
EU-enlargement 2004		
More advantages	29	19
More disadvantages	66	72
EU-annoyance		
Very annoyed	42	41
Somewhat annoyed	44	34
Not annoyed	13	25
Daily newspapers		
NKZ readers	77	53
Readers of other papers	23	47

Source: Plasser/Ulram 2004b: 22.

As a main candidate *HPM* mobilized 66 percent of his voters who saw him as a very important motive for voting this list. He was followed by Ursula Stenzel of the *OEVP* (49 percent), the Green Johannes Voggenhuber (36 percent), the *FPOE* candidate Hans Kronberger, and *SPOE* representative Hannes Swoboda (32 percent each). As far as Swoboda is concerned, it must be pointed out that such a result for a party which is vying for first place is clearly too low.

4. Conclusions

As declared by the editor, Hans Dichand, the *NKZ* as a supporter of *HPM* demonstrated its basic competence of scanning, picking up and channelling the mood and the current protest opinions of the electorate. This has always been a part of its success story and also helped *HPM* in 2004. Nearly three-quarters of the *HPM* voters were readers of the *NKZ*. Nevertheless, it is surprising that *HPM*'s success came about solely through a mobilization of voters via the mass media. Although everywhere in Europe media campaigns, especially for populist candidates or groups, are the centre of every election campaign and the key factor for their success, only in few cases, such as with *HPM*, they could renounce the classical mobilization through a traditional election campaign by parties.

In addition, an information deficit for the EU still exists in Austria, critique of which is certainly justified. After five years of neglecting to inform and educate the public on this topic, which is a responsibility of the state and politics, it could not be expected that five weeks of an election campaign would be enough to improve this situation. The low turnout figures should be seen as a good reason to improve civic education. In this connection, the role of the media is very problematic, as on the one hand their reports have the character of horse race journalism and on the other hand they broadcast inappropriate topics as in the case of *ORF* radio, which reported on porno star Dolly Buster as a candidate instead of democratic and political issues in the week before election day. In a campaign where half the readers are not interested in the EU-topic, this is the only chance to increase newspaper readership figures. *HPM* also benefits from the phenomenon of personal stories.

Austria has a market leading newspaper which is able to strongly influence the results of political campaigns under certain conditions, especially in case of a low turnout with a corresponding great need for mobilization. During the European parliamentary elections of 2004 the *NKZ* mutated to a pseudo political party as so many times before. It extensively used all kinds of campaign journalism including single-subject and inter-departmental coverage ranging from articles to commentaries, dramatization and (negative) emotionalization, appeals etc. (see Plasser/Ulram 2002: 184).

Weird moods among the electorate (annoyance with mismanagement and fears of European influence) in fact created the basis for the *HPM* success but only managed to become effective through the editorial mobilization platform of the *NKZ*. The boundaries between politics and journalism dissolved because competitive newspapers picked up the issue and the person *HPM* and made it their central focus too, instead of ignoring *HPM* altogether.

The indifference of the Austrian population in European/international politics is clearly shown by its media usage. The majority of all readers is interested in local or domestic politics: in 2003 38 percent stated that they prefer local reports, 26 percent were very interested in domestic politics, but only 24 percent wanted to know more about international politics (see Media-Analysis 2004). Further, only 23 percent would like to be supplied with detailed background information on issues concerning EU politics in daily coverage on TV and news. 33 percent felt well-informed by brief reports with some background information, 37 percent saw bulletins as sufficient information (see Plasser/Ulram 2004a). The connection to the *NKZ* indicates that the readers were not really interested in politics but in a person like *HPM*. As 41 percent of the *NKZ* readers were interested in local coverage and only 25 percent respectively 21 percent

preferred Austrian and international politics reports, the extended coverage of *HPM* was nevertheless a high risk for the *NKZ*.
The final question is whether *HPM* will be able to repeat his success in other elections. For Austria this means that despite decreasing turnout figures and the "*NKZ* factor", this development cannot be ruled out, although both phenomena, the low turnout und the *NKZ* factor, will not appear in the same intensity. In the whole of Europe, there is no comparable situation.

References

Altendorfer, Otto (2004): Die Macht der Bilder. Visualisierung. In: Kreyer, Volker J. (Ed.): Handbuch Politisches Marketing. Impulse und Strategien für Politik, Wirtschaft und Gesellschaft. Baden-Baden: Nomos, 345-354 [Altendorfer: The Power of Pictures. Visualization. In: Kreyer: Handbook for Political Marketing. Impulses and Strategies for Politics, Economy, and Society].
Althaus, Marco/Cecere, Vito (Eds.) (2003): Kampagne 2! Neue Strategien für Wahlkampf, PR und Lobbying. Münster: Lit Publishers [Campaign 2! New Strategies for Election Campaign, PR, and Lobbying].
European Commission (Ed.) (2004): Eurobarometer. Public Opinion in the EU 15, Brussels. At: http://europa.eu.int/comm/public_opinion/, retrieval December 4th 2005.
Filzmaier, Peter (2004a): Politische Trends im Wahljahr 2003. In: Khol, Andreas/Ofner, Günther/Burkert-Dottolo, Günther R. (Eds.): Österreichisches Jahrbuch für Politik 2003. Wien: Verlag für Geschichte und Politik, 4-18 [Filzmaier: Political Trends in the Election Year of 2003. In: Khol et al.: Austrian Yearbook for Politics 2003].
Filzmaier, Peter (2004b): Wahlen und politischer Wettbewerb in der Mediengesellschaft. In: Forum Politische Bildung (Ed.): Von Wahl zu Wahl. Wien/ München: Studienverlag, Informationen zur Politischen Bildung ‚No. 21, 13-21 [Filzmaier: Elections and Political Competition in a Media Society. In: Forum Politische Bildung: From Election to Election].
Filzmaier, Peter/Hajek, Peter (2004a): Wahlen zum Europäischen Parlament in Österreich 2004. Wien. At: http://www.ogm.at and http://polbil.uni-klu.ac.at, last retrieval September 30th 2005 [European Parliamentary Elections in Austria 2004].
Filzmaier, Peter/Hajek, Peter (2004b): Wien ist anders? Die Wahlen zum Europäischen Parlament 2004. In: Häupl, Michael/Oxonitsch, Christian/Millmann, Gerd (Eds.): Wiener Jahrbuch für Politik 2004. Wien: Echo-Verlag, 321-342 [Filzmaier/Hajek: Vienna is different? The European Parliamentary Elections 2004. In: Häupl et al.: Viennese Yearbook for Politics 2004].
Filzmaier, Peter/Hajek, Peter (2005a): Bundespräsidentschafts- und Europawahlen 2004. In: Khol, Andreas/Ofner, Günther/Burkert-Dottolo, Günther R.

(Eds.): Österreichisches Jahrbuch für Politik 2004. Wien: Verlag für Geschichte und Politik, 29-53 [Filzmaier/Hajek: Presidential and European Elections 2004. In: Khol et al.: Austrian Yearbook for Politics 2004].

Filzmaier, Peter/Hajek, Peter (2005b): Das österreichische Wahljahr 2004. In: SWS-Rundschau, Vol. 45, No. 1, 6-36 [The Austrian Election Year of 2004].

Green, Donald P./Gerber, Alan S. (2004): Get Out the Vote! How to Increase Voter Turnout. Washington D.C.: CQ Press.

OGM – Österreichische Gesellschaft für Marketing (2004): Zeit im Bild. Wahltagsbefragung zu den österreichischen Wahlen zum Europäischen Parlament im Auftrag des ORF. At: http://www.ogm.at, retrieval September 30th 2005 [Zeit im Bild. Exit Poll for the European Parliamentary Elections 2004 on behalf of the Austrian Broadcasting Union (ORF)].

ORF-Medienforschung (2004): ORF-Teletest und ORF-Radiotest. At: http://mediaresearch.orf.at, retrieval September 30th 2005 [Television- and Radio-Test].

Pelinka, Peter/Duchkowitsch, Wolfgang/Hausjell, Fritz (Eds.) (1992): Zeitung-Los. Essays zur Pressepolitik und -konzentration in Österreich. Salzburg: Müller [Without Newspapers. Essays on Politics and Concentration of the Press in Austria].

Plasser, Fritz/Ulram, Peter (2002): Das österreichische Politikverständnis. Von der Konsens- zur Konfliktkultur? Wien: WUV-Verlag [Political Culture in Austria. From Consensus to Conflict?].

Plasser, Fritz/Ulram, Peter (2004a): Öffentliche Aufmerksamkeit in der Mediendemokratie. In: Plasser, Fritz (Ed.): Politische Kommunikation in Österreich. Ein praxisnahes Handbuch. Wien: WUV-Verlag, 37-99 [Plasser/Ulram: Public Attention in a Media Democracy. In: Plasser: Political Communication in Austria. A Practical Handbook].

Plasser, Fritz/Ulram, Peter (2004b): Analyse der Europawahl 2004. Wähler, Nichtwähler, Motive. Wien. At: http://www.polimatrix.at, retrieval October 31th 2004 [An Analysis of the European Elections 2004. Voters, Non-Voters, and Motives].

Röper, Horst (2004): Zeitungsmarkt in der Krise. Ein Fall für die Medienregulierung. In: Aus Politik und Zeitgeschichte, Vol. 54, No. 12-13, 7-13 [Newspaper Market in a Crisis – A Case for Media Regulation].

SORA – Institute for Social Research and Analysis (2004): Wählerstromanalyse der EU-Wahl 2004 im Auftrag des ORF. At: http://www.sora.at, retrieval December 4th 2005 [Analysis of Voter Transition in the European Parliamentary Elections 2004 on Behalf of the Austrian Broadcasting Union (ORF)].

Verein Arbeitsgemeinschaft Media-Analysen (2004): Media-Analyse 2003: Jahresbericht. At: http://www.media-analyse.at, retrieval December 4th 2005 [Media Analysis 2003: Annual Report].

[1] A comparison with the print media market in Germany also illustrates the unparalleled leading position of the *NKZ*. The *Bild-Zeitung* had nearly 4 million readers, which corresponds to a market share of 17 percent. The *NKZ* with its 43 percent exceeds the share of the five largest German publishing groups (see Röper 2004: 8-10). In other words: If the *NKZ* campaigns for *HPM* this is at least twice or three times more powerful than any initiative by German newspapers.

Media Coverage and Voting in the European Parliamentary Elections in France 2004[1]

*Jacques Gerstlé, Raul Magni-Berton & Christophe Piar**

1. Introduction

In countries where voting is not compulsory, abstention in the European Parliamentary elections is a kind of tradition. Abstention is growing everywhere in Europe. But in France during the last European elections in June 2004, abstention reached the record of 57.2 percent up from 53.8 percent in 1999; it was the highest abstention rate ever seen, except for the referendums. A second particularity of these elections was the overwhelming victory of the *Socialist Party* (*PS*) over the *Union for a Popular Movement* (*UMP*), the party of the president: 29 percent of the votes for the *PS* versus 17 percent for the *UMP*.[2]

In the comparative research conducted for the 1999 European Elections, Gerstlé et al. (2001) showed how low the media coverage of the campaign was in the different countries of "Old Europe". The European campaign was overshadowed by various problems of overbooked national agendas and the saturation coverage of the Kosovo crisis. For this reason we decided to look at the relationship between news media and French electoral behaviour.

The 2004 European Elections occurred two years after the presidential and legislative elections in France and two and a half months after the defeat of the majority in the regional elections. The government led by the *UMP* was very unpopular. Because of the European Election PR rules, almost all parties ran independently, except those on the extreme left. Table 1 shows the results. The electoral system has been modified since the 1999 elections. For the first time in a European election, France was divided into eight regions instead of only one national electoral district. This change has led to a multiplication of lists (168) and of candidates (3.432) without known leaders (see Gerstlé et al. 2005).

In reference to the media system, we focus here on television. In France there are two principal TV channels for political information, *France 2* and *TF1*. In general, the *TF1* news audience is larger than the *France 2* news audience (for example, in June, *TF1* audience reached 32.2 percent against only 20.9 per-

---

* Jacques Gerstlé, PhD. *1948. Professor of Political Science at the Université de Paris I Panthéon-Sorbonne, Centre de Recherches Politiques de la Sorbonne, email: gerstle. jacques@wanadoo.fr
Raul Magni-Berton. *1973. Maître de conférences à l'IEP de Bordeaux, email: magniberton@free.fr
Christophe Piar. *1977. Phd.-Student at the Université de Paris I Panthéon-Sorbonne, Centre de Recherches Politiques de la Sorbonne, email: christophepiar@club-internet.fr

cent for *F2*, see Médiamétrie, Médiamat 2004). In the post-electoral survey, 55 percent of the respondents said they watched *TF1* TV news, and 40 percent watched *France 2*. However, the content of the news of the private channel is generally more dominated by infotainment than the news of the public channel (see Gerstlé 2001). The public channel (*F2*) broadcasts more news about the EU and the elections than the private one (*TF1*) (approximately twice as much, four hours versus two hours). On the other hand, we know that the audience of *TF1* is more oriented towards the right. The content analysis of the news shows that *TF1* devoted more time to the right parties of the government (39 percent) than *F2* (23 percent).

Table 1: Results of European Parliamentary elections in France (2004)

Parties	% vote
Extreme Left	
Lutte Ouvrière – Ligue Communiste Révolutionnaire	2.56
Others extreme left	0.77
Left	
Parti Communiste Français	5.24
Parti Socialiste	28.89
Others Left	1.35
Green	7.4
Right	
Union pour un Mouvement Populaire	16.64
Union pour la Démocratie Française	11.95
Others right	8.83
Extreme Right	
Front National	9.81
Others extreme right	0.31
Others	**4.51**
Total	**99.99**

The analysis reports here a post-electoral survey carried out on a representative sample of 1.406 registered voters in France by the "Institut Français d'Opinion Publique" (IFOP). Using these individual data units, it was possible to implement a logistic regression analysis with different models testing hypotheses about dummy dependent variables: turnout and voting choices (protest voting, left voting, and right voting). In order to explain the differences between left and right voting, we link the survey data to the results of a content analysis of TV news conducted during ten weeks (from April 5th to June 12th) before election day, which *was* June 13th in France. We chose both main evening news programs in France, broadcasted at the same hour (8 pm) on *TF1* (the main private channel) and *France 2* (the main public channel). These 138 newscasts were recorded, watched, and coded. This paper focuses on the election coverage, which encompasses all stories that mentioned political actors (government, political parties, President). The content of these reports was coded in different categories to study how television covered European parliamentary elections in 2004. Important in this connection is the fact that news' production is influenced by different people. With news management, politicians and their spin doctors try to control or, at least, to influence the construction and content of information. They create pseudo-events to attract journalists and try to get coverage in accordance with their campaign strategies. On the other hand, journalists withstand such attempts by following their professional norms and because they fear being manipulated. Thus, election coverage is the result of an interactive process that nobody can completely control (see Gerstlé 2004a).

First, we will present the independent variables used and the specifications of the models, and then we will look at the results about abstention and protest voting (that is, voting for fringe parties, which are not intended to govern, in contrast to parties intended to govern, called "partis de gouvernement" in France). Third, we will turn to the prediction of left and right voting. Finally, we will discuss the link between campaign, mobilization, and volatility.

2. Independent variables and specification of the models

Our hypothesis is that if media coverage of European campaigns was low and the European issues not very salient, we can expect that this situation would lead to either abstention (because of weak interest) or protest voting against the government. That is why we consider abstention and protest voting together before considering the left/right voting. Table 2 shows all of the dependent and independent variables, a short description, their name, the scale, and the model the variable refers to.

The first set of independent variables is political in nature and deals with *party identification, ideological self placement* of the respondents, *popularity* of the government, and *chances to vote* (more or less than 70 percent). A second group of variables takes into account the media variables: *knowledge* of the positions taken by the parties, *awareness* defined as the attention paid to the press and TV news controlled by political interest, *EU awareness* (looking for information about the EU controlled by political interest), the *assessment of the media's attention to the EU, respondents' preference for the public or private channel*, and *exposure to public or private TV news*. The third group identifies two socio-demographic characteristics of the respondents: *age* and *educational level*.

Because of multicollinearity, we do not use political awareness and EU awareness in the same model. There is the same constraint concerning the preference for a channel and the exposure to its news. In reference to awareness, there are three variables: knowledge or "objective awareness", which means "how do people master frames to interpret politics"; awareness in the sense of a "subjective awareness" since it is controlled by political interest, and EU awareness which is especially devoted to European issues.

Table 2: Variables of models 1 and 2

Variable	Description	Name	Scale	Model's Type
Vote Choices	To vote for protest parties	Protest Voting	1 = Parties not intended to govern. 0 = Parties intended to govern.	Dependent Variable in the 1st Model.
	To vote for the Left (far left, Pcf, Ps, Greens) or for the Right (Udf, Ump, Mpf)	Left Voting	1= Left 0= Right	Dependent Variable in the 2d Model.
Abstention	Abstention	Abstention	1= Abstention 0= Voting	Dependent Variable in the 1st Model.
Party Identification	Do people lean toward a particular party?	Partisanship	1 = Identification 0= No Identification	Political Independent Variable in the 1st and 2d Model.
Self Placement	Left-Right Self Placement	Left - Right Self Placement	1= Strong Left 10= Strong Right	Political Independent Variable in the 1st and 2d Model.
Popularity	Do people approve or disapprove of the government's job performance?	Popularity	1 = Approve 0 = Disapprove	Political Independent Variable in the 1st and 2d Model.
Probability of Voting	People saying that there are at least 0.7 chances to vote for a party	0.7 Chances to Vote for a Party	0= None of the parties 4=4 Parties for which one can vote	Political Independent Variable in the 1st and 2d Model.
Political Knowledge	Knowledge about the political parties positions	Political Knowledge	0= Low Level of Knowledge 3= High Level of Knowledge	Media Independent Variable in the 1st and 2d Model.
Political Awareness	Frequency of reading newspaper per week + watching TV news per week) / lack of interest in politics	Political Awareness	More or less linear : The higher its value, the more aware people are	Media Independent Variable in the 1st and 2d Model.
EU Awareness	Do people try to get some information on the EU/ lack of interest in politics	EU Awareness	More or less linear : The higher its value, the more aware people are of the EU	Media Independent Variable in the 1st and 2d Model. (Alternative to the Variable « Awareness »)
Media's Attention to the EU	Do people think that the media pay too much or too little attention to the EU?	Media's Little Attention to the EU	1= Too Much 3= Too Little	Media Independent Variable in the 1st and 2d Model.
France2/TF1	Do people watch France 2 or TF1?	France 2 (versus TF1)	2 = France 2 1 = Both 0 = TF1	Media Independent Variable in the 1st and 2d Model.
Exposure to Evening TV News	Do people watch Evening TV News (on France 2 or TF1)?	Evening TV News	1 = Yes 0 = No	Media Independent Variable in the 1st and 2d Model. (Alternative to the Variable "France2/TF1")
Educational Level	Person's level of Education	Education	1 = No Diploma. 10 = Master Degree or More.	Socio-demographic Independent Variable in the 1st and 2d Model.
Age	Year of Birth	Year of Birth	Depending on the Year of Birth: 1920-1984	Socio-demographic Independent Variable in the 1st and 2d Model.

In the following section, we explore the importance of media in explaining abstention and protest voting. In the fourth section, we analyze the vote choice for the principal parties involved in governing coalitions. Finally, we present the major consequences of the relationship between the media and the European elections in France.

3. Abstention and protest voting

Table 3 shows only the variables which are predictive of these behaviours (abstention versus protest voting) as they are our dependent variables. So first, we know that among the political variables, self-placement and government approval do not play a significant role. Second, it is confirmed that the most significant variables are the "media" variables both for abstention and protest voting (12 percent of the voters).

Table 3: Results for abstention and protest voting

	Abstention (b)	Protest Voting (b)
Political Variables		
Partisanship	-.83***	-.75**
0.7 Chance to vote for a Party	-.25***	-.19
Media Variables		
Political Knowledge	-.28***	-.42**
Political Awareness	-.13***	-.14*
Media's Little Attention to the EU	-.31***	-.33
Socio-demographic Variables		
Year of Birth	.02***	.02*
Education	-.05*	-.11*
Constant	1.81***	.36
N	1340	666
LR chi2	262.73	59.27
Prob > chi2	.0000	.0000
Pseudo R2	0.1414	0.1276
Correctly Predicted Cases	68%	89%

***P<.000, **P<.01, *P<.05

Results of the simulations in order to establish the importance of each variable in the model

	Abstention	Protest Voting
Political Variables	39%	15%
Partisanship	19%	7%
0.7 chance to vote for a party	11%	3%
Media Variables	84%	48%
Political Awareness	37%	14%
Political Knowledge	18%	13%
Media's Little Attention to the EU	13%	6%
Socio-demographic Variables	53%	20%
Education	39%	12%
Year of Birth	29%	8%

According to the simulation, the individuals who go from the lowest to the highest scores in the media variables will have an 84 percent chance to change from abstention to voting. The socio-demographic factors come in second position. Abstention is characteristic of young people with a low level of education and a low amount of information and exposure.
1. Focusing on *media variables*, knowledge obviously has the strongest impact both on abstention and protest voting. The coefficients for these variables always have the same sign. It allows us to describe abstentionists and protest voters as less knowledgeable and less aware people.
2. Regarding *socio-demographic variables*, age and education are both significant. What about other traditional long-term factors such as professional occupation, residence, or social stratification? Religion was considered but was not significant at all. In our opinion, the variables of age and education best represent the dichotomy revealed by the referendum for the Maastricht Treaty (1992) between a dynamic part of France projecting itself into a European future and a fragile part, in economic, cultural, and social terms, for which Europe presents a threat. The impact of these variables is in line with expectations: young people with a low level of education tend more toward abstention and protest voting than older people.

In summary, in reference to abstention and protest voting, media variables explain these electoral behaviours best. It is important to note that the same structure is seen to explain both of these behaviours. Therefore, the meaning of protest voting is quite clear: it is more about punishing politicians than supporting a small party. Protest voters are less likely to be partisan and, compared to other voters, they are less aware and less well informed.

Because there were modifications in the electoral system for these European elections (eight districts instead of one), it seems that the role of knowledge and awareness was especially important. These modifications probably confused voters with little electoral experience or weak cultural capital. In addition, the media did not fulfil their civic responsibility, since they did not spend much time on the presentation and explanation of the new electoral system based on regional criteria which was applied for the first time in France for this kind of election.

4. Left/right voting

The *French Communist Party* (*PCF*), the *PS*, and the *Greens* represent the major left-wing parties since they belonged to the coalition "la Gauche Plurielle", which was in charge of the government from 1997 to 2002. Preferences for the *UDF* (the most federalist party), the *UMP*, and the other right parties represent right-wing voting.

In Table 4 we consider three regression models taking into account different kinds of independent variables: in the first model, we check the impact of political awareness associated to the preference for the public channel (*France 2*); in the second model, we associate EU awareness with this same preference; and in the last one, we check the effect of exposure to evening TV news with EU awareness.

Table 4: Results for left voting

Left Voting	Coef.1	Coef.2	Coef.3
Political Variables			
Self-Placement	-.88***	-.89***	-.82***
Popularity	-2.2***	-2.18***	-2.33***
Media Variables			
Pol. Awareness	-.13**		
EU Awareness		-.59**	-.43**
France2 (vs TF1)	1.54**	1.75**	
TV news of 20h (evening tv news)			-.74*
Socio-demographic Variables			
Education	-.23***	-.24***	-.21***
Year of Birth	.03*	.03**	.03***
Constant	5.16***	5.15***	6.29***
N	479	479	613
LR chi2(7)	410.57	412.28	485.42
Prob > chi2	0.0000	0.0000	0.0000
Pseudo R2	0.6334	0.6361	0.5941
Corr. Predicted Cases	90,6%	90,2%	88,7%

***P<.000, **P<.01, *P<.05

Results of the simulations in order to establish the importance of each variable in the second part

	Variant 1	Variant 2	Variant 3
Political Variables	98%	98%	98%
Self Placement	91%	91%	89%
Popularity	22%	22%	27%
Media Variables	25%	34%	23%
Political Awareness	14%		
EU Awareness		21%	17%
France 2	9%	10%	
TV news of 20h			6%
Socio-demographic Variables	31%	43%	38%
Education	15%	16%	15%
Year of Birth	15%	20%	22%

The three models are really good at predicting the vote. The variables with the highest impact are the political variables, with a score of 98 percent (cf. the simulation). The non-significant political variables are party identification and chances to vote, and the non-significant media variables are assessment of the media's attention to the EU and political knowledge.

4.1 Impact of political and socio-demographic variables

Self-placement is by far the most predictive variable. Approval of the government's job performance is also significant and indicates retrospective voting, supporting the predominant interpretation of the election outcomes as punishment voting.

Finally, the oldest voters and those with the highest socio-cultural capital were those who were mostly in favour of the right parties.

4.2 Impact of media variables

Political awareness and exposure to evening TV news are more associated with the tendency to vote right. However, TV news viewing must be further differentiated: the exposure to public TV news is associated with left voting, but the audience of *TF1* is more oriented towards the right (see Gerstlé 2004a). Moreover, in this analysis we observe that the right voters have a higher degree of awareness.

Table 5: Coverage of European Parliamentary elections by both main evening news programs (April 5th – June 12th)

	Coverage of European elections (minutes)	Coverage of European elections (number of stories)	Game frame	Issue frame	National frame	European frame
TF1 (private channel)	124 minutes = 7 % of total news coverage	37	29 minutes = 23 % of election coverage	95 minutes = 77 % of election coverage	71 minutes = 57 % of election coverage	53 minutes = 43 % of election coverage
France 2 (public channel)	198 minutes = 11 % of total news coverage	72	102 minutes = 52 % of election coverage	96 minutes = 48 % of election coverage	126 minutes = 64 % of election coverage	72 minutes = 36 % of election coverage
Total	322 minutes = 9 % of total news coverage	109	131 minutes = 41 % of election coverage	191 minutes = 59 % of election coverage	197 minutes = 61 % of election coverage	125 minutes = 39 % of election coverage

So, there is a paradox that encourages us to examine the contents of the news broadcasted by both channels (see Table 5). We know that France 2 (the public channel) offered twice as much information about the EU during the campaign than did TF1. On the other hand, our findings reveal that 1) those who watch France 2 news are more likely to vote left, but 2) awareness increases the tendency to vote right. Variables France 2 and awareness do not have the same di-

rection, and this is contrary to our expectations based on the results of the content analysis. Two processes could explain this paradox:
1. We have distinguished between two kinds of frames of information: issue frames are focused on EU issues, while game frames are focused on stories, meetings, or anecdotes about parties and politicians. 77 percent of the contents of *TF1* news were based on issue frames because journalists decided to cover the election most of the time by inviting political leaders to speak in the studio, while *France 2* had only 48 percent issue stories. The differential in favour of issue stories (versus game stories) is (66') on *TF1* and (-6') on *F2*. Our hypothesis is that awareness about the EU increases with the exposition to issue frames information. This could explain why right voters, being more exposed to *TF1* news, are more politically aware.
2. The second explanation is more political. The leaders of the right parties, who were governing at the time, may have strategically decided to avoid an electoral mobilization for the European elections in order to prevent a protest or punishment voting. So, they allowed little time for the election as a game, unlike the left parties. In short, the media logic of infotainment and the political logic of mobilization converged in these two different types of TV coverage of the election. The public news devoted more time to the elections with an emphasis on the game aspects of the competition and the lists of the *Left* as well as a strong emphasis on national considerations. This coverage has encouraged the punishment of a largely unpopular government at that time. The private news devoted less time to the elections, with a less national framing and an emphasis on the leaders of the *Right* and on issues which are supposedly less attractive for a mainly disinterested audience and therefore more efficient to demobilize voters. The high level of abstention indicates that demobilization was effective, but it was associated with an unexpected effect for the *Right*: opening the "choice space" to speak like Paul Sniderman (2000).

5. European campaigns, mobilization, and volatility

Our analysis of the 1999 European campaigns in different countries confirmed the conclusion that Jay Blumler (1983) drew from the first elections of 1979. "The 1999 campaign confirms that a certain degree of visibility is required to launch a mobilization process, as Blumler observed twenty years ago: the turnout rate increases in proportion to campaign activity. The intensity of communication and support for the European Community constituted the two essential factors for explaining differences among national turnout levels. For instance, in Holland where people widely supported the EC, there was no alternative but to attribute the low level of turnout to the weakness of the campaign. Similarly and contrasting to the British case, in Germany the strong support for the EC and a rather active campaign led to a high level of turnout" (see Gerstlé et al. 2001:

76). Of course, there is the enlargement and the low level of electoral participation in the new member states of the EU, but that is only a part of the story to explain the decline of voting since 1979. The last European campaigns revealed what we called a "loose political obligation" (Gerstlé et al. 2005) which combined the disaffection towards politics and the difficulties for the people in the new member countries of the EU to feel any "political obligation" as political theory understands the concept. This election revealed a gap between the "moral community" and the "legal community" to use Michaël Walzer's terms.

In 2002, Banducci et al. examined the different factors explaining why the turnout in these elections is low. They proposed the second-order nature of EP elections, negative attitudes about European integration, negative news, and a lack of mobilization. But the authors adopted an exclusive "mediacentric" view of the electoral process concentrating on the "contingent effects of the media". They suggested to assess four variables to characterize news content and its impact: the volume of campaign coverage, the tone (positive, neutral, and negative) towards the EU, the intensity of strategic frame, and the importance of national versus European focus in the stories. We argue here that they are wrong, as well as other authors who are convinced about the importance of the tone analysis, and not only in reference to its methodological shortcomings. Visibility, predispositions, and news framing are sufficient to explain the level of turnout. Regarding visibility and predispositions, the observations of Blumler (1983) seem to be relevant. In reference to news framing, these authors have a very limited understanding of frames, because they only consider strategic ones. In contrast, the typology of frames we implemented to analyse the news coverage of the presidential elections of 1988 in the US and France is much more differentiated (see Gerstlé et al. 1992): there were *positioning stories* in which the politicians supported or attacked the candidates taking place in the electoral battlefield; *staging stories* in which the events of the campaigns were more or less transformed into spectacles; *appraisal stories* in which the journalists described the electoral process in progress particularly with the help of voting intention surveys; and *agenda-setting stories* in which the policy issues were taken into account by the candidates and the parties. In Table 6, we apply this typology to the 2004 European Parliamentary elections with these four categories: *positioning news*, *staging news*, *appraisal news* (which together form the game frame), and *agenda-setting news* (which corresponds to the issue frame).

Table 6: Framing of the European Parliamentary elections by both main evening news programs (April 5th – June 12th)

	Positioning news	Staging news	Appraisal news	Agenda-setting news
TF1 (private channel)	6 min. = 5 % *	17 min. = 14 %	3 min. = 2 %	95 min. = 77 %
France 2 (public channel)	16 min. = 8 %	76 min. = 38 %	5 min. = 3 %	96 min. = 48 %
Total	22 min. = 7 %	93 min. = 29 %	8 min. = 2 %	191 min. = 59 %

* percent of election coverage

Second, we contend that frame analysis is central to the understanding of the interpretation, favourable or not, proposed to the public by the media. The implementation of this argument to the coverage of the European construction process: "Trapped in the European dialectic of integration and fragmentation, information reveals the resistance of national public spaces in two different but convergent ways: on the one hand, a dominating common frame[3], which carries homogeneous transnational representations, which means common media bias; on the other hand, specific national frames, which means national media bias. In other words, common characteristics make the European information homogeneous, while national specificities make it heterogeneous" (Gerstlé 2004b: 132).[4] Six common media biases are found in information about the European Union: eventalization, spectacularization, intermittent broadcasting, nationalization of the news, professionalization of the European political elites, institutionalization, plus national media bias which generate reactions of national interests defence. These common and specific biases do not produce a "shared understanding" in the sense of Walzer, but on the contrary, delegitimize the European construction and obstruct the emergence of a European public space. Thus, there is no need to use an unpredictable tone analysis to reveal that news framing is responsible for this process of delegitimization.

6. Conclusions

The regression analysis leads to the following results:
1. First, the media variables are the most important variables to explain abstention. Further, it is not a trivial result to explain such a record (the highest abstention rate in French election history) by a media variable. We admit that the model does not explain abstention as well as the model explains the direction of the vote. But, we are convinced that there is a way to a more powerful model of voting behaviour by including media variables.
2. Second, to explain the choice between voting for "protest parties" or for parties intended to govern ("partis de gouvernement"), the media variables still dominate.
3. To explain left/right voting, the traditional and well-documented importance of political and socio-demographic variables is once again demonstrated.
4. By comparing the outcomes of this election with those of previous European elections and with recent regional elections, we can verify how mobilization benefited the *Left* or how interbloc volatility handicapped the *Right*. Since the 1999 European elections, the *Left* has added 4 percent to the total of its votes, and since the last regional elections two months prior to the EU elections, it added 2 percent. So, media variables can be very efficient because they influence the instability of particular segments of the electorate, while stressing specific issues and framing them according to "issue ownership",

for example social issues in connection with European affairs in favour of the *Socialists*.

But if we try to broaden the analysis to the questions posed by the contingent effects of the media, the political strategies, and the mobilization of the voters, it is possible to go further and take a synoptic view of this electoral process in France.

The high level of abstention is the result of a limited visibility of the campaign in France (see Gerstlé et al. forthcoming), and protest voting appeared to be an opportunity to punish politicians by dispersing votes among competing lists.

Concerning the mixture of the news devoted to the *Left* and the *Right*, we can observe that both kinds of news together have an effect which explains the general election outcome. On the one hand, left parties led a more visible campaign emphasizing strategic frames to mobilize the punishment vote against the government and stressing social issues to reinforce party allegiance. On the other hand, right parties led a less visible campaign primarily focused on a general discourse about European affairs to distract the public from making any assessment of current domestic policy by the government.

The survey of the IFOP provides us with data about the effectiveness of these strategies. Of the 440 individuals who declared any identification with a left party, 251 really went to vote and voted for a party of the *Left* (i.e. 100 percent). In contrast, of the 240 individuals who declared an identification with any right party, 178 went to the polling station (that means more mobilization in the camp of the right voters), but only 153 voted for a party of the *Right* (i.e. 86 percent). In short, there were 14 percent right voters who had withdrawn their support, and this is in accordance with the role of popularity measured in the Table 3.

In sum, by giving priority to the media tone, Banducci et al. (2002) make the mistake to underestimate political strategies, even in instrumentalizing the media. It is not the tone of the news which is decisive but the blend of visibility, political predispositions, and frame choices. According to Mark Turner (2001: 17), "'new meaning' is 'emergent' in the sense that it is not available in either of the influencing spaces but instead emerges in the blended space by means of blending those influencing spaces. The blend inherits some of its elements and some of its meaning from the influencing spaces [...]". This is exactly what we intend to demonstrate when we argue about the interweaving of controlled political communication and media news as sources of influencing spaces in the political realm (see Gerstlé 2004a).

References

Banducci, Susan/Semetko, Holli A. (2002): Negative News, Mobilization and European Elections. Paper Prepared for Presentation at the Meeting of The APSA. Boston: Mass. September.
Blumler, Jay G. (1983): Communicating to Voters. Television in the First European Parliamentary Elections. London : Sage.
Déloye, Yves (2005): Dictionnaire des élections européennes. Paris: Economica. [Dictionary of European Elections].
Gerstlé, Jacques (1995): La dynamique nationale d'une campagne européenne. In: Perrineau, Pascal/Ysmal, Colette (Eds.): Le Vote des Douze. Les élections européennes de juin 1994. Paris: Presses de Science-po, 203-228. [Gerstlé: The National Dynamic of A European Campaign. In: Perrineau/Ysmal: The Twelve's Voting. The European Elections of June 1994].
Gerstlé, Jacques (2001): Les effets d'information en politique. Paris: L'Harmattan [Information Effects in Politics].
Gerstlé, Jacques (2004a): La communication politique. Paris: Armand Colin. [Political Communication].
Gerstlé, Jacques (2004b): L'information, entre fragmentation et intégration des espaces publics en Europe. In: Bockel, Alain/Karakas, Isil (Eds.): Diversité culturelle en Turquie et en Europe. Paris: L'Harmattan, 129-143. [Gerstlé: Information, between Fragmentation and Integration of Public Spaces in Europe. In: Bockel/Karakas: Cultural Diversity in Turkey and Europe].
Gerstlé, Jacques/Davis, Dennis K./Duhamel, Olivier (1992): Television News and the Construction of Political Reality in France and the United States. In: Kaid, Lynda Lee/Gerstlé, Jacques/ Sanders, Keith R. (Eds.): Mediated Politics in Two Cultures. Presidential Campaigning in the United States and France. New York: Praeger, 119-143.
Gerstlé, Jacques/Magni-Berton, Raul/Piar, Christophe (forthcoming): Information et vote dans le cadre des élections au Parlement Européen. Communication au colloque «La construction européenne au prisme des élections au Parlement européen de juin 2004», 18-19th November 2004, AFSP/GSPE, Strasbourg. [Information and Voting in European Parliamentary Elections. Paper prepared for the symposium "The European Construction at the prism of the European Parliamentary Elections of June 2004"].
Gerstlé, Jacques/Neumayer, Laure/Colomé, Jean-Gabriel (2005): Les campagnes électorales européennes ou «l'obligation politique relachée». In: Perrineau, Pascal (Ed.): Le Vote européen 2004-2005. De l'élargissement au référendum français. Paris: Presses de Sciences Po, 17-44. [Gerstlé et al.: The European Electoral Campaigns or "the Loose Political Obligation". In: Perrineau: The European Vote 2004-2005. From Enlargement to the French Referendum].
Gerstlé, Jacques/Semetko, Holli A./Schönbach, Klaus/Villa, Marina (2001): The Faltering Europeanization of National Campaigns. In: Grunberg, Gerard/Per-

rineau, Pascal/Ysmal, Colette (Eds.): Europe at the Polls. The European Elections of 1999. New York: Palgrave, 59-77.

Perrineau, Pascal (2005): Les élections européennes de juin 2004 en France. In: Delwit, Pascal/Poirier, Philippe (Eds.): Parlement puissant, électeurs absents? Les élections européennes de juin 2004. Bruxelles, Ed.de l'Université de Bruxelles [Perrineau: The European Elections of June 2004 in France. In: Delwit/Poirier: Powerful Parliament, Absent Voters? The European Elections of June 2004].

Sniderman, Paul (2000): Taking Sides: a Fixed Choice Theory of Political Reasoning. In: Lupia, Arthur/McCubbins, Mathew D./Popkin, Samuel L./Kuklinski, James H./ Chong, Dennis (Eds.): Elements of Reason. Cognition, Choice and the Bounds of Rationality. Cambridge: Cambridge University Press, 67-107.

Turner, Mark (2001): Cognitive Dimensions of Social Science. The Way We Think about Politics, Economics, Law and Society. Oxford: Oxford University Press.

---

[1] We would like to thank Cyrille Thiébaut (CRPS) for helping us to translate this paper into English.

[2] For more general information about European elections in France see Déloye (2005); Perrineau (2005).

[3] Frame means a way to present information, which, by its discriminatory aspect, gives a dominating interpretation of an issue (see Gerstlé 2001).

[4] "Prise dans la dialectique européenne de l'intégration et de la fragmentation, l'information révèle la résistance des espaces publics nationaux de deux manières différentes et convergentes: un cadrage commun dominant qui porte des représentations transnationales homogènes, c'est-à-dire des biais médiatiques communs d'une part, des cadrages nationaux à caractère particulier, c'est-à-dire des biais médiatiques nationaux, d'autre part. Autrement dit, des caractéristiques communes donnent son homogénéité au traitement de l'information européenne, des spécificités nationales génèrent son hétérogénéité."

Let Us Entertain You!
Perception and Evaluation of the European Election Campaign Spots 2004 in Germany

Michaela Maier & Jürgen Maier*

1. Introduction

In Germany the European Parliamentary Election 2004 turned into a disaster for the *Social Democratic Party* (senior partner of the governing coalition in Berlin) and its most visible exponent, chancellor Gerhard Schröder. With 21.5 percent the *SPD* obtained the worst result ever in nationwide elections. On the other hand, the major opposition party, the *CDU/CSU*, was able to achieve similar good results as in preceding state and local elections and received 44.5 percent of the votes. *Bündnis 90/Die Grünen*, the minor partner of the Berlin coalition, improved to 11.9 percent which was a victory in their eyes, the same as for the liberal *FDP* (reaching 6.1 percent), which was also able to make it into the new European Parliament. Likewise, the post-communist *PDS* obtained 6.1 percent of the votes and is now also present in Strasbourg.

Thus, the trend of the last decades (to be precise, since 1979) that government parties lose votes in European Elections (see, e.g., Schmitt/Reif 2003) continued in 2004 – not only in Germany, but also in numerous other European countries, as comparative analyses of the election results show (see Freudenstein 2004: 3). This phenomenon is usually explained by the fact that European Elections are only secondary in importance. Therefore, European elections are often called "second-order elections" (see, e.g., Reif/Schmitt 1980).

The disinterest in European Elections in Germany did not only show on the voters' side, the majority of which again did not cast their vote on June 13th 2004 (the turnout rate was 43.0 percent); it was also evident in mass media reporting. At the beginning of 2004 clearly less than five percent of all statements given in television and by the press concerned European politics.[1] Only three percent of these statements dealt with the upcoming European Election (see Rettich 2004). Considering the low media response, e.g. the low consideration of statements by the parties' top candidates for the European Election 2004 (see Rettich 2004), all parties were challenged to draw attention to the upcoming election and their positions regarding European politics by their own means.

---

* Michaela Maier, PhD. *1973. Junior Professor for Applied Communication Psychology, University of Koblenz-Landau, email: mmaier@uni-landau.de
Jürgen Maier, PhD. *1968. Junior Professor for Methods in Social Sciences Research, Kaiserslautern University of Technology, email: jmaier@rhrk.uni-kl.de

"Own means" denotes first and foremost campaign advertising, through which all parties try to impose the public their interpretation of reality.[2] It is the parties' primary goal to mobilize their own supporters and to convince voters who either have no party attachment or are still undecided. The same holds true for the attempt to either improve the own candidate's image via campaign advertising or to weaken the opponent's reputation through "negative campaigning" – a strategy very prominent in the United States (see, e.g., Benoit et al. 2003). In contrast, attempts to woo away voters from other parties, to set political agendas taken up by the mass media, or to claim long-term "issue ownerships" (Petrocik 1996) – thereby influencing the political culture of a society – are of secondary importance (on the latter aspect see Holtz-Bacha 2000). The persuasive function of campaign advertising gains more and more importance, since the proportion of unaffiliated voters is increasing (see, e.g., Falter/Rattinger 2001), as is the number of "late deciders", while turnout is declining due to less acceptance of the democratic principle that it is one's duty to vote in elections (see Rattinger/ Krämer 1995). Because willingness to vote is particularly low in European Elections compared to state or local elections, a considerably higher potential effect of campaign advertising can be assumed here.

As shown in the past, posters and televised commercials are usually the most important means of campaign advertising (see Schmitt-Beck 2002). Televised commercials have a special advantage in this context: Although they are not subject to the process of journalistic selection and revision, they still profit from being broadcast in a journalistic context. Campaign spots do not appear within blocks of regular commercials but are broadcasted around newscasts and often between early evening entertainment programs. Both formats draw a large audience which – and this is another argument supporting the potential effectiveness of campaign advertising – also consists of politically indifferent citizens, who are informed of an upcoming election and learn about a party's message by coincidental reception of a campaign spot (see Holtz-Bacha 2000: 59-60). In times where the tenor of journalistic reporting is considered unpredictable (see Holtz-Bacha 2000: 14), televised campaign spots obviously seem to offer an ideal background for taking influence on electoral decisions. If one believes the advertising industry's claim that "the spending probability of persons who watch television commercials is 36 percent higher than persons who do not watch television commercials" (Werben & Verkaufen 1995: 44), then one could expect all parties who run televised campaign spots to achieve outstanding election results.

However, the simple logic of the stimulus-response-model suggested in this statement cannot be a realistic explanation of the causal effects between advertisement and behaviour, which is, of course, much more complex. All current models of advertising effect research underline the consideration of cognitive and affective process components. Furthermore, the barrier of selective perception must be overcome and the reception of information ensured before there is a chance for the intended reaction to occur.

Concerning the question of a campaign spot's capability to generate *political knowledge* there are no further research results available in the context of European Election campaigns. According to numerous studies conducted in the United States it can generally be assumed that campaign spots help voters to recognize the names of parties and candidates and that they inform them about the main campaign topics and the positions held by the different political actors (for a summary see Kaid 2004: 167-169). This is the case especially for candidates and parties that are not members of the parliament and thus not present in the mass media. A number of authors even believe that television viewers learn more from campaign spots than from other political television formats such as newscasts (see, e.g., Patterson/McClure 1976) or televised debates (see, e.g., Just et al. 1990). Other studies, however, show that the reception of campaign spots has little to do with political knowledge and that other information channels have considerably stronger cognitive effects (see, e.g., Weaver/Drew 2001; Zhao/Chaffee 1995). Again, other research clearly shows that the influence of televised campaign advertisement depends on recipients' characteristics (see, e.g., Bowen 1994; Rothschild/Ray 1974) and also on the contents and design of an ad (see, e.g., Biocca 1991c).

For the process component of *political attitudes* Holtz-Bacha (1990) has shown that campaign spots televised in the context of the 1989 European Parliamentary Election caused (positive) changes in the evaluation of the European Parliament, of Germany's membership in the European Union, and of the speed of the European integration process. Holtz-Bacha's findings, however, cannot be considered convincing evidence of *general* effects of campaign spots on political attitudes, as she also calls attention to the possibility that party advertising may be of greater importance for European Elections than for federal ones because of the voter's lower familiarity with the European Union and its institutions (see Holtz-Bacha 2000: 87). Campaign research from the United States, however, indicates that campaign spots are very likely to influence perception and evaluation of candidates (see, e.g., West 1993; for a short summary of current research see Kaid 2004: 169-170). Here, too, it holds true that the recipients' characteristics as well as contents and design of a spot have considerable influence on the evaluation of candidates.

This overview of literature concerning the potential effect of campaign spots supports the general assumption that televised ads can influence political orientations – and thus political behaviour – as long as they attract recipients' attention. The enormous costs involved in conducting advertising campaigns for candidates running for office show that this assumption is also held by campaign managers. The question of how the parties go about this and how voters perceive and evaluate their efforts in the struggle to achieve majorities has not yet been studied in the context of European Election campaigns in Germany.

This is the topic which our paper addresses. Within the framework of an experiment we will try to answer the question of which reactions German campaign spots for the 2004 European Election produced in recipients. So, we will first describe the design of the study and our sample. Second, we will give a short summary of the content and the style of the campaign spots analyzed in this paper. Third, we will examine the reception and evaluation of those spots and deal with the question of which characteristics of a campaign spot decide whether it is rated successful or not.

2. Design of the study

On June 7th 2004 – one week before the European Election – various experiments were conducted at the University of Koblenz-Landau[3] dealing with the reception and effects of European Election campaign spots broadcasted on the two public television channels *ARD* and *ZDF* on behalf of the five German parties represented in the national parliament: the two governing parties, i.e. the *Social Democrats* (*SPD*) and the *Greens* (*Bündnis 90/Die Grünen*); the major opposition party, i.e. the *Christian Democrats* (*CDU*); the *Liberals* (*FDP*); and the post-communist *PDS*, a party successful only in the Eastern part of Germany.[4]

Table 1: Overview of the experimental design

Wave	Time	Contents
1	Before showing the spots	Political involvement (interest, attention for the campaign); political knowledge; political attitudes (evaluation of parties, issues, Europe); prior voting behaviour, voting intention; party identification; media usage; socio-demographic data.
2	After the first spot (SPD)	Voting intention; evaluation of the spot; comprehension of the spot; political attitudes (issues, evaluation of parties).
3	After the second spot (PDS)	Voting intention; evaluation of the spot; comprehension of the spot; political attitudes (issues, evaluation of parties).
4	After the third spot (FDP)	Voting intention; evaluation of the spot; comprehension of the spot; political attitudes (issues, evaluation of parties).
5	After the fourth spot (Bündnis 90/Die Grünen)	Voting intention; evaluation of the spot; comprehension of the spot; political attitudes (issues, evaluation of parties).
6	After the fifth spot (CDU)	Evaluation and comprehension of the spot; political involvement (interest); political knowledge and attitudes (evaluation of parties, issues, Europe); voting intention.

One of the experiments was conducted among 53 citizens from Landau and the surrounding area.[5] The following procedure was applied: Before watching the first campaign spot all participants were asked to complete an extensive questionnaire inquiring about their political involvement (among other things, their political interest and attention for the campaign), their political knowledge and political attitude (towards parties, issues, and Europe in general), their voting behaviour at previous national and European elections, how they intended to vote at the upcoming European Election as well as their media usage and socio-demographic data. Afterwards they were shown the campaign spot of the *SPD*, followed by the spots of the *PDS*, the *FDP*, and *Bündnis 90/Die Grünen*. The last spot they were shown was that of the *CDU*. After each campaign spot participants were given a short questionnaire asking if they had seen the particular spot before[6] and containing questions concerning the evaluation and comprehension of the spot and evaluation of the political parties. Following the final questionnaire concerning the reception and evaluation of the *CDU*-campaign spot, participants were requested to answer certain questions from the initial questionnaire once more (see Table 1).

3. Description of the campaign spots[7]

The study referred to the campaign spots of the five major German parties (*SPD*, *CDU*, *FDP*, *Bündnis 90/Die Grünen*, and *PDS*) which had nominated candidates for the European election, and considered only the spots broadcasted on public television. On *ARD* and *ZDF* each party had up to eight broadcasting spots which were watched by up to 5.3 million viewers (see Table 2).

Table 2: TV audience ratings of televised campaign spots[a]

Party	Number of spots		Max. number of viewers in million	Date of Broadcast
	ARD	ZDF		
CDU	8	8	3.6	Tu, 06/01/04, 9:53 p.m.
SPD	7	7	5.3	Tu, 06/01/04, 9:03 p.m.
FDP	4	4	3.5	Th, 06/10/04, 9:43 p.m.
Bündnis 90/Grüne	4	4	5.1	Tu, 05/18/04, 9:03 p.m.
PDS	3	3	3.9	Fr, 05/21/04, 9:13 p.m.

Sources: media control; Westdeutscher Rundfunk Köln

The *SPD* European Election campaign slogan was "New Power" (German: "Neue Stärke"). In a black and white spot with relatively unobtrusive background music, six citizens from different age groups gave short statements (so called "testimonials") about important topics, namely economic security in old age, opportunities for youth, international competitiveness through better education, economic growth through innovation, compatibility of family and career, and responsibility for peace. A longer statement by chancellor Gerhard Schröder, speaking directly into the camera, on the importance of Europe as a peace force and on justice in Europe, and a flash of the *SPD*-logo accompanied by the slogan "New Power" (a so-called "pack shot"[8]) finished this campaign spot.

In a much more dynamic spot in reference to cuts and background music the *CDU* advertised its motto "Europe 2004: Germany can do better" ("Deutschland kann mehr"). While images of more than a dozen citizens from different age groups and with different skin colour alternated on the screen in rapid succession or were fitted together, a female and a male voice in the background spoke on behalf of the citizens, complaining about unemployment, pension fraud, and the government not keeping its promises but causing chaos instead, wishing for politics that would "do it better". Concrete goals mentioned were job security, a simplified tax system, better education, a more important role of Germany in Europe, and general progress for Germany. The spot ended with a flash of the two claims "Europe 2004: Germany can do better," and "Better for the people: *CDU*" ("Besser für die Menschen"). Although both spots of *CDU* and *SPD* had citizens speaking and both spots were similar in that they were shot in the studio or on a stage set respectively, the *CDU* campaign spot was considerably more dynamic and also – because of the explicit verbal attacks against the government – more aggressive.

The theme of the campaign spot of *Bündnis 90/Die Grünen* was "For more green everywhere in Europe" ("Für mehr Grün in ganz Europa") and in a combination of fitted images and video clip showed the meaning of the colour green, or the meaning this colour could have in everyday life. The pictures included green (or coloured green) landscapes, microchips, glass bottles, sprouts, street cars, different foods, etc., alternating with flashes of the *Green* members of the national government, Jürgen Trittin, Renate Künast, and Joschka Fischer. Interestingly – the same as in the ads of *CDU* and *SPD* – the top *Green* candidate for the European Parliament, Rebecca Harms, was not shown in the spot. The images alternated quickly, and the whole spot was accompanied by a lively song. The spot ended with a flash of the slogan "You decide: for more green everywhere in Europe," ("Du enscheidest: Für mehr Grün in ganz Europa") showing the logo of the *Green* parties in Europe (*European Greens*) first and then the logo of the German *Bündnis 90/Die Grünen*.

In its campaign spot the *FDP* showed a parody from a scene in an employment office in which two seemingly almighty employment service officials turn down a job seeker whose idea is to open up a restaurant or snack bar or become a chef. In a final statement the top candidate of the *FDP* for the European Parliamentary Election, Silvana Koch-Mehrin, promoted less bureaucracy and more freedom and opportunities instead. The spot ended with a flash of the party logo and the slogan "We can make Europe better."

As in the federal election of 2002 the campaign spot of the *PDS* followed the film "Run Lola, Run". In the first part of the spot the young woman is still lying in bed and repeatedly turns off a radio alarm clock; in between one hears parts of a radio newscast reporting about cuts in social welfare, expensive contracts between the government and consulting firms, and the PISA Study. At 5:55 pm on June 13th (i.e. five minutes before the polling stations close) she jumps out of bed and sprints to the polling station to vote "Socially – *PDS*". The second part of the spot shows the top candidate of the *PDS*, Sylvia-Yvonne Kaufmann, as she explains the election program of the party to the actress who plays Lola in a kind of "citizen consultation" in the make-up room: The *PDS* objective is a social, democratic, civic Europe, without wage dumping and without participation in the American wars of aggression. The spot ends with the actress leaving the make-up room and shutting the door with the party logo on it behind her. A voice in the background says: "Vote socially on June 13th. *PDS.*" ("Am 13. Juni sozial wählen. *PDS.*")

In general, the spots of the five most important German political parties hardly focused on European issues. For example, neither the discussion about the enlargement of the European Union from 15 to 25 members on May 1st, nor very important topics for Germany, like the role of the European Union in coordinating the foreign and security policy of their member states, immigration, the stability of the Euro, possible consequences of national budget deficits, and the discussion about the sanctions for violating the Maastricht criteria, were highlighted in these spots. On the contrary, the party ads aired on public television predominantly emphasized national issues – e.g. unemployment, the economic situation, questions of social policy or education.

4. Reception and evaluation of the campaign spots

After having watched each spot the participants of our study were asked to evaluate each one separately. First, they were asked to indicate on a five point-scale how they liked the spot they had just watched, and then to evaluate that spot – also on a five point-scale – in reference to 14 pre-defined characteristics.

The results from Table 3 show that the spot of *Bündnis 90/Die Grünen* was the best-rated spot receiving an average score of 2.3. The spot of the *SPD* was evaluated with 3.0 (i.e. the mean point of the scale), followed by the ads of *CDU* (3.1) and *FDP* (3.2). Least liked by the viewers was the *PDS*-spot with an average score of 3.3 (which is not surprising if one keeps in mind that the study was conducted in West Germany while the *PDS* can still be considered a party which exclusively represents East German interests and therefore its supporters are predominantly found in the new *Bundesländer*).

Generally speaking, the overall spot rating for the five parties was rather low; this was mainly due to the negative evaluation of content and style. The participants in our study perceived the spots in the following way: In reference to the focus on persons, the average score was 2.8 in direction that they put persons in the centre of attention (especially for the *SPD* spot rated with 2.5). The spots were only of average creativeness (3.0; most imaginative: *Bündnis 90/Die Grünen* with 2.1; least imaginative: *CDU* and *SPD* with 3.6 and 3.7), and had even less to offer in terms of humour (3.2; most funny: *Bündnis 90/Die Grünen* and *FDP* with 2.1 and 2.2; least funny: *SPD* with 4.7), credibility (3.3; most credible: *Bündnis 90/Die Grünen* with 2.9; least credible: FDP with 3.8), their informational content (3.5; most informative: *CDU* with 3.0; least informative: *FDP* with 4.1), and their objectivity (3.5; most objective: *SPD* with 2.8; least objective: *FDP* with 4.3). The spots were not perceived as boring (3.6; least boring: *Bündnis 90/Die Grünen* with 4.1; most boring: *SPD* with 3.1) and predominantly as non-attacking (3.7; most attacking: *CDU* with 1.9; least attacking: *SPD* with 4.9) and non-aggressive (3.7; most aggressive: *FDP* and *CDU* with 2.7 and 2.8; least aggressive: *Bündnis 90/Die Grünen* and *SPD* with 4.5 and 4.8). Not only did the spots lack information about Europe (3.7; most European: *PDS* with 3.2; least European: *FDP* with 4.4), they also were not very convincing (3.7; most convincing: *Bündnis 90/Die Grünen* with 3.2; least convincing: *FDP* with 4.2), and left the participants of the study uncertain (3.7; most confident: *Bündnis 90/Die Grünen* with 3.2; least confident: *PDS* and *FDP* with 4.0 and 4.1). Although the spots did not show any solutions for the most pressing political problems (4.0; the worst rating appeared for the *FDP* with 4.5), the recipients were not worried by them (4.2; most alarming: *CDU* with 3.6; least alarming: *Bündnis 90/Die Grünen* with 4.7).

Table 3: Evaluation of the campaign spots

	All spots	CDU	SPD	FDP	B90/Grüne	PDS
Overall spot evaluation[a]	3.0	3.1	3.0	3.2	2.3	3.3
The campaign spot...[b]						
...focused on persons	2.8	2.9	2.5	3.1	2.7	3.0
...was imaginative	3.0	3.6	3.7	2.6	2.1	2.9
...was funny	3.2	3.8	4.7	2.2	2.1	3.0
...was credible	3.3	3.4	3.1	3.8	2.9	3.4
...was informative	3.5	3.0	3.2	4.1	3.6	3.6
...was objective	3.5	3.5	2.8	4.3	3.7	3.3
...was boring	3.6	3.5	3.1	3.7	4.1	3.4
...attacked the political opponent	3.7	1.9	4.9	4.0	3.6	4.0
...was aggressive	3.7	2.8	4.8	2.7	4.5	3.7
...dealt with Europe a lot	3.7	3.6	3.4	4.4	3.7	3.2
...was convincing	3.7	3.7	3.4	4.2	3.2	3.8
...left me confident	3.7	3.8	3.5	4.1	3.2	4.0
...showed solutions	4.0	3.9	3.8	4.5	3.9	3.9
...left me worried	4.2	3.6	4.4	4.1	4.7	4.1

[a] Measured on a five-point-scale from 1 "like it very much" to 5 "don't like it at all".
[b] Measured on a five-point-scale from 1 "statement fully applies" to 5 "statement does not apply at all".

With the exception of *Bündnis 90/Die Grünen*, recipients' general impression of the spots was highly unfavourable. In sum, the spots appeared relatively uninformative, not very credible or convincing, and did not offer any suggestions about how to solve the most pressing problems. Although the spots were not characterized as boring, they lacked fantasy and humour. The spots failed to emotionalize the recipients since they hardly attacked the opponent and were obviously not very effective in their use of personalization strategies. As a consequence, the spots left recipients without any emotional involvement, i.e. without a feeling of confidence or anxiety. Finally, the participants of our study clearly noticed that European issues were ignored in the spots. The election campaigns of the political parties did not make any attempt to close the information gap on European Politics and the European Parliamentary Election created by the insufficient mass media coverage. This leads to the somewhat bizarre situation where citizens were asked to vote for parties competing in the context of the European Election but had not been informed about their political goals on the European level. In addition, by focusing on national topics in their campaign advertising, all parties highlighted the status of European Elections as "second-order elections".

5. Structures of the reception of the campaign spots

An interesting question which we will examine in this section is if the very different aspects of spot evaluation applied in this study can be assigned to more abstract dimensions of evaluation. Technically speaking, we are searching for common factors behind these 14 campaign spot characteristics. Furthermore, we want to examine if the structures underlying the perception of the spots of the different parties are different or similar. If the latter is the case, it would indicate that recipients of campaign spots have common standards for rating such spots.

Table 4: Overview of the results of factor analysis

The campaign spot...	CDU	SPD	FDP	B90/Grüne	PDS	Dimension
...was informative	(1)	(1)	(1)	(1)	(1)	
...was convincing	(1)	(1)	(1)	(1)	(1)	
...was credible	(1)	(1)	(1)	(1)	(1)	
...was objective	(1)	(1)	(1)	(1)	(1)	Information (1)
...left me confident	(1)	(1)	(1)	(1)	(1)	
...showed solutions	(1)	(1)	(1)	(1)	(2)	
...dealt with Europe a lot	(1)	(2)	(2)	(1)	(1)	
...focused on persons	(2)	(2)	(2)	(2)	(2)	Personalization (2)
...was boring[a]	(3)	(2)	(3)	(3)	(2)	
...was funny	(3)	(3)	(3)	(3)	(3)	Entertainment (3)
...was imaginative	(3)	(3)	(3)	(3)	(3)	
...left me worried	(4)	(4)	(4)	(4)	(4)	
...was aggressive	(4)	(4)	(4)	(4)	(4)	Aggression (4)
...attacked the political opponent	(4)	(4)	(4)	(4)	(2)	

[a] Item was recoded.

The results of factor analysis make clear that all 14 items can almost consistently be assigned to an underlying dimension (see Table 4).[9] The indicators informational content, persuasive power, credibility, objectivity, assuredness, suggestions for problem solving, and reference to European issues loaded on a common factor labelled "information orientation". The variables entertainment, humour, and fantasy comprise a factor called "entertainment". The impression that recipients were left worried, that the spot was aggressive and attacking the political opponent make up the factor "aggression". The perception that the campaign spot focused on persons built a factor of its own called "personalization".

For the subsequent analysis, the items loading on each of the four factors were summed up to indices.[10] The descriptive analysis of these indices (see Table 5) once again clearly shows that the spots were perceived in direction of personalization (especially for the *SPD* spot) and entertainment (especially for the spots of *FDP* and *Bündnis 90/Die Grünen*). In contrast to this, not one of the spots was rated informative by participants of our study (this is especially the case for the *FDP* spot). Finally, with the exception of the *CDU*, all spots were perceived as low on aggression.

Table 5: Mean evaluation of the dimensions information, entertainment, aggression, and personalization

Index[a]	All spots	CDU	SPD	FDP	B90/Grüne	PDS
Personalization	2.8	2.9	2.5	3.1	2.7	3.0
Entertainment	2.9	3.3	3.8	2.4	2.0	2.9
Information	3.6	3.6	3.3	4.2	3.5	3.6
Aggression	3.9	2.8	4.7	3.6	4.3	3.9

[a] Scales from 1 ("attribute fully applies") to 5 ("attribute does not apply at all").

Table 6 shows the correlation between the different dimensions. Of special interest is the finding that high positive intercorrelations between the dimensions information and entertainment were attained. In the eyes of the participants, entertaining campaign spots seem to transmit information; informative spots, in turn, are rated entertaining. This is especially the case for the spots of *CDU* and *Bündnis 90/Die Grünen*. Information as well as entertainment positively correlate with the personalization perceived in a spot. This holds true for *CDU* and *FDP* in particular, to some extent also for *Bündnis 90/Die Grünen* and the *PDS*. Putting persons in the centre of attention could also support the transmission of a high content of information or entertaining elements then. Only the spot of the *SPD*, which was perceived as the most personalized spot, does not succeed in either informing or entertaining viewers with this strategy. Finally, aggression seems to be unentertaining – especially for the *CDU*; in this case both attributes correlate strongly negative with each other.

Table 6: Correlation between the dimensions

	Information	Entertainment	Aggression
All spots			
Entertainment	.48		
Aggression	-.04	-.12	
Personalization	.09	.13	.01
CDU			
Entertainment	.59		
Aggression	-.16	-.43	
Personalization	.18	.24	-.21
SPD			
Entertainment	.41		
Aggression	.02	-.06	
Personalization	-.08	-.01	.14
FDP			
Entertainment	.46		
Aggression	.08	.01	
Personalization	.24	.16	.19
B90/Grüne			
Entertainment	.51		
Aggression	.07	-.05	
Personalization	.09	.10	-.08
PDS			
Entertainment	.43		
Aggression	-.22	-.08	
Personalization	.00	.18	-.01

6. The impact of the campaign spot characteristics on the evaluation of campaign spots

Now, the interesting question is which of the characteristics ascribed to the campaign spots have an effect on the general spot rating. In other words: Which individual features lead to a positive evaluation of the spot? The answer to this question has far-reaching consequences: Only if a spot receives favourable ratings does it have the chance to evoke positive impressions of the party or the candidate it is promoting. This is a necessary condition for mobilizing party supporters and reinforcing their attitudes and voting intentions. If, in addition, a spot pursues the goal to convince undecided voters and change the voting intensions of the supporters of other parties or candidates, there is no doubt that here too a favourable evaluation of the spot is indispensable.

The results of the regression analysis shown in Table 7 clearly demonstrate that in particular the two dimensions information and entertainment are responsible for how a campaign spot is judged. In all cases they are significant predictors of the general evaluation of the campaign spot. With the exception of the *PDS*, the effect of entertainment is larger than that of informational content. In other words: In the eyes of the recipients a good spot is in the first place entertaining. In contrast, the question of whether a spot contains enough information for the recipient to form attitudes and make electoral decisions is regarded as less important. Interestingly, the effects of aggression as well as personalization are insignificant. Neither attacking a political opponent nor the much praised strategy of personalization has consequences for the evaluation of televised campaign advertising.

Table 7: Impact of the dimensions on the overall spot evaluation[d]

	CDU	SPD	FDP	B90/Grüne	PDS
R^2	.71	.71	.69	.69	.73
Information	.43[c]	.34[b]	.20	.31[b]	.47[c]
Entertainment	.52[c]	.55[c]	.55[c]	.41[c]	.44[c]
Aggression	.10	.10	-.08	-.12	-.08
Personalization	-.08	-.16	.05	.02	.01

Significance levels: a: p<.05, b: p<.01, c: p<.001
[d] Standardized regression coefficients are shown; all models control for party identification, sex, age, education, and prior spot viewing.

7. Summary and conclusions

Four weeks before the 2004 European Parliamentary election, the political parties in Germany aired campaign spots in the public television stations for free. Those spots had the major function to mobilize voters, to reinforce attitudes and voting intentions of own supporters, to convince undecided voters, and – but only as a secondary task – to change voting intentions of the supporters of other parties.

To fulfil this function, an essential prerequisite is that campaign spots are favourably evaluated by recipients. The campaign spots shown to the participants of our study largely failed to fulfil this demand. Moreover, they were perceived as relatively uninformative and not very credible, objective, or convincing. Compared to national topics, European issues were only of minor importance, and the spots failed to show any solutions for the problems they put in the centre of discussion. Because the media did not focus extensively on the European Union and especially not on the upcoming European election this led to the absurd situation that people should cast their vote for parties competing for seats in the European parliament without knowing very much about European issues and related party positions.

In contrast, most spots were perceived as entertaining (although they failed to emotionalize). The dimensions of spot evaluation entertainment and information were strongly correlated but were almost unrelated with the factors aggression and personalization. Therefore, it seems that attacking strategies as well as personalization strategies (both strategies were scarcely used in the European election campaign spots) were inadequate to transmit humour or information.

When it comes to the question which aspects determine a spot's overall evaluation, it turned out that the perception of a spot as entertaining was the most important criterion for almost all parties. Second in importance was information, whereas attacking and personalization appeared to be rather unimportant for the evaluation of a spot.

References

Anderson, John R./Bower, Gordon H. (1972): Recognition and Retrieval Processes in Free Recall. In: Psychological Review, Vol. 79, 97-123.
Benoit, William L./McHale, John P./Hansen, Glenn J./Pier, P.M./McGuire, John P. (2003): Campaign 2000. A Functional Analysis of Presidential Campaign Discourse. Lanham: Rowman & Littlefield.
Binder, Tanja/Wüst, Andreas (2004): Inhalte der Europawahlprogramme deutscher Parteien 1979-1999. In: Aus Politik und Zeitgeschichte, No. 17, 38-45 [Content of the European Manifestos of German Political Parties].
Biocca, Frank (1991a): Models of Successful and Unsuccessful Ad: An Exploratory Analysis. In: Biocca, Frank (Ed.): Television and Political Advertising, Vol. 1. Hillsdale, NJ: Erlbaum, 91-122.
Biocca, Frank (1991b): Viewers' Mental Models of Political Messages. Toward a Theory of the Semantic Processing of Television. In: Biocca, Frank. (Ed.): Television and Political Advertising. Vol. 1. Hillsdale, NJ: Erlbaum, 27-89.
Biocca, Frank (Ed.) (1991c): Television and Political Advertising. Vol. 1. Hillsdale, NJ: Erlbaum.
Biocca, Frank/David, Prabu/West, Mark (1994): Continuous Response Measurement (CRM). A Computerized Tool for Research in the Cognitive Processing of Communication Messages. In: Lang, Annie. (Ed.): Measuring Psychological Responses to Media. Hillsdale, NJ: Erlbaum, 15-64.
Bowen, Lawrence (1994): Time of Voting Decision and Use of Political Advertising. The Slade Gorton-Brock Adams Senatorial Campaign. In: Journalism Quarterly, Vol. 71, 665-575.
Buss, Malte (1994): Manipulation mit Millionen. TV-Werbung intern. Frankfurt: Ullstein [Manipulation with Millions. TV-Advertisement – a View from Inside].
Falter, Jürgen W./Rattinger, Hans (2001^2): Die deutschen Parteien im Urteil der öffentlichen Meinung 1977-1999. In: Gabriel, Oscar W./Niedermayer, Oskar/Stöss, Richard (Eds.): Parteiendemokratie in Deutschland. Bonn: Bundeszentrale für politische Bildung, 484-503 [Falter/Rattinger: German Political Parties in Public Opinion. In: Gabriel/Niedermayer: Party Democracy in Germany].
Freudenstein, Roland (2004): Übergreifende Trends. In: Reifeld, Helmut (Ed.): Europawahlen 2004. Ergebnisse und Bewertungen der Außenstellen der Konrad-Adenauer-Stiftung. St. Augustin: Konrad-Adenauer-Stiftung, Haup-

tabteilung Internationale Zusammenarbeit/Hauptabteilung Politik und Beratung, 3-4 [Freudenstein: Comprehensive Trends. In: Reifeld: European Elections 2004].

Friedrichsen, Mike (1999): Grundlagen der Wirkung von Werbung im Fernsehen. In: Friedrichsen, Mike/Jenzowsky, Stefan (Eds.): Fernsehwerbung. Theoretische Analysen und empirische Befunde. Opladen: Westdeutscher Verlag, 89-120 [Friedrichsen: Foundations of Advertising Effects in Television. In: Friedrichsen/Jenzowsky: TV Advertising. Theoretical Analyses and Empirical Results].

Holicki, Sabine (1993): Pressefoto und Pressetext im Wirkungsvergleich. Eine experimentelle Untersuchung am Beispiel von Politikerdarstellungen. München: Fischer [Press Photo and Press Text in Comparison. An Experimental Analysis on the Depiction of Politicians].

Holtz-Bacha, Christina (1990): Nur bei den Wasserwerken Effekte? Eine Studie zur parteipolitischen Spot-Werbung vor Europawahlen. In: medium, Vol. 20, 50-53 [Effects Only for the Waterworks? A Study of Parties' TV-ads in the Context of European Elections].

Holtz-Bacha, Christina (2000): Wahlwerbung als politische Kultur. Parteienspots im Fernsehen 1957-1998. Wiesbaden: Westdeutscher Verlag [Election Advertising as Political Culture. Party-Spots on Television 1957-1998].

Just, Marion/Crigler, Ann/Wallach, Lori (1990): Thirty Seconds or Thirty Minutes. What Viewers Learn from Spot Advertisements and Candidate Debates. In: Journal of Communication, Vol. 40, 120-133.

Kaid, Lynda Lee (1996): "Und dann, auf der Wahlparty..." Reaktionen auf Wahlwerbespots: Computergestützte Messungen. In: Holtz-Bacha, Christina/ Kaid, Lynda Lee (Eds.): Wahlen und Wahlkampf in den Medien. Opladen: Westdeutscher Verlag, 208-224 [Kaid: "And later at the Election Party..." Reactions to the TV Advertising. Computer Based Measurements. In: Holtz-Bacha/Kaid: Elections and Campaigns in the Media].

Kaid, Lynda Lee (2004): Political Advertising. In: Kaid, Lynda Lee (Eds.): Handbook of Political Communication Research, Mahwah, NJ: Erlbaum, 155-202.

Kaid, Lynda Lee/Tedesco, John (1999): Die Arbeit am Image: Kanzlerkandidaten in der Wahlwerbung. Die Rezeption der Fernsehspots von SPD und CDU. In: Holtz-Bacha, Christina (Ed.): Wahlkampf in den Medien – Wahlkampf mit den Medien. Opladen: Westdeutscher Verlag, 218-241 [Kaid/Tedesco: Working on the Image. Reception of TV Aads of SPD and CDU. In: Holtz-Bacha: Campaigning in the Media – Campaigning with the Media].

Kolmer, Christian (2004): Vernichtung eines Ideals – Fallstudie: Das Medienbild der EU 01/2003-06/2004. In: Medien Tenor, Forschungsbericht No. 147, 10-13 [Destruction of an Ideal – Case Study: The Picture of the EU in the Media].

Kroeber-Riel, Werner (1991): Strategie und Technik der Werbung. Stuttgart: Kohlhammer [Strategy and Technique of Advertising].

Kroeber-Riel, Werner (1992^5): Konsumentenverhalten. München: Vahlen [Consumer Behaviour].
Levy, Mark R. (1982): The Lazarsfeld-Stanton Program Analyzer. A Historical Note. In: Journal of Communication, Vol. 30, No. 4, 30-38.
Maier, Michaela/Maier, Jürgen (2005): Inhalt und Wahrnehmung der Wahlwerbesendungen zur Europawahl 2004 der im Bundestag vertretenen Parteien. Eine Dokumentation. Kaiserslautern: Technische Universität Kaiserslautern [Content and Perception of the 2004 European Election Campaign Spots of the Parties Represented in the German National Government].
Mattenklott, Axel (2004): Werbung. In: Mangold, Roland/Vorderer, Peter/Bente, Gary (Eds.): Lehrbuch der Medienpsychologie. Göttingen: Hogrefe, 619-642 [Mattenklott: Advertising. In: Mangold et al.: Media Psychology – a Textbook].
Medien Tenor (2004): Verzerrtes Bild. Nebensache Europa – Jahresrückblick 2003 und Langzeitanalyse von sieben Jahren EU-Berichterstattung. Forschungsbericht No. 140, 18-19 [A Distorted Picture. Looking Back at the Year 2004 and on Seven Years of Reporting on the EU].
Paivio, Allan (1971): Imagery and Verbal Processes, New York: Holt, Rinehart & Winston.
Paivio, Allan (1975): Imagery and Long-term Memory. In: Kennedy, Alan/Wilkes, Alan (Eds.): Studies in Long-Term Memory. London: Wiley, 57-85.
Patterson, Thomas E./McClure, Robert D. (1976): The Unseeing Eye: Myth of Television Power in Politics, New York: Putnam.
Petrocik, John R. (1996): Issue Ownership in Presidential Elections with a 1980 Case Study. In: American Journal of Political Science, Vol. 40, 825-850.
Pylshyn, Zenon W. (1977): What the Mind's Eye tells the Mind's Brain: A Critique of Mental Imagery. In: Nicholas, John (Ed.): Images, Perception, and Knowledge. Dordrecht: Reidel, 1-36.
Rattinger, Hans/Krämer, Jürgen (1995): Wahlbeteiligung und Wahlnorm in der Bundesrepublik Deutschland. Eine Kausalanalyse. In: Politische Vierteljahresschrift, Vol. 36, 267-285 [Turnout and Citizen's Duty to Vote in Germany. A Causal Aanalysis].
Reif, Karlheinz/Schmitt, Hermann (1980): Nine Second-order Elections. A Conceptual Framework for the Analysis of European Election Results. In: European Journal of Political Research, Vol. 8, 3-44.
Reinemann, Carsten/Maier, Jürgen/Faas, Thorsten/Maurer, Marcus (2005): Reliabilität und Validität von RTR-Messungen. Ein Vergleich zweier Studien zur zweiten Fernsehdebatte im Bundestagswahlkampf 2002. In: Publizistik, Vol. 50, 56-73 [Reliability and Validity of RTR-Measurement. A Comparison of Two Studies on the Second Televised Debate in the 2002 German National Election Campaign].
Rettich, Markus (2004): EU-Wahlen gibt es nicht. In: Politik & Kommunikation, No. 4, 42-43 [There are no European Elections].

Rölle, Daniel (2002): Nichts Genaues weiß man nicht? Über die Perzeption von Wahlprogrammen in der Öffentlichkeit. In: Kölner Zeitschrift für Soziologie und Sozialpsychologie, Vol. 54, 264-280 [Don't Know Anything? On the Perception of Manifestos by the Public].
Rothschild, Michael L./Ray, Michael L. (1974): Involvement and Political Advertising Effect: An Exploratory Experiment. In: Communication Research, Vol. 1, 264-285.
Schmitt, Hermann/Reif, Karlheinz (2003): Der Hauptwahlzyklus und die Ergebnisse von Nebenwahlen: Konzeptuelle und empirische Rekonstruktionen am Beispiel der Europawahlen im Wahlzyklus der Bundesrepublik. In: Wüst, Andreas (Hrsg.): Politbarometer. Opladen: Leske + Budrich, 239-256 [Schmitt/Reif: The First-order Electoral Cycle and the Results of Second-order Elections. Conceptual and Empirical Reconstructions on the Example of European Elections within the German Election Cycle. In: Wüst: Politbarometer].
Schmitt-Beck, Rüdiger (2002): Das Nadelöhr am Ende. Die Aufmerksamkeit der Wähler für die Wahlkampfkommunikation als Voraussetzung wirksamer Kampagnen. In: Machnig, Matthias (Hrsg.): Politik – Medien – Wähler. Wahlkampf im Medienzeitalter. Leverkusen: Leske + Budrich, 21-48 [Schmitt-Beck: The Eye at the End. The Attention of Voters for Campaign Communication as a Prerequisite of Effective Campaigns. In: Machnig: Politics – Media – Voters. Election Campaigns in the Era of Media].
Thorson, Esther/Reeves, Bryan (1985): Effects of Over-time Measures of Viewer Liking and Activity during Programs and Commercials on Memory for Commercials. In: Lutz, Richard (Ed.): Advances in Consumer Research XIII, New York: Association of Consumer Research, 549-553.
Weaver, David/Drew, Dan (2001): Voter Learning and Interest in the 2000 Presidential Election: Did the Media Matter? In: Journalism & Mass Communication Quarterly, Vol. 78, 787-798.
Werben & Verkaufen News (1995): Werbespots je nach Sportart. In: Werben und Verkaufen, Vol. 46, 42 [Advertising Spots Depending on the Discipline].
West, Darrell M. (1993): Air Wars. Television Advertising and News Coverage in Election Campaigns, 1952-1992. Washington, D.C.: CQ.
Zhao, Xinshu/Chaffee, Steven M. (1995): Campaign Advertisements versus Television News as Sources of Political Issue Information. In: Public Opinion Quarterly, Vol. 59, 41-65.

---

[1] As a longitudinal analysis of mass media reports on the European Union shows, the low media coverage of the European Union during January 2004 was not an exception (see Kolmer 2004; Medien Tenor 2004).
[2] The base for a political campaign is, of course, a party or specific election program in which political goals are formulated. In the context of European Parliamentary Elections, the party programs do not predominantly focus on national issues but increasingly contain

topics from the European political agenda (see Binder/Wüst 2004: 40). Nevertheless, party programs are usually poorly perceived by voters (see, e.g., Rölle 2002). Thus, transmitting information from party programs to voters is a task of mass media.

3   The study was funded by the Ministry of Science, Education, Research and Culture of the Land Rheinland-Pfalz.

4   The *SPD* and the *CDU* also broadcasted campaign spots on private commercial television channels. The spots' topics were identical in content but shorter in length than those shown on *ARD* and *ZDF*, because – in contrast to a certain amount of free advertising time on public channels – broadcasting time on private commercial channels costs money.

5   Recruitment of subjects took place according to a previously set up sampling plan which controlled for sex, age, and education. Whereas men and women were represented almost equally among the participants (51 vs. 49 percent), there were minor divergences in reference to participants' age (18-29: 30 percent; 30-44: 30 percent; 45-59: 11 percent; 60 and above: 28 percent), and education (elementary education: 26 percent; modern secondary school education: 30 percent; A levels/high school education: 45 percent). In reference to party affiliation, what was not checked beforehand, it was found that government supporters participated in the survey significantly more often than supporters of the opposition party (*CDU/CSU*: 17 percent; *SPD*: 34 percent; *FDP*: 6 percent; *Bündnis 90/Die Grünen*: 26 percent; *PDS*: 2 percent; identification with a different party: 2 percent; no indication: 6 percent; no party identification: 8 percent). All participants applied for the study in response to ads published in the daily newspaper "*Die Rheinpfalz*" and in a free weekly local newspaper and received a compensation of 15 Euros. For further details about the design of the study see Maier/Maier (2005).

6   23 percent of the participants had seen the *CDU*-campaign spot before; 43 percent had previously seen the *SPD* spot, 13 percent the *FDP* spot, 8 percent the *Bündnis 90/Die Grünen* spot, and 11 percent the *PDS* spot. The fact that the *CDU*- and *SPD*-spots were known by a wider audience has two reasons: On the one hand, both parties had more broadcasting time to their disposal on public TV channels than the smaller parties, and on the other hand they bought additional broadcasting time from the private commercial TV channels.

7   For a detailed analysis of the visual and verbal content of the spots shown to the participants of the study see Maier/Maier (2005).

8   This format of "pack shots" was taken from commercial advertising, where the advertised product is often shown again in the final shot. In political party advertising this "usually concerns shots showing a party logo, often added by a slogan or other party identifying elements" (Buss 1994: 229; see also Holtz-Bacha 2000: 161).

9   Missing values were eliminated via mean substitution. The extracted factor solution was Varimax-rotated.

10 The scales are relatively reliable in this context. For the dimension "information" the reliability coefficient α varies between .83 (*FDP*) and .91 (*CDU*). For the entertainment dimension the coefficients vary between .62 (*SPD*) and .80 (*Bündnis 90/Die Grünen*). Except for the *SPD* (α=.17; the reliability of the scale could have been improved by changing the composition of the index; this was not done to maintain comparability to the spots of the other parties) the reliability coefficients for the dimension "aggression" vary between .51 (*Bündnis 90/Die Grünen*) and .69 (*CDU*).

Advertising Effects:
Polish Elections to the European Parliament

*Wojciech Cwalina, Andrzej Falkowski & Paweł Koniak**

1. Introduction

In the accession referendum (June 7th-8th 2003) Poles expressed their wish to join the European Union. At the same time, it was the first step toward full participation in the EU. The next stage of integration with EU structures included the election of representatives to the European Parliament. The President of the Republic of Poland, Alexander Kwasniewski, set June 13th 2004 as the date for the election. Fifty-four representatives to the European Parliament were to be elected in 13 multi-seat constituencies across Poland.

The first election to the European Parliament in Poland was connected with both establishing political representation in the EU and administering the respective election law. The aim of the first part of this article is to describe the election law with special consideration of the regulations concerning the electoral campaign in public and commercial media. Next, a detailed description of the electoral competition between the most important political groups is given, and the final results are presented. Particular attention is paid to the analysis of the importance of political ads for forming voters' electoral preferences. In order to determine the influence of ads on Poles' political preferences during the election to the European Parliament, experimental research was carried out. The purpose of this analysis is an attempt to answer two questions. First, do the ads of a particular party have an influence on voters changing their attitude towards this party? Second, does the exposure to political ads lead to changes in the perception of the party's image? Also presented is an analysis of the evaluation of political ads broadcasted by three political parties during the electoral campaign. Attention is drawn to the manner with which images and issues are presented in these ads. Furthermore, we answer the question whether viewing political ads contributes to increasing the voters' political knowledge and political self-expertise. The detailed description of the research design and the obtained results are presented in the second part of the article.

---

* Wojciech Cwalina, PhD. *1971. Associate Professor, Department of Marketing Psychology, Warsaw School of Social Psychology, email: wojciech.cwalina@swps.edu.pl
Andrzej Falkowski, PhD. *1953. Professor, Department of Marketing Psychology, Warsaw School of Social Psychology, email: andrzej.falkowski@swps.edu.pl
Paweł Koniak, MA. *1978. Assistant Professor, Department of Marketing Psychology, Warsaw School of Social Psychology, email: pawel.koniak@swps.edu.pl

2. Polish law on election to the European Parliament

Ordynacja wyborcza do Parlamentu Europejskiego (The Act of January 23rd, 2004, on Elections to the European Parliament) specifies that the candidates to the European Parliament are proposed by party election committees or voter groups. Each committee may propose one list of candidates in each constituency. The list may include no less than five and no more than ten persons. In addition, each party must collect at least 100.000 signatures of voters living permanently in a given constituency. Each voter may express his or her support for more than one committee. In the case of election committees which registered their lists in at least half of the constituencies, their candidates were automatically registered in the other constituencies. The registration of election committees must be finished 40 days before the elections.

The election campaign commenced following the announcement of the date of the elections. According to Polish law, campaign activities must be brought to an end 24 hours before the polling stations open on election day. The last 24 hours is the period of so-called "voting silence". From the end of the election campaign until the polling stations close, it is forbidden to make public the outcomes of pre-election surveys concerning probable voting behavior and tentative results of the elections to the European Parliament in the European Union.

Election committees should have the right to broadcast their election programs on radio and television free of charge. The total free airtime allotted for broadcasting election spots is: 1) on nationwide channels – 15 hours broadcasted by the Polish Television Joint Stock Company between 17:00 and 23:00 o'clock and 20 hours by the Polish Radio Joint Stock Company; 2) on every regional channel – 10 hours broadcasted by the Polish Television Joint Stock Company and 20 hours by regional broadcasting companies (see Ordynacja wyborcza do Parlamentu Europejskiego 2004).

An election committee has the right to broadcast its election materials on nationwide channels for free if it has registered constituency lists in at least nine electoral constituencies. In the case where the election committee has registered a constituency list in at least one electoral constituency but less than nine, then it has the right to broadcast its election materials for free only on regional channels. Airtime for broadcasting election materials should be divided into equal parts amongst the election committees. No later than on the 18th day before the election should the editors-in-chief of the respective national television channels, including *Television Polonia* and regional programs, as well as radio programs, draw up the timetable of election programs to be broadcasted each day in the presence of the persons who submitted the lists (see Ordynacja wyborcza do Parlamentu Europejskiego 2004). In addition to the free broadcasting time, once the voting campaign has been opened each committee may run paid voting advertisements on radio and television. The fees charged for voting advertisements and airtime must be the same for all election committees and set according to the price list effective on the day of the announcement of the date of the election.

These are the same rules which apply to Polish parliament elections (see Ordynacja wyborcza do Sejmu Rzeczypospolitej Polskiej i do Senatu Rzeczypospolitej Polskiej 2001).

3. Election campaign to the European Parliament

The political parties in Poland represent a broad range of public consensus, with groups which may be classified as social-democratic, liberal, conservative, national, rural-interest, or populist. There are also radical groups with a negligible amount of public sympathy. The major political parties in Poland are: the *Alliance of the Democratic Left* (*Sojusz Lewicy Demokratycznej*), the *Civic Platform* (*Platforma Obywatelska*), *Law and Justice* (*Prawo i Sprawiedliwosc*), the *League of Polish Families* (*Liga Polskich Rodzin*), the *Polish Peasant Party* (*Polskie Stronnictwo Ludowe*), *Self-Defense* (*Samoobrona*), and *Polish Social Democracy* (*Socjaldemokracja Polska*). Representatives of these groups and smaller parties make up the Polish parliament, which is divided into two chambers, Sejm and Senate. The Sejm is composed of 460 deputies chosen for four-year terms of office according to the principle of proportional representation. There are 100 Senators who are also elected for four years on the principle of majority vote (see www.sejm.gov.pl/english).

Twenty-one lists of election committees were registered for the elections to the European Parliament in 2004. Fifteen of them had access to free airtime on Polish public television.

Two weeks before Election Day more than half of those persons eligible for voting (57 percent) stated that they were not interested in the election to the European Parliament. Only 41 percent of the voters expressed a moderate interest in the elections. The relatively low level of interest in the elections – particularly when compared with other types of elections – did not increase despite the fact that the date of the election was coming closer. It remained almost on the same level as a few months earlier. Forty-five percent of the polled persons stated that they would participate in the elections (see Wybory do Parlamentu Europejskiego 2004).

One of the crucial factors determining people's willingness to participate in the elections was their attitude toward Poland's membership in the European Union. The persons supporting Poland's membership in the EU declared that they wanted to participate in the elections, in contrast to those who opposed integration. And despite the fact that compared to their declarations from March, the number of people not supporting Poland's membership in the EU but wanting to participate in the elections increased, there were still more opponents to integration not wishing to participate in the elections (see Wybory do Parlamentu Europejskiego 2004).

Results of pre-election polls, conducted by The Public Opinion Research Center two weeks before Election Day, suggested that the *Civic Platform* could count on the highest number of seats in the European Parliament as 24 percent of the respondents declared their support for it. Compared to the declarations in March, the support for the *Civic Platform* had hardly changed. Many candidates from the following parties also had a high chance of being elected: Self-Defense 13 percent and *Law and Justice* 12 percent. Next in the poll were the *League of Polish Families* and the *Polish Peasants' Party* with 7 percent each, the coalition *Alliance of Democratic Left-Labor Union* (*Sojusz Lewicy Demokratycznej-Unia Pracy*) 6 percent, and also *Polish Social Democracy* 5 percent (see Wybory do Parlamentu Europejskiego 2004).

It should be pointed out that the leading positions in pre-election polls were taken by opposition parties against the ruling left coalition (*Self-Defense, Law and Justice* and *League of Polish Families*). The voting campaign was running at a time where support for the ruling left-wing parties was rapidly declining.

The parties running in the European Parliament elections focused on different aspects in their campaigns. The *Civic Platform* focused on domestic issues. One could get the impression that for the *CP* it was more important to take over power in Poland than to be represented in the European Parliament. Its campaign was accompanied by such slogans as: "the government of Leszek Miller [former Polish prime minister] was bad for Poland" or "we have a coherent vision of Poland" – and sometimes there was a gloss saying "and for Europe" (see Czaplicki 2004).

Law and Justice appealed mainly to national and patriotic feelings of the electorate. It stressed in its campaign that the EU should be an organization that serves Poland and not the other way around. Therefore, it would have been difficult to talk about any European common interest or compromises with other EU countries.

The strongest anti-Union stance was adopted by the *League of Polish Families* (*LPF*) as reflected in its campaign slogan "Yesterday Moscow and today Brussels". The message of the *LPF* was dominated by national and patriotic rhetoric, and the politicians from this party suggested that the EU was a threat to the Polish state and Polish tradition. They claimed that the only defender of Poland from secular Europe was the *LPF*.

Self-Defense treated the elections to the European Parliament in a similar way. The key person of the party's campaign was its leader – Andrzej Lepper. He was presented as the only person in the country capable of making the EU treat Poland on a par with its "old members." Lepper claimed that "the EU has gotten between our clean sheets with its dirty legs" (Czaplicki 2004).

The ruling *Alliance of Democratic Left-Labor Union* adopted a different election strategy. With the support of the Poles constantly decreasing, they tried to present themselves as being pro-European and caring, in this context, for the country. At the same time they emphasized their economic achievements and the fact that it was the Alliance who had led Poland to the EU. The campaign of *ADF-LU* was one of the few campaigns free from critique of the EU.

Despite the fact that the focus of the campaigns of the particular parties varied, their content was about the same in reference to the rhetoric they used in order to secure seats in Polish parliament (i.e. Sejm and Senate). On the one hand, this style of campaigning was connected with Poles' limited knowledge of the European Parliament and its function in the EU-system, making it difficult for people to distinguish between the European Parliament and the Polish Parliament. On the other hand, Polish parties gave the impression that they had no conception of what their position and function in the European Parliament were to be.

Besides, both from politicians' statements and from the selection of the candidates for members of the European Parliament (including popular persons from public life having nothing to do with politics), it was obvious that the parties did not consider the results of these elections as very important. It seems that for the political elites the result of voting was more important (which party will be winner) than what particular persons would be representing Poland in the European Parliament. Therefore, one should not be surprised that Poles were hardly interested in these elections and that what they saw in them was only a certain procedure making it possible for the representatives of particular political parties to obtain highly paid positions (see Czaplicki 2004).

Another factor pointing to the low relevance given to the elections to the European Parliament were the issues connected with the expenses of the election campaign. Theoretically, each party could have spent 9 million PLN (about 2.2 million Euro) – approx. 0.3 PLN per voter. According to Czaplicki's (2004) estimates, the spending was much lower. For instance, *LPF* spent around 2 million PLN (about 485.000 Euro), *LaJ*, 1 to 3 million (243.000 to 728.000 Euro), and *Union of Freedom* (*Unia Wolnosci*) 0.8 million PLN (about 194.000 Euro).

On the other hand, in Poland there was no information campaign before the elections to the European Parliament. The state administration did not show any initiative in this matter. Also, the Information Office of the European Parliament did not make any active attempts to inform the Poles about the elections and the function of the European Parliament in the European Union (see Czaplicki 2004).

4. The results of the election

The opposition parties were most successful in the elections, in which only 20.9 percent of the eligible Polish voters participated. The prerequisite for obtaining a seat is that the specific party list received at least 5 percent of the vote across Poland. The liberal *Civic Platform* got the most support – 24.1 percent (15 seats). The second place was taken by the anti-European, right-wing *League of Polish Families*, connected with Catholic and national ideology (15.9 percent; ten seats), and *Law and Justice* (12.7 percent; seven seats) placed third. The following parties also won seats in the Parliament: the populist and anti-European

Self-Defense, representing a mainly rural electorate (10.8 percent; six seats); left-wing parties connected with the government – the coalition *Alliance of Democratic Left-Labor Union* (9.4 percent; five seats) and *Polish Social Democracy* (5.3 percent, three seats); the centrist *Union of Freedom* (7.3 percent; four seats) and the *Polish Peasant Party* mainly representing farmers (6.3 percent; four seats) (see Obwieszczenie Państwowej Komisji Wyborczej 2004).

The first elections to the European Parliament in Poland were accompanied by relatively low voter participation. Only one person out of five who were eligible to vote fulfilled his or her "civic duty". It seems that the factor that may have led to such a low turnout was the lack of reliable and comprehensive information about the EU and the European Parliament.

The voting campaign did not fulfill its educational function. The issues widely discussed in other countries were not brought up in the Polish campaign. Such issues included the war in Iraq, Turkey's potential membership in the EU, and the problems of migration. No one raised the issue of joining the monetary union (Euro-zone) by Poland.

For the majority of Polish political parties the elections to the European Parliament were of less importance than the government crisis and the debate on earlier parliamentary elections in Poland. They saw these elections as a first step in taking over governmental power in Poland.

For the media as well, the elections were not a priority subject. Nevertheless, the media tried to provide extensive coverage of the voting campaign. The Polish newspapers usually wrote about the voting campaign as a whole, whereas the local media focused on the presentation of candidates from a specific region. Television also broadcasted programs about the course and development of the campaign. However, such programs were few in number (see Czaplicki 2004).

5. The influence of political advertising on voter preferences

Many studies have demonstrated that political advertising has an important influence on the forming of voters' evaluations of candidates and their preferences (see Cwalina/Falkowski 2000, 2003; Cwalina et al. 2000, 2005; Kaid/Holtz-Bacha 1995; Kern 1989).

The results of cross-cultural research on the influence of political advertising on voters' preferences conducted by Cwalina et al. (2000) during the presidential elections in Poland and France in 1995 and during the parliamentary elections in Germany in 1994 show that it is possible to distinguish three types of influence. Firstly, advertisements may strengthen already existing voting preferences. The supporters of a specific candidate consolidate themselves in their support for their candidate, whereas the opponents consolidate themselves in their opposition. In other words, the polarization of voting convictions increases. It can also be connected with a certain reshaping of the candidate's image in the minds of his or her electorate.

Secondly, advertisements may weaken already existing voting preferences and, in extreme cases, may even cause a change. This leads to increasing uncertainty among voters about whom to support. It is usually accompanied by a reconfiguration of the candidate's image. After watching the advertisements, certain features of the candidates, other than the ones he or she perceived as important before, become relevant for the voter. So he or she must re-consider arguments for a specific decision.

Thirdly, advertisements may neither weaken nor strengthen political preferences, but they may lead to a reconfiguration of the candidate's image in voters' minds. This type of influence can be called cognitive influence because, as a result of it, the reasoning behind the earlier decision changes, but the direction of the decision and the conviction with which it was made remain the same. From the point of view of political marketing, and thus, from the point of view of shaping political preferences, this type of promotional influence during a presidential or parliamentary campaign can be evaluated as inefficient. But leading to the change of a politician's image can be treated as the first and necessary step to the strategy preparing him for the successful fight for power.

Besides, the key factor influencing for whom persons cast their vote seems to be their emotional attitude towards candidates. If a politician or a party is capable of evoking positive emotions in a large part of the electorate, this can translate into their election success. Current research suggests that the main factor influencing human behavior are emotions (see Zajonc 1980), and many studies have revealed that the emotional attitude toward candidates or political parties is a very good predictor of voters' decisions (see Cwalina/Falkowski 1999, 2003; Cwalina et al. 2000, 2005; Falkowski/Cwalina 1999). Aronson et al. (1994) even metaphorically suggest that people vote with their hearts rather than with their minds. Wattenberg (1987) found out that one third of voters know almost nothing about particular politicians, although he or she has strong feelings towards them.

The task of analysis of the influence of advertising on voting preferences should be to answer two questions. First of all, do the ads of a particular candidate have an influence on voters' changing their attitude towards him or her? And secondly, does the exposure to political ads lead to changes in the perception of his or her image?

6. Empirical research

In each democratic state political parties and candidates face the fundamental decision of how to communicate with their voters and influence them in such a way that citizens accept their leadership. In order to achieve this goal, political parties and leaders most often use political advertising (see Cwalina/Falkowski 2005; Kaid/Holtz-Bacha 1995; Newman 1999). Apart from legal constraints, the only other limitation when using television in political promotion is the financial resources needed to pay for air time and to produce a television spot (see Brams 1976; Devlin 1995).

6.1 Research methodology

In order to analyze the effectiveness of political advertisements in gaining voter support, experimental research was conducted four days prior to the elections to the European Parliament. Seventy-three subjects (59 women and 14 men) participated anonymously in the study. The sample consisted of students of psychology at the Catholic University of Lublin in the southeastern part of Poland. The average age of the respondents was 20.4 years.

The experimental design included a pre-and posttest and consisted of three stages. In the first stage the experimental group completed the first part of a research questionnaire (pretest). Subjects then watched three political advertisements of the *League of Polish Families*, *Self-Defense,* and the *Civic Platform* on a large TV-screen. The presented advertisements were chosen at random from the advertisements that each of the parties used in its television campaign. After the subjects had watched the spots, they were given the second part of the research questionnaires (posttest).

The pretest questionnaire included questions concerning demographic data of the subjects and items measuring the extent to which the parties represented subjects' political beliefs and subjects' reported support for the parties running in parliamentary elections. In the pretest there were also questions concerned with subjects' interest in the European Election and their knowledge of this event (five-point scale). Furthermore, in the posttest subjects were asked to evaluate the usefulness of electoral information provided by such media sources as TV news and debates, newspapers, news magazines, radio, internet, TV ads sponsored by candidates and independent organizations, campaign mailings and brochures, talking with friends and family, and going to rallies or public speeches. Both assessment phases included questions concerning political cynicism (eight items) and political self-expertise (four items).

Besides, in the pretest and posttest identical semantic differentials were administered. They consisted of 13 bipolar seven-point scales (unqualified-qualified; unsophisticated-sophisticated, dishonest-honest, unbelievable-believable, unsuccessful-successful, unattractive-attractive, unfriendly-friendly, insincere-sincere, excitable-calm, aggressive-unaggressive, weak-strong, inactive-active, not believing-believing Christian). Subjects were asked to evaluate each of the parties on each of the scales, before and after ads exposure. The semantic differentials were the measure of the perceived party image.

In order to assess the emotional attitude toward these three political parties, a so-called thermometer of feelings was used, ranging from 0 to 100 degrees. The scales were included in both parts of the questionnaire (see Cwalina et al. 2000; Falkowski/Cwalina 1999).

Apart from that, the research method included questions referring to subjects' knowledge about the elections to the European Parliament and their interest in them and the sources from which they obtained information about these elections. In all these items the evaluation was conducted on five-point scales.

6.2 Results

6.2.1 Party preferences

In reference to party preferences, most support was given to the *Civic Platform* – 42.5 percent of the subjects considered this party as the one which best represented their interests, followed by 16.4 percent of the subjects stating *Law and Justice* to be their favored party. Further, 5.5 percent of the students indicated the *Union of Real Politics* (*Unia Polityki Realnej*) and 4.2 percent the *League of Polish Families* as their favorites. Interestingly, almost 21.9 percent of the participants stated that none of the parties running for the European Parliament represented the views they identified with. Other responses included other political groups.

As far as students' voting preferences for the elections were concerned, the distribution was different. 21.9 percent of the respondents stated that they were not going to participate in the coming elections. From the remaining group, 30.1 percent of the respondents expressed their support for the *Civic Platform*, 6.8 percent for the *League of Polish Families,* and 5.4 percent for *Law and Justice.* Besides, 23.3 percent of the students claimed that they were still uncertain about which parties to vote for. Such a distribution of support is clearly different from the distribution of "closeness" of the researched persons' views to political parties. It is suggested that despite having some concrete program preferences, most of the respondents were going to vote against them. One could put forward a hypothesis here that subjects were willing to postpone their decision whom to support until the last moments of the election campaign depending on how the general situation developed in the meantime. In other words, their final decision may be an expression of strategic voting (see, e.g., Johnston 2002).

6.2.2 Knowledge about the elections

Subjects answered the questions on political cynicism, interest in the election to the EP, their knowledge about this election, and evaluated the usefulness of information provided by different media on five-point scales.

The interest of the subjects in the first elections in Poland to the European Parliament was moderate (M=3.1). It was accompanied by their relatively low knowledge about the event (M=2.4). Besides, in the week preceding the elections students had not been exposed very often to media coverage (press, radio and TV) of the EU Parliamentary elections (M=3.1) nor had talked with other people about them (M=3.1). The subjects considered television debates with representatives of individual parties running for the European Parliament as the most useful source of information about the elections (M=4.0). Less relevance was given in this respect to newspapers (M=2.9), informal communication with family and friends (M=2.9), and also TV news coverage (M=2.9) as well as radio (M=2.8).

The least useful source of election information was, according to the respondents, direct mail distributed by political parties (M=1.4) and political advertising (M=1.4).

Another factor pointing to students' low involvement in the elections to the European Parliament was their level of political cynicism, which was somewhat above average (M=3.7) This was expressed through their acceptance of such views as: "Whether I vote or not has no influence on what politicians do", "People like me don't have any say about what the government does", or "One cannot always trust what politicians say".

6.2.3 The evaluation of political advertising

The respondents were asked to define which type of appeal dominated in the spots they were shown. Their task was to determine on a five–point scale whether the spots of a particular political group focused more on the image of the party (coded as "1") or on the party's attitude towards specific issues (coded as "5"). In order to analyze the differences between the evaluation of the spots of the *League of Polish Families*, *Self-Defense*, and the *Civic Platform*, analysis of variance (ANOVA) was conducted.

The results show that respondents perceived the spots of these parties to be significantly different as far as ways the type of appeal was concerned [$F(2, 134)=7.48$; $p<0.001$]. The comparisons with Scheffe's post hoc test proved that *Self-Defense's* spots were more focused on the image (M=2.2) than the spots of the *League of Polish Families* (M=2.8, $p<0.05$) and those of the *Civic Platform* (M=3.0, $p<0.01$).

The respondents were also asked to evaluate to what extent the spots of particular parties did a good job of discussing issues that were important to them. Answers were provided on five-point scales (1 = "not discussed" to 5 = "well discussed"). Analysis of variance shows that in this case too the evaluations of the spots differ significantly [$F(2, 132)=32.69$; $p<0.001$]. The results of Scheffe's test prove that such issues were best presented by the spots of the *CP* (M=3.3), despite the fact that – according to the respondents – it was not a satisfactory presentation of the party's program. The spots of the *CP* were significantly different from the spots of other parties ($p<0.01$). The lowest ratings were given to *SD*'s message (M=1.9) with the *LPF*'s lying in between (M=2.7). The latter two messages were significantly different from each other (p<0.01). The results are illustrated in Figure 1.

Figure 1: The evaluation of the issues presented in the spots of the *League of Polish Families*, *Self-Defense* and the *Civic Platform*

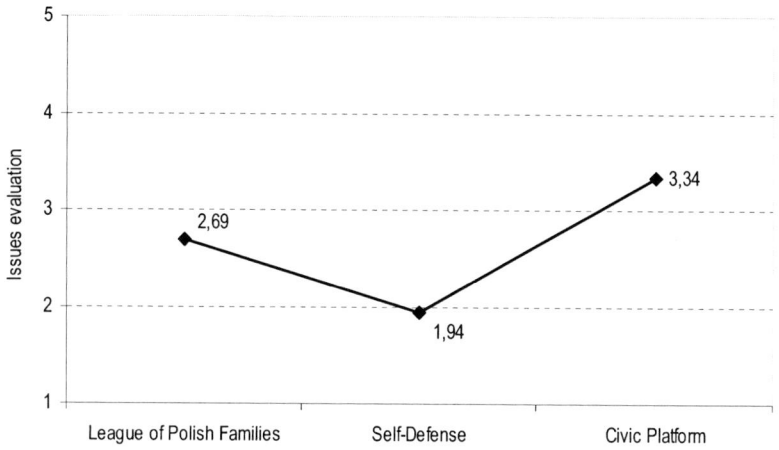

Issues in the spots: 1 – "not discussed" to 5 - "well discussed"

6.2.4 The influence of political advertising on the sense of political self-expertise

Political expertise represents accumulated knowledge in a political domain. It includes an accumulation of raw facts, but this is not all. Expertise also includes well-structured and organized concepts and exposure to relevant information. In politics this is likely to occur via the print and electronic media. Moreover, expertise entails practice and direct experience – political activities that are undertaken. And it means involvement, both in terms of expressed interest in one's chosen domain and perceived identity as the sort of person who knows and cares about the area (see Fiske et al. 1990). As far as a politician's expertise is concerned, it resembles football very much; each voter/fan believes he or she has the best qualifications to form the lineup of the winning team. And what is characteristic is the fact that it is not automatically accompanied by the necessary abilities. One could then assume that each person has their own sense of political self-expertise, based to a larger or smaller degree on knowledge and skills. No matter what the level of knowledge and skills might be, this sense of political expertise is always one of the key elements influencing the evaluations and behaviors in a given sphere, including the world of politics.

During the experiment the participants were asked twice to rate their own political self-expertise on five-point scales – before and after ads exposure. It helps to determine the level of the changes in this sense of political self-expertise brought about by the spots. In order to determine the level of this influence, a t-test for dependent samples was performed.

Although the subjects claimed that political advertising was not an important source of information about the elections to the European Parliament for them, being exposed to political ads had an important influence on their sense of political self-expertise [$M=2,8$ and $M=2,9$, respectively for pre- and posttest; t-test(66)=-2,7; $p<0,01$].

This result suggests that political communication does not only have a persuasive function. It may also increase voters' conviction of their competence in making political judgments. In turn, it could become the foundation for overcoming political cynicism. Another possibility could be that the voters, having familiarized themselves with the political message, are strengthened in their conviction that their former views were right. In other words, their cynicism is by all means justified.

6.2.5 The influence of political advertising on the perception of political parties

The purpose of analysis of the influence of advertising on voting preferences and perception of political parties is an attempt to answer two questions. First, do the ads of a particular candidate have an influence on voters' changing their attitude towards him or her? Second, does the exposure to political ads lead to changes in the perception of the candidate's image?

In order to analyze the changes in the emotional attitude toward the *LPF*, *SD*, and the *CP* under the influence of their spots, three t-tests were performed for dependent samples on the basis of the feeling thermometer included in pre- and posttest.

In the case of all three parties it was determined that the spots did not result in any significant changes in subjects' emotional attitude towards the parties. Thus, the answer to the first question about the influence of political advertising on voters is negative. No such influence was observed.

In order to determine whether political advertising led to a reconfiguration of the perception of the image of particular parties, six forward stepwise regression analyses were conducted for each party in the pre- and posttest. The dependent variable was the "feeling thermometer" score. This measurement was taken for each of the candidates by asking the subjects to mark the point on the thermometer (ranging from 0 to 100 degrees) which corresponds to their "feeling temperature" in reference to the party being advertised. The independent variables were the particular scales of the semantic differentials.

The results clearly demonstrate that the images of the parties presented in their voting advertisements influence people's affective attitude towards them. In each of the three cases a reconfiguration of the characteristics explaining attitudes towards these parties occurred. Detailed results of regression analysis are presented in Table 1.

Table 1: Adjectives explaining the variance of the feeling thermometer based on the multiple regression analysis

Party	Experimental conditions	R²	Characteristics	Beta (β)
League of Polish Families	pretest	0.61	friendly***	0.34
			qualified*	0.23
			active*	0.20
	posttest	0.71	attractive***	0.38
			aggressive**	-0.30
			qualified*	0.23
Civic Platform	pretest	0.32	qualified*	0.29
	posttest	0.44	credible**	0.43
			strong*	0.29
			sophisticated*	0.26
Self-Defense	pretest	0.44	honest**	0.36
			believable*	0.30
	posttest	0.56	honest*	0.35
			qualified*	0.29
			successful**	0.21

Levels of significance: *p<0.05; **p<0.01; ***p<0.001

In the case of the *League of Polish Families* important preference predictors for emotional attitude towards the party in the pretest ($R^2=0.61$) were characteristics such as "friendly", "qualified", and "active". However, after watching the advertisements, respondent's attitude towards the party was determined ($R^2=0.71$) by a different set of characteristics. They included "attractive", "aggressive", and "qualified".

These results suggest that the *LPF*'s political advertising led to a reconfiguration of the important elements of the party's image. The importance of features initially important to the subjects ("friendly" and "active") disappeared completely. The voters began to focus on the evaluation of the *LPF* according to its attractiveness and aggressiveness. And the core element of the party's image was its qualification.

In the case of the *Civic Platform* the only important image characteristic in the pretest influencing subjects' attitude towards the party ($R^2=0.32$) was "qualified". After watching the advertisements the voters became sensitive to a completely different pattern of the characteristics (R^2=0.44). They included "believable/credible?", "strong", and "sophisticated". A full reconstruction of the perception of the *CP's* image took place. All the features which finally came out as the final predictors of people's attitude towards the party had not been relevant until the subjects familiarized themselves with the party's voting message.

In turn, the characteristics influencing the attitude towards *Self-Defense* in the pretest (R^2=0.44) were "honesty" and "believable/credible". After presenting the advertisements, a good predictor of emotional attitude (R^2=0.56) still was "honesty", but, in addition to that, the following characteristics emerged: "qualified" and "successful".

In all analyzed parties, political advertisements led to a significant change in the perception of their image. The importance of particular characteristics for forming the attitude towards a specific party changed as well. It seems that in the case of the political spots used during the European Parliament campaign by the *LPF*, *SD*, and the *CP* cognitive influence occurred. Advertisements neither weaken nor strengthen political preferences, but they lead to a reconfiguration of the candidate's image in voters' minds. In other words, the argumentative basis for the earlier made decision changed, but the direction and certainty with which it was made remained the same (see Holbrook et al. 2001; Rahn et al. 1994).

7. Conclusion

Despite the fact that the first elections to the European Parliament in Poland were accompanied by relatively little interest of the voters, the promotional materials prepared by particular parties had some influence on forming the decisions of those voters who decided to take part in the elections. The research presented here suggests that political advertising led to an increase in the self-ratings of political expertise among young voters. They also had some influence on the perception and the evaluation of the image of various parties. However, they were too weak to modify people's attitude towards the competing groups.

Thus, it seems that a well-conducted information campaign, accompanied by a more active election campaign, could have brought more benefits to the mutual understanding for the citizens of Poland (and European Union) than it did in reality.

References

Aronson, Elliot/Wilson, Timothy D./Akert, Robin M. (1994): Social Psychology: The Heart and the Mind. New York: HarperCollins College Publishers.

Brams, Steven J. (1976): Paradoxes in Politics. An Introduction to the Nonobvious in Political Science. New York: Free Press.

Cwalina, Wojciech/Falkowski, Andrzej (1999): Decision Processes in Perception in Political Preferences Research. A Comparative Analysis of Poland, France, and Germany. In: Journal for Mental Changes, Vol. 5, No. 2, 27-49.
Cwalina, Wojciech/Falkowski, Andrzej (2000): Psychological Mechanisms of Political Persuasion: The Influence of Political Advertising on Voting Behaviour. In: Polish Psychological Bulletin, Vol. 31, No. 3, 203-222.
Cwalina, Wojciech/Falkowski, Andrzej (2003): Advertising and the Image of Politicians. National Elections in Poland, France, and Germany. In: Hansen, Flemming/Christensen, Lars Bech (Eds.): Branding and Advertising. Copenhagen: Copenhagen Business School Press, 205-231.
Cwalina, Wojciech/Falkowski, Andrzej (2005): Marketing Polityczny. Perspektywa Psychologiczna. Gdansk: GWP [Political Marketing. A Psychological Perspective].
Cwalina, Wojciech/Falkowski, Andrzej/Kaid, Lynda Lee (2000): Role of Advertising in Forming the Image of Politicians. Comparative Analysis of Poland, France, and Germany. In: Media Psychology, Vol. 2, No. 2, 119-146.
Cwalina, Wojciech/Falkowski, Andrzej/Kaid, Lynda Lee (2005): Advertising and the Image of Politicians in Evolving and Established Democracies. Comparative Study of the Polish and the U.S. Presidential Elections in 2000. In: Journal of Political Marketing, Vol. 4, No. 2/3, 29-54.
Czaplicki, Michal (2004): Pierwsze wybory europejskie w Polsce. In: Analizy i Opinie, No. 25, 1-10 [Czaplicki: The First European Election in Poland].
Devlin, L. Patrick (1995): Political Commercials in American Presidential Elections. In: Kaid, Lynda Lee/Holtz-Bacha, Christina (Eds.): Political Advertising in Western Democracies: Parties and Candidates on Television. Thousand Oaks: Sage Publications, 186-205.
Falkowski, Andrzej/Cwalina, Wojciech (1999): Methodology of Constructing Effective Political Advertising. An Empirical Study of the Polish Presidential Election in 1995. In: Newman, Bruce I. (Ed.): Handbook of Political Marketing. Thousand Oaks: Sage Publications, 283-304.
Fiske, Susan T./Lau, Richard R./Smith, Richard A. (1990): On the Varieties and Utilities of Political Expertise. In: Social Cognition, Vol. 8, No. 1, 31-48.
Holbrook, Allyson L./Krosnick, Jon A./Visser, Penny S./Gardner, Wendi L./Cacioppo, John T. (2001): Attitudes toward Presidential Candidates and Political Parties. Initial Optimism, Inertial First Impressions, and Focus on Flaws. In: American Journal of Political Science, Vol. 45, No. 4, 930-950.
Johnston, Ron (2002). Manipulating Maps and Winning Elections. Measuring the Impact of Malapportionment and Gerrymandering. In: Political Geography, Vol. 21, No. 1, 1-31.
Kaid, Lynda Lee/Holtz-Bacha, Christina (1995): Political Advertising in Western Democracies. Parties and Candidates on Television. Thousand Oaks: Sage Publications.
Kern, Montague (1989): 30-Second Politics: Political Advertising in the Eighties. New York: Praeger.

Newman, Bruce I. (1999): Handbook of Political Marketing. Thousand Oaks: Sage Publications.
Obwieszczenie Państwowej Komisji Wyborczej z dnia 15 czerwca 2004 r. o wynikach wyborów posłów do Parlamentu Europejskiego przeprowadzonych w dniu 13 czerwca 2004 r. (2004). In: Dziennik Ustaw, June 16th 2004; No. 137, item 1460 [Polish Election Committee Announcement. Results of the European Parliament Election. In: Journal of Laws of the Republic of Poland].
Ordynacja wyborcza do Parlamentu Europejskiego. Ustawa z dnia 23 stycznia 2004r. (2004). In: Dziennik Ustaw, February 23rd, 2004, No. 25, item 219 [The Act of 23 January 2004 on Elections to the European Parliament. In: Journal of Laws of the Republic of Poland].
Ordynacja wyborcza do Sejmu Rzeczypospolitej Polskiej i do Senatu Rzeczypospolitej Polskiej. Ustawa z dnia 12 kwietnia 2001 r. (2001). In: Dziennik Ustaw, May 16th No. 46, item 499 [The Act of April 12th 2004 on Elections to the Polish Parliament. In: Journal of Laws of the Republic of Poland].
Rahn, Wendy M./Krosnick, Jon A./Breuning, Marijke (1994): Rationalization and Derivation Processes in Survey Studies of Political Candidate Evaluation. In: American Journal of Political Science, Vol. 38, No. 3, 582-600.
Wattenberg, Martin P. (1987): The Hollow Realignment: Partisan Change in a Candidate-Centered Era. In: Public Opinion Quarterly, Vol. 51, 58-74.
Wybory do Parlamentu Europejskiego. Komunikat z badań (2004): Centrum Badania Opinii Społecznej, BS/95/2004, June 2004 [Election to the European Parliament. Research Report. In: The Public Opinion Research Center].
Zajonc, Robert B. (1980): Feeling and Thinking. Preferences Need Not Inferences. In: American Psychologist, Vol. 35, 151-175.

The European Parliament Elections in Estonia 2004: Party Spots and the Effects of Advertising

Mart Raudsaar & Külli-Riin Tigasson*

1. Introduction

By the end of the 1990s, when Estonian accession negotiations with the EU had just started and the negotiations with NATO had not yet begun, the Estonian foreign minister at the time, Toomas Hendrik Ilves, liked to emphasize that Estonia belonged to Northern rather than to Eastern Europe. It would be a mistake to underestimate the identity-building power of this sentence, which served in the broader context of the foreign policy strategy of Estonia aiming to represent itself in the world not as a simple "post-communist country", but as a "normal country" sharing Western values.

By spring 2004 the two most important foreign political aims of Estonia were fulfilled: Since the 29th of March 2004, Estonia has been a full member of the NATO, and since the 1st of May 2004, Estonia enjoys full membership in the EU. On the 13th of June, Estonia held its first elections to the European Parliament (EP) – and these elections provide a good basis to compare Estonia with the other EU member states.

The EP-elections in Estonia were rather untypical – and this not only because these were the first EP-elections in this country. In the international context, the EP-elections in Estonia were also remarkable because Estonia belonged (and still belongs) to the most Eurosceptical member states of the EU (see Eurobarometer 2004). Whereas the political elite of Estonia has continuously supported its membership in the EU (although not all political parties that support the membership in the EU, also support the further political integration of the EU, being especially reluctant to adopt the ideas to harmonize the social policy and direct taxes at the EU-level), a considerable proportion of the population can be characterized more by Euroscepticism and even by resistance against EU-membership – and this attribute shaped the whole direction of the EP-campaign.

The other main reason why the elections in Estonia can be described as rather untypical in the European context is the regulation of political advertising in this country. In contrast to most Western democracies, Estonia has not enacted specific and tight regulations for political advertising. For instance, whereas in the Scandinavian countries "political advertising is generally per-

---

* Mart Raudsaar, M.Phil. *1973. PhD student and Lecturer at Department of Media and Communication, Tartu University, email: mart.raudsaar@ut.ee
Külli-Riin Tigasson, M.A. *1975. PhD student at the Department of Media and Communication, Tartu University, email: kylli.riin.tigasson@epl.ee

ceived as a threat to the principles of democracy" (Siune 1995: 124), in Estonia efforts to restrict political advertising are perceived as a threat to the principles of freedom of expression. In Estonia electoral advertising in the press and in broadcasting underlies the same principles applying to commercial advertising. Estonia allows parties unlimited purchasing of advertising time in commercial TV and radio channels as well as advertising space in print and outdoor media.[1]

Thus, Estonian political parties have good possibilities to influence and shape the communicative situation before the elections. The liberal regulation of political advertising provides a good breeding ground for what is called a "professionalization" and "commercialisation" of campaign communication and political communication in general. The term "professionalization" means that the election campaigns have become more and more technical and professional. This includes the growing importance of expert-work, communication that relies on journalistic news values, the design of political advertising, the design and interpretation of public opinion surveys as well as the increasing orientation of campaign communication to certain "target groups" (see Meadow 1989: 270), the growing use of entertaining strategies (see Holtz-Bacha 1994: 190), and increasing negativity and personalization of the campaign communication. Under "commercialisation" is meant that the political parties increasingly rely on marketing strategies typically used by the private sector and the voters are perceived more as clients whose support is to be won, but not as citizens who need to participate in the public debate (see Blumler/Gurevitch 1995: 207-208).

Despite the omnipresence of political advertising, almost no work has been done in Estonia in investigating its possible effects and influences. However, this question is particularly relevant in Estonia due to the fact that the links between electorate and parties are very weak in this country, and the elections are characterized by high vote volatility and decreasing voter turnouts (see Grofman et al. 2000: 346). Various surveys of political campaigns have indicated that the campaigns and advertising tend to have more influence among "volatile" voters, for instance, voters without a certain candidate preference tend to assess the candidate attacked in a negative campaign more negatively than the voters with a stable candidate preference (see Garramone et al. 1990; Kahn/Kenney 1999).

In this article, the focus will be on political TV-spots and their effects on voters on the basis of an experiment. The results of the experiment are compared for two different age groups (students and retired persons) to examine whether there are age differences in the reception of political spots. Additionally, to investigate whether the reception of political advertising depends on the level of being informed about politics, the respondents were divided in two further groups according to their self-evaluation of their political interest and informedness about political and EU-issues.

Before turning to the specific issues of the experiment, first a general overview about the Estonian political and media system and its regulation will be given, followed by a description of EP-campaign issues and the content of TV-spots.

2. The political and legal framework of the EP-campaign

2.1 Estonian political and election system and the results of the EP-elections

Estonia is a parliamentary democracy with a one-house parliament (*Riigikogu*) that has 101 members. The duties of the president are largely ceremonial. The Estonian government and prime minister are responsible to the parliament.

Political parties play a key role in the Estonian political system. However, as the first free elections in re-independent Estonia were held in 1992, after 50 years of Soviet occupation and a one-party reign, the party system has been rapidly changing, and electoral allegiances are relatively weak. After the collapse of communism Estonian politics faced "a defining vacuum" (Grofman et al. 2000: 348): The Estonian parties could not emerge "naturally" from social organizations, such as trade unions or religious groups, or from class cleavages. The association with communism had discredited the trade unions, the religious groups could barely exist under Soviet rule, and the notion of "class" was relatively unimportant, because in the beginning of the 1990's the democratisation and marketization caused economic hardships and role reversals in Estonia, so that the basic identifiers of socio-economic "class" became fuzzy (ibid.).

Thus, Estonian party politics tend to focus more on top leaders and their personalities than on political programmes. The Estonian party landscape has been characterized by "fission and fusion of parties" (ibid.) and by the emergence of new ones. By the end of the 1990s there was already some evidence of a stabilizing party system as well as a classical right-left patterning: Five to six bigger parliamentary parties and one dozen non-parliamentary parties shaped the picture. However, the illusion of "stabilization" was shattered by the unexpected success of a new conservative party, *Res Publica*, formed in the year 2001 that used the slogan "new politics" and immediately jumped to second place in the elections to local government councils in 2002. *Res Publica* succeeded in repeating its success in the 2003 national elections as well: Under the slogan "Choose order!" the party gained 24.6 percent of the votes and again reached second place.

Before the EP elections 2004 each party was allowed to nominate no more than 12 candidates. According to the European Parliamentary Elections Act, candidates can be nominated as candidate lists of political parties or as independent candidates. Unlike national elections, where there are 12 constituencies in Estonia, in the European Elections the whole country forms a single constituency. This leads to an increased personalization of the elections campaign: Public attention is drawn to the top-candidates of the parties to a greater extent than in national elections.

The main players of the 2004 EP-election campaign were six parliamentary parties: leftist *Centre Party* (member of the ELDR Group at the European Parliament), liberal *Reform Party* (the same), conservative *Res Publica* (EPP-ED

Group), national-conservative *Pro Patria Union* (the same), rural *Estonian People's Union* (*Union for Europe of the Nations*), and *Estonian Social Democratic Party* (PES). A total of 95 candidates were nominated; 91 candidates from ten parties as well as four single candidates (see Table 1):

Table 1: Number of candidates and mandates at the EP-elections in Estonia 2004

	Number of candidates	Mandates
Estonian People's Union	12	0
Reform Party	12	1
Res Publica	12	0
Social Democratic Party	12	3
Pro Patria Union	12	1
Centre Party	12	1
Russian Party in Estonia	12	0
Estonian Democratic Party	3	0
Social-Democratic Labour Party	3	0
Estonian Pensioner's Party	1	0
Independent candidates	4	0

Source: Estonian National Electoral Committee

The election results are determined according to the principle of proportionality. The threshold is five percent, but gaining five percent of the votes does not automatically mean access to the elected body. Mandates are distributed using the d'Hondt distribution method that favours the parties that have proportionally gained more votes.[2] This distribution method has been used in Estonia since the beginning of the 1990s to facilitate the consolidation of the "kaleidoscopic" (see Grofman et al. 2000: 329-357) party landscape.

Figure 1: Turnout in the national elections 1992-2003 and in the European Parliament elections 2004 (percent of eligible voters (≥18 years old))

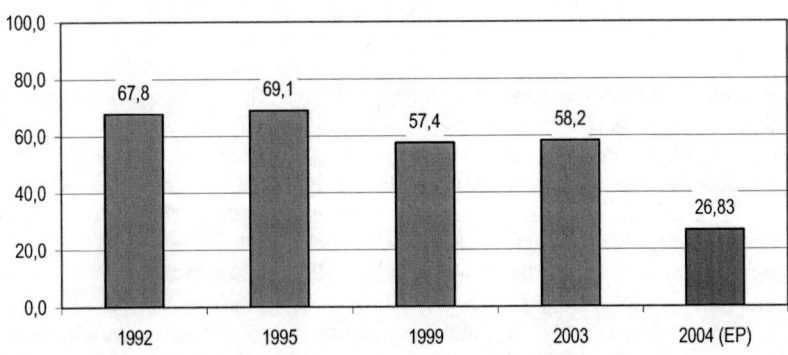

Source: Estonian National Electoral Committee

The turnout in the EP-elections was a record low – only 26.83 percent, that is less than half the turnout generally seen in Estonian elections (see Figure 1). The record low turnout can be explained in many ways. According to a Eurobarometer survey that was conducted in May 2004, the main reasons for abstention in Estonia were the belief that the vote of the respondent would not change anything (58 percent of respondents not planning to go to vote), lack of interest in the European elections (52 percent), belief that the European Parliament would not sufficiently deal with problems that concern the respondent (51 percent), and the feeling of not being sufficiently represented by the Members of the European Parliament (51 percent). 28 percent of the respondents who intended not to vote explained their decision with their being against Europe, the European Union, and the European construction.

One important factor that was probably one of the reasons for high election abstention was the remarkable negativity of the campaign: Many political parties who had launched massive campaigns to ensure "yes" to the EU before the referendum on EU membership (on the 14th of September 2003) had changed their strategy now, before the EP elections. Hoping to get support from the Eurosceptical voters, many parties used a negative strategy, largely presenting the European Union, its institutions, and the constitutional treaty in a negative way, as a threat to Estonian independence (see Tigasson 2005).

Table 2: The intention to vote (percent of those eligible to vote)

"Are you planning to vote in the European Parliament Elections on the 13th of June?"			
	February 2004 (759 Respondents)	March 2004 (756 Respondents)	Mai 2004 (760 Respondents)
Yes, definitely	38	37	29
Probably yes	35	31	29
Probably no	6	12	14
Certainly no	8	13	19
I do not know	13	7	9

Source: Survey Research Center Faktum

The negativity of the EP-campaign in Estonia 2004 manifested itself foremost in political advertising: in TV-spots and in outdoor advertising as well as in the party websites. Several studies of the influence of political advertising have indicated that negative advertising can increase the abstinence from voting (see Garramone et al. 1990; Kahn/Kenney 1999). It seems that this negative strategy led to a certain "cognitive dissonance" among voters (because the parties that had campaigned for the EU before the EU-referendum built their strategy for the EP-elections on criticising the EU) and increased the abstinence from voting. Public opinion surveys conducted during the campaign period demonstrate that the proportion of people saying they would certainly go to the polls decreased continuously during the campaign (see Table 2).

2.2 The media system and regulation of electoral advertising

Despite the fact that Estonia has only 1.347 million inhabitants, the country's media landscape is rather rich – there are many commercial media channels as well as strong public broadcasting stations.

There are two quality national daily newspapers in Estonia – *Postimees* and *Eesti Päevaleht*. There is also a national tabloid – *SL Õhtuleht*. The largest national weekly is *Eesti Ekspress*. Estonia is divided into 15 counties, and each county has at least one local newspaper.[3]

Besides the print media, there are three national TV-channels in Estonia: the state-owned public *Estonian TV* (*ETV*) and two private channels *Kanal 2* and *TV3*. Both commercial TV-channels belong to foreign companies: Norwegian Schibsted Group owns *Kanal 2*, and *TV3* belongs to Swedish Modern Times Group. There is also a public broadcasting radio station and about 30 private radio stations run by less than 20 companies.

According to legislation, electoral advertising in the press and broadcasting underlies the principles similar to those governing commercial advertising. Separate and strict regulations on political advertising have been enacted only for public service broadcasting. Since 1999, there have been no paid political spots on *ETV*. The purchase of advertising time on private broadcasting channels (or in newspapers) has not been limited, and the parties can buy an infinite number of spots (or advertisements in the print media).

The private media in Estonia is not obligated to treat all political parties equally when selling broadcast time. This gives the larger (and richer) parties that are able to buy more airtime a further advantage, because they receive additional volume discounts.

3. The European elections: strategies, messages, and effects

3.1 The political atmosphere before the EP-elections

The election campaign for the European Parliament was the most negative political campaign that Estonia has witnessed since restoration of its independence in 1992. The attacks of the political parties were directed not only against their political adversaries, but also (and overwhelmingly) against the EU. It seemed that many parties built their strategy on gaining the support of "Eurosceptical" voters. Therefore, the campaign was characterized by EU-critical messages. This strategy fitted in well with the Eurosceptical attitude of Estonian voters: According to a Eurobarometer-poll published shortly before the EP-elections, Estonia shared with Latvia the position of the most Eurosceptical member state (see Eurobarometer 2004).

In summer 2003, some months before the referendum on EU-membership, the reluctance of the Estonians towards joining the EU was so high that there existed a real chance that half of the voters would say "no" to the EU (see Figure 2).

Figure 2: Support for the EU in Estonia, 2001-2005 (percent of those eligible to vote, N varies between 730-760)

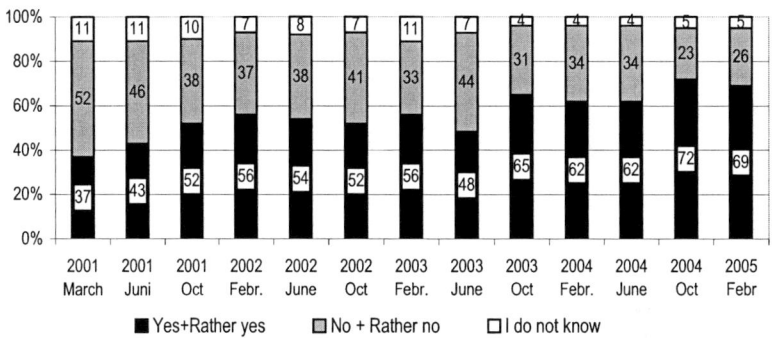

Sources: Estonian State Chancellery, TNS Emor (EU Monitoring)

To increase the changes for "yes", the larger parties launched a pro-EU-campaign before the referendum. None of the Estonian parliamentary parties could be marked as "contra-EU" – and five of the six largest parties campaigned for the EU accession (using slogans like e.g. "Yes to Estonia, yes to Europe!", "Life is going to get better", "It's better to be there", and somewhat provocatively, "More handsome men"). Only the *Centre Party* did not launch such a campaign, because this parliamentary party could not find an inner-party consensus about the Estonian accession to the EU.

During the campaign for Estonian accession to the EU, the attitude of Estonians towards the EU gradually became more positive, and finally, 66.83 percent of voters voted for accession to the EU. However, the referendum turnout was only 64.06 percent. Only Malta and Latvia had similarly low voting activity. It seems that despite the successful referendum, a considerable part of Estonian society still remained sceptical towards the EU. Toots and Vettik (2004: 35-40) argue that according to the opinion polls the attitude towards the EU is dependent upon trust in the state and its institutions as well as the social-economical position of the respondent and his or her knowledge about the EU. Those persons who are satisfied with the Estonian government and national parliament are also more positive about European integration. The same is also true for those persons who have a higher socio-economical status and better knowledge about the EU. Therefore, it can be concluded that the EU-opponents mostly belong to socially disadvantaged groups.

However, not only those who were disadvantaged by the transition processes were positioned against the EU, but also a portion of the "winners" who argued that the EU is "overregulated", too "protectionist", and in comparison to Estonia "not liberal enough". This opinion was also voiced by Martin Helme und Ivar Raig, the main organizers of the anti-EU-campaign before the referendum. Helme und Raig claimed that the tempo of the Estonian "economic miracle" could be slowed down by accession to the "overregulated" EU (see Maaleht 2003).

Besides the above-mentioned (primarily economical and social) factors, the EU-reluctance of Estonians was (and is) also based on the fear to lose sovereignty: Opinion polls conducted by the Survey Research Center Faktum in June 2003 demonstrate that three quarters of those positioned against the EU and one third of pro-EU people were afraid that Estonian independence would now "move" to Brussels.

3.2 The TV-spots: content and reach

Considering the established and continuous Euroscepticism of the population, it is not surprising that many parliamentary parties, which had launched massive pro-EU campaigns in summer 2003 before the referendum on the Estonian access to the EU, completely changed their campaign strategy for the EP-campaign in spring 2004. In their campaign many parties presented an (alleged) conflict between the national interests of Estonia on the one side and the European Union on the other side and suggested that they were the current solution to this conflict (see Tigasson 2005).

Table 3: Reach of electoral TV-advertising during the EP-election campaign 2004

	Population of voting age (over 18)
Quantity*	1.965
Frequency**	92.1
Reach***	942.000
Reach (% of target group)****	91.5%

* Total number of political TV spots broadcasted (incl. repetitions)
** Average number of perceived political TV spots per voter
*** Total number of voters who have seen a political TV spot at least once
**** Percentage of voters who have seen a political TV spot at least once
Source: TNS Emor TV Audience Meter Survey, 2004

The Estonian political parties invested ca. 1.3 million Euros in the EU-campaign, the biggest expenditures being outdoor advertising and TV-spots.[4] Six parties represented in the Estonian parliament produced a total of 41 TV-spots for the EP election campaign. The smaller parties that were not represented in the Estonian parliament produced no TV advertisements. The governing *Res Publica* produced the highest number of spots – 17, and the smaller parties each produced 1-3 spots. The 41 spots were broadcasted 1.965 times, and paid TV-advertising reached 91.5 percent of the population of voting age (see Table 3). The medium length of one electoral TV-spot was 24.5 seconds.

The issues addressed most often in the spots were EU-integration (this topic was closely connected with the debate about the Constitutional Treaty of the EU and the question which influences would the Treaty and the possible deeper political integration have on the national sovereignty of Estonia), technical information about the elections (e.g. general "mobilizing" appeals to increase election turnout, information about the election date, etc.), and the social policy in the EU (especially the influence of the EU structural funds for Estonian society). Additionally, the spots also addressed "Eurobureaucracy", tax policy (the proposal for so-called "Europe-tax"[5] as well as the harmonization of direct taxes), and some other minor issues (see Table 4). The only issue which was presented as an advantage was the social policy in the EU, whereas for all other issues the EU was seen as having predominantly negative effects. A deeper political integration of the EU was generally presented as a danger to the national sovereignty of Estonia, under the topic "Eurobureaucracy" the EU was presented as "over-regulated" and not flexible enough, and under the issue "tax" policy the parties expressed their disapproval of the proposals for "European tax" as well as the harmonization of direct taxes in the EU (for more detailed analysis of spots, see Tigasson 2005).

Table 4:   Issues in the EP election spots

Issues	Number
Deeper integration of the EU/National sovereignty	12
Technical information (election date, etc.)	11
Social policy in the EU	9
Eurobureaucracy	6
Immigration, Russian minority in Estonia	5
Tax policy	5
Other	11

The hierarchy of the relevance of the issues presented in the TV-spots did not coincide with the media agenda. In the context of the EP elections, the newspapers mostly addressed the "adventurous" aspects of the campaign (e.g. campaign strategies of various parties, campaign costs) and the course of the campaign in the other EU member states; deeper integration of the EU and national sovereignty; the functions of the EP; public opinion polls and the forecasts of election turnout (for a more detailed analysis of the media agenda, see Tigasson 2005).

3.3 Does political advertising matter? Results from an experiment

To assess the micro-level effects[6] of political advertising, an experiment was designed to study the reception of the TV-spots and the changes in the perceptions of candidate images. However, it is important to underline that such experiments can reflect only short-term changes in perceptions and attitudes, but not long-term influences (e.g. on the voters behavior). Additionally, as the experiment was conducted in an artificial environment instead of in the "natural" environment of watching TV (and election spots), the results may not accurately reflect the assumed influence of seeing the political advertising. Despite these shortcomings, this kind of experiment is one of the few possibilities to obtain quantitative data about the reception of the political advertising.

In order to study the reception of political TV-spots, the respondents were asked to fill out a questionnaire, which was split up into a pretest and posttest part. After filling out the first part, the respondents were shown 10 TV spots. After this, the respondents were asked to complete the second part of the questionnaire.

Spots were shown for all major Estonian parties, i.e. all six parties represented in Parliament had at least one spot. The experimental sessions were conducted in two groups on the same day, June 5th 2004 (thus, eight days before the EP-elections). Two groups were formed according to age: One group consisted of students, the other of retired persons.

The first group consisted of 28 respondents between 19-28 years; the average age was 21.8 years. They were primarily students of Tartu University, and most were students at the Department of Media and Communication, i. e. the majority of this group has had some media training before, making them more able to critically assess adverstisement spots. It should be noted that the interest of these respondents in Estonian political life is above average.

The second group also consisted of 28 persons, but their age was between 50-85 years; the average age was 71.1 years. They were all visitors of an activity center for retired persons in Tartu, and so the group consisted primarily of retired persons. Thus, there was a striking difference in age between the two groups. It is important to emphasize that – unlike the first group – the members of this group had lived most of their adult lives under Soviet totalitarian rule where the mass media was strictly controlled and non-pluralistic content-wise. Therefore, it could be assumed that this group – who had spent most of their lives in a society where virtually no commercial media and political advertising in the Western sense existed – could be more vulnerable to contemporary political advertising than the (communication) students. On the other hand, this fact can also be interpreted conversely: In the Soviet system the people became "trained to see through the veils of media representation" (see Lõhmus 2002: 47). Indeed, Vihalemm (1999) argues that the art of reading critically was dominant in the totalitarian system. Thus, the Soviet system trained people to "read between the lines" and – using the terminology of Stuart Hall (1980) – to use sophisticated "negotiated" and "oppositional" decoding when consuming media.

Besides the groups based on age, two more groups were composed on the basis of being informed about politics and the EU. In order to divide the participants according to their degree of informedness, the cumulative index of being informed was created (0-5 points), counting respondents' positive answers ("*agree totally*" or "*agree partly*") to five questions designed to measure the level of political interest and being informed about political and EU-issues based on respondents' self-evaluation (e. g. *I believe that I can quite well understand political issues having significance for Estonia*). According to the results, there were 25 less informed respondents (index 0-2 points) and 31 highly informed respondents (3-5 points).

It is important to underline the fact that the two dividing lines – first, between the younger and older respondents, and second, between the less and highly informed persons – are not one-to-one identical (see Table 5).

Table 5: Respondent's age and level of being informed

	Index of being informed		Total
	Less informed	Highly informed	
19-28 years old	11 44.0%	17 54.8%	28 50.0%
50-85 years old	14 56.0%	14 45.2%	28 50.0%
Total	25 100.0%	31 100.0%	56 100.0%

Half of the students reported having seen each spot before, whereas two-thirds of the retired persons stated they had seen most of the spots previously. There were only a few respondents who had not seen any spots before. Unfortunately, the sample consisted of 25 percent males and 75 percent females, so that it was not possible to conduct any further analyses on the basis of gender.

The questionnaire was similar to the one applied by Christina Holtz-Bacha and Lynda Lee Kaid (1995: 61-88) but was adapted to the Estonian political landscape. The pretest questionnaire consisted of demographic information, political interest and measures related to the level of being informed, media use variables, and a thermometer scale (0-100) to ascertain respondent's general feelings towards seven MEP candidates[7] and the Prime Minister (Prime Minister Juhan Parts did not run in the EP-elections himself but had a central role in the *Res Publica* spot). In addition, these seven MEP candidates and the Prime Minister were evaluated by respondents in the pretest, using a semantic differential scale.

The posttest questionnaire basically repeated all questions, including the "feelings' thermometer" and the semantic differential. Finally, respondent's political preference concerning parties and support of Estonian MEP candidates were assessed, as well as their general impression concerning the usefulness of the spots as a source for political information.

The semantic differential scale used to evaluate candidate's image consisted of twelve sets of bipolar adjectives (e. g. qualified-unqualified), each rated on a seven-point scale. The list of these adjectives is found in Table 7 (see below). The semantic differential scale is the same scale used by Holtz-Bacha and Kaid (ibid.).

3.3.1 Does age and level of being informed matter?

All data has been analysed comparing pretest and posttest results over all respondents. More detailed analysis has been done by splitting the respondents by age and their informational level, i. e. students vs. retired persons and groups of less informed vs. highly informed respondents have been compared.

All respondents were questioned about their party affiliation. Similarly, their general satisfaction with the shown spots was assessed. A tendency was found for supporters of particular parties to give a more positive evaluation of those spots that were produced by their "favourite" party. However, party affiliation did not fully coincide with respondents' support of MEP candidates. Most support was given to Toomas Hendrik Ilves (19 respondents out of 56) independent of respondent's party affiliation, whereas only five respondents would have voted for Toomas Savi and none of them for Carmen Kass. No respondent changed his or her MEP candidate preference during the test.

The results for three of the eight political figures assessed in the questionnaire will be presented in the scope of this article, namely the MEP candidates Toomas Hendrik Ilves, former Estonian foreign minister; Toomas Savi, former chairman of the Estonian parliament; and Carmen Kass, international supermodel of Estonian origin, having no previous political background. Toomas Hendrik Ilves (*Social Democratic Party*) and Toomas Savi (*Reform Party*) were elected as MEPs, collecting 76.120 and 11.198 votes respectively (first and fourth position), while Carmen Kass (*Res Publica*) was not successful with only 2.319 votes (21st position).

Their positions on the thermometer relative to each other (see Figure 3) correspond to their positions on the list of electoral results. This picture did not change significantly during the course of the experiment. However, the evaluation of Toomas Hendrik Ilves on the thermometer had its peak in the pretest and decreased slightly afterwards, whereas the evaluation of Toomas Savi and Carmen Kass became somewhat more positive.

Figure 3: Pretest and posttest ratings for three MEP candidates, all respondents

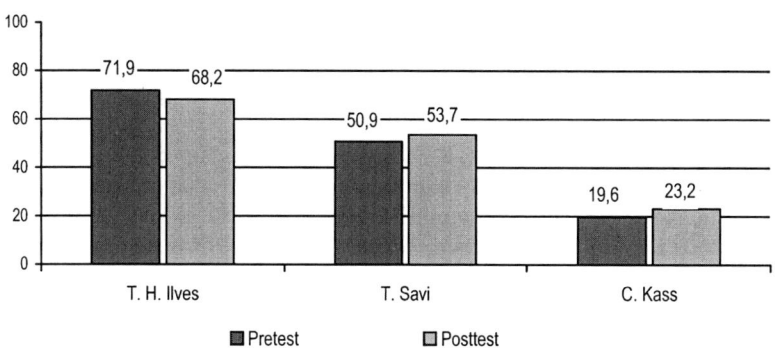

Note: Thermometer measures respondents' general feelings toward each party's MEP candidate. The respondents were asked to indicate their feelings on a scale of 0-100, whereby 51-100 points means "warm feelings" towards a candidate. 0 points means "complete dislike" and 100 points means "absolute sympathy".

If age groups and the groups composed according to informational level are compared, significant differences emerge (see Table 6). The evaluation of Toomas Hendrik Ilves decreased in all groups after the presentation of the spots, but more among retired persons and especially among highly informed persons (-5.6 points). One possible explanation is higher pre-test expectations towards Ilves compared to the other candidates.

The evaluation of Toomas Savi decreased among students (-6 points) but increased significantly among retired persons (+12.1 points). It increased both among less informed respondents (+5.2 points) and highly informed respondents (+1.5 points).

Table 6: Pretest and posttest ratings for three MEP candidates, age group, and level of being informed.

	Pretest		Posttest		Pretest		Posttest	
	19-28 y.	50-85 y.	19-28 y.	50-85 y.	Less inf.	Highly inf.	Less inf.	Highly inf.
Toomas H. Ilves	73.3	70.2	70.7	65.4	68.6	74.4	67.4	68.8
Toomas Savi	59.0	42.5	53.0	54.6	54.3	48.5	59.5	49.9
Carmen Kass	22.2	16.6	22.1	24.5	15.7	21.9	20.1	25.2

Note: Thermometer scale 0-100

The evaluation of Carmen Kass was rather modest compared to Ilves and Savi. Among students there was almost no change after the presentation of the spots, but among retired persons her evaluation increased by 7.9 points. The increase among less informed and highly informed respondents was more or less the same (+4.4 and +3.3 points respectively). Kass gained most among retired persons, perhaps because the students were studying communication science and therefore more aware of the effects of advertising.

3.3.2 The informed people: a difficult "target group"

The results of the semantic differential are displayed in Table 7. Toomas Hendrik Ilves enjoyed the highest pretest ratings on all 12 attribute scales with the exception of *honest* (mean 5.2 points versus 5.3 in favour of Toomas Savi), *calm* (5.4 versus 5.7 in favour of Toomas Savi), and *attractive* (5.4 versus 5.5 in favour of Carmen Kass). Top model Carmen Kass had the lowest ratings among these three MEP candidates on all attribute scales with the exception of the already mentioned *attractiveness*.

Table 7: Pretest and posttest ratings for three MEP candidates, all respondents

	Toomas Hendrik Ilves		Toomas Savi		Carmen Kass	
	Pretest All respondents	Posttest All respondents	Pretest All respondents	Posttest All respondents	Pretest All respondents	Posttest All respondents
Qualified	6.2	6.2	5.3	5.2	2.1	2.5
Educated	6.4	6.5	5.9	5.8	2.6	2.8
Honest	5.2	5.5	5.3	5.3	3.7	3.7
Believable	5.2	5.4	5.1	4.8	3.1	3.6
Successful	5.9	6.0	5.8	5.7	5.2	5.4
Attractive	5.4	5.4	5.0	4.7	5.5	5.4
Friendly	5.7	5.6	5.4	5.6	4.3	4.8
Sincere	5.4	5.1	5.2	5.0	3.6	3.7
Calm	5.4	5.9	5.7	5.8	4.8	5.0
Not aggressive	5.0	5.2	5.0	5.0	4.5	4.4
Strong	5.8	5.8	5.4	5.2	4.5	4.7
Active	5.5	5.4	5.2	5.0	4.8	5.1
Total change		+0.9		-1.3		+2.4

Note: Minimum value 1, maximum value 7 points

However, if the total change of ratings in all attribute scales is calculated, Carmen Kass gained more than Ilves or Savi. The total change in her evaluation on the differential attribute scales (the sum of all changes of attribute scales) is +2.4 points, while Ilves has +0.9 points, and Savi has -1.3. Generally speaking, it seems that the presentation of the spots helped Carmen Kass' image the most and had a somewhat detrimental effect on Savi's image.

Carmen Kass became significantly more *qualified, believable, friendly,* and *active* while Savi became significantly less *believable* and *attractive*. Toomas Hendrik Ilves became more *honest* but less *sincere*. A possible explanation for this may be the fact that the copywriters induced Ilves – former minister of foreign affairs, who in Estonia has a reputation of being an "intellectual" – to wear the typical clothing of various occupational groups in his TV-spot, such as a policeman's uniform, farmer's clothing, etc., which recipients probably immediately detected as being a "fake context".

Tables 8a-8c: Pretest and posttest ratings for three MEP candidates according to age groups

Toomas Hendrik Ilves	Pretest		Posttest	
	19-28 y.	50-85 y.	19-28 y.	50-85 y.
Qualified	6.3	6.1	6.1	6.4
Educated	6.6	6.1	6.5	6.4
Honest	4.9	5.5	5.3	5.8
Believable	5.3	5.1	5.2	5.6
Successful	5.9	5.9	5.8	6.2
Attractive	5.1	5.7	5.3	5.4
Friendly	5.7	5.7	5.6	5.6
Sincere	5.3	5.5	4.8	5.5
Calm	5.4	5.4	5.9	6.0
Not aggressive	5.1	5.0	5.3	5.1
Strong	5.5	6.2	5.4	6.1
Active	5.0	6.1	4.8	6.0
Total change			-0.2	+1.5

Note: Total change has been calculated by subtracting posttest results from pretest results and summing up all changes

Toomas Savi	Pretest		Posttest	
	19-28 y.	50-85 y.	19-28 y.	50-85 y.
Qualified	5.0	5.7	4.6	5.8
Educated	5.6	6.1	5.3	6.3
Honest	5.2	5.4	5.1	5.5
Believable	5.1	5.0	4.4	5.4
Successful	5.8	5.7	5.6	5.9
Attractive	5.0	4.9	4.6	4.9
Friendly	5.3	5.5	5.4	5.9
Sincere	5.1	5.3	4.6	5.6
Calm	5.7	5.7	5.7	5.9
Not aggressive	5.2	4.8	5.2	4.9
Strong	5.1	5.7	4.7	5.8
Active	4.6	5.7	4.5	5.6
Total change			-3.0	+2.0

Note: Total change has been calculated by subtracting posttest results from pretest results and summing up all changes

Carmen Kass	Pretest		Posttest	
	19-28 y.	50-85 y.	19-28 y.	50-85 y.
Qualified	1.7	2.6	2.2	3.0
Educated	2.0	3.1	2.3	3.4
Honest	3.9	3.6	3.7	3.8
Believable	2.4	3.8	3.1	4.2
Successful	5.7	4.7	5.6	5.1
Attractive	5.4	5.5	5.6	5.1
Friendly	4.5	4.0	4.6	5.1
Sincere	3.8	3.4	3.7	3.8
Calm	5.1	4.4	5.2	4.6
Not aggressive	4.7	4.2	4.4	4.4
Strong	4.3	4.7	4.6	4.9
Active	4.8	4.7	5.1	5.2
Total change			+1.8	+3.9

Note: Total change has been calculated by subtracting posttest results from pretest results and summing up all changes

Concerning the public perception of Carmen Kass, one should keep on mind that Ilves and Savi both had previous records as politicians in Estonia while Kass made her debut in politics (joining the *Res Publica* party only a few months before the elections), and Estonian media often argued that her party used the celebrity status of Kass merely to gain votes. However, the change of Kass' perception among the respondents during the test is noteworthy. The total change of her ratings over all attribute scales was positive both among students and retired persons (Tables 8a-8c), +1.8 points and +3.9 points, respectively.

Tables 9a-9c: Pretest and posttest ratings for three MEP candidates according to informational level

Toomas Hendrik Ilves	Pretest		Posttest	
	Less informed*	Highly informed	Less informed	Highly informed
Qualified	5.9	6.4	6.3	6.2
Educated	6.5	6.3	6.5	6.5
Honest	5.2	5.2	5.6	5.5
Believable	5.2	5.3	5.5	5.4
Successful	6.0	5.9	6.1	6.0
Attractive	5.3	5.4	5.3	5.4
Friendly	5.9	5.7	5.6	5.7
Sincere	5.3	5.4	4.9	5.3
Calm	5.8	5.2	6.1	5.8
Not aggressive	5.1	5.0	5.2	5.2
Strong	5.9	5.8	5.9	5.7
Active	5.6	5.5	5.6	5.2
Total change			+0.9	+0.8

Note: Total change has been calculated by subtracting posttest results from pretest results and summing up all changes

Toomas Savi	Pretest		Posttest	
	Less informed*	Highly informed	Less informed	Highly informed
Qualified	5.5	5.3	5.8	4.8
Educated	6.2	5.7	6.3	5.5
Honest	5.5	5.2	5.6	5.1
Believable	5.2	5.0	5.3	4.6
Successful	5.8	5.7	6.0	5.6
Attractive	5.1	4.9	4.8	4.7
Friendly	5.6	5.3	5.9	5.4
Sincere	5.3	5.1	5.4	4.7
Calm	5.6	5.8	5.8	5.7
Not aggressive	5.0	5.0	5.5	4.8
Strong	5.4	5.4	5.6	5.0
Active	5.5	5.0	5.4	4.7
Total change			+1.1	-3.0

Note: Total change has been calculated by subtracting posttest results from pretest results and summing up all changes

Carmen Kass	Pretest		Posttest	
	Less informed*	Highly informed	Less informed	Highly informed
Qualified	2.3	2.0	2.9	2.2
Educated	2.4	2.7	2.7	2.8
Honest	3.5	3.9	3.2	4.0
Believable	2.9	3.2	3.6	3.6
Successful	4.7	5.6	5.6	5.2
Attractive	5.4	5.6	5.1	5.6
Friendly	3.7	4.7	4.4	5.1
Sincere	3.2	3.9	3.2	4.0
Calm	4.3	5.1	4.5	5.2
Not aggressive	4.0	4.8	4.7	4.3
Strong	4.4	4.5	4.1	5.0
Active	4.0	5.3	5.0	5.2
Total change			+3.3	+0.9

Note: Total change has been calculated by subtracting posttest results from pretest results and summing up all changes
* less informed = index of being informed is 0-2 points, highly informed = index is 3-5 points.

In groups based on informational level (see Tables 9a-9c), the highly informed group is more critical towards all three MEP candidates. Probably they have more information for argumentation and critical assessment of spots as they read more newspapers than less informed respondents (among the less informed group 12.5 percent of the respondents do not read newspaper at all versus 3.2 percent among the highly informed group; 16.7 percent of the less informed respondents stated that they had not received any information about EP elections via media for a week versus 0 percent of highly informed respondents). In case of cognitive dissonance the previous opinion of highly informed respondents prevails, and they may assess conflicting messages more negatively.

This seems to have happened with the spot of Toomas Savi. His total change of ratings associated with "positive" personal characteristics across all attribute scales decreased by 3.0 points among highly informed respondents. He has become significantly less *qualified, believable, sincere,* and *strong,* while less informed respondents evaluate him as being *less aggressive.*

3.3.3 Concluding remarks: personalities matter more than parties

The sample consisted of 56 respondents who voluntarily participated in an experiment in response to advertisement posted on the bulletin board of the university communication department or in an activity centre for retired persons. Therefore, the sample is not totally representative because it consists of a higher percentage of active persons and persons with higher interest towards politics.

However, the objective of the experiment – to compare image shift for different age groups and for groups with different levels of information – was achieved. Significant differences between students (19-28 years old) and retired persons (50-85 years old) were found. Both in responses to a thermometer and semantic differential, retired persons became more sympathetic toward candidates after watching spots. Students became more critical towards MEP candidates, but one should not forget that most of them were communication students, possessing analytical skills and trained to be critical.

Still, the shift in the evaluations did not depend only on respondent's age. A similar significant shift appeared when comparing less informed with highly informed respondents, whereby both age groups were almost equally represented in less and highly informed respondents. Less informed respondents became more sympathetic towards MEP candidates after watching spots, no matter if they were students or retired persons. This effect was most clear in the case of Carmen Kass because her public image as a politician was just in the middle of formation. Highly informed respondents did not demonstrate such a significant shift towards being more sympathetic towards candidates after seeing the spots, and in the case of liberal Toomas Savi they even became even less sympathetic towards him than before.

When respondents' support of candidates was assessed after they had viewed the spots, 19 respondents supported Toomas Hendrik Ilves, five Toomas Savi, and none supported Carmen Kass. Thus, it seems that most of the respondents had made their choice previously, while twelve respondents either had no choice or refrained from answering the question. The support given to candidates had no strong correlation to the support given to his or her party.

Therefore, personalities and their presentation through TV spots were most crucial for this campaign. Since Toomas Hendrik Ilves already had a good position, it is possible that the spots did not do much to improve his standing and were of minimal value. Toomas Savi was not recognized as such an EU expert as Ilves, and the attempt of the copywriters to emphasize his domestic achievements had a rather negative impact in the sample group. Carmen Kass' advantage was her appearance and the fact that she is well-known internationally, and her image improved the most in the sample studied. However, her previous political achievements were too modest to have any consequences worth mentioning in the fight for voters.

The shifts in evaluation after having viewed the political advertising may seem minimal, but it is important to keep in mind that in the course of the campaign spots are broadcasted many times a day (the 41 TV spots produced for the EP elections were broadcasted a total of 1.965 times, thus the statistical mean number of broadcasts for each spot is 48).

4. Conclusions

The experiment designed to measure the micro-level effects of political advertising demonstrated that there were modest, but noteworthy changes after seeing political TV-spots. It seems that political TV spots achieve the positive effects intended by their producers to a greater extent among recipients who consider themselves poorly informed about politics. Also, age matters: Retired persons became more sympathetic to candidates after watching spots.

However, this experiment cannot answer the question whether and how much political advertising influences the real electoral behaviour of voters. Indeed, on the macro-level, the Estonian EP-election campaign that was characterized by negativity (especially towards the EU itself) seemed to increase the abstinence from voting. Before the referendum on EU membership, Estonian political parties had campaigned for the EU, but before the EP-elections many major political parties used a "Eurocritical" strategy designed to get the votes from "Eurosceptical" voters. It can be said that the negative strategy led to a certain "cognitive dissonance" among voters, and the public opinion surveys conducted during the campaign period demonstrate that the proportion of people saying they would certainly go to the polls continuously decreased during the campaign.

References

Blumler, Jay G./Gurevitch, Michael (1995): The Crisis of Public Communication. London/New York: Routledge.
Eurobarometer (2004): Flash EB 161. European Elections 2004 Barometer.
Garramone, Gina M./Atkin, Charles K./Pinkleton, Bruce E./Cole, Richard T. (1990): Effects of Negative Political Advertising on the Political Process. In: Journal of Broadcasting and Electronic Media, Vol. 34, 299-311.
Grofman, Bernard/Mikkel, Evald/ Taagepera, Rein (1999): Electoral Systems Change in Estonia, 1989-1993. In: Journal of Baltic Studies, Vol. 30, No. 3, 227-249.

Grofman, Bernard/Mikkel, Evald/Taagepera, Rein (2000): Fission and Fusion of Parties in Estonia, 1987-1999. In: Journal of Baltic Studies, Vol. 31, No. 4, 329-357.
Hall, Stuart (1980): Encoding/Decoding. In: Hall, Stuart/Hobson, Dorothy/Lowe, Andrew/Willis, Paul (Eds.): Culture, Media, Language: Working Papers in Cultural Studies 1972-79. London: Hutchinson, 128-138.
Holtz-Bacha, Christina (1994): Massenmedien und Politikvermittlung. Ist die Videomalaise-Hypothese ein adäquates Konzept? In: Jäckel, Michael/Winterhoff-Spurk, Peter (Eds.): Politik und Medien. Analysen zur Entwicklung politischer Kommunikation. Berlin: Vistas, 181-191 [Holtz-Bacha: Mass Media and Political Communication. Is the Videomalaise Hypothesis an Adequate Concept? In: Jäckel/Winterhoff-Spurk: Politics and Media. Analyses on the Development of Political Communication].
Holtz-Bacha, Christina/Kaid, Lynda Lee (1995): Television Spots in German National Elections. Content and Effects. In: Kaid, Lynda Lee/Holtz-Bacha, Christina (Eds.): Political Advertising in Western Democracies. Parties and Candidates on Television. London/New Delhi: Sage, 61-88.
Kahn, Kim Fridkin/Kenney, Patrick J. (1999): Do Negative Campaigns Mobilize or Suppress Turnout? Clarifying the Relationship between Negativity and Participation. In: American Political Science Review, Vol. 93, 877-889.
Lõhmus, Maarja (2002): Transformation of Public Text in Totalitarian System. A Socio-Semiotic Study of Soviet Censorship Practices in Estonian Radio in the 1980s. Turku: Turun yliopisto.
Maaleht (2003): Maalehe suur eurodebatt. Peaminister Juhan Parts väitles eurovastastega. Sep. 4th 2003, 3 [The Big EU-Debate of Weekly Maaleht. Prime Minister Juhan Parts in Debate with Eurosceptics].
Meadow, Robert G. (1989): Political Campaigns. In: Rice, Ronald E./Charles K. Atkin (Eds.): Public Communication Campaigns. London/Newbury Park/ New Delhi: Sage, 253-272.
Siune, Karen (1995): Political Advertising in Denmark. In: Kaid, Lynda Lee/ Holtz-Bacha, Christina (1995): Political Advertising in Western Democracies. Parties and Candidates on Television. London/New Delhi: Sage, 124-142.
Tigasson, Külli-Riin (2005): Wahlkampf gegen Europa. Die Wahlen zum Europäischen Parlament in Estland 2004. In: Tenscher, Jens (Ed.): Wahl-Kampf um Europa. Analysen aus Anlass der Wahlen zum Europäischen Parlament 2004. Wiesbaden: Verlag Sozialwissenschaften, 293-315 [Tigasson: Campaigning against Europe. The Elections to the European Parliament in Estonia 2004. In: Tenscher: Campaigning for Europe. Analyses on the Occasion of the 2004 European Parliament Elections].
TNS Emor (2004): TV Audience Meter Survey.
Toots, Anu/Raivo Vetik (2004): Estland vor dem EU-Beitritt. In: Aus Politik und Zeitgeschichte, No. 5-6, 35-40 [Estonia before the EU-Accession].

Vihalemm, Peeter (1999): Changing Baltic Space. Estonia and its Neighbours. In: Journal of Baltic Studies, Vol. 30, No. 3, 250-269.

---

[1] However, according to an election law amendment that came on force in July 2005, political outdoor advertising is banned in Estonia.

[2] According to d'Hondt divisors, in a multiseat district the first seat is allocated to the largest party, but then its vote share is divided by two. The next seat is allocated to the largest of the shares thus resulting. Whenever a party gets a second seat, its vote share is divided by three, etc, until all seats are allocated. Compared to other proportional representation rules, this one favours large parties (see Grofman et al. 1999: 227-249).

[3] About one third of the Estonian population is Russian-speaking and several newspapers are published in Russian.

[4] Because not all parties differentiated between the expenditures for TV-, radio, and outdoor advertising in their election cost declarations, it is not possible to present the exact proportions of expenditures for various advertising channels.

[5] Under "Europe-tax" is meant the proposal of Belgian Prime Minister Guy Verhofstadt (made in winter 2001) that European citizens pay a EU tax directly to Brussels – an issue that had very little relevance at the time of the EP election campaign in the European Union, but that was indeed heavily used in the Estonian EP campaign.

[6] One of the possible macro-level influences of advertising (high level of negativity of the EP-campaign seemed to decrease the turnout) was discussed in Chapter 2.1.

[7] Six of the seven MEP candidates selected for the test were the top candidates of the candidate lists of the parties represented in the Estonian Parliament. Additionally, the seventh candidate was included to measure the reactions of recipients towards this rather untypical political personality (supermodel Carmen Kass).